Praise for *A Finer Future*

A Finer Future brings hope by showing us a vision of a future with greater wellbeing, deep engagement with nature and each other, and the enormous economic benefit in transforming how we deliver energy, grow food, and finance industry. A manifesto for the future we must create.

—Jennifer Holmgren, CEO, LanzaTech

A Finer Future is an important book for our times. The world is facing deep environmental and social challenges that threaten our collective well-being. These thought leaders provide the clearest explanation I've seen of how the world got to this point—the culprit is a fatally flawed story about what makes economies hum and people happy. This me-first philosophy now dominates the thinking in governments and businesses around the world, and it's dead wrong. But *A Finer Future* offers us some optimism, giving us a new and better story about how to build a thriving future. And like all good stories, this one is well-told—it feels a lot like sitting down with Hunter Lovins to talk about the future of humanity over a good drink.

—Andrew Winston, author, *The Big Pivot* and *Green to Gold*

Join the movement for an economy driven by sustainable wellbeing rather than consumerism, profit and growth. This book is your introduction to a movement for sustainable wellbeing and a better world.

—Kate E. Pickett, Professor of Epidemiology,
and Deputy Director, Centre for Future Health,
University of York

—Richard Wilkinson, OBE, founder, Equality Trust

Amidst the wreckage of the industrial economy, a better, more humane, more just, and more durable economy is emerging. The obstacles and the economic alternatives and alternatives are laid out here by four of the most observant and prescient thinkers of our time. Indeed, there is a regenerative economy to be built and it will be the keystone of a finer future.

— David W. Orr, Paul Sears Distinguished Professor of
Environmental Studies and Politics, Oberlin College,
and author, *Dangerous Years: Climate Change,
the Long Emergency, and the Way Forward*

A Finer Future provides a thought-provoking perspective and a call to action on the role of sustainability as a key factor in driving value. It challenges all of us to find strategies that truly align our economic, community, and environmental stakeholders.

— Rob Katz, CEO, Vail Resorts, Inc.

The end of the exploitive, and the rise of the regenerative: that's the clarion call in this must-read book. Our consumptive status quo is too costly for the economy and it's past-time we mainstream a new way. What we eat, wear, ride, fly, and build must be regenerative. How? This book shows the way. An authoritative nod towards a much-needed norm and narrative, this book is a masterful mix of the hard and soft sciences, putting solid numbers behind sound narratives. For anyone wanting to save people and the planet, this book is the path to pursue and the story to tell.

— Nils Moe, Managing Director,
Urban Sustainability Directors Network

Beautifully comprehensive and inspiring. What we need.

— Dr Eban Goodstein, Director, Bard Center for Environmental Policy

Hunter Lovins is a pragmatic visionary, and the strategy she lays out in this book is the best chance we have to date of actualizing a regenerative future. One of the most luminary thought leaders of our time. Simply a must-read if you are interested in the future of the planet and your role in it!

— Brenna St. Onge, Executive Director, The Alliance Center

A Finer Future captures the reason we created our company. Hunter Lovins is a much needed elder telling a new story that can galvanize the largest "we" in human history. This book calls us to serve sanity, justice, and every living thing.

— Donna Morton, CEO, Change Finance

Rarely has economics been so fun and exhilarating to read about. Four scholars at the forefront of the wellbeing economy agenda have crafted a pacy, captivating book. It blends vision with insightful analysis of why our world is in such a perilous state, with a good helping of tangible examples of the changes so vitally needed. Anyone reading it will soon find assurance that a finer, more functional and more fun future is entirely possible.

— Dr Katherine Trebeck, Research Director,
Wellbeing Economy Alliance

We spend too much time discussing problems without getting to solutions. This book provides the solutions needed to transform our economy into one that actually serves all of humanity, instead of only the rich. It's a must-read for anyone that cares about creating a better world not only for themselves but their children and grand-children.

— Ida Kubiszewski, Ph.D., Associate Professor,
Crawford School of Public Policy,
The Australian National University

A Finer Future is a work of refined synthesis and insightful visioning. Rooted in a stark analysis of current development trends its authors rapidly move beyond critique to developing an inspiring yet deeply practical narrative about transitioning to a regenerative economy. More than a guide or blueprint—it is an enlightened, pragmatic, and empowering roadmap through life as we know it, the choices we make, and the future we want.

— Achim Steiner, Administrator,
United Nations Development Programme

A Finer Future is a brilliant and well-researched book that guides readers to rethink what the future will look like once we shatter old narratives, paradigms, and models that no longer serve humanity and the planet. We are through with the waste and the inefficiencies and inequities that have been the unintended consequences of the last 100 years. This is a roadmap to a truly sustainable future.

— Catherine Greener, VP Sustainability,
Xanterra Travel Collection and
Founder, Greener Solutions Inc

To build a better world, first we must imagine one. In this book, the authors do just that, laying out a vision for a better life and, crucially, a practical roadmap to get there. If you're disillusioned with today, this deeply researched book offers the path forward. I'll see you in our finer future…

— Freya Williams, CEO, Futerra North America

In this most compelling text Hunter Lovins delivers an engaging walk through what is possible for achieving—and excelling—in delivering products and services that are good for planet and people! It is a must-have for students and practitioners seeking to accelerate and amplify the transition to economies around the world where humanity and nature thrive.

— Professor Cheryl Desha,
Head of Civil Engineering (Nathan),
Griffith University

This is the book we've been waiting for. With clarity and vision, Hunter and her co-authors give us the playbook for how we can craft the future in which we want to live. Buy it, read it, and live it.

— John Steiner and Margo King, founders, Bridge Alliance.

A Finer Future is the best book out on how to reform capitalism in the direction of more fundamental changes and to buy much-needed time.

—Randy Hayes, Executive Director, Foundation Earth;
and founder, Rainforest Action Network

A much-needed book with a call for constructive collaboration towards a finer future we all yearn for. We have all the technological solutions we need we just need to implement them. Lovins and colleagues show a path forward that allows all those of good will, some smarts, and stamina to get us out of the mess we are in towards an economy and society that works for 100% of humanity.

— Dr Michael Pirson, Director, Center for Humanistic Management;
Director, Master of Science in Management, Fordham University;
and author, *Humanistic Management: Protecting Dignity
and Promoting Well Being*

This book will make you smarter about creating real, lasting, generational value. If you know in your gut that we can prosper and restore our environment at the same time, but are told by politics you're wrong, then this book is for you.

— Will Semmes, former Chief Deputy Director,
California Department of General Services;
and CEO, Bellwether Consultants

This book gives us the map, a voice, and the reassurance that we are on the right course. It has all come full circle; *Natural Capitalism* inspired us to start Waste Farmers, and Hunter's latest book provides the necessary roadmap for an economy that supports companies like ours and all of the stakeholders we serve.

— John-Paul Maxfield, Founder & CEO, Waste Farmers

A Finer Future is perhaps the most important book of this century: the future of humanity may well rest on the achievement of the recommendations. If you care about the future of our species and our biosphere—really about the future of everything we hold dear—read this book, then roll up your sleeves and get to work.

— Kim Coupounas, social entrepreneur and
Director of B Lab, the certifying body
behind B Corporations

A FINER FUTURE

A FINER FUTURE

CREATING AN ECONOMY IN SERVICE TO LIFE

L. HUNTER LOVINS • STEWART WALLIS
ANDERS WIJKMAN • JOHN FULLERTON

new society
PUBLISHERS

Cover design by Diane McIntosh.
Cover images: © iStock butterfly: 509188822; paper texture: 903280608;
currency engraving texture: 120750114.

Printed in Canada. First printing August 2018.

Inquiries regarding requests to reprint all or part of *A Finer Future*
should be addressed to New Society Publishers at the address below.
To order directly from the publishers, please call toll-free (North America)
1-800-567-6772, or order online at www.newsociety.com.

Any other inquiries can be directed by mail to

New Society Publishers
P.O. Box 189, Gabriola Island, BC V0R 1X0, Canada
(250) 247-9737

LIBRARY AND ARCHIVES CANADA CATALOGUING IN PUBLICATION

Lovins, L. Hunter, 1950– , author
A finer future : creating an economy in service to life / L. Hunter Lovins,
Stewart Wallis, Anders Wijkman, John Fullerton.

Includes bibliographical references and index.
Issued in print and electronic formats.
ISBN 978-0-86571-898-2 (softcover).—ISBN 978-1-55092-691-0 (PDF).—
ISBN 978-1-77142-287-1 (EPUB)

1. Sustainable development.   2. Entrepreneurship—Environmental aspects.
3. Entrepreneurship—Social aspects.   I. Wallis, Stewart, author   II. Wijkman,
Anders, 1944– , author   III. Fullerton, John, (John B.), author   IV. Title.

HC79.E5L75 2018   338.9'27   C2018-903969-8
                                                        C2018-903970-1

Funded by the   Financé par le
Government   gouvernement
of Canada   du Canada

Canada

New Society Publishers' mission is to publish books that contribute in fundamental
ways to building an ecologically sustainable and just society, and to do so with the least
possible impact on the environment, in a manner that models this vision.

new society
PUBLISHERS

Certified
B
Corporation

MIX
Paper from
responsible sources
FSC® C016245

Contents

Foreword

by Kate Raworth

On a bright May morning in 2015 a little boat carried a group of travellers, including the four authors of this book and me, to the shores of Ekskäret, a tiny island in Stockholm's archipelago. Ekskäret, meaning 'where the oak trees grow', welcomed us with its clear waters, rocky shoreline, pristine forest and stunning views. These were indeed ideal conditions for the metaphorical oaks that we intended to start growing in our coming days of discussion together.

The meeting, convened by the Club of Rome, focused our minds for three days on one issue: is it possible to transform the current global economic system without facing collapse—and if so, how? Take my advice: if you are going to spend three days focused on the possibilities of civilizational collapse, do it in the company of people who have, for decades, considered its risks, tracked its trends, and are not afraid to stare it fully in the face. But far more importantly, do it with people who understand this: believing that collapse is inevitable is one of the best ways to make it so, while believing that an alternative future is possible is one of the only ways of giving it a chance of actually being realised.

It is not hard to be overwhelmed by the possibility of collapse because at a global scale today the world is severely out of balance, caught in a state of simultaneous shortfall and overshoot. Despite decades of global economic growth and poverty reduction, many millions of people worldwide still fall short of the resources they need to meet their most basic of needs, from food, water and healthcare to education, energy and housing. At the same time, the pressure of humanity's collective resource use has already overshot the boundaries of some of Earth's most critical life-supporting systems, resulting in climate change, extensive forest loss, ocean dead-zones and rapid biodiversity loss.

Thanks to huge strides in Earth-systems science over the past forty years, we are the first generation to know that we face unprecedented global environmental risks, says Johan Rockström, one of the leading scientists in this field, but at the same time we are most likely the last generation with a significant chance to do something about it. So will we step up to this challenge? Will we be the turn-around generation that acts to avert very real risks of collapse and, instead, starts to put humanity on track to meet the needs of all people within the means of this delicately balanced living planet? We certainly have the choice to do just that, and this book—which began as a mere idea on Ekskäret—sets out a powerfully compelling contemporary vision for how it could be done.

Writing the foreword is a particular pleasure for me because all four of the book's authors have been among my sources of inspiration for years. Hunter Lovins—never without a Stetson on her head, or an ambitious plan up her sleeve—has for decades been an irrepressible champion of reinventing business to create an economy in service to life. John Fullerton's extraordinary personal journey, which compelled him to walk away from Wall Street economics to pioneer the field of regenerative economics, has given him a rare ability to span the transformations needed across business and finance. Anders Wijkman's influential and life-long career in politics and diplomacy—from his nation's parliament to the United Nations—gives him invaluable insight into the political realities of forging lasting institutional change. And Stewart Wallis—whose fascinating experience spanning Rio Tinto and Oxfam, new economics and interfaith dialogue—conveys the humility of someone who knows that there are always many perspectives but also, within humanity's great diversity, many shared values. Few books have the luck of being written by such an eclectic and insightful team as this one, and it shows, in their ability to connect decades of transformative thinking to contemporary politics, and in the sheer vision and breadth of practical policies for sector-specific transformations that they lay out.

Seventy years ago a profoundly influential meeting was held not on a Swedish island but in the Swiss mountain village of Mont Pelerin. There, Friedrich Hayek, Milton Friedman, Ludwig von Mises, Lionel Robbins and others met to craft a founding narrative for neoliberalism. Given the times, it is little surprise that the delegates at that first meeting of the Mont Pelerin Society were all men. But neoliberalism's foundational female voices continued to be few — the exceptions being Ayn Rand, who turned the narrative into novels, and Margaret Thatcher who, together with Ronald Reagan, turned it into economic policy and put it firmly on the international stage.

As I read the powerful, alternative narrative set out in *A Finer Future*, what struck me was the unmistakable intellectual leadership of many extraordinary women. Foundational thinkers since the 1960s include Jane Jacobs, Rachel Carson, Donella Meadows, Wangari Maathai, Elinor Ostrom, and Hazel Henderson — women whose ideas and insights were decades ahead of their times but are now finding their true recognition and resonance in a growing worldwide movement. I was equally struck, however, by the leadership of women today working at the heart of transforming design, finance, politics and business — from Janine Benyus and Christiana Figueres to Donna Morton, Ellen MacArthur and Hunter Lovins herself — all of whom are exemplary pioneers demonstrating that it is possible to bring a new economy into being. Their ideas and actions have profoundly inspired me over the years and I hope many future generations of women — be they academics, business leaders, designers, scientists, politicians or civic leaders — are similarly inspired to commit their own energy to continuing this work.

Since the idea of this book was seeded in Ekskäret — that place where the oak trees grow — I hope that the island's inspiration helps its vision and ambition to grow, spread and flourish just like an oak, in the way that only a future economy based on regenerative design possibly can.

— Kate Raworth
July 2018

Acknowledgments

This work would not have been possible without the support given by the Club of Rome and the KR Foundation. Thank you for your courage to support the inquiry into whether it is possible for humanity to avoid total systems collapse. We hope that this book will help answer that question in the affirmative. Many members of the Club of Rome were most gracious in donating their time and wisdom, most especially Dr. Ernst von Weizsäcker. Thank you, friend.

The genesis of this book was a meeting of 15 international experts who convened to explore whether collapse might be avoided.[1] They found that it is essential to delay collapse as long as possible, to give humanity time to make the necessary societal and economic shifts. Thanks to Alan AtKisson (President and CEO of AtKisson Group), Nora Bateson (President of the International Bateson Institute), Tomas Björkman (Director and co-founder of Fri Tanke Förlag), Jo Confino (Executive Editor of Huffington Post), Holly Dublin (Senior Advisor at The B Team), John Fullerton (President and founder of the Capital Institute), Oliver Greenfield (Convenor of the Green Economy Coalition), Graeme Maxton (Secretary General of the Club of Rome), Hunter Lovins (President Natural Capitalism Solutions), Rebecca Oliver (Acting Deputy Director of the Future Earth Secretariat, Swedish Global Hub), David Orr (Counselor to the President at Oberlin College), Kristina Persson (Sweden's Minister for Strategic Development and Nordic Cooperation), Kate Raworth (Lecturer, Oxford University's Environmental Change Institute), Stewart Wallis (executive chair of the Wellbeing Economy Alliance), Anders Wijkman (Co-president of the Club of Rome).

Much of the content, and indeed the commitment to transform the global economy, grew out of an invitation by the King of Bhutan to join an International Expert Working Group to make Bhutan's concept of Gross National Happiness the basis for international development. At this meeting in Thimphu, Bhutan, H. E. Jigmi Y. Thinley, Prime Minister of Bhutan, said to Hunter Lovins, "Your job is to reinvent the global economy." Out of this meeting, a group of us created the Alliance for Sustainability and Prosperity (ASAP).[2] This led to many of the formative discussions that resulted in this book. To all of the ASAP members, but especially to Dr. Robert Costanza, Dr. Ida Kubiszewski, Dr. Jacqueline McGlade, Dr. Kate Pickett, Dr. Richard Wilkinson, Dr. Ashok Khosla, Dr. Enrico Giovonini, Dr. Vala Ragnarsdottir, and Dr. Lorenzo Fioramonti, thanks so much for all of the great intelligence and the even better times celebrating life together.

In 2014, to blend the work of ASAP with the growing Humanistic Management movement, we created Leading for Wellbeing. (L4WB).[3] To Dr. Michael Pirson, who has tirelessly hosted us at Fordham, a special thank you, friend. This would not have been possible without you. Thanks, also to Matt Schottenfeld of Fordham TV, who helped bring our ideas to visual life.[4] Thank you so much to our hosts in Monterrey, Mexico: Osmar Arandia, Luis Portales, and Consuelo Garcia de la Torre; to Claus Dierksmeir, who hosted us at the Global Institute in Tubingen Germany; and Romina Boarini, who hosted us at OECD. Deep gratitude to the Steering Committee: Andrew Winston, David Levine, and Chris Laszlo. And to all who made L4WB possible, thank you, including Freya Williams and Solitaire Townsend of Futerra, Donna Hicks, Jonas Haertle of Global Business Network, James Stoner, Salvador Paiz, Christopher Albrigo, Ernestina Guidici, Vince Siciliano, Sandra Waddock, Vincent Stanley of Patagonia, and Russell Greene. To the hundreds of people around the world who contributed to the various L4WB conferences, our deep gratitude for helping create the Meadows Memorandum described in this book and for your faith in humanity.

In spring 2017, it seemed to many of us that the proliferation of these groups, while it brought us to where we were, was not the best route forward. At Natural Capitalism Solutions' Regenerative Future Summit, ASAP and L4WB merged to create the Wellbeing Economy Alliance.[5] Chaired by Stewart Wallis, WEAll formed its secretariat at the WE-Africa[6] gathering in Pretoria, South Africa. It has now assembled dozens of organizations to work together to create an economy in service to life, generously funded by Velcro Fasteners. Thank you to all of you who have labored to create this blending of some of the world's great new economy movements, including, as well as all of those mentioned above, especially our Amplifiers: Katherine Trebeck of Oxfam, Diego Isabel of New Economics Social Innovation, Michael Weatherhead of the New Economics Foundation, and the growing group of conveners who are committing their organizations to be part of this.

Any manuscript benefits from having diverse eyes on it. A group called the Finer Future Forum debated the thesis, read early versions, and made extremely useful edits. We are deeply grateful to Jim Davidson, Joe Breddan, Anne Butterfield, Lynn Israel, Elizabeth Caniglia, Praful Shah, John Paul Maxfield, Randy Compton, Brenna St. Onge, John Powers, Mark Lewis, Cody Oreck, Joellen and Scott Radersdorff, Joel Serface, Eli Feldman, Governor Bill Ritter, Diane Rosenthal, Bill Kramer, John Lo Porto, John Steiner, Margo King, Donna Morton, Catherine Greener, and A.J. Grant.

Thanks also to the whole staff at Natural Capitalism Solutions: Isabel Nuesse, A.J. Grosenbaugh, Marguerite Berringer, Meghan Altman, Jeff Hohensee, and Robert Noiles. Artim Nikulkov of Earth Coast Productions was invaluable in overseeing our Kickstarter campaign, video production, and social media.

No book makes it to print without countless unseen helpers. You know who you are. Please know that we are deeply grateful for all that you did in this process.

Prologue:
The Parable of the Caterpillar

Consider the caterpillar. It goes happily about its waddly little green-and-yellow life munching milkweed, until one day it stops, adheres itself to a twig and begins a staggering transformation.

At the moment that the caterpillar enters the chrysalis, it has no earthly idea what's fixing to happen to it, no conception of the beautiful creature it is about to become.

As the chrysalis hardens, the poor worm dissolves.

Have you ever broken one of those things apart? There's no worm in there; there's no butterfly in there; it's just goo.

But if you're patient, a miraculous transformation takes place. Within the now translucent chrysalis, the folded image of its future becomes visible.

The emergent creature must struggle heroically to break free from the shards of what once protected it. That fight is essential to give the fragile new life its strength to spread its wings to warm and dry in the sun. Then, light as the milkweed down that carries seeds from the plant that sustained its prior life, the monarch flies.

So, if our world feels a bit gooey just now, perhaps it's because we are entering a time of transformation unimaginable to those of us who are in it. We're leaving the pedestrian world of crawling consumption to become beings of grace and elegance.

May this book help you take flight beyond the wildest dreams of a humble caterpillar.

Introduction:
Welcome to the Anthropocene

The future is already here,
it's just not evenly distributed.

WILLIAM GIBSON[1]

This book is a warning. At the same time, it is a vision of the way forward for humanity to survive. It is mostly good news: we have a vision and all the technologies we need to make a good start at crafting a life of dignity and quality for all people on Earth. If we choose this route, we can relieve the social tensions we are now suffering, and even support careful increases in population and economic growth.

But let's not kid ourselves: a daunting array of challenges faces us, driven by exponential growth in population, the overuse of resources, and the resulting pollution, loss of biodiversity, and declining availability of life-support systems. The ideological belief that we have to maintain exponential growth in gross domestic product (GDP) will result in economic collapse.[2] Baked into mental models of most everyone in business, academia, and policy, this belief is driving humanity over a cliff.

In 2000, scientists Paul Crutzen and Eugene Stoermer coined the term "Anthropocene" to argue that humans are now the dominant geological force on planet Earth.[3]

The International Commission on Stratigraphy (ICS), the scientific body that names geological epochs, is debating whether humanity has left the Holocene, the relatively stable geological epoch in

1

which humanity evolved from hunter-gatherers to agriculturalists, built cities, and initiated space travel.[4] Regardless of the conclusion, evidence of human impact on the planet is undeniable.[5]

Human-caused changes to the Earth, argues the principal geologist of the British Geological Survey, are greater than the changes that marked the end of the last ice age.[6] Radioactive residue of atmospheric nuclear testing is now found in geologic deposits. Human releases of CO_2 from fossil fuel combustion have changed atmospheric and oceanic chemistry. DuPont's chemical perfluorooctinoic acid is in the tissues of polar bears and all humans on Earth.[7] Plastic pollutes the guts of 90 percent of seabirds,[8] and microplastics, the decomposition of the millions of tons of plastic waste generated every year, are now ubiquitous.[9] More concrete has been used in the past 20 years than in all of human history. Ninety percent of all oil burned by humans has been since 1958; 50 percent of it since 1984.[10] It has left a permanent record of black carbon in glacial ice—assuming that any glaciers remain for future scientists to measure.

Today's economy relies on a "fast turnover" principle that promotes early obsolescence. The faster we replace almost everything we consume, the faster the economy grows, built on the principle of maximum speed and volume of resource flows. But so too does pollution, loss of ecosystems, and substantial losses of value with each product disposed.

A report from Trucost, commissioned by The Economics of Ecosystems and Biodiversity, found that if environmental costs are counted, almost no industry is profitable.[11] The hundred biggest ways in which companies are harming natural capital are costing the economy at least $4.7 trillion every year in lost ecosystem services and pollution costs, none of which are ever repaid by business. These are real costs: sick people and lost services like clean water or fertile soils that nature used to provide for free but for which we now must pay.

This is crazy. It's not even good business. The Trucost report warned that treating the Earth as a business in liquidation poses risks for investors. Companies that are not properly accounting for their actions will be called to account, especially as a growing global middle class demands that companies clean up their act.

But the issue runs deeper. Our mental model of how the world works tells us we're winning when we're really losing. GDP measures nothing more than the speed with which money and stuff pass through the economy. Even its inventor, Simon Kuznets, observed that it is a lousy measure of whether or not we are better off.[12] It's like a speedometer in a car: useful but wholly insufficient as a compass, a map, fuel or heat gauge. How fast are we going? GDP has the answer. Are we heading in the right direction? Have we sufficient fuel to make it? Is our Earth overheating? Can money buy happiness? GDP simply cannot tell you that.

Based on the growth fixation, and flawed philosophy, we've created an economy to maximize financial and built capital as doing this destroys our life-support systems. Money and stuff are useful, but increasing them by sacrificing human and natural capital is daft. Intact community and ecosystems are far more valuable forms of capital. Without them, there is no social stability and no life and thus no economy.

So, the real question is, do we have the courage to change our economic system, to create an economy in service to life, not consumption? If you are one of those recreationally challenged and beady-eyed sorts who has read every Club of Rome report,[13] Earth Policy Institute book,[14] and UN publication as they are released, if you are sick to death of bad news, and know all too well how the ideology of neoliberalism has put a stranglehold on humanity,[15] skip to chapter 3 and get on with the solutions.

If you think things are pretty fine where you live and can't understand what all the fuss is about, chapter 1 sketches the extent to which we need to come to grips with some daunting challenges. It makes clear that the mess is real. It warns that conditions very like those we face have led to total system collapse before and are likely to do so again. It profiles the NASA-funded Human And Nature DYnamical[16] (HANDY) study, which examined the prevalence throughout history of collapses and their causes. It demonstrates that the two factors that drove many if not all of past civilizational collapses—society overrunning its resource base, or high levels of inequality, or both—pretty well describe where we are now.

Yes, it's sobering to realize the peril we are in, but the chapter also invites you to imagine what life will be like when we win. It juxtaposes current reality with vision.

The rest of the book argues that, to build this new world, our narrative must provide a clear alternative to the very tempting desire now sweeping the world to surrender to authoritarian rule and just turn back the clock to an imagined past that never existed. It sets forth the basics of a narrative of a Regenerative Economy.

The second section describes how we can buy time by using resources dramatically more efficiently. The third section explores the transformations needed, and in many cases already underway, in finance, corporations, agriculture, and energy. These are not the only realms of human life that need to be changed, but if we address these four, we will be well on our way to forestalling the worst crises facing us. The fourth section then navigates the murky waters of policy, challenging us to reengage with politics and governance, and to rebuild trust in the institutions we created to guide us.

Finally, the book returns to the realm of vision, urging us to gain clarity about the world we want.

Achieving this is the challenge for every human alive today. It is our great work and, as Bucky also said, our final exam.

We invite you to join us.

It'll Do
Til the Mess Arrives

SOME PEOPLE LOOK at the scary statistics coming at us and say, "There's nothing I can do about it, I'll just party til it's all over."[2]

This is perhaps the most profoundly irresponsible thing you can do. *You* are the result of 4 billion years of evolutionary history.

Act like it.

Further, it is intellectually dishonest. There *is* a route forward. Rabbits freeze when confronted by a threat. Humans invent a new solution. Throughout our history, we have come together to create a better world. Hominids, before we were even fully human, nearly died out. Archeologists believe that the population was reduced to only a few thousand individuals.[3] They survived, and you are here, because your ancestors bonded. Those individuals cared more for the well-being of their whole group than any one cared for his or her personal success.[4] We, you and I, say the evolutionary biologists, are alive today because our ancestors created solutions together. The imperative to work together, to care for one another,

It's a mess…
If it's not,
it'll do til the
mess arrives.

TOMMY LEE JONES[1]

and to begin again is in our DNA. These features, they say, are not flaws: they define what it means to be human.

It *is* possible for humanity to avoid collapse. We've done it before. We *can* do it again.

For this to happen, however, we need a new narrative to counter the one that says we are rugged individuals, locked in mortal competition. This myth, more than anything else, has put us in peril. This book sets forth the basics of a Finer Future, what John Fullerton calls a Regenerative Economy.[5]

So, brace yourself, challenge yourself, read chapter 1.

Everything is changing.

Except us.

We remain the complex, creative, courageous, fearful, insular, but remarkable creatures we have always been.

It is the world around us that is morphing at warp speed into a future we only dimly imagine.

Then turn to chapter 2 to see how we created this mess we're in by telling ourselves a silly story. It may reassure you to realize that a small group of men crafted the narrative that has set the world on its current collision course. But if they did that, we can create a better story. Chapter 2 turns from the grim statistics set forth in chapter 1 and sketches what it will take if we are to avoid collapse.

Then smile to realize in chapter 3 that we have a better story. Because we too are changing. By facing our fears, we can evolve and gain greater consciousness. We have the ability to adapt to our new context and craft a Finer Future.

CHAPTER ONE

IMAGINE

Vision is the most vital step in the policy process.
If we don't know where we want to go,
it makes little difference that we make great progress....
The best goal most of us who work toward sustainability offer
is the avoidance of catastrophe. We promise survival
and not much more. That is a failure of vision.

DONELLA (DANA) MEADOWS[1]

Imagine....

The day dawns fine and clear. You stretch your 87-year-old bones in your bed, luxuriating in the tropical sun pouring in through the super-insulated windows in your Passivhaus co-housing unit in Indonesia.[2] Initially designed for northern climates, the concept of super-efficient buildings has, with some modifications,[3] transplanted well to the hotter weather of the Global South. These structures keep residents comfortable year-around[4] with only solar energy gathered by rooftop units to power them. Small, but suited to your needs, your unit is part of a larger community committed to working together. This has allowed you to stay in your own home as you age, eating communally with your neighbors when you wish but able to fix your own meals in the trim kitchen when you want privacy.

You were alive in 2015, when a group of applied mathematicians released the HANDY study.[5] It warned that cases of severe civilizational disruption due to "precipitous collapse—often lasting centuries—have been quite common." The title, Human And Nature DYnamical Study (HANDY), was clearly chosen for the acronym, but the subtitle, Is Industrial Civilization Headed for Irreversible Collapse, crisply set forth the thesis. Using a NASA-funded climate model, it explored the history of collapses. It did not set out to make short-term predictions, but the warning is stark: under conditions "closely reflecting the reality of the world today...we find that collapse is difficult to avoid."

The study described prior collapses variably as population decline, economic deterioration, intellectual regression, and the disappearance of literacy (Roman collapse), serious collapse of political authority and socioeconomic progress (repeated Chinese collapses), and disappearance of up to 90 percent of the population (Mayan). Some collapses the study profiled were so complete that the forest swallowed any trace until archaeologists rediscovered what had clearly been a complex society (many Asian collapses).

The authors concluded that despite the common impression that societal collapse is rare, or even largely fictional, collapse is real; "the picture that emerges is of a process recurrent in history, and global in its distribution."

Historic collapses, the study argued, were neither inevitable nor natural; they were human caused. They inflicted massive misery, often for centuries following. The study identified two underlying causes of collapse throughout human history:

1. "**the stretching of resources** due to the strain placed on the ecological carrying capacity" [emphasis added] and
2. "**the economic stratification of society** into Elites [rich] and Masses (or "Commoners") [poor]." [emphasis added]

These causes, the study concluded, have played "*a central role in the process of the collapse.*" This finding was reached based on all of the cases over "*the last five thousand years*" the authors examined.

The study elicited reams of criticism, most posted on ideological websites.[6] Critics objected that the study's use of mathematical models made collapse seem unavoidable. To be fair, the HANDY authors stated, in terms, that collapse is not inevitable.

The analysis led you to change your life. And today, in 2050, it feels very distant.

Children play outside in the central spaces, safe from cars, which, as in the early car-free city of Vauban, Germany,[7] are banned from this and many neighborhoods. A few residents still own electric cars, although they pay handsomely for the privilege—and wonder why they do, as their vehicles reside in a garage where the carshare program used to live. Now almost no one drives herself: driverless cars deliver last-mile services,[8] and regional transit works spectacularly well.

Today the air is clean. When you moved here, 34 years ago, 100,000 people died each year of acute air pollution across Indonesia.[9] The killing smoke spread across Southeast Asia from forests burned to clear land for palm oil plantations. Since Unilever[10] and other major users of the oil shifted in 2020 entirely to sustainable soy[11] and algae oil, the palm oil market collapsed, except for a vibrant smallholder palm industry.[12] Their trees are integrated into sustainable forestry initiatives that support rural communities. Tied closely to the ecotourism industry,[13] this has enabled Indonesia to ensure that the once-endangered orangutans and tigers have plenty of forest home in which to flourish, adding to visitor appeal. Indonesia once exported almost half of the world's palm oil.[14] Unilever[15] and governments like Norway's funded the creation of an algae oil industry that now employs twice the number of people who once worked on plantations.

But it was not always so....

Collapse Is a Serious Risk

New York Times columnist Tom Friedman opened 2016 with the query: what if "the recent turmoil in international markets isn't just the product of tremors but rather of seismic shifts in the foundational pillars of the global system, with highly unpredictable consequences?"[16]

He cited the bursting of the Chinese economic growth bubble,[17] the likelihood of durably low oil prices,[18] the end of Cold War support for banana republic nations, the rise of artificial intelligence and the destruction of the jobs market by robots,[19] the dissolution of European Union[20] under the flood of refugees,[21] American political polarization and the resulting populism,[22] and the inability of central banks to prop up faltering economies.[23] Are these tectonic plates all moving at once, he wondered, overwhelming the ability of our civilization to cope?

Humanity was on a bus hurtling toward a cliff, and we, the passengers, were looking out the windows remarking at the pretty view. An array of studies found worrying signs that if we did not change course quickly, we risked total civilizational collapse. We had left it until too late, these voices said; our speed was too great to brake in time and turn the bus without just rolling it off the cliff: collapse was inevitable. A Web search for "economic collapse," delivered something like 35 million claims that we were doomed. From *The Moron's Guide to Global Collapse*[24] to books on *Surviving the Coming Collapse*,[25] depressing literature was widely available.[26]

Stop a moment and think about that: total civilizational collapse.

The loss of everything that you care about.

Impossible?

Consider the global forces that combined to make such systemic collapse likely.

Collapse was already a reality for millions of people around the globe. In the developing world, in areas racked by civil war, totalitarianism, or increasingly common natural disasters, societal breakdown was commonplace. Poor communities hit by violent weather and developing countries without infrastructure to withstand sudden shocks or failed states experienced various levels of collapse. Millions of Chinese[27] and Indians[28] died every year from acute air pollution. In the wake of Hurricane Maria, 3.5 million Americans in Puerto Rico suffered collapse. Months later, many citizens of the wealthiest nation on Earth remained without electricity, fuel, clean water, or reliable supplies of food.[29] The world around, such storms became more frequent and more violent.

Religious conflicts and civil wars from Africa to Syria and Iraq to Afghanistan were all worsened by climate change.[30] This unleashed a flood of 67 million refugees,[31] estimated by Mercy Corps in 2016 as growing at 24 new refugees every minute.[32] This was more people on the move than the population of Italy, and more than at any time since World War II.[33] Threatening the stability of the European Union,[34] this flow of humanity drove xenophobic populism around the world.[35]

Life was not much better for those left behind. One hundred and twenty-five million people needed an estimated $35 billion each year in humanitarian assistance because of conflict or disasters.[36] This exhausted the willingness of even the most generous donor nations to react. And this was before counting the estimated $1.4 trillion a year needed to implement the Sustainable Development Goals (SDGs).[37] Frustrated young men with nowhere to go, no jobs, and no prospects were increasingly easy to radicalize, resulting in predictable attacks, for which there was no defense.[38]

Former UN official Christiana Figueres put it this way:

> People have lost trust that their lives can get better and that institutions are on their side. This in turn is leading to apathy, depression, despair and in some cases to the development of radical views. This cycle must be stopped, before it consumes our collective future.[39]

This ought to have been unacceptable, but the crass reality seemed to be that only when various aspects of collapse became more common in the developed world would policy elites pay attention.

Collapse was coming to a community near you. Despite people begging on the streets in major cities,[40] infrastructure crumbling,[41] and American cities unable to supply clean drinking water to their citizens,[42] companies, communities, and countries said, "We cannot afford to solve these crises."

So they worsened.

Kids asked if they were going to have a future. They feared that climate change and other environmental harm would cut short their lives.[43] Young people suffered record rates of affective anxiety disorder (fear of the future); some said as high as 25 percent of the youth population. Suicide, after years of falling rates, was at its highest level in 50 years, triple that of US homicides.[44] Suicide was the second-largest cause of death for youths aged 15 to 24.[45] Suicide rates in the US grew at two percent per year, higher in 2016 than any time since 1986.

They were not just scared of monsters under the bed. The failure of the nations of the world to reduce their nuclear arsenals had led to nuclear brinksmanship and scares of actual launches. In 2018, a false alarm gave Hawaiian citizens 38 minutes of terror as the governor scrambled to remember his Twitter password to tell panicked residents that someone had pushed the wrong button.[46]

Science told us that humanity was living beyond the planetary boundaries.[47] According to the 2015 *Esquire* article "When the End of Human Civilization Is Your Day Job," "Among many climate scientists, gloom has set in. Things are worse than we think, but they can't really talk about it."

It profiled the emotional trauma, nightmares, and depression felt by climatologists who tracked the indicators that showed that climate change was happening far faster, even, than their most pessimistic models. They had the scientific knowledge of just how bad things were going to get but could only watch in frustration as ever-more-frightening science failed to rouse a somnolent population to do anything about it.[48]

It all seemed just too much.

But take a deep breath, close your eyes, and remember, we created a better world.

What It Will Be Like When We Win

A world away from your snug co-housing unit in Indonesia, New York City is settling into autumn. Arjana, a young African graduate student, steps off the electric trolley that now runs down the middle of Broadway. An urban farm adjoins the rails, running the length of Manhattan. What were once concrete canyons echo with birdsong.

Part of a program begun back in 2016 called Growing Roots,[49] the farm is one of many across Manhattan and dozens of other

Green Cityscape. Credit: Mitchell Joachim, Terreform ONE.

major cities. Like your neighborhood in Jakarta, Manhattan is car-free, with the space once taken up by vehicles freed for housing and local food production.

Arjana stops a few blocks north of Wall Street to chat with the previously incarcerated young woman who is just ending her day weeding the kale patch, suggesting that they should try growing cassava.

They both laugh as Arjana hurries off to her classes at the Bard MBA in Sustainable Management.[50] Sent to study social entrepreneuring and sustainable development, she is only the latest of thousands of students funded by WE-Africa[51] to study at innovative programs that teach young Africans how to regenerate their continent.

It's working. With stronger, locally based economies prospering across Africa, the temptation for young men to hire themselves out to terrorists has plummeted. Renewable energy now powers Africa, and because it creates ten times the number of jobs per dollar invested than central fossil-fueled power plants,[52] it has become one of many job-creation engines for the continent. Refugees who once believed that their only option was to flee to Europe can now create a flourishing life at home.

In North Africa, Nur Energy[53] successfully deployed solar technologies that supply not only energy for Morocco, Tunisia, and much of the Maghreb but also cable low-carbon energy (instead of migrants) across the Mediterranean to power Greece, Italy, Spain, and France. Nur also develops renewable energy projects in these Southern European countries, creating jobs, ending the crushing economic collapse there,[54] which had seen youth unemployment above 60 percent.

The whole world now runs entirely on renewable energy, as Stanford's Professor Tony Seba predicted back in 2014.[55] (See chapter 10: Triumph of the Sun, for how we did it.) In the years following his predictions, hundreds of companies, from Google and Apple to Ikea and Unilever, led the conversion to 100 percent renewable power.[56] They realized that failing to act on climate change exposed them to increased risks, from physical disruption to financial loss.[57]

Countries like Scotland,[58] Costa Rica,[59] Denmark,[60] Dubai,[61] Germany, and finally even Saudi Arabia[62] followed suit. Cities joined the race.[63] It was better business to shift off the fossil fuels that were threatening the climate and implement the cheaper, job-creating renewable technologies.

Coupled with regenerative agriculture pioneered by the Africa Centre for Holistic Management at Dimbangombe, near Victoria Falls,[64] we are rolling climate change backwards. The practice of holistic grazing actually takes carbon from the air and returns it to the soil, where it is needed as the building block of life. (See chapter 9, Growing a Finer Future, for details on how this works.) Coupled with the success of renewable energy, over the past 30 years, the world is beginning to cool and the climate become more stable. Soon concentrations of carbon dioxide in the atmosphere will have returned to preindustrial levels.

The approach of regenerative development not only enabled Africa to produce sufficient food for all its citizens, it is ending hunger around the world. The recognition that achieving food security is the basis for implementing the Sustainable Development Goals[65] enabled the world to meet the targets set back in 2014, well before 2030.[66]

But you sigh deeply, thinking about just how close it was. We turned from collapse only at the last moment.

What Could Have Been

In 2018, it looked as if the collapse scenario of *The Limits to Growth* was coming to pass. Principally authored by Dana Meadows, the 1972 report[67] set forth work she and her co-authors did using the massive MIT computer model, World 3. Incorporating all that was then known about the world, they examined four primary runs of the model using different assumptions: business as usual, high growth, low growth, and a transition to what they called "sustainability." The latter was the first known use of that word in the English language. They found that in every one of nine runs (mostly variants of the first three) humanity collapses. Unless we implement "sustainability."

In the business-as-usual run of the model, use of resources grew, population grew, and availability of non-renewable resources began to fall, until at some point, estimated to be in the mid-2030s, it all came apart. At that point, human activity and, indeed, population was projected to decline, in some cases precipitously.

In 1992, in *Beyond the Limits*,[68] the 20-year update of *The Limits to Growth*, Meadows warned that society was then in a state of overshoot and that the result would likely not be a single massive collapse but the compounding of growing numbers of smaller crises, collectively overwhelming the ability of the world's managers to cope.

In 2012, *Smithsonian Magazine* was so unkind as to resurrect the old *Limits* collapse graph, plotting on top of it the actual data from 1972 until 2000.[69] The results were a rather nasty warning: we were right on track for collapse.

The modeling was brought up to date in Graham Turner's 2014 report, "Is Collapse Imminent?" It reiterated that humanity was continuing on the business-as-usual (BAU) trend line, warning,

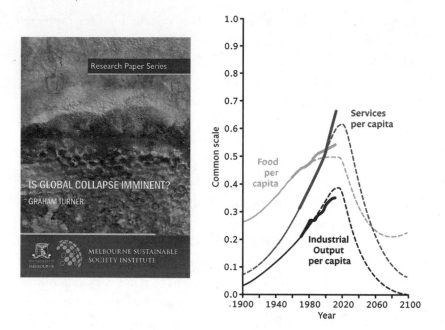

Credit: Graham Turner, *Is Global Collapse Imminent?* August 4, 2014.

The BAU scenario results in collapse of the global economy and environment (where standards of living fall at rates faster than they have historically risen due to disruption of normal economic functions), subsequently forcing population down. Although the modeled fall in population occurs after about 2030—with death rates rising from 2020 onward, reversing contemporary trends—the general onset of collapse first appears at about 2015 when per capita industrial output begins a sharp decline.[70]

Exceeding the Planetary Boundaries

In 2009, Professor Johan Rockström, at Stockholm Resilience Centre, and 27 leading academics from around the world identified nine "planetary life-support systems" essential for human survival.[71] They proposed that these be used as a framework of planetary boundaries, designed to define a "safe operating space for humanity." The

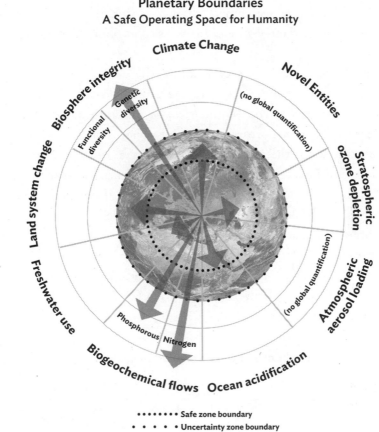

Rockstrom's Planetary Boundaries. Credit: Johan Rockström et al., "A Safe Operating Space for Humanity," *Nature*, Vol. 461, September 24, 2009.

group sought to quantify just how close human activity had come to the limits of these systems and how much further we could go before our survival was threatened. Breaching the planetary boundaries, they warned, "could see human activities push the earth system outside the stable environmental state of the Holocene, with consequences that are detrimental or even catastrophic for large parts of the world." Understanding and staying below these limits, the scientists said, could enable humanity to return to the stability of Holocene-like conditions.

Rockström's team showed that humanity had already crossed four of the nine boundaries: climate change, biosphere integrity, land-system change, and biogeochemical cycles (phosphorus and nitrogen cycle).

The scientists were very clear about the dangers of exceeding some of the nine boundaries. They described climate change and biosphere integrity as "core boundaries." Significantly altering either of these would "drive the earth system into a new state."[72] They were less certain about the risk of exceeding others. However, the Precautionary Principle argued that people must learn to live within all nine of these boundaries. The scientists stated, "If one boundary is transgressed, then other boundaries are also under serious risk. For instance, significant land use changes in the Amazon could influence water resources as far away as Tibet."[73]

This work echoed earlier analysis by Club of Rome members William Rees, at the University of British Columbia, and Mathis

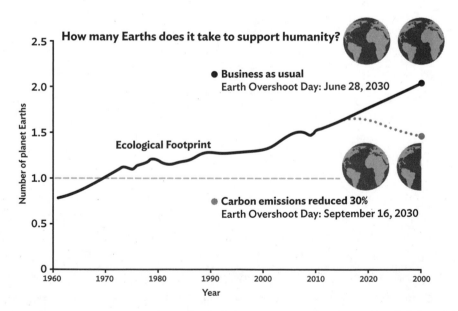

Global Footprint Network. Credit: footprintnetwork.org/en/index.php/GFN/page/world_footprint/

Wackernagel, who created what they called the ecological footprint. They point out that humans have inhabited this planet for approximately 200,000 years. During most of these, we lived within the planet's ability to regenerate itself...until about 40 years ago. Rees and Wackernagel calculated that by 2008 humanity had used the equivalent of 1.5 planets to provide the resources humans used and to absorb our wastes.[74] The approach became popular among scientists, businesses, governments, agencies, individuals, and institutions, who used it to measure the "footprint" of various populations—individuals, cities, businesses, nations, and all of humanity. Assessing the pressure on the planet enabled them to manage ecological assets more wisely and to take personal and collective action to support a world where humanity lives within the Earth's bounds.

As Dana Meadows had pointed out in *Beyond the Limits*, turning resources into waste faster than waste could be turned back into resources was driving global ecological "overshoot," depleting the resources on which human life and biodiversity depended. The impacts of overshoot were well-documented, especially the buildup of carbon dioxide and greenhouse gases in the atmosphere; the acidification of oceans, together with coral reef destruction; collapsing fisheries; the risk to pollination systems; and the depletion of fresh water. Groundwater tables in many parts of the world fell meters a year, much more rapidly than they could be regenerated.

In 100 years of industrial agriculture, we had consumed and dissipated 50 to 70 percent of the organic material and natural nutrients that had required 10,000 years of post-glacial building to accumulate.[75] These losses exemplified the warnings in the HANDY study.

Moderate UN scenarios suggested that, if current population and consumption trends continued, by the 2050s, we would have needed the equivalent of three Earths to support us.[77] Of course, we have only one.[78]

Now, today in 2050, we use far fewer resources, leaving enough to enable the natural world to flourish.[79] But it took humanity a rather severe learning curve to realize the value of intact nature.

So Many Problems: Where Did We Start?

Virtually every scientist who looked at the deteriorating state of the Earth's environment sounded the alarm. The Smithsonian Institution's massive Global Biodiversity Outlook 3 (GBO-3) analysis by hundreds of scientists warned, "We continue to lose biodiversity at a rate never before seen in history—extinction rates may be up to 1,000 times higher than the historical background rate."[80]

There were many factors driving this loss, but GBO-3 warned that climate change was forcing ecosystems to "tipping points" where they rapidly become less useful to humanity. Three ecosystems were at particular risk: coral reefs—sorry, scuba divers—business as usual and warming oceans would mean that there would be no living coral reefs on planet Earth by perhaps as early as 2030. Second, the Amazon was drying out and burning. And third, the emissions of CO_2 in the atmosphere were accumulating in the oceans, acidifying them and risking global devastation.[81]

Recognizing the risk, the 2016 annual survey of CEOs at the World Economic Forum (WEF) at Davos agreed that climate change was the greatest challenge facing humanity.[82] Bishop Desmond Tutu said that climate change has become "the human rights challenge of our time," responsible for many of the challenges that the impoverished face, including loss of life, lack of fresh water, the spread of disease, and rising food prices.[83]

The US National Academy of Science stated that every degree of warming would drive 5- to 15-percent reductions in crop yields, 3- to 10-percent increases in rainfall in some regions, and increased flooding. Conversely, it would also cause 5- to 10-percent decreases in streamflow, leading to decreases in potable water; 200- to 400-percent increases in the acreage burned in wildfires, 15-percent loss in Arctic sea ice, and 25-percent decreases in the annual minimum extent of ice in September.[84] Even if all CO_2 emissions stopped, the report stated,

> Climate would continue to warm for several more centuries. Over thousands of years this could unleash amplifying feed-

backs leading to the disappearance of the polar ice sheets and other dramatic changes. In the meantime, the risk of catastrophic wild cards "such as the potential large-scale release of methane from deep-sea sediments" or permafrost, is impossible to quantify.

Scientists showed that shifting monsoons might have caused the 2015 Himalayan earthquake that killed 9,000 people and the Sendai earthquake that unleashed the Fukushima disaster. They predicted that the world would suffer more and more violent quakes. "Climate change may play a critical role in triggering certain faults in certain places where they could kill a hell of a lot of people," said University College London's Professor Bill McGuire in 2015.[85]

That same year, Pope Francis, in his Encyclical, *Laudato Si*,[86] called on all humanity to respond to the climate crisis. More, however, he called on all people to address the failure of the current economic system to care for humans or the Earth. The Holy Father stated, "In the face of the emergencies of human-induced climate change, social exclusion and extreme poverty, we join together to declare that: Human-induced climate change is a scientific reality, and its decisive mitigation is a moral and religious imperative for humanity."

Religious leaders of essentially all of the world's great faiths joined the UN in acknowledging that climate change hurts the poorest first and worst,[87] as Typhoon Haiyan left 10,000 dead in the Philippines, mostly from rural villages. Periodic flooding in India displaced millions of poor villagers.

Climate chaos was recognized as a likely trigger for collapse. In a 2015 speech in Alaska, then president Obama observed,

Climate change is no longer some far-off problem. It is happening here. It is happening now. Climate change is already disrupting our agriculture and ecosystems, our water and food supplies, our energy, our infrastructure, human health, human safety—now. Today. And climate change is a trend

that affects all trends—economic trends, security trends.
Everything will be impacted...few things will disrupt our
lives as profoundly as climate change. Few things can have as
negative an impact on our economy as climate change.[88]

Climate change dramatically worsened food shortages. Lester
Brown's *Full Planet, Empty Plates: The New Geopolitics of Food Scarcity* warned that "grain stocks have dropped to a dangerously low
level, while the World Food Price Index has doubled in a decade....
We are only one poor harvest away from chaos in the world grain
markets."[89]

A food riot in Tunisia touched off the Arab Spring, and drought
fueled conflict in Syria and across North Africa that triggered the
flow of millions of refugees. Research published in the British medical journal *Lancet* warned that unchecked climate change would lead
to half a million deaths a year by 2050 from food shortages.[90]

In November 2017, 15,000 scientists reissued a warning to humanity of "widespread misery and catastrophic biodiversity loss" unless business-as-usual is changed.

By failing to adequately limit population growth, reassess
the role of an economy rooted in growth, reduce greenhouse
gases, incentivize renewable energy, protect habitat, restore
ecosystems, curb pollution, halt defaunation, and constrain
invasive alien species, humanity is not taking the urgent steps
needed to safeguard our imperiled biosphere.[91]

Former UN climate chief Christiana Figueres and physicist Stefan
Rahmstorf warned[92] that the world had approximately three years
before the worst effects of climate change would become inevitable.
In an open letter, they urged companies, communities, countries,
and citizens to cut carbon emissions now, arguing that failure means
fires, floods, droughts, rising sea levels, extreme weather, agricultural
losses, and massive insurance costs.

Back then, climate change seemed an existential threat.
But close your eyes again. Relax back into the world of 2050.
We solved it.

We live better lives, abundant lives supplied by local food and renewable energy. Chapters 9 and 10 spell out how we did this. Given that whatever exists is possible, it's time to start believing we can win this one.

Inequality

It was harder to reduce inequality. The HANDY study was clear: throughout history collapse has been driven not only by civilizations overrunning their resource base but also by rising inequality.[93]

The study laid out the ways past civilizations collapsed:

> [It] appears to be on a sustainable path for quite a long time, but even using an optimal depletion rate and starting with a very small number of Elites, the Elites eventually consume too much, resulting in a famine among Commoners that eventually causes the collapse of society.
>
> [Or]…with a larger depletion rate, the decline of the Commoners occurs faster, while the Elites are still thriving, but eventually the Commoners collapse completely, followed by the Elites.

Either way, geopolitical chaos ensues. In 2018, inequality was at crisis levels.

In 2016, Oxfam estimated that 8 people had as much wealth as the poorest 3.5 billion people on the planet.[94] This number replaced Oxfam's estimate just a year before of 62 people being richer than the bottom half.

By 2017, the number had shrunk to eight men who had the same wealth as the bottom half of the world:[95] Bill Gates ($75 billion, source of wealth, Microsoft); Amancio Ortega ($67 billion, Zara); Warren Buffett ($60.8 billion, Berkshire Hathaway); Carlos Slim Helu ($50 billion, Telecom); Jeff Bezos ($45.2 billion, Amazon); Mark Zuckerberg ($44.6 billion, Facebook); Larry Ellison ($43.6 billion, Oracle); and Michael Bloomberg ($40 billion, Bloomberg LP).[96]

Such inequality was a relatively recent phenomenon, as chapter 2 describes, dating only from 1980. After the 2008 financial collapse, however, it began to attract attention. In 2011, thousands of young people occupied Zucotti Park, a block away from Wall Street in New York, to fight the power of the major banks that had driven the financial system, and thus the rest of the world, into collapse.[97] Calling themselves Occupy Wall Street,[98] the movement rose from nowhere to 70 percent brand recognition in three months. It spread to a thousand cities around the world, durably framing the concept that one percent have as much wealth as the other 99 percent. This was not strictly true in 2011 but became so by 2016.[99]

The Spirit Level,[100] written by epidemiologists Richard Wilkinson and Kate Pickett, showed that people in more equal societies lived longer and had better mental health and more chances for a good education, regardless of background. Community life was stronger where the income gap was narrower. Children did better at school and were less likely to become teenage parents. When inequality was reduced, people trusted each other more, there was less violence, and rates of imprisonment were lower.

High levels of inequality were recognized not only to be immoral but to threaten social stability. Inequality worsened all social problems we wished to redress. Health and social problems were worse in more unequal countries.[101] Inequality eroded trust, increased anxiety and illness, and encouraged excessive consumption.

Wilkinson and Pickett showed that outcomes were significantly worse in more unequal rich countries for each of 11 different health and social problems: physical health, mental health, drug abuse, education, imprisonment, obesity, social mobility, trust and community life, violence, teenage pregnancies, and child well-being.

Their 2014 paper, "A Convenient Truth," laid out a business case for reducing inequality: companies that pay a living wage enjoy such increased productivity that it more than pays for giving their workers a life of dignity.[102]

In 2018, governments seemed incapable of acting. Tens of millions of people lacked a job or an income, while a small number of people had more money than they knew what to do with. The $25 billion in bonuses paid to Wall Street bankers in 2015 would have

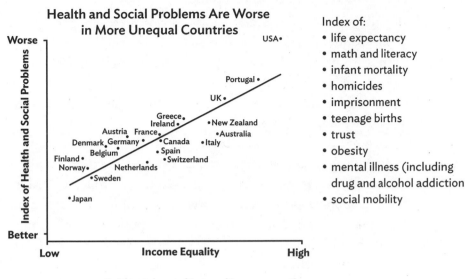

Epidemiology of inequality regenerative.

been enough, if distributed to every minimum wage worker in the US, to double their pay to a living wage.[103]

Companies began to respond. Dan Price, 31-year-old CEO of Gravity, a payment-processing company in Seattle, cut his own salary by $1.3 million, to $70,000 a year, so that everyone in the company could get that same salary. Outraged critics predicted collapse, but the company prospered so well that it had to add staff.[104]

As societies around the globe recognized that inequality was as critical a threat to their existence as climate change, they began to implement the sorts of policies that the New Economics Foundation in the UK had been setting forth for years. (These are described in chapters 11 and 12.) With the implementation, first, of minimum wages,[105] inequality began to lessen. In 2017, Finland initiated an experiment in universal basic income.[106] In the ensuing years, most European nations implemented a variant of this program, as it turned out to cost far less than administering other forms of social support. Now almost all nations provide their citizens with basic support as a human right, and inequality is no longer a driver of collapse.[107] Section 4 describes the policy measures that led to this outcome.

All Roads Did Not Lead to Collapse

HANDY warned that under conditions "closely reflecting the reality of the world today…We find that collapse is difficult to avoid."

But it observed, "Collapse can be avoided and population can reach equilibrium if the per capita rate of depletion of nature is reduced to a sustainable level, and if resources are distributed in a reasonably equitable fashion." [108]

In 2018, much of the world seemed poised for systemic collapse. In 2016, temperatures had been the hottest ever, the third such year in a row. [109] The 35 megacities were growing uncontrollably. [110] More than a billion people lived in shantytowns, projected to be two billion by 2030. This included 90 percent of the populations of Uganda, Malawi, and Ethiopia. In 1950, Lagos was a village of 300,000. By 2016, it struggled to serve 21 million. [111] The world's cities required enormous resources to keep them running. They also emitted almost 70 percent of the world's greenhouse gasses. [112]

National governments, unable to deal with rising demand for resources (energy, metals, fish stocks, etc.), competition for capital, unrepayable debt, and falling oil prices, created a situation in which their economies began to fail one by one. They followed the path of Egypt, Syria, Iraq, and Greece into political and economic chaos. Damages from storms, flooding, and heat waves cost their economies billions of dollars. Accelerating climate change and ecological degradation were recognized to be creating uneconomic growth—damages caused by growth exceeded the benefits, and ecological turmoil began to take national economies down. Unable to cope, they forced local governments to take matters into their own hands.

But cities turned out to be key to the answer. Recognizing that roughly 80 percent of the world's economic activity came from cities, mayors around the world joined together to supplant the increasingly incapable national governments. [113] By 2025, Asia had reached 29 megacities, and because of a combination of renewable energy and local food production, they succeeded in becoming regionally self-reliant.

Mayors took seriously the numbers set forth in such reports as *Risky Business*,[114] put forth by American business leaders Tom Steyer, Hank Paulsen, and Michael Bloomberg. This showed that solving the climate crisis would unleash billions of dollars in investment and create millions of jobs.

Globally, the Stern report[115] showed that significant investment to solve the crisis would be only 1 to 5 percent global GDP annually, compared to global costs of up to 20 percent if humanity did nothing. In 2018, a report showed that keeping global temperature rise below 1.5°C would save the world $30 trillion in avoided damages.[116]

Business leaders from across the political spectrum joined mayors to use actionable data at geographically granular levels.[117] They invested in climate protection,[118] renewable energy,[119] and local food production in their companies,[120] and in their communities.[121]

Belatedly countries began to realize that what the mayors of the world were doing made better sense than the austerity the nations had pursued. Costa Rica became the first nation to be entirely powered by renewable energy, followed by Greece.[122]

Yes, things looked grim in 2018, but trend is not destiny.

Even in that old book *The Limits to Growth*, which sounded the alarm that we had to change course, Meadows and her colleagues set forth one scenario in which humanity did not collapse. Since then Dana, as she was known to her friends, focused on this outcome, tirelessly devoting herself to organizing—from her community to the global level. In 2000, the effort killed her.[123] But her writings about solutions, and the devoted following who carried on her work, gave us the Finer Future we are crafting today.

Dana believed that we can avoid collapse. She observed,

> People don't need enormous cars; they need respect. They don't need closetsful of clothes; they need to feel attractive and they need excitement, variety, and beauty. People need identity, community, challenge, acknowledgement, love, joy. To try to fill these needs with material things is to set up an

unquenchable appetite for false solutions to real and never-satisfied problems. The resulting psychological emptiness is one of the major forces behind the desire for material growth. A society that can admit and articulate its nonmaterial needs and find nonmaterial ways to satisfy them would require much lower material and energy throughputs and would provide much higher levels of human fulfillment.[124]

Dana believed that a sustainable world is possible. The sustainability vision[125] she outlined looked very like what the world has now adopted.

Dana's belief in human potential and the power of telling optimistic stories is the basis for the rest of this book.

CHAPTER TWO

THE STORY THAT GOT US IN TROUBLE

Like Slavery and Apartheid, poverty is not natural.
It is man-made and it can be overcome and
eradicated by actions of human beings.

NELSON MANDELA[1]

If the Looming Collapse Is Human Made, Then We Can Unmake It

To set forth a better economic system, we need to understand how we got into the one we have.

Humanity has been trending toward unsustainable behavior for a long time, some say since the advent of agriculture.[2] (Chapter 9 describes this challenge and what to do about it.)

The immediate risk to human survival, however, arose more recently. It is a truism to say that the cause of problems is often prior solutions,[3] but that's precisely what has happened, and it is important to understand how it was caused if we are to fix it.

The Making of the Dominant Paradigm

The economic system that has brought us to the brink was made by men, 36 of them to be precise, who met in 1947. In the wake of a devastating world war, they set out to frame the economic system that they believed would deliver prosperity. Ludwig von Mises, Fredrich von Hayek, Milton Friedman, and 33 of their intellectual associates met for ten days at the Mont Pelerin Hotel, outside of Montreux, Switzerland. The ideology they built, which they called neoliberalism, now underpins essentially all national economic policies, even in countries with an economy nominally labeled something else. It also forms the basis for economics courses the world around, and if you've taken one, this stuff is in your head.

Ludwig von Mises was appalled at what National Socialism had done to trash Europe. Friedrich Hayek was terrified of the rise in the East of Soviet collectivism. Milton Friedman championed the freedom of the individual to make economic decisions. Together, they laid out their belief that government interference in economics was unmitigated evil, that there should be no meddling by government in individuals' choices. The best way, they felt, to express preference was in as unfettered a market as possible. Strong property rights and free trade, they argued, are the best institutional means through which to achieve liberty and freedom.

Friedman stated,

> Government has three primary functions. It should provide for military defense of the nation. It should enforce contracts between individuals. It should protect citizens from crimes against themselves or their property. When government—in pursuit of good intentions—tries to rearrange the economy, legislate morality, or help special interests, the costs come in inefficiency, lack of motivation, and loss of freedom.[4]

Theirs was not a universally held belief at that time. Following the triumph of the New Deal, in a world fresh from the success of Western governments in winning World War II (incidentally thereby ending the Great Depression), most people had a lot of faith in governments.

But the small group persevered. The Mont Pelerin Society they founded worked with the newly created Nobel Prize for Economics to get eight of its members chosen as winners and named as advisors to essentially every head of state on the planet. Three of them became heads of state, and others central bankers.[5]

The narrative is appealingly simple: you, as an individual, are the only legitimate economic actor. Money is the measure of success, and your unfettered freedom to go get it is the paramount value. An article in the Mises Institute publication quotes Mises to say, "The only method of economic calculation is by individuals through the pricing process. Therefore, government investment is inherently inferior to free-market investment."[6] "Markets may not be perfect," says the Mises institute, "But they are superior to any alternative, and individuals acting in their own selfish interests will sort things out better without interference. People are, says this interpretation of psychology, essentially selfish beings fighting it out in a Neo-Darwinist 'survival of the fittest.'"

The Mises Institute argues,

> Whether some degree of government is necessary to allow the market to operate, while being outside the scope of this essay, deserves commentary. The belief that government is necessary to at least guarantee individuals's [sic] property rights is not uncommon. However, knowing that property rights are absolutely essential for a working coordination process, it seems difficult to think that individuals themselves would consider the allotment of resources toward the end of securing their property rights as having secondary importance to something else—especially since the attainment of "something else" may require secure property rights.[7]

Neoliberals believe that maximizing individual desires is the force that drives maximization of what economists call "utility." Their narrative tells us that

+ the sole goal of the economy and business is to generate financial wealth;
+ the freedom of the individual (person or corporation) is the primary societal value;
+ government should be small, protecting individuals and their private property.
+ if we just let the free market sort things out, all will be well.

The men who gathered at Mont Pelerin acted out of the best intentions. They believed that any form of collective action, particularly when imposed by government, resulted in tyranny. Their approach, they felt, was the only way to ensure freedom and dignity. Citing the murders in Germany and Russia of millions of people who dared oppose collectivism, they questioned any role for the state. The path to happiness, they said, is the maximization of private ownership.

Proponents of this worldview find inequality not only inevitable but entirely acceptable. The Mises Institute writes,

> If, then, inequality of income is the inevitable corollary of freedom, then so too is inequality of control. In any organization, whether it be a business firm, a lodge, or a bridge club, there will always be a minority of people who will rise to the position of leaders and others who will remain as followers in the rank and file. Robert Michels declared this as one of the great laws of sociology, "The Iron Law of Oligarchy." In every organized activity, no matter the sphere, a small number will become the "oligarchical" leaders and the others will follow.[8] Theirs is clearly a top-down view of the world, in which the only way to increase wealth is to empower the wealthy to get as rich as they can, which deliver wealth to all. It is a linear and mechanistic view of the world, associated with a patriarchal sense that it is the right of white males to dominate. The non-white, non-male is the "other."[9]

Any deviation from this is a sign of weakness, a sentiment now echoed in modern demagoguery.[10] The framing also draws from the old Calvinist belief that being rich was a sign of being blessed.[11] It was a sign of adherence in meeting the command of Genesis 9:7 as stated in the King James Bible, "And you, be fruitful and multiply; bring forth abundantly in the earth and multiply therein."[12]

The steady drumbeat of this argument led to a conviction that the only legitimate goal of business is to maximize shareholder (owners) value in the short term.[13] Milton Friedman declared that any other action by a company is philanthropy at the expense of the corporate owners.[14] This framing guides politicians to cut taxes, especially on corporations and the wealthy.[15] If wealth is the sign of success, shouldn't we do everything that we can to promote and increase it?

Institutionalizing Greed

Given the ability of government in the years following World War II to lift people from poverty and create an increasingly prosperous middle class in the US and in Europe, how did a rather wonkish ideology that flew in the face of that success come to rule the world?

The answer appears to be story and strategy. Neoliberalism found its storyteller in novelist Ayn Rand. Her books *Atlas Shrugged* and *The Fountainhead* sell in the hundreds of thousands still today and were credited by Alan Greenspan, the Tea Party, and the Speaker of the US Congress, secretary of state, and president as foundational. Her dismissal of the poor as parasites and celebration of naked greed have been described as the philosophy of a psychopath but have been read by one-third of Americans.[16]

The strategy arose in 1971 when Lewis Powell, a corporate lawyer who, two months later, would become a justice on the United States Supreme Court, penned a strategy at the request of the head of the US Chamber of Commerce, describing how business could relegitimize itself. The Chamber was concerned that, in the wake of the 1960s, young people, radicalized on the college campuses, were rejecting the central role of business. Powell, also concerned by student activism and the rise of public interest lawyers, penned "Attack on the American Free Enterprise System."[17] Available today on the Web, it was the strategy for engaging corporate America to enshrine the neoliberal ideology.

In his memo, Powell stated,

> Business must learn the lesson...that political power is necessary; that such power must be assiduously cultivated; and that when necessary, it must be used aggressively and with determination—without embarrassment and without the reluctance which has been so characteristic of American business.... Strength lies in organization, in careful

long-range planning and implementation, in consistency of action over an indefinite period of years, in the scale of financing available only through joint effort, and in the political power available only through united action and national organizations.[18]

Powell got the funding and consistency of action he desired. On the strength of the Memorandum, a variety of foundations and donors assembled staggering amounts of money to implement the strategy that Powell laid out.[19] On the East Coast of the US, the Koch brothers founded and endowed the Heritage Foundation and the Cato Institute, American Enterprise, Hudson, Hoover, and similar think tanks. Millions of dollars created and endowed such organizations as the Pacific Legal Foundation. It embedded the concept of tax cutting and protection of property rights into California law, and groomed a young actor named Ronald Reagan to gain the governorship of the state.[20] Together, such organizations took the neoliberal principles, previously found only in academic conversations, hired the best marketing firms to massage them, sold them, and created the intellectual architecture that made market fundamentalism commonplace and propelled neoliberal ideology to dominance.

It is somewhat chilling to read the Powell Memorandum today and realize that the systematic dismantling, over the past 50 years, of American democracy[21] and government policies around the world designed to protect the well-being of people all flowed from this strategy.[22] Powell targeted almost 30 institutions for transformation, from local school districts to local judges to local and national media.

In 1980, with the election of Ronald Reagan in the US and Margaret Thatcher in the UK, neoliberalism won. It became the global economic ideology.

In the Reagan Era of the 1980s, deregulation was implemented in many countries. Directors of corporations assumed greater control and initiated a flurry of hostile takeovers of many smaller companies.

Club of Rome co-president Ernst von Weizsäcker argues, however, that acceptance of neoliberalism became truly global only after the fall of the Berlin Wall and the collapse of the Soviet Union. He points out,

> British and Americans see the Thatcher/Reagan revolution (+ Mont Pelerin, Hayek, Friedman, etc.) as the cause of it all. I insist that until 1990 only Chile and the Anglo-Saxon countries (including, significantly, New Zealand) fell to the neoliberal doctrine. In Japan, Germany, Scandinavia, etc., the *social* market doctrine remained stronger. Most developing countries, suffering terribly under the "Washington Consensus" regime of the World Bank, IMF and US Treasury, found neoliberalism deadly wrong. Of course, neoliberal economists began flooding the universities but were not politically successful except in the Anglo countries. In the Netherlands, Ruud Lubbers created the "Polder Model" of consensus among all relevant parties, which eliminated *some* social privileges although it did not question the rule-making power of the State. But when the Soviet Union and the Soviet influence over Eastern Europe collapsed (and China began to emerge as a *market* power), the world changed completely. The Uruguay Round of the GATT, initiated by Ronald Reagan, had been as "hopeless" as now the Doha Round is, until 1990. But immediately after the Soviet collapse, absolutely sweeping neoliberal changes were brought into the trade regime, as all the mentioned European and Asian countries and essentially all developing countries that had blocked "progress" on Reagan's Round, grudgingly conceded that "there was no alternative" to free and deregulated trade and capitalism. That made the Uruguay Round more effective than all previous seven GATT Rounds combined and led to the creation of the WTO.

This historical analysis is important because the kind of "benign capitalism" that some people advocate flourished in many countries as long as everybody knew that there *was* an alternative to capitalism—albeit one that no one in his/her right mind would prefer. But the very existence of communism forced capitalists in nearly all countries to accept social (and later ecological) restrictions to market forces. Remember during the first decade of the Cold War, i.e., Eisenhower's Presidency, marginal tax rates for the rich were 90 percent.[23]

Regardless of when you decide that neoliberalism won, by the 1990s and 2000s, it was dominant, and the consequences became manifest. Deregulation allowed accounting scandals from the 1998 near-death of Long-Term Capital Management,[24] to the collapse of Enron in 2001[25] and of Worldcom in 2002.[26] Financialization swept the economy[27] (see chapter 7). Companies engaged in an orgy of outsourcing and offshoring of jobs, costs, and profits, costing millions of American jobs.[28] The 2008 financial collapse was a predictable result of the systematic dismantling by adherents of neoliberalism of a wide array of government protections.[29] The "Great Recession" resulted in the evaporation of $50 trillion and the loss of 80 million jobs.[30] All of this sowed the seeds of Brexit in the UK, the 2016 Electoral College victory in the US, and populist nationalism across Europe.

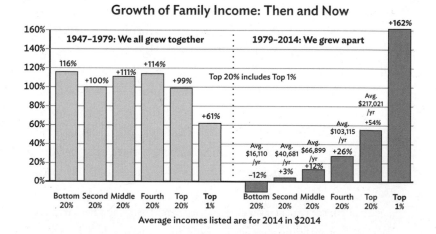

Inequality pre/post 1980. Source: 1947–1979: United for a Fair Economy (FairEconomy.org): Analysis of US Census Bureau data; 1979–2016: Census Bureau, Table F03AR (Census.gov); Top 1%: Piketty & Saez, World Top Incomes (wid.world).

It also lifted inequality to unheard of heights. After World War II, as New Deal policies took root, income disparities fell in the US, and most of the Western world. They remained low until about 1980. During this time, all classes of Americans rose together. The poorest actually did a bit better than other classes.

It was only after the neoliberals came into power that incomes diverged and the staggering levels of inequality described in the prior chapter came to be the norm.

Nobel laureate Paul Krugman observed,

> Before World War One the one percent received around a fifth of total income in both Britain and the United States. By 1950 that share had been cut by more than half. But since 1980 the one percent has seen its income share surge again—and in the United States it's back to what it was a century ago.[31]

From 2000 to 2007, it got worse: incomes for the bottom 90 percent of earners rose only about four percent, adjusted for inflation. For the top one-tenth of one percent, incomes climbed about 94 percent.[32] Following the 2008 financial crash, 93 percent of all income gains went to the richest one percent of the US population.[33] "The richest one percent now has more wealth than the rest of the world combined."[34]

The Republican tax cuts of 2017 give 83 percent of the gains to the richest one percent and raise taxes on 92 million middle-income families. To pay for this largesse, cuts are mandated to health care for the poor and elderly.[35]

Inequality is a complex issue. Thomas Piketty's *Capital in the 21st Century* put the discussion of inequality squarely on the map.[36] The book's popularity—its 700 pages of arcane economics statistics translated from the French became the number one best seller on Amazon and the *New York Times* list for weeks—has to be a tribute to the framing by Occupy Wall Street of the one percent versus the 99 percent. It wasn't true at the time but has become so. What Nicholas Kristof[37] called "the least read, best seller in history"—all of the Kindle quotes about the book are drawn from its first 26 pages—put the issue of inequality squarely on the map.

Piketty showed that the nature of the financial world today means that unless you have capital, you are essentially excluded from a route to real prosperity. He argued that this fact will drive ever-greater inequality at a terrifying rate. Such inequality, he observed, corrodes our democratic institutions and is causative of collapse.[38]

But his solutions fell short. The only real answer he proposed was a global wealth tax to repay public debt and redistribute income. He proposed rates of at least 80 percent on top marginal income—roughly what was true under Ronald Reagan in the US. Most observers give it a slim chance of passage.

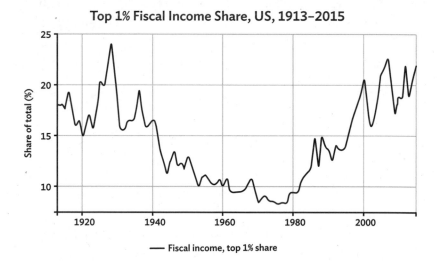

Top 1% Fiscal Income Share, US, 1913–2015

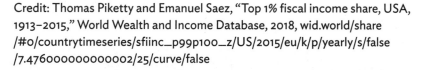

Credit: Thomas Piketty and Emanuel Saez, "Top 1% fiscal income share, USA, 1913–2015," World Wealth and Income Database, 2018, wid.world/share /#0/countrytimeseries/sfiinc_p99p100_z/US/2015/eu/k/p/yearly/s/false /7.476000000000002/25/curve/false

Nobel laureate Joseph Stiglitz, who has been writing about inequality since the 1960s, celebrated Piketty's acclaim, which reinforces much of what he has said for decades. He argued that the inequality in the US is driven by market manipulations. "Much of America's inequality," Stiglitz warns, "is the result of market distortions, with incentives directed not at creating new wealth but at taking it from others."[39] He observed,

The top 1 percent have the best houses, the best educations, the best doctors, and the best lifestyles, but there is one thing that money doesn't seem to have bought: an understanding that their fate is bound up with how the other 99 percent live. Throughout history, this is something that the top one percent eventually do learn. Too late.[40]

But social instability is starting to make even the wealthiest a little nervous. In early 2017, a *New Yorker* article profiled the uber-rich "preppers," who are laying in ammunition, buying land on islands in the Northwest US, and in rapidly increasing numbers, buying "boltholes" in New Zealand to escape the coming collapse, or the uprising of the underclasses.[41]

Nick Hanauer is an investor who hit it big. Seeing the power of the internet to disrupt bricks-and-mortar stores, he invested in Amazon and, as he puts it, now owns a yacht. His take on the collapse of the middle class is that it is engendering anger and will soon trigger class warfare. In a stark article titled "The Pitchforks Are Coming...for Us Plutocrats," he wrote,

At the same time that people like you and me are thriving beyond the dreams of any plutocrats in history, the rest of the country—the 99.99 percent—is lagging far behind. The divide between the haves and have-nots is getting worse really, really fast. In 1980, the top one percent controlled about 8 percent of US national income. The bottom 50 percent shared about 18 percent. Today the top one percent share about 20 percent; the bottom 50 percent, just 12 percent.[42]

Austerity and Why It Is Not the Answer

To a neoliberal, the answer is always less government. Inequality? Reduce government borrowing, spending, and debt so that there is more money for businesses to spend and the economy will grow. Best way to reduce debt? Austerity. Cut back all government action. Cut taxes, especially on the wealthy, because with more money in their pockets, the rich will invest, creating jobs and greater economic activity, lifting everyone. Given that free markets are by definition perfect, we should increase the freedom in markets globally through free trade agreements.

That narrative is, as H. L. Mencken put it, clear, simple, and wrong.

Austerity increases unemployment and inequality. Lower interest rates do increase bank profits, but these get invested in speculation, not the real economy. Lower taxes increase inequality, and they cut the government services that those who have little money depend on to survive.[43]

Despite the mounting proof of the failure of neoliberals' ideological commitment to austerity, it got intellectual support in analysis by Harvard academics Carmen Reinhart and Kenneth Rogoff. They claimed that when a country's gross debt exceeds 90 percent of its GDP, "median growth rates fall by one percent, and average growth falls considerably more." They claimed that allowing high debt drives constraints on growth, and that deficit cutting is the only obligation of nations.[44] This argument convinced austerians across the world, even as poverty rose and economies crumbled, to redouble their efforts.

But in 2013, Nobel economist Paul Krugman figured out why the pair were wrong. Turns out they not only had deleted relevant data, and used sketchy statistical procedures, but they also had made a freshman math error that rendered their conclusion not merely wrong but dangerous.

This came to light because researchers who tried to replicate the Reinhart and Rogoff conclusions consistently failed. When they got access to the spreadsheets, they found why no one could replicate their results. Krugman lamented,

> Austerity enthusiasts trumpeted that supposed 90 percent tipping point as a proven fact and a reason to slash government spending even in the face of mass unemployment. So, the Reinhart-Rogoff fiasco needs to be seen in the broader context of austerity mania: the obviously intense desire of policy-makers, politicians and pundits across the Western world to turn their backs on the unemployed and instead

use the economic crisis as an excuse to slash social programs. What the Reinhart-Rogoff affair shows is the extent to which austerity has been sold on false pretenses. For three years, the turn to austerity has been presented not as a choice but as a necessity.[45]

Krugman, who had argued that austerity is a route to ruin, was vindicated. He, like most economists, retains a fixation with growth, but he showed that neoliberalism and austerity will not deliver shared prosperity.

Austerity has clearly not solved the Greek crisis. Economic analyst Bradford DeLong showed that the greater the austerity imposed, the greater the fall in GDP. He quotes Paul Krugman's estimate that €1.00 of spending cuts in Europe produces only €0.40 of debt reduction relative to baseline and produces a €1.25 fall in production in the short run.[46]

Economists at the International Monetary Fund have also shown that austerity drives inequality,[47] one of the causative factors of collapse. In a study of 17 OECD (Organization for Economic Cooperation and Development) countries between 1978 and 2009, they found that fiscal belt-tightening redistributed income and jobs to those in society who already have more of the resources. It decreased wages and increased long-term unemployment, worsening inequality.[48] Conversely, Oxfam found that although inequality rose in Norway after the financial crisis of 2008, the government's willingness to extend the social safety net enabled their economy to emerge relatively unscathed from the crisis, with low unemployment and falling poverty.[49] In 2017, Norway was named the happiest country on Earth, a measure, as described in chapter 12, of aggregate well-being.[50]

In contrast, Belgium and the UK followed the austerity orthodoxy of the EU at the time and now face rising inequality, more people driven into poverty, and a threat to social stability.[51] In the UK, Oxfam found[52] that the Thatcher-led shift to market capitalism doubled the number of people living in poverty and raised inequality to levels unseen since just before the Great Depression.[53]

Who's in Charge Here?

Such statistics raise the specter that the 2008 collapse was a dress rehearsal for something more sinister.

Neoliberal ideology argued that such a downturn was impossible. Alan Greenspan, a staunch disciple of Mont Pelerin, admitted that he had not believed such a collapse possible and had, as a result, put too much faith in the self-correcting power of free markets. He stated, "Those of us who have looked to the self-interest of lending institutions to protect shareholders' equity, myself included, are in a state of shocked disbelief."[54] Appointed by Ronald Reagan in the first flush of neoliberal victory, Greenspan, called the Maestro when he was chair of the US Federal Reserve Bank because it was thought that he was the one who held it all together, still struggles to reconcile that his ideology had betrayed him. For millions of citizens worldwide, the result was a bit more devastating.[55]

The workings of the world are weird.

For example, who would have believed that the collapse of a bank none of us have ever heard of, on an island (Cyprus) most Americans would have trouble locating on a map, could threaten the existence of the euro?[56] Or that when Angela Merkel, now the world's banker, proposed to give the depositors a "haircut," Vladimir Putin was soon on the phone telling her not to reduce the holdings of what turned out to be Russian mafia bosses.[57] In the end, depositors with large accounts lost most of their money, although people with deposits under $100,000 were untouched. The euro was saved, but Merkel got a more than a few grey hairs.[58]

OK, then just who *is* running the global economy?

Much to the delight of the neoliberals, it appears that no one is.

An article in the *Financial Times* was headlined "Central Bankers Say They Are Flying Blind." A former European Central Banker was quoted as saying, "We don't fully understand what is happening in advanced economies."[59] Turns out that the economic chaos perplexed even those who ran it.

Even that couldn't convince neoliberals to accept oversight. Alan Greenspan, although admitting to having found market imperfections after the 2008 collapse, resisted additional regulation: "Those markets for an indefinite future will be far more restrained than would any currently contemplated new regulatory regime."[60]

Let us hope so. A decade after the collapse, the too-big-to-fail banks are even bigger,[61] and the unrestrained trading that drove the 2008 collapse is back.[62]

To neoliberals, this is just fine. If the rich have plenty of money, that's the way it is supposed to be. But when the economy is 70 percent based on consumption, and ordinary people lack the money to buy stuff, the wheels start to come off the enterprise. In June 2011, the *Financial Times* blamed "zombie US consumers for menacing the world economy."[63]

We have created a situation in which if people in Western countries stop shopping, the economy actually is at risk. After the tragic attack on the Twin Towers on 9/11, George Bush implored American's to "Go shopping."[64] And he was right, in a perverse way: if, in a shock, you act as if nothing has happened, economically nothing *has* happened.

Cracks in the Paradigm

Stock markets spiral ever upwards. But even "irrational exuberance" cannot prop things up indefinitely. The system is increasingly brittle, and any surprise sends investors scurrying.[65] Prevailing belief holds that a collapse in economic (GDP) growth would likely drive a social collapse, as expectations of rising prosperity are denied. But as HANDY warned, collapse is more likely from too much growth inequitably distributed. Unless some way is found to ensure that consumers have incomes, a downward spiral is a risk.

Nick Hanauer put it,

> But the problem isn't that we have inequality. Some inequality is intrinsic to any high-functioning capitalist economy. The problem is that inequality is at historically high levels and getting worse every day. Our country is rapidly becoming less a capitalist society and more a feudal society. Unless our

policies change dramatically, the middle class will disappear, and we will be back to late 18th-century France. Before the revolution.

And so I have a message for my fellow filthy rich, for all of us who live in our gated bubble worlds: Wake up, people. It won't last.

If we don't do something to fix the glaring inequities in this economy, the pitchforks are going to come for us. No society can sustain this kind of rising inequality. In fact, there is no example in human history where wealth accumulated like this and the pitchforks didn't eventually come out. You show me a highly unequal society, and I will show you a police state. Or an uprising. There are no counterexamples. None. It's not if, it's when.[66]

There's an old joke that says a recession is when your neighbor loses his job, a depression is when you lose yours. Perhaps the definition of collapse is that we're all out of a job.

Such concerns have reached even the halls of the International Monetary Fund. In an unusually thoughtful piece in summer 2016, the IMF's own journal asked whether neoliberalism has been oversold. While repeating the neoliberals' claims that their approach has lifted millions out of poverty, increased efficiency, and spread modern technology across the globe, the report turned its attention particularly to the results of neoliberalism's commitment to global and instantaneous movement of capital and austerity as the tools to deliver prosperity. It stated,

> An assessment of these specific policies (rather than the broad neoliberal agenda) reaches three disquieting conclusions:
> + The benefits in terms of increased growth seem fairly difficult to establish when looking at a broad group of countries.
> + The costs in terms of increased inequality are prominent. Such costs epitomize the trade-off between the growth and equity effects of some aspects of the neoliberal agenda.

+ Increased inequality in turn hurts the level and sustainability of growth. Even if growth is the sole or main purpose of the neoliberal agenda, advocates of that agenda
still need to pay attention to the distributional effects.[67]

The report goes on to admit: Austerity policies not only generate
substantial welfare costs due to supply-side channels, they also hurt
demand—and thus worsen employment and unemployment.

The GDP growth that the austerity advocates had promised,
and that the IMF continues to believe is essential and beneficial,
would not, the IMF conceded, result from neoliberalism.

This led the IMF to walk back its doctrinaire espousal of the
tenets of Mont Pelerin:

On capital account liberalization, the IMF's view has also
changed—from one that considered capital controls as almost
always counterproductive to greater acceptance of controls to
deal with the volatility of capital flows. The IMF also recognizes that full capital flow liberalization is not always an
appropriate end-goal, and that further liberalization is more
beneficial and less risky if countries have reached certain
thresholds of financial and institutional development.

When the entity that has done the most to impose the neoliberal
agenda on the nations of the world begins, publicly, to question its
own paradigm, perhaps the time is right for a new narrative.

CHAPTER 3

TELL ME A BETTER STORY: REGENERATIVE ECONOMICS

You never change things by fighting the existing reality.
To change something, build a new model
that makes the existing model obsolete.

BUCKMINSTER FULLER[1]

Is It Possible to Change the System and Avoid Collapse?

Yes.

There is no silver bullet, but we sure have plenty of silver buckshot. To use it effectively, we need a new story.

The cultural historian Thomas Berry said,

> We are in trouble just now because we do not have a good story....
>
> The old story—the account of how the world came to be and how we fit into it...sustained us for a long period of time. It shaped our emotional attitudes, provided us with a life purpose, energized action. It consecrated suffering, integrated knowledge, guided education....
>
> We need a (new) story that will educate man, heal him, guide him.[2]

The neoliberal narrative profiled in chapter 2 brought humanity to the verge of ruin. But the Keynesian narrative of government stimulation and regulation of the economy to ensure growth, if allowed to continue, would drive to much the same outcome, if slower and more humanely. So would socialism. Both lessened inequality but drove equally hard for growth and the overuse of resources. Communism, similarly, resulted in ecological[3] and human mayhem. One account estimates that communist regimes were responsible for 94 million deaths between 1900 and 2000, more than three times the number killed by fascist regimes.[4]

The economy of consumption has not delivered the quality of life promised. Instead, people struggle to make ends meet and find purpose in their lives. The annual Gallup Healthways survey of global workplace satisfaction[5] warns that workers are unhappier than at any time since Gallup began taking such polls. They feel worse about their jobs than before, with 87 percent saying that they are disengaged from their work.[6] Good Company estimates that this dissatisfaction costs US companies up to $550 billion every year in lost productivity.[7]

In addition, there are the truly disaffected people that J. D. Vance writes about in *Hillbilly Elegy*.[8] Even conservative commentator David Brooks acknowledged that such people are in pain and that the failure of the system to hear this has led to the rise of extremist politics. He, too, calls for a new story:

> I don't know what the new national story will be. But maybe it will be less individualistic and more redemptive. Maybe it will be a story about communities that heal those who suffer from addiction, broken homes, trauma, prison and loss, a story of those who triumph over the isolation, social instability and dislocation so common today.[9]

This isn't an ideology of the right or the left; it is a matter of the survival of modern human civilization as we know it.

History shows that the construction of a new story or narrative is the critical first step to achieving system change. If we know where we want to get to, then we can make it happen.

Dana Meadows said of visioning,

Vision is the most vital step in the policy process. If we don't know where we want to go, it makes little difference that we make great progress. Yet vision is not only missing almost entirely from policy discussions; it is missing from our whole culture. We talk about our fears, frustrations, and doubts endlessly, but we talk only rarely and with embarrassment about our dreams. Environmentalists have been especially ineffective in creating any shared vision of the world they are working toward—a sustainable world in which people live within nature in a way that meets human needs while not degrading natural systems. Hardly anyone can imagine that world, especially not as a world they'd actively like to live in. The process of building a responsible vision of a sustainable world is not a rational one. It comes from values, not logic.[10]

In the absence of positive vision, voices of fear fill the vacuum. Populist politicians blame economic migrants, refugees, trade from other countries, the "other"—the "outsider"—and build stories based on taking back control and making their country great again. History shows us that this is a dangerous path. Protectionism, iron curtains and walls, and populist nationalism have all caused massive harm in the much less interconnected world of the 20th century. In this new century where so many of our problems are global in scope, where our technologies and communication systems are similarly global, and where we face huge population and resource pressures, the consequences are likely to be disastrous.

Failure to ensure that the billions of people who feel left behind by the system can not only find a sense of self-worth but also support themselves and their families will have severe political consequences.[11]

Populist, authoritarian agitators speak to the pain of feeling unwanted, threatened by modernity, technological change, and issue-based politics. The mass of increasingly unemployed blue-collar workers was especially receptive to the antiestablishment movement in the US, but the phenomenon is global. From Brexit in the UK to the Austrian and Italian referenda, from Orban in Hungary and Duterte in the Philippines to the US, populist nationalism is on the rise. The predictable rise in populism, racism, xenophobia, and nativism portrays migrants as threats to jobs, and a source of crime, drugs, and rising welfare costs.

As the books of novelist Alan Furst show, fringe movements of such disaffected people in "near history" have the capacity to wreak real havoc.[12]

No one knows how close we are to collapse, although historical scientist Peter Turchin claims that it will happen within the decade.[13] Many people are feeling on edge, wondering what shock might tip the global system into an unstoppable slide to dissolution.

Abundant evidence shows that it *is* possible to avoid collapse, that it *is* possible to shift to a better economic system without collapse. But unless people believe this, and act as if this is true, we'll get to find out just how close to collapse we really are.

Let's not go there. We have all of the technologies we need to make a good start at solving the challenges facing humanity. Chapters 9 and 10 detail some of the exciting opportunities to slow, then reverse, climate change. They show how doing this will create delightful cities, meet our needs for energy and food in ways that generate jobs and build community. The best of these are market based, and more profitable than what we are doing now. The question is whether we can find the political will to implement the solutions in time.

For these necessary shifts to occur, there must be a powerful new story, one that resonates with our definition of who we are as people and with our aspirations of how we want to live. The task is to create a narrative of human well-being. Recent history has shown that it is not enough to publish scientific reports or amass data. Humans have always learned from story. Brexit won in the UK because the Leave advocates told a better story. In the US, the president told a story of how he would improve the lives of those feeling left behind. Hilary Clinton only asked her supporters to avow, "I'm With Her."

The best stories are never about you. They are about your audience. People must see themselves in the new story and want to live it. Then they must demand that their governments create policies and practices to give it to them.

Rethinking Economic Theory

Humanity's collision with planetary boundaries requires a radical rethink of economic theory and practice. Economics as taught and used by politicians is littered with myths and half-truths. This is not a failure unique to economics as a discipline. But the power of the dismal discipline compels politicians and other economic actors to base political decisions on these "half-baked" theories. As John Maynard Keynes, one of the most famous economists, stated, "Practical men who believe themselves exempt from any intellectual influences are usually the slaves of some defunct economist."[14] The myths and half-truths to which politicians frequently fall prey include the beliefs that

+ we can have infinite growth on a finite planet;
+ markets are fair;
+ prices tell the truth;
+ more income equals more happiness.

These are particularly acute in neoliberalism but pervade all of conventional economics, where they contribute significantly to the malfunctioning of the current economic system.

Robert Nadeau[15] makes clear the extent to which not only is the current economic narrative unsuited to our needs, it is based on fantasy:

> Neoclassical economic theory is predicated on unscientific assumptions that massively frustrate or effectively undermine efforts to implement scientifically viable economic policies and solutions.... The strategy used by the creators of neoclassical economics was as simple as it was absurd—the economists copied the physics equations and changed the names of the variables. In the resulting mathematical formalism, utility

becomes synonymous with the amorphous field of energy described in the equations taken from the physics, and the sum of utility and expenditure, like the sum of potential and kinetic energy in the physical equations, is conserved. Forces associated with the field of utility (or, in physics, energy) allegedly determine prices, and spatial coordinates correspond with quantities of goods.

Thomas Piketty, author of *Capital in the 21st Century*, agrees that such "physics envy" by the economics profession had driven its "immoderate use of mathematical models, which are frequently no more than an excuse for occupying the terrain and masking the vacuity of the content."[16]

Even Piketty underestimates the magnitude of the failing, however. Nowhere in the production functions and prices of the mathematical models beloved by economists is the value of ecological resources and human well-being counted. Infinite growth is assumed to be possible even when based on non-renewable resources. Economists routinely assign what they call a "discount rate" to their calculations of the future worth of a project to reflect their belief that you would rather have a reward today than tomorrow. But under this highly questionable practice, any future becomes worthless.

Stewart Wallis, in his chapter in the recently published *Why Love Matters: Values in Governance*, adds,

> These problems are exacerbated by the fact that economics is now treated as a science where outcomes are predicted mathematically. Just some of the reasons why this is not the case are: the fact that most economists don't recognise that the economy is a subset of the eco-system; economic theory is not based on explicit values, it mixes means and ends (GDP is a means and not an end); it is not focused on meeting human needs (physical and psychological); the theory is insufficiently focused on economic inequality, and there is a lack of an explicit power analysis. In addition, neoclassical economics is

based on a number of dangerously simplistic assumptions that distort reality. These include: that humans are rational utility maximising actors; that markets tend toward equilibrium and market failures are exceptional; and that sufficient money is always provided when there is demand. I could go on, but I believe that neo-classical and neo-liberal economics, in many ways, are practically, intellectually and morally bankrupt.[17]

The old narrative, also called the "economistic paradigm,"[18] tells us that people are essentially greedy. The framers of neoliberal ideology saw humans as uncaring, and narrowly self-interested. And to them, that was OK. It was the genius of the market that such people pursuing their individual desires would aggregate to deliver the greatest good for the greatest number.

People like that exist. Science tells us that about one percent of the population accurately fits the description of neoliberal perfection. Psychologists label such people psychopaths.

Robert Hare, a leading researcher on psychopathy describes them as

> social predators who charm, manipulate, and ruthlessly plow their way through life, leaving a broad trail of broken hearts, shattered expectations, and empty wallets. Completely lacking in conscience and in feelings for others, they selfishly take what they want and do as they please, violating social norms and expectations without the slightest sense of guilt or regret.[19]

Most of us, however, are not like that. We yearn for more than just money.

The economistic narrative of the economy extols competition, perfect markets, and unfettered growth in a world in which the rugged individual is seen as the economic epitome. This view of human nature, and how to achieve success, is dogmatically taught in most economics courses and in business schools around the world.

John Harvey, writing in *Forbes Magazine*, goes so far as to blame this version of economic theory for the problems facing the world today:

> The fault lies not with the rich, not with corporations, not with China, not with the Illuminati, not with Al Qaeda, but with the economics discipline. Bad ideas have done at least as much damage to our world as anyone's bad intentions. Decades of misguided policy from both political parties and in other nations has critically weakened the core of our economy and left us in a situation where, despite our tremendous level of technological achievement, we seem to be regressing. Just as in the Great Depression, we have the ability to solve these problems practically overnight. What we lack is sound theory to guide our actions.[20]

The result of professional economists getting social science wrong is an economy that doesn't work for most people on Earth. We have created a society that seeks to meet non-material needs with material things, celebrating consumerism. It's called "shopping therapy" and "He who dies with the most toys wins." We have huge inequality. Too big to fail crushes local self-determination, and millions of people hate their jobs.

Ellen Goodman explains:

> Normal is getting dressed in clothes that you buy for work and driving through traffic in a car that you are still paying for in order to get to the job that you need to pay for the clothes and the car and the house that you leave vacant all day so you can afford to live in it.[21]

And we grow lonelier.

Pope Francis warned, "The external deserts in the world are growing, because the internal deserts have become so vast."[22] He quotes the Earth Charter that challenges humanity to do better:

> As never before in history, common destiny beckons us to seek a new beginning.... Let ours be a time remembered for

the awakening of a new reverence for life, the firm resolve to achieve sustainability, the quickening of the struggle for justice and peace, and the joyful celebration of life.[23]

The brilliant scholar Elinor Ostrom became the first woman to win the Nobel Prize in Economics[24] in part because she so adroitly debunked the shortcomings of economics. The fact that her doctorate is in political science may have enabled her to become an effective critic of economics. Her friend David Sloan Wilson described the profound nature of her challenge:

> The mathematical empire [of economics] was founded on the assumption that self-interest automatically leads to collective wellbeing. Lin's work was founded upon a stubborn fact of life: self-interest often leads to the overexploitation of resources and other problems that make life worse for everyone, not better. When everyone was allowed to suck as much water out of the ground as they pleased, there was no invisible hand to rescue the situation.... [T]he import of the Nobel Prize going to Lin Ostrom...signaled that something was rotten about the mathematical empire and that a new paradigm needs to begin from a different starting point. But what would the new paradigm look like and what would be its theoretical foundation?[25]

An Economy in Service to Finance

The current economy is exceptionally efficient at doing what it is designed to do. In the language of finance, it "optimizes the risk adjusted return to capital." This means that the system facilitates the accumulation of money and flows it to those who had money to start with. As Thomas Piketty showed,[26] access to money is what enables you to make more money and drives the finance sector that manipulates that money.

In other words, more than bad or greedy capitalists being "at fault," the fault lies in the system we have designed, which delivers the outcomes we are experiencing. We're in a prosperous dilemma

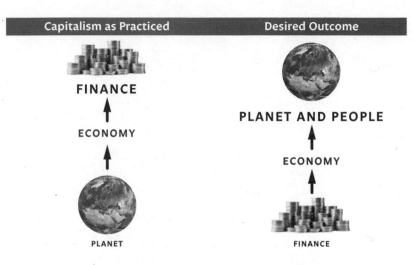

Credit: John Fullerton, Capital Institute.

of our own making.[27] We, the people and the planet, are in service to the economy, which is in service to finance. This is precisely the wrong way around.

As described in chapter 1, this system is a clear and present danger to our collective well-being and even our survival.

Finance should be a nested subsystem of the economy, not its purpose. It should serve as a tool to deliver essential productive investments and liquidity (money) to the real economy, which should function in such a way as to be in service to life.

What Do We Want?

The new narrative must tell us how to
  1. achieve a flourishing life within ecological limits;
  2. deliver universal well-being as we meet the basic needs of all humans; and
  3. deliver sufficient equality to maintain social stability and provide the basis for genuine security.[28]

The first step in turning away from the threat of collapse is to imagine an alternative economic system.

Try it.

It's not easy. William Allen, former chancellor of the Delaware Court of Chancellery, notes, "One of the marks of a truly dominant intellectual paradigm is the difficulty people have in even imagining an alternative view."

Dana Meadows argued,

> Imagine for a moment that in every bioregion (think: the watershed in which you live) there is an organization that is creating an economy that brings wellbeing to everyone within it (both the human communities and the "beyond human" life). Think for a moment about the economy that hums around you? What does it consist of? Sure, people make and sell and buy things. So far so good. But does the economy ensure that everyone who wants one has a job? Do people have enough money to meet their needs and a bit left over for the luxuries of life? Is the natural world flourishing and increasing? Or do you live in a world of pollution and poverty? What if teams of people were identifying all that you love about your present economy and protecting that, while assessing what isn't working and fixing that? Impossible? That opinion is a failure of vision. Now, today, in four bioregions of Costa Rica, and in almost 20 other communities around the world such "Regenerative Hubs" are forming and functioning.[29]

We are limited by our belief that the current system is all that is possible. Bernard Lietaer points out that Homo sapiens is an interesting species:

> We have incredible power to transform our environment to meet our needs. And yet we have this odd tendency to create a world, forget that we have created it, and then throw up our hands and proclaim our inability to change the system. Capitalism (and socialism for that matter, which is equally unsustainable) is not a set of natural laws that Adam Smith discovered. It is our creation, constantly evolving and changing—consciously or unconsciously.[30]

Creating that different reality is the purpose of the rest of the book.

Ladder to a Better World

The second step is to realize that we are all in this together, that no one approach will definitively be the right one, and that a lot of experimentation will be needed. Only by working together, by appreciating our diversity and differences and still working collaboratively will, we find our way forward.

Imagine a pool of muck.

That's not far wrong from the situation in which humanity now resides. The pool has been created by the old narrative and the resulting excesses of a degenerative economy practicing business as usual.[31]

Imagine that rising from this sewage lagoon is a ladder. On the foundational rungs are activists seeking to stop some of the destruction facing us: the scientists,[32] businesspeople[33] and professors[34] calling for a new approach, and the young people[35] willing to get arrested to stop the mining of tar sands—the massive carving away of the earth to mine Canadian bitumen—and opposing the pipelines to ship tar sands sludge or fracked oil.[36] Students and clergy[37] demand that their universities and churches divest from ownership in fossil fuels, and human rights activists[38] fight inhumane conditions in Bangladeshi factories or biopiracy in India[39] on similar rungs.

On adjacent rungs are conservationists saving remnants of intact ecosystems[40] and agency personnel enforcing pollution regulations.[41] Several rungs later are the business leaders implementing corporate social responsibility, driving enhanced profits by shifting business practices,[42] and ensuring that workers and communities are treated decently.[43]

Organizations like CDP[44] and the Global Reporting Initiative[45] set standards, measure reduction of impacts, and occupy neighboring rungs. New accounting systems like the International Integrated Reporting Council,[46] the Sustainability Accounting Standards Board,[47] and other metrics sit on rungs proving the business case for more responsible behavior. The Sustainable Development Goals[48] call to all of humanity to deliver basic quality of life in ways that can endure.

In the same area are green developers creating less wasteful, more delightful structures that offer higher productivity because employees are happier and healthier and perform better in cleaner, more natural environments.[49] A few rungs on are the architects of Platinum LEED buildings and Living Buildings,[50] and the WELL Building Standard.[51]

These servants of what is known as "sustainability" are bringing the system back to neutral—able, unlike now, to endure indefinitely without destroying itself. All of this work to achieve what we have been calling sustainability or sustainable development is essential to getting our noses above the muck.

Such activism is more than noble. It brings the world back toward balance, mitigating the destruction of life our activities are causing on this little planet. But it will never achieve the balance we seek.

Increasingly, there is a palpable change afoot. Even those doing this important work sense that it is not enough. It is failing to meet the crises accelerating around us. It is essential, necessary, and insufficient.

It has become fashionable to denigrate sustainability because it is only "less bad." Some fault "green" activities as being "uninspiring." This is facile, and as the founder of the modern environmental movement, David Brower,[52] warned, such circular firing squads deliver only despair. He observed if you are standing on the edge of a cliff, the only progressive move is to turn around and then step forward, what he called the ecological U-turn. A bus speeding toward the cliff's edge must first slow down before it picks a new heading. The foundational rungs of the ladder are as crucial as those above them. Cut the legs off the ladder, and we sink further into the mire. Break too many of the rungs, and the integrity of the ladder collapses.

The turf squabbles engaged in by change agents confuse people facing a world skidding into catastrophe. As Jo Confino, executive editor of *Huffington Post* puts it, "The status quo is a huge beast with claws sharpened and teeth bared. All the new models that people are pushing, because they aren't working together, are just like little mice running around bumping into each other."[53]

The disparate efforts for change are essential foundations, the vital hard work on the ground to place "sustainability" as a necessary midpoint of the climb. Humanity is hungry for "a vision all living things can share."[54] But what is above the middle rung of the ladder? What can unite all of the disparate efforts into a new narrative?

An Economy in Service to Life

We haven't got all of the answers, but the ladder's destination might better be described not as sustainability but as a Regenerative Economy: an economy in service to life.

Viewed from the vast potential that exists but is not yet manifest in the present economic system, sustainability is an outcome, not the objective. Looking to natural systems as the model, it is obvious that nature didn't set out to be sustainable. It achieves that only because it is regenerative. The essence of life and the evolutionary process of all life is regeneration.

This vision of an economy aligned with how the universe works can supply missing clarity of vision needed to inspire the commitment that will enable change groups to work together transformatively, in a dynamic, creative mosaic.

If we combine what is known about how transformations occur with the best science of what is necessary and who we are as human beings, the outline of a way to avoid collapse emerges.

The new story begins with the principles of living systems.

It includes the equitable distribution of scarce resources to maximize well-being for all within planetary limits.

The narrative shows how humanity can ascend out of the degenerative world in which we have sunk. It goes beyond "sustainability" to a world that is regenerative of life.

To avoid collapse, for example, it is helpful but insufficient to construct greener buildings and build various metrics that detail our progress toward a less wasteful world. Each of these measures is a rung on the ladder, but without the potential represented from the "regenerative" vision, humanity is unlikely to avoid collapse.

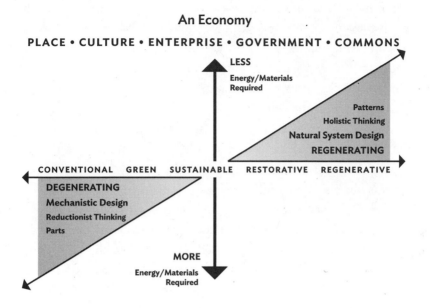

Credit: John Fullerton, Capital Institute.

"Regenerative," as a term, is cropping up everywhere now. Its first known use in a design context was by Buckminster Fuller. More recently, the financier John Fullerton applied it to economics. After an 18-year career at JP Morgan, Fullerton walked away. During the ensuing decade of deep study and awakening, he learned that the essence of life and the evolutionary process is regeneration. Inspired by his learnings in the fields of regenerative agriculture, systems science, and ecological economics, he sought to extend the principles from agricultural systems to economic systems. As a result, we are now experiencing the birth of "Regenerative Economics."

He realized that sustainability is the result, not the means of getting the system right.

In 2010, Fullerton created Capital Institute to "seek a more just and sustainable way of living on this earth through the transformation of finance."[55] His 2015 landmark paper, "Regenerative Capitalism: How Universal Principles and Patterns Will Shape the New

Economy,"[56] is an articulation of what an economy aligned with living systems principles and the laws (not theories) of physics would look like. He points out that, according to leading evolutionary theorists,[57] there are patterns and principles that nature (living and non-living alike) uses to build stable, healthy, and sustainable systems throughout the world.

Capital Institute defines Regenerative Economics as "the application of nature's laws and patterns of systemic health, self-organization, self-renewal, and regenerative vitality to socioeconomic systems." In his paper, Fullerton set forth eight principles:

1. Right Relationship:[58] This principle holds the continuation of life sacred and recognizes that the human economy is embedded in human culture, which is itself embedded in the biosphere.[59] All systems—from molecular scale all the way to cosmic scale—are nested, interconnected, and defined by overarching relationships of mutualism,[60] within which day-to-day exchanges take place.

2. Innovative, Adaptive, and Responsive: This draws on the innate ability of human beings to innovate and "create anew" across all sectors of society. Humans are innately creative and entrepreneurial.[61] Even in failure, we "begin again."

3. Views Wealth Holistically: True wealth is not money in the bank. It is defined in terms of the well-being of the "whole," achieved through the harmonization of the multiple forms of capital, with systemic health only as strong as the weakest link. Well-being depends on belonging, on community, and on an array of community-stewarded assets.[62]

4. Empowered Participation: All participants in a system must be empowered to participate in and contribute to the health of the whole.[63] As people, we long to be part of something bigger than ourselves.[64] Therefore, beyond whatever moral beliefs one may hold, financial and non-financial wealth must be equitably (although not necessarily equally) distributed in the context of an expanded understanding of systemic health.

5. Robust Circulatory Flow: Like the metabolism of any healthy

system, resources (material and non-material) must circulate up and down the system efficiently and effectively.[65] Circular economy concepts for material and energy described in chapters 4 and 10 are one important aspect of this principle at work.

6. "Edge Effect" Abundance: In nature the most abundant ecosystems occur where two come together—where a river meets the ocean in an estuary—because there is diversity. Similarly, creative collaborations across sectors of the economy increase value-adding wealth creation through a diversity of relationships, exchanges, and resiliency.[66]

7. Seeks Balance: This balances resilience, the long-run ability to learn and grow stronger from shocks, with efficiency, which, while more dynamic, can create brittle concentrations of power.[67] Living within planetary boundaries, without collapse, requires economic systems that are designed for a balance of efficiency and resilience and are built on patterns and principles that mirror those found in healthy, resilient natural systems.[68]

8. Honors Community and Place: There can be a dynamic, global economy so long as it ensures that every place, every ecosystem has integrity. This principle nurtures healthy, stable communities and regions, both real and virtual, in a connected mosaic of place-centered economies.[69]

Fullerton's principles are not absolutes. They are part of a rapidly emerging field of holistic thinking. They are interconnected and necessarily work together. They are a limited description of a complex pattern that is beyond linear description. But as a start, they guide us in creating an economy that operates in accordance with the rest of the world, creating conditions conducive to life.[70]

They are the essential first step to grounding this new field of Regenerative Economics. They draw from the best thinking in evolutionary biology,[71] ecological economics,[72] positive psychology,[73] economic democracy,[74] and the emerging discipline of humanistic management[75] to offer a new story of who we are as human beings, and how we can craft a Finer Future.

Who Are We As Human Beings?

Neoliberal ideology arose at a time when economists, seeking to be seen as legitimate scientists, tied their thinking to the social fashions of the day: physics and Darwinian evolution. David Sloan Wilson observes,

> Evolutionary theory's individualistic turn coincided with individualistic turns in other areas of thought. Economics in the postwar decades was dominated by rational choice theory, which used individual self-interest as a grand explanatory principle. The social sciences were dominated by a position known as methodological individualism, which treated all social phenomena as reducible to individual-level phenomena, as if groups were not legitimate units of analysis in their own right (Campbell 1990). And UK Prime Minister Margaret Thatcher became notorious for saying during a speech in 1987 that "there is no such thing as society; only individuals and families." It was as if the entire culture had become individualistic and the formal scientific theories were obediently following suit.[76]

People who subscribe to the view that the world is a nasty, brutish, competitive place are quick to cite Charles Darwin's frequently misquoted "survival of the fittest." By which they mean that the strongest, toughest, meanest individuals will triumph, and that this is the way the way of nature.

This position ignores the fact that Darwin actually wrote about the "survival of the best adaptive." In 1909, he stated,

> Any animal whatever, endowed with well-marked social instincts, the parental and filial affections being here included, would inevitably acquire a moral sense or conscience, as soon as its intellectual powers had become as well, or nearly as well developed, as in man. For, firstly, the social instincts lead an animal to take pleasure in the society of its fellows, to feel a certain amount of sympathy with them, and to perform various services for them.[77]

Darwin also observed,

> The small strength and speed of man, his want of natural
> weapons, etc., are more than counterbalanced by his intellec-
> tual powers, through which he has formed himself weapons,
> tools, etc., and secondly by his *social qualities* which lead him
> to give and receive aid from his fellow-men.[78]

Since then, biologists have discovered that nature is much more
about cooperation than it is about competition.[79] Evolutionary biologists, anthropologists, psychologists, and social scientists have
studied what makes humans unique as a species. The best of modern
science now tells us that the neoliberal narrative is fatally incomplete.

In his 2010 book, *Driven to Lead: Good, Bad, and Misguided
Leadership*,[80] Paul Lawrence sets forth what he calls Renewed Darwinism, a correction to the neoliberal belief that the rugged individual is all that matters, that people just want to acquire money, and
that the job of government is solely to defend their ability to do this.
Yes, Lawrence says, there is a human drive to acquire and defend,
but, he adds, what distinguishes us from many other animals that
share these drives is that, as Darwin noted, humans have an equally
powerful drive to bond. They also have a drive to comprehend, to
create, to innovate. To be happy, says Lawrence, to be truly fulfilled,
humans need to meet each and all of these drives.

This suite of drives, say the evolutionary biologists, is baked into
what enabled prehumans to survive. When the first hominids came
down out of the trees in Africa, we were naked. Our claws were
pretty inadequate, our teeth puny. Anthropologists theorize, based
on fossil record, that the earliest humans were not fearsome warriors
but rather were prey animals, dependent for their survival on working together creatively. "Lacking size or weapons, this early human
species most likely used brains, agility, and social skills to escape
from predators," says Robert Sussman, author of *Man, the Hunted*.[81]

Our ancestors were kind and moral, more prone to empathy and
collaboration than the neoliberal narrative believes.

We faced species extinction on at least several occasions, with
the number of humans reduced to a breeding population of perhaps

18,000, fewer than the endangered population of gorillas today.[82] Yet we survived lions, bear-sized hyenas, volcanic eruptions, and ice ages. We survived because we formed tribes, we worked together, and we were creative, entrepreneurial creatures.[83] We're storytellers, meaning-makers. We're puzzle-solvers and communitarians. Today, the fascination with Facebook and Pokémon GO are just as much a part of what makes us happy as are acquisitions of new Porsches and the ability to thump our chests at rivals.

E.O. Wilson, one of the planet's most famous biologists, states that early human prehistory supports this thesis. He makes clear that we are the dominant species on Earth now only because we are inherently social beings, "super-cooperators, groupies of the group, willing to set aside our small, selfish desires and I-minded drive to join forces and seize opportunity as a self-sacrificing, hive-minded tribe."[84]

Wilson's book *The Social Conquest of Earth*[85] argues that the dominant species that inhabited Earth prior to the emergence of the human species were what he calls "eusocial," or truly social, like ants and bees. He compares vertebrates' and invertebrates' ways of spreading across the planet, showing that both were successful to the extent that they collaborated. To Ed Wilson, group and tribe formation is a fundamental human trait.[86]

The emotions that economists are fond of saying only cloud the mind of rational, utility-maximizing Homo economicus are actually, says Wilson, traits hardwired into us as decision-making tools. These emotions guide us toward the sorts of cooperative outcomes we call "morality." We behave in ways that are genuinely altruistic because it is in our genes to benefit the group, not the individual.

So, then, why aren't we all kind and loving? Wilson argues that these behaviors are "prepared" and ready to be developed as part of our genetic makeup but that the implementation of them needs to be learned.[87]

Economists have sought for decades to school such caring out of us, to convince us that normal humans seek only to maximize and defend their possessions, that wealth is the only measure of worth.

But in so doing, they are denying half of what makes us human. Education and socialization can make us more like the economic model of perfection, but doing that is making us miserable. What has for millennia been critical for human survival is also essential to making us happy.

Michael Pirson, founder of the Humanistic Management Network,[88] a global network of scientists and academics, states,

> One can make more sense of this by looking at daily experience in which humans find that they care about each other (in family, work and friendship circles) and about society at large (reading the news, checking in with "friends" on social media, etc.). A life devoid of care leads to misery in many ways. Humans have long determined that isolation is the cruelest punishment, whether physical isolation on a remote island (exiled like Napoleon), in a solitary confinement cell, or psychologically isolated through feelings of shame. Being alone is considered a tragedy and leads many to depression, dysfunction, or even suicide, rendering isolation crueler than death.[89]

Pirson's discipline, humanistic management, emphasizes the importance of respect for human dignity and the scientific evidence that humans survived only when they organized for the common good. This approach envisions organizations as caring communities that converge to produce wider benefits.[90] Based on the best of modern science,[91] it says,

+ Most people are happy.
+ Happiness is a cause of good things in life. People who are satisfied with life eventually have even more reason to be satisfied, because happiness leads to desirable outcomes.
+ Most people are resilient.
+ Happiness, strengths of character, and good social relationships are buffers against the damaging effects of disappointments and setbacks.
+ Crisis reveals character.

+ Other people matter mightily if we want to understand what makes like most worth living.
+ Religion matters.
+ Work matters as well if it engages the worker and provides meaning and purpose.
+ Money makes an ever-diminishing contribution to well-being, but money can buy happiness if it is spent on other people.
+ As a route to a satisfying life, well-being is superior to hedonism.
+ The "heart" matters more than the "head." Schools explicitly teach critical thinking; they should also teach unconditional caring.
+ Good days have common features: feeling autonomous, competent, and connected to others.
+ The good life can be taught.

This approach is spreading. Positive Psychology practitioners[92] study what makes people happy, fully functioning humans, not what makes them neurotic and self-destructive. Leading business thinkers (see chapter 8 for more) speak of flourishing[93] and of Conscious Capitalism,[94] Natural Capitalism,[95] Regenerative Capitalism,[96] and the need for a Big Pivot.[97] Biologists explore the "wood-wide web,"[98] the notion that in nature organisms communicate and cooperate more than they engage in cut-throat competition. Policy officials at OECD and in various national governments develop Better Life Initiatives,[99] move beyond GDP,[100] and create happiness indexes.[101]

People hunger for a sense of who they are, where they belong, and what they believe in. Think about it. You are here because your distant ancestors cared more for the good of the whole than any one of them cared for himself. It's literally in your DNA to care and to act to create a greater good.

The "Zero Draft Narrative"

The proponents of neoliberalism worked for more than 30 years to achieve dominance for their narrative. As described in chapter 2, they found only limited success until the US Chamber of Commerce commissioned the Powell Memorandum. It then took less than a decade for neoliberalism to become the dominant global ideology.

Many advocates of human survival have tried to overcome the juggernaut of neoliberalism. But without a compelling alternative narrative, none of the organizing, agitating, lobbying, litigation, and legislation has succeeded. Progress has been achieved, but as the Alt-Right movement in the US, the forces backing Brexit in the UK, and the various anti-immigrant parties across Europe have shown, the desire to turn the clock back is strong. Meanwhile, the rending of the social fabric wrought by inequality, and the havoc of climate change is upon us. Going back won't work. It simply is not an option. As David Brooks put it, the future of the US (and many other countries) "is not going to be found in protecting jobs that are long gone or in catering to the fears of aging whites. There is a raging need for a movement that embraces economic dynamism, global engagement and social support."[102]

An international consortium, the Wellbeing Economy Alliance (WEAll),[103] has stepped up to do just that. It seeks to replicate the process that brought neoliberalism to power. Through gatherings on diverse continents, it is framing a new narrative for a world that works for all of humanity. It is developing a strategy to bring into being the following narrative:

> True freedom and success depend on creating a world where we all prosper and flourish. Institutions serve humanity best when they recognize our individual dignity and enhance our interconnectedness. To thrive, businesses and society must pivot toward a new purpose: shared well-being on a healthy planet.[104]

The Wellbeing Economy Alliance stands for
+ the possibility that institutions can evolve and transform; that revolution/tearing down the entire system and building new structures from scratch should only be a last resort. We honor those who resist degenerative practices, but seek to build bridges

where possible and create opportunities for our movement to experiment and learn together;

+ amplifying, supporting, building upon, and bringing greater coherence to efforts already in motion: a "movement of movements" even if it lacks a single name;
+ being constructive; building a wide and strong foundation;
+ recognizing the value of individual entrepreneurship and human creativity;
+ a strategy that understands complex adaptive systems, versus command and control;
+ working iteratively, guided by a long-term vision of what is possible/necessary;
+ channeling resources toward what is working, or what we sense should be tested.

This narrative starts from the recognition that people are basically good, that what all of us want is to be happy. It understands that we derive the greatest happiness from being in service to something greater than ourselves. What it takes to be happy is not especially costly, either in financial terms or ecological destruction. It turns out that good lives do not have to cost the Earth.[105]

The "Zero Draft Strategy"

To achieve a Finer Future, we need a strategy.

WEAll has set forth a draft strategy. To answer the Powell Memorandum, it proposes the Meadows Memorandum, named in honor of the gentle Vermont farmer, great scientist, and writer, Dana Meadows.[106]

The strategy will

+ accelerate the decline of the dominant neoliberal narrative, particularly in Western economic thought;
+ connect the millions of people pursuing a Finer Future and let them know that they're not alone.

It proposes to shift the world's major institutions, including governments, but especially businesses, so that they operate in service to the well-being of all. This will reliably increase human health and productivity, as it fosters sustainability. It will give change agents a vision of the future we want, a definition of who we are as humans, and a route to implement well-being at work and in society. It will shift businesses, governments, and the institutions of cultural creation to be part of the solution, not a cause of problems.

The strategy

+ reframes the economic narrative around how we achieve well-being, dignity, and a healthy planet;
+ invites diverse groups of people and organizations from all parts of society to co-create, adapt, and interpret the narrative;
+ maps key stakeholders and gatekeepers who shape our current economic narrative;
+ convenes stakeholders and collaboratively serves the movement's ability to find coherence;
+ crowdsources strategies that change agents around the globe can use to frame locally appropriate strategies to take their work to scale;
+ shifts corporate behavior to implement the new narrative;
+ shifts flows of capital to companies and organizations behaving in ways that enhance well-being;
+ identifies and connects institutions and leaders for whom well-being is a core mission,
  • amplify their stories by showcasing successes and helping them pay it forward;
  • build on their strengths and bring their work to scale;
+ agrees on key qualitative/quantitative measures of well-being that institutions can leverage;
+ designs and executes on a plan to,
  • make that new narrative the default in our institutions so that choices that promote well-being (i.e., prosperity and flourishing)—in people's lives, in business, and in government and systems—flow naturally;
+ combines the story of who we are as humans with how we can organize to solve the challenges facing us. This details how businesses and all organizations can better manage people. It shifts

our purpose from exploitation for short-term profit to delivering holistic well-being as the basis for sustainable returns *and* a healthier society.

Objectives:
+ Spread the new narrative to inspire people and empower institutions to pursue an economy in service to life;
+ Replace incentives for exploitation for short-term profit with rewards for long-lasting, regenerative wealth creation;
+ Use the new narrative to shape the policies needed at all levels of government, including corporate reporting, investor oversight, and rewards for behavior that serves us all;
+ Shift flows of capital to organizations behaving in ways that enhance well-being, by moving money from harm to healing;
+ Change our consciousness (our deeper-level understanding of who we are and the world we live in) through practices and positive routines that connect us to individual purpose, to each other, and to the natural environment;
+ Enlist young people, business leaders, teachers, civil society leaders, communities of faith, regulators, policy-makers, scientists, economists and economic thought leaders, storytellers, marketers, the media, advertisers, and cultural icons to refine and spread the new narrative.

The neoliberal ideology's storyteller was Ayn Rand.[107] While the Finer Future yet lacks a novelist, it has found voice in the work of renegade economist Kate Raworth. Her book *Doughnut Economics*[108] has taken the economics world by storm. It quantifies a social foundation for the human economy based on meeting the basic needs of all humans.[109] She lays out how humanity must operate below the planetary boundaries but above the minimum foundation needed to ensure human well-being and dignity. She calls this the sweet spot, the "safe and just operating space for humanity."[110]

To supplement the book, Kate produced a series of videos[111] that detail her Seven Ways to Think Like a 21st Century Economist:

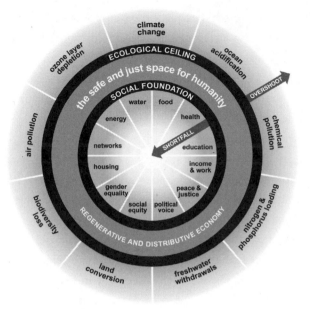

Credit Kate Raworth, *Doughnut Economics*.

+ Change the Goal: From GDP to the Doughnut
+ Tell a New Story: From the neoliberal narrative to a story fit for our times
+ Nurture Human Nature: From rational economic man to social adaptable human
+ Get Savvy with Systems: From mechanical equilibrium to dynamic complexity
+ Design to Distribute: From "growth will even it up again" to distributive by design
+ Create to Regenerate: From "growth will clean it up again" to regenerative by design
+ Be Agnostic about Growth: From growth addicted to growth agnostic
+ And Now...It's Time for Planetary Economics: Why it's time to think big about the economy[112]

Kate calls on us to tell a new story about a sweeter view of economics. The neoliberal narrative is based on assumptions that scientists now reject. Psychologists, evolutionary biologists, and anthropologists and others find that most people are not greedy, rugged individualists.[113] We seek to meet our needs, yes, but more, people seek goodness, connection, and caring.[114] We desire to be rewarded for meaningful contributions with a decent living[115] but are not primarily motivated by acquiring wealth.

Unlike neoliberalism, which is based on an incomplete view of what it means to be human,[116] the new economic model must balance our innate entrepreneurialism and individualism with a more holistic view that recognizes the human instinct for fairness and our desire to bond with others.

There is a business case for this view: purpose-driven organizations[117] that respect dignity and implement more sustainable practices better engage all stakeholders and enjoy increasing productivity. More sustainable brands and ethical investments deliver higher profitability.[118]

There is a quality-of-life reason, as well. Science now tells us that life itself is not separate, competitive, or based on random chance[119] but interconnected[120] and mutualistic. Implementing more regenerative practices drawn from natural systems is a better way to achieve both the true freedom that the original neoliberals cherished, as well as a world that works for everyone.

That inclination you feel to help, that yearning to be part of something bigger than yourself, is not a flaw. More than language, more than the fact that you stand tall, this is what makes you human. *You* are the descendent of those who survived. Ever wanted to get the call to be a superhero? That's not a foolish fantasy. The world needs you. Answer that call.

It's literally in your blood.

George Bernard Shaw once said,

This is the true joy in life, the being used for a purpose recognized by yourself as a mighty one; the being a force of nature instead of a feverish selfish little clod of ailments and grievances complaining that the world will not devote itself to making you happy.

I am of the opinion that my life belongs to the whole community and as long as I live it is my privilege to do for it whatever I can. I want to be thoroughly used up when I die for the harder I work the more I live. I rejoice in life for its own sake. Life is no "brief candle" for me. It is a sort of splendid torch which I have got hold of for the moment and I want to make it burn as brightly as possible before handing it on to future generations.[121]

Buying Time
to Fix the Mess

IN ANY CRISIS, what you really need is time to find and put in place the answers. This section describes how resource productivity can buy time and give humanity the opportunity to implement durable solutions to challenges that narrow our possibilities. Technological solutions exist that can push back the most proximate threats. Essentially, all of these alternative approaches make money, which means that even if we faced no crises, we should do them anyway. They buy us time, but only if we use that time, and the resources they afford us, wisely to implement fundamental change.

An array of technologies and new business models can deliver clean energy, feed us, transform how we do business, and solve essentially all of the worst challenges facing humanity. Many of these are already growing exponentially (see the energy section in chapter 10), but as any student of disruptive technologies knows, the slope of the growth curve of what will become any rapidly rising exponential growth starts shallow. It takes time for that growth rate to deliver significant change.[1] We need ways to buy this time. The

The first rule
of holes is
when you
find you are
in one,
stop digging.

ANONYMOUS

77

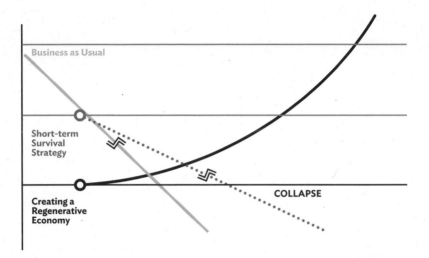

Business as Usual

Short-term
Survival
Strategy

Creating a
Regenerative
Economy

COLLAPSE

Credit: Natural Capitalism Solutions.

fastest, cheapest way to do that is to use all resources dramatically
more productively.

In the image above, the light gray line is the one humanity is now
on. We're going down. Using resources dramatically more efficiently
(the dotted line) will not change the ultimate outcome until the
black line diverts us (the squiggles) from collapse.

Following the light gray line, collapse cannot be avoided and happens fast (Turchin's prediction of ten years). But by delaying the
crises, we give the regenerative economy time to take root.

Efficiency measures per se are only part of the solution. As is the
case for all productivity enhancements, an increase in resource efficiency—be it materials or energy—will lead to resources being freed
up. This can result in some increased resource demand over time
through rebound effects and by stimulating growth. This is what
we have experienced in the past, i.e., relative decoupling but rarely
absolute decoupling. Consequently, what has to be stressed much
more than is now done is the need *to combine* enhanced resource
efficiency with the structural shifts created by (1) circular material
flows, (2) material substitution, primarily through the increased use
of renewable materials, (3) technology innovation, and (4) the in-

troduction of taxes to keep prices up for bad practices and balance demand. This not only buys us time, it sets us on the path to a regenerative economy.

Chapter 4 describes the work that is being done to close the loops in material flows. This approach, called the circular economy, slows the use of the Earth's scarce material resources as it creates jobs and cuts carbon emissions that are driving climate change.

Chapters 5 and 6 celebrate the workhorse of the transition to a new economy: energy efficiency, first in buildings and then in vehicles. Again, each of these sets of measures is profitable right now, and collectively, they go a long way to forestall the most proximate crisis facing us.

CHAPTER FOUR

EVERYONE WINS:
THE CIRCULAR ECONOMY

Any sufficiently advanced technology
is indistinguishable from magic.

ARTHUR C. CLARKE[1]

Resource Efficiency: Cornerstone to Buying Time

In a business-as-usual world, resource extraction rates are projected to double or even triple by 2050. This is not unreasonable, given past trends. Annual extraction of construction materials grew by a factor of 34 during the 20th century. Similarly, we used 27 times more ores and minerals. Fossil fuels use grew twelvefold and biomass use by a factor of four. Given that an estimated 50 percent of the urban infrastructure that will be needed in 2050 has not been built yet, in a business-as-usual world resource use could reasonably be expected to keep growing. The resulting cost, waste, and emissions from this trajectory, not least of which is CO_2, would ensure that the worst *Limits to Growth* scenario comes true. Collapse would be essentially inevitable.

A way must be found to reduce material throughput in the economy dramatically, but at the same time generate jobs and flourishing livelihoods for nine or ten billion people.

Today, more than 40 years after the publication of *Limits*, the world is at a crossroads. Wasteful lifestyles, primarily in the rich North, have used up most of the "environmental space": the capacity of the planet to absorb our pollution or supply rich raw materials.

The only way to deal with a growing population, and at the same time enable the much-needed increases of per capita income in low-income countries, is to use efficiency-promoting technology in combination with circular material flows, economic instruments to curb demand, behavioral change, and, as chapter 10 shows, new technologies to enable us to prosper in fundamentally different ways. There are many opportunities for behavior change, often complemented by technology innovation. But policies to promote such changes are rare. Almost all policy focus has been on promoting labor productivity instead of resource productivity or, better, total factor productivity. Market prices fail to reflect the true costs of both production and consumption. Pollution has been cheaper than responsibility.

We now find ourselves in the somewhat absurd situation that it has been OK to extract resources from nature, turn them into products, and profit from their sale without paying for the costs of the external effects, like pollution. Such costs have been transferred to society and drive the destruction of vital ecosystems and the pollution of the atmosphere. This can no longer go on.

Closing the Loops

One effective way forward is a revolution in the way we use both energy and materials. The landmark report, *Resource Efficiency: Potential and Economic Implications*, issued by the International Resource Panel (IRP) and launched at the G7 meeting in May 2016 in Japan, makes this clear.[2] It explains the risks we face with today's more or less linear production systems and advocates a radical shift in mind-sets as well as production and consumption systems. Today's economy is built on a "fast turnover" principle, characterized by huge inefficiencies and the principle of maximum speed and volume of resource flows. This often promotes cheap disposable items and early obsolescence. The faster we replace our gadgets, the better, growth advocates argue. But if we are to have any hope of creating a Finer Future, we will need to manufacture heritage products that last longer and design them to be easily recycled, reused, and remade.

It's also just better business. The economic values lost because of linear material flows are seldom talked about, but they are huge. In Europe, for instance, an estimated 95 percent of the value of virgin materials is lost after one use cycle. This remains an average across all material categories, in spite of recycling efforts.[3] Even in the best systems, far from all materials produced are reused or recycled, and those that are recycled often have lost their value because of poor design, contamination, or the absence of standards. Electronics is a good example. Most electronic products are designed in such a way that they cannot be dismantled. The rare earth materials are inextricably baked into low-value plastics, so the whole thing is thrown away. The high-quality steel in cars usually becomes so contaminated in the scrapping process that it is primarily used as lower-value construction steel. The same story could be told about the construction sector, amounting to 30 to 40 percent of material flows in society. Visit a building renovation project, and you will find that most materials are dumped or incinerated, not used again. Substantial losses of value occur when products and materials that could have a second life are disposed of.

A study in Sweden done by the Swedish Recycling Association and Material Economics (2018) established that only 8 percent of the original value of plastics remained after one use. The rest was either incinerated or the value lost because of contamination and too many different qualities being mixed during recycling. But the Swedish Statistical Office—basing its data on recycling rates in terms of tons of plastics collected—gives a different picture. According to its data, more than 60 percent of the plastics used is being recycled. This demonstrates that the policies pursued—aiming at high recycling rates but not really caring for quality and value—fool us into believing our economy is far more circular than is the case. The Swedish study shows a similar situation for other materials, such as aluminium, steel, and textiles. The inefficiencies described above result in increasing levels of pollution, resource depletion, and loss of ecosystems.

From a climate-change-mitigation perspective, the present linear economic model means we won't make it. The production of basic materials—like steel, cement, plastics, and aluminum—accounts for almost 20 percent of global carbon emissions. Switching to renewables (described in chapter 10) and improved energy efficiency in production processes will help. But just as important will be to reduce material throughput by reuse, recycling, extended product life, and remanufacturing. In many sectors and for many applications, material substitution can play a major role, like using wood or bamboo instead of steel and cement in construction.[4] Given all the infrastructure needs in developing countries, a revolution in the way we use materials—not least basic materials—is very much needed.

Fortunately, there is an enormous scope for using resources more elegantly. This was set forth in *The Future of Industry in Asia*, a report commissioned by the UN Industrial Development Organization (UNIDO).[5] It detailed the extent to which radically sustainable manufacturing, based in dramatic increases in materials reuse and resource productivity, is the best way to deliver prosperity for Asia.

This approach is the foundation of balancing growth and development with protection of the environment, essential if we are to reduce greenhouse gasses enough to save ourselves. Moving in this direction will create more jobs. An economy favoring reuse and recycling of materials, as well as product-life extension, is, by definition, more labor-intensive than one based on the disposal philosophy of linear resource flows.

Leveraging technology for enhancing productivity is nothing new. Labor productivity, which increased by at least a factor of 20 since the Industrial Revolution began, is a case in point. To quote Ernst von Weizsäcker, author of *Factor Four*[6] and *Factor Five*,[7] leading books on increased resource productivity, "It is not labor that is in short supply in the future but rather basic resources, like energy, soil and water. The same level of innovation must now go into using technology for resource productivity as was the case with labor."

Many Winners in a Circular Economy

The concept of the circular economy was first set out in the 1970s by the Swiss architect Walter Stahel.[8] He pointed out that closing loops in manufacturing is no threat to competitiveness or jobs: in the current economy, 75 percent of environmental impact comes from extraction of raw materials, most of which are quickly thrown away. But this produces only 25 percent as many jobs as would be created by repurposing the waste. A circular economy produces 75 percent more jobs reusing, remanufacturing, and recycling materials, according to his estimate.

Moving toward a circular economy is one of the best ways to counter traditional fears held by some in the business community that environmental policy-making is a threat to competitiveness. Likewise, trade unions have seen environment protection as a threat to jobs. California would already have voted to become 100 percent renewably powered had not the powerful union of the electrical workers partnered with the utilities to defeat (for now) the measure.[9] While competition in a globalized economy is a challenge, there are very strong reasons not to view resource efficiency and moving toward a circular economy as a threat—rather the opposite. Evidence is strong that a much more resource-efficient economy will offer many more—not fewer—jobs.

The economics of the circular economy are increasingly compelling to companies. Calls for this new model of production and consumption are becoming more frequent. Increasingly, countries seeking to overcome a legacy of traditional industrialization are adopting it: the Chinese made the circular economy the basis of development policy in the 11 Party Congress.[10] The process is slow, however. One of the reasons is that the head of the EU Commission, Jean-Claude Juncker, views any efforts to oblige companies to improve product design, do away with obsolescence, and/or change business models in favor of offering services rather than selling more stuff as "excessive regulation." Juncker, who is yesterday's man and should never have been elevated to his position in the first place, wants to be remembered as someone who "cut red tape" for the business community through deregulation. To introduce new regulation in terms of product requirements is therefore seen by Juncker as a step in the wrong direction, and this in spite of the fact that there is so much cost to be saved and pollution to be reduced!

Regardless, in January 2018 the European Commission adopted a new set of measures, including the following:

+ A Europe-wide EU Strategy for Plastics in the Circular Economy[11] and annex to transform the way plastics and plastics products are designed, produced, used, and recycled. By 2030, all plastics packaging should be recyclable. The Strategy also highlights the need for specific measures, possibly a legislative instrument, to reduce the impact of single-use plastics, particularly in our seas and oceans. A public consultation was held. To reduce the leakage of plastics into the environment, the Commission adopted a new proposal on Port Reception Facilities to tackle sea-based marine litter and published a report on the impact of the use of oxo-degradable plastic, including oxo-degradable plastic carrier bags, on the environment.

+ A communication on options to address the interface between chemical, product, and waste legislation[12] that assesses how the rules on waste, products, and chemicals relate to each other.

+ A monitoring framework on progress toward a circular economy[13] at EU and national levels. It is composed of a set of ten key indicators that cover each phase—i.e., production, consumption, waste management, and secondary raw materials—as well as economic aspects—investments and jobs—and innovation.

+ A *Report on Critical Raw Materials and the Circular Economy*[14] that highlights the potential to make the use of the 27 critical materials in our economy more circular.

Recent studies by the Ellen MacArthur Foundation, the EU Commission, and the Club of Rome highlight that moving to a much more material-efficient economy by using and reusing materials, rather than depleting resources, would yield multiple benefits. The

Ellen MacArthur Foundation report describes how doing this would net the European manufacturing sector $630 billion by 2025.[15]

Anders Wijkman's study, "The Circular Economy and Benefits for Society," looks at the energy and employment impacts of a circular economy.[16] Altogether eight countries in Europe—Finland, France, the Netherlands, Norway, Poland, Spain, Sweden, and the Czech Republic—were analyzed through a traditional input/output model. The study considers three decoupling strategies: increasing the share of renewable energy and enhancing energy as well as material efficiency. It asked how the economies would perform today if they were 25 percent more energy efficient, had reduced the use of fossil fuels by 50 percent in favor of renewable energy, and achieved a far more efficient use of materials.[17]

The results are significant: moving toward a circular economy would support efforts to build economic competitiveness, increase jobs, and cut carbon emissions. If the countries studied introduced all the three actions in parallel, carbon emissions would be cut between 65 and 70 percent. An estimated 75,000 additional jobs in Finland, 100,000 in Sweden, 200,000 in Holland, 400,000 in Spain, and 500,000 in France would be created, in the range of 1 to 3 percent of these countries' labor forces. The situation is similar in Norway, Poland, and the Czech Republic.

The result should not come as a surprise. An economy giving priority to caring for what has already been produced—through repair, maintenance, upgrading, and remanufacturing—is more labor-intensive than both mining and manufacturing (often done in highly automated and robotized facilities).

A similar study found that the circular economy, implemented in the UK, could create 205,000 new jobs.[18] It found that electronics designed for reuse and remanufacturing created 8 to 20 jobs per thousand tonnes of product; those designed for recycling created 5 to 10 jobs per tonne. Products designed for landfill created 0.1 jobs per thousand tonnes of waste.

Circular economy companies run on a different business logic. Products are designed for ease of recycling, reuse, disassembly, and remanufacturing. This replaces the traditional, linear "take, make and dispose" model that has dominated all modern economies to date. The basic principle of closing the loops is simple: electronics are designed for longer life and for components to be used again; car plants, as is the case with Renault, take back old engines, renovate them, and use them in new vehicles.[19] Multistorey buildings are built of wood with materials that are used and reused; low-energy buildings are well insulated and designed for distributed energy. This approach of returning useful materials to the economy and eliminating the concept of waste is becoming standard practice in many factories.[20]

As we replace the linear economy, business models will shift as well: customers will buy what it is that they really want, the service, not the thing. For example, Philips provides lighting as a service.[21] Tire manufacturers, like Michelin, lease their products, charging per kilometer of use.[22] A wide array of consumer products, from computers, cell phones, household appliances, cars, and furniture, to textiles, can be delivered using this model. In the property market, the same principles apply: Airbnb is a multibillion dollar business built on monetizing previously unvalued resources and providing them as a service when needed.[23] Clothing companies like Mud Jeans,[24] Houdini,[25] and H&M[26] are offering clothing for rent and/or offering to take old textiles back for recycling and reuse, as Patagonia does in the US.[27] The principle of "earning revenue by selling more stuff" is being replaced by a logic in which revenue results from quality of service.

Walter Stahel defines it this way:

> Societal wealth and well-being should be measured in stock instead of flow, in capital instead of sales. Growth then corresponds to a rise in the quality and quantity of all stocks— natural, cultural, human and manufactured. For example, sustainable forestry management augments natural capital, deforestation destroys it; recovering phosphorus or metals from waste streams maintains natural capital, but dumping it increases pollution; retrofitting buildings reduces energy consumption and increases the quality of built stock.[28]

Getting the circular economy right is the first step to replacing growth in GDP with indicators that give prominence to quality, not quantity. It is a foundational element of any strategy to deliver excellence in business and craft a better world.[29]

Making It Happen

There are a number of policy options and investments that would help advance a circular economy and the climate and job benefits that it would bring about:

+ Address the flawed cost structure of the economy by letting external costs, like pollution and loss of natural capital, be reflected in market prices;
+ Strengthen recycling and reuse targets to help reduce and process waste and residues. Put limits on waste incineration — ideally capturing as well the values captured after the first use cycle;
+ Introduce or strengthen existing policies to promote renewable energy, such as feed-in tariffs, tax credits or tax cuts, and green certificates;
+ Introduce design requirements for new products for ease of repair and maintenance, dismantling, and countering obsolescence;
+ Introduce standards for many product categories to make reuse and recycling more feasible. Plastics recycling for instance is highly ineffective simply because there are too many different qualities on the market. Of equal importance will be product design requirements and standards that will facilitate reuse and recycling.
+ Use public procurement to incentivize new business models, moving from selling products to selling performance;
+ Make material efficiency a core part of climate mitigation policies. Most climate change mitigation strategies are sector-based, with a primary focus on energy use. But the studies above demonstrate the obvious benefits in terms of emission reductions from using products longer and from enhanced rates of recycling and reuse;
+ Launch investments to support the circular economy;

+ Rethink taxation. Taxes are best applied to items that society does not want, to discourage them. So another proposal is to reduce taxes on labor and income and tax instead those activities, like excessive energy and resource use, that are undesirable. Such a tax shift would accelerate the transition to a circular economy. It would also help balance the threat of losing jobs in an increasingly digitized economy;

+ Create a market for secondary materials. This could be achieved, for example, by removing VAT on recycled materials and/or by requiring a certain ratio of recycled materials in new production;

+ Extend minimum legal warranties for products from 2 to 3 years to 8 to 10 years (depending on the product); and

+ Phase out the use of toxic materials.

Efficiency: The First Fuel

An even faster way to buy time and cut carbon emissions is energy efficiency. A 2009 McKinsey report concluded that, in the US, an investment of $520 billion in ways to use less energy would unlock savings of $1.2 trillion.[30] By 2010, McKinsey calculated that such efficiency could cut 40 percent of global greenhouse gas emissions at a cost below €60 a metric ton of carbon dioxide equivalent.[31] Doing this would save trillions.

Had the US implemented the proposed 2009 climate protection legislation (Waxman-Markey Bill) to cut emissions by 5 to 8 percent by 2020, it would have saved $750 per household by 2020 and $3,900 by 2030. Doing this would have created 250,000 jobs by 2020 and 650,000 jobs by 2030. Increasing reductions to 10 percent by 2020 could have added $50 billion in total savings by 2030.[32]

The International Energy Agency (IEA) points out that such opportunities are still with us. Its 2014 *Energy Efficiency Market Report* puts the international value of efficiency at $310 billion a year, and growing.

And it's happening. Calling energy savings "the world's first fuel," IEA estimates,

[In the] eighteen IEA countries evaluated in the report, total final energy consumption was down 5 percent between 2001 and 2011 primarily as a result of investments in energy efficiency. Cumulative avoided energy consumption over the decade from energy efficiency in IEA countries was 1,732 million tonnes of oil equivalent—larger than the energy demand of the United States and Germany combined in 2012.[33]

Energy efficiency investments over the past four decades have avoided more energy consumption than the total consumption of the European Union in 2011.[34]

In 2015, Fatih Birol, executive director of the IEA, stated,

Per capita energy consumption in IEA countries has dropped to levels not seen since the 1980s yet income per capita is at its highest level, access to energy services is continually expanding, and GDP has expanded by USD 8.5 trillion, an increase of 26 percent. This is why energy efficiency is so important. It is improving prosperity with a domestic, clean "source" of energy. Energy efficiency investments across the IEA since 1990 avoided USD 5.7 trillion of energy expenditure. But the benefits of improving energy efficiency extend well beyond financial savings, relating also to improved energy security, higher productivity for businesses and reduced greenhouse gas emissions. Approximately 40 percent of the emissions reductions required by 2050 to limit global temperature increase to less than 2 degrees centigrade would potentially come from energy efficiency.[35]

Many people think that only developed nations have opportunities to cut waste, but efficiency is an international resource. The United States is far from the most energy efficient nation—it ranks 13th of the 16 countries profiled by the American Council for an Energy Efficient Economy's annual ranking of country efficiency,[36] well behind China, which is fourth. But Brazil and Mexico, and most African countries, have far more opportunities to save than does the US.

China is the energy efficiency powerhouse in the making. In the 1990s, it had three times the energy intensity of Japan, but energy shortages that idled up to a third of its manufacturing capacity at any given time encouraged it to embrace efficiency.[37] By 2006, China recognized that climate change was a threat, as well, with the potential to cut 10 percent of its grain production. Air pollution causing an estimated 4,400 deaths in China every day[38] was threatening Party legitimacy. China began discussing the concept of a "Green GDP,"[39] and pledged to cut energy intensity by 4 percent a year through 2010. It set a target to reduce energy consumption per unit GDP by 20 percent between 2006 and 2010.[40]

In 2007, even as it built two coal plants every week, China announced the creation of over a billion-dollar fund to encourage energy efficiency and renewables.[41] A Chinese solar entrepreneur became the world's first green billionaire.

China also announced in 2007 that it intended to become the "Ecological Civilization," a concept that it wrote into its constitution in 2012.[42]

By 2009, the China Greentech Initiative projected that resource efficiency and other green measures could be a trillion-dollar a year market by 2013.[43]

As part of its 2015 Green Horizon's program, China pledged to cut its carbon almost in half from 2005 levels by 2020. In the first three months of 2015, coal imports fell by 42 percent from a year before.[44]

In 2016, China released its thirteenth Five-Year Plan.[45] It called for 6.5 percent economic growth per year but coming increasingly from services, which are less energy intensive, and from more innovative and efficient manufacturing. It pledged an 18 percent reduction in carbon intensity, but analysts predict that it will exceed that, achieving a 48 percent cut from 2005 levels by 2020, en route to achieving its Paris pledge of peaking its carbon emissions, cutting carbon intensity 60 to 65 percent by 2030.[46]

In 2013, China struck a deal with the State of California to cooperate on cutting carbon by linking its seven pilot carbon markets with California's more mature market.[47] By 2016, the European Union was in conversations to link its carbon market, then the world's largest, with both China and California to create a global market. In late 2017, China declared that its market would begin operation with the power sector, covering one-third of its emissions, making its market the largest in the world.[48]

China announced that it was mothballing 250 projects to build 170 gigawatts worth of coal-fired power plants in 15 regions because of over-capacity of electric supply. In the wake of the US administration's moves to reverse American climate policies, China indicated that it will lead the world to a low carbon future.[49] In 2017, analysts estimated that China, and the entire world, had already hit peak coal use,[50] although in Inner Mongolia, bitcoin mining operations use more coal-fired electricity than three million American homes.[51]

Indeed, it is hard to see how China can avoid its own form of collapse if it does not get vastly more efficient: projections warn that, in the next decade or so, China will seek to move more people than there are in the US into cities yet unbuilt.[52] Just the copper wire this would require is more than current world copper production.[53] Business as usual, by 2030, China will want more oil than the world now extracts. And more cars, cotton, concrete, and essentially all other commodities.[54]

India is not far behind. The second most populous country in the world, it is the fourth-largest energy consumer. Extremely dependent on energy imports, it ranks 11th globally in terms of energy efficiency[55] but bottom of the list in environmental performance and 177th of 180 in air quality.[56] In a country where 25 percent of its people lack electricity and more than 50 percent use wood, dung, or charcoal for cooking, electricity consumption per capita is only about 566 kilowatt hours a person (kWh), a quarter of the world average of 2,782 kWh. Blackouts, brownouts, and electricity shortages are common, costing the country around 7 percent of GDP each year.[57] In this situation, no solution makes sense without energy efficiency. The great Indian energy expert Amulya Reddy reported that in one instance when a south Indian village switched from kerosene to compact fluorescent lamps, illumination rose nineteenfold, energy input decreased ninefold, and household lighting expenditure fell by half. LEDs would cut that by another two-thirds.

In response, and increasingly to deal with air pollution now ten times worse than in China,[58] Indian Prime Minister Modi has set ambitious targets for energy access (providing power to the 300 million Indians currently without electricity). The Indian Bureau of Energy Efficiency created the Perform, Achieve, and Trade program, a scheme very much like carbon trading, to incentivize energy efficiency in 500 plants in eight industries. Energy savings create tradable permits that can be sold to less efficient companies.[59]

Before the Paris Climate Summit, Modi pledged to cut Indian emissions 35 percent by 2030.[60] By 2017, all buildings had to meet the Energy Building Conservation Code. By 2030, this alone could save the output of 17 coal-fired power plants.[61]

Brazil is the eighth-largest energy consumer in the world and the third largest in the Americas, behind the United States and Canada. Fossil fuels represent about 60 percent of Brazil's domestic electricity supply. Renewable energy delivers about 40 percent of its electricity, primarily from hydroelectric dams. Brazil has, until recently, focused on renewable energy and devoted little organizational effort to energy efficiency at a national level.[62] This, however, is changing as the worst drought in 80 years eliminated much of the country's hydro capacity.[63]

States and regions can join in on the efficiency boom. Joe Romm, author of *Climate Change: What Everyone Needs to Know*,[64] describes efficiency as "the core climate solution; the biggest, cheapest, fastest, renewable energy resource." It is limitless, he argues, and effective. His blog, *Climate Progress*, has repeatedly profiled California's success in keeping energy use per capita level for over three decades. Supported by both Democratic and Republican administrations, cost-effective energy efficiency measures have been implemented statewide through 56 different regulatory programs. And it was cheap, averaging 1.4 to 3¢ per kWh to achieve the efficiency, one-fifth the cost of new natural gas plants to do the same job. In contrast, electricity use in the rest of the country rose 60 percent, imposing costs, emitting immense amounts of carbon, and decreasing the country's resilience. If all Americans used electricity as efficiently as California, it would cut electricity consumption by 40 percent and save billions of dollars.[65]

Erasing energy waste in essentially every human activity is cost-effective. A report on 17 US federal research and development programs in energy efficiency and 22 programs in fossil energy estimated that these programs yielded economic returns of $40 billion from an investment of $13 billion.

> Three energy-efficiency programs, costing approximately $11 million, produced nearly three-quarters of this benefit. Most significant were advances made in compressors for refrigerators and freezers, energy-efficient fluorescent-lighting components called electronic ballasts, and low-emission, or heat-resistant, window glass. Standards and regulations incorporating efficiencies attainable by these new technologies ensured that the technologies would be adopted nationwide, thus dramatically compounding their impact.[66]

Of course, America's Child in Chief is intent on cutting all such programs.[67]

CHAPTER FIVE

BUILDING A BETTER WORLD

Happiness can be found even in the darkest of times,
if only one remembers to turn on the light.

ALBUS DUMBLEDORE[1]

The building sector benefits enormously from resource productivity.[2] Buildings use more energy and therefore emit more greenhouse gasses than any other sector of the economy (16 percent globally and 40 percent in the US and most developed countries). One of the heaviest consumers of natural resources, they account for 40 percent of raw material use globally. They use 74 percent of all electricity, emit 40 percent of greenhouse gasses, and can be made dramatically more efficient while also becoming more profitable.[3]

Almost any existing building can be made three to four times more efficient, new ones ten times more efficient than conventional practice.[4] The US Green Building Council[5] reports that owners of existing buildings enjoyed a 19.2 percent return on investment for efficiency improvements. One conservative report calculated that investing $400,000 in efficiency in a 100,000-square-foot building would deliver $1.50 per square foot in reduced energy costs over a similar building without the productivity measures.[6] That $150,000 per year savings would pay back any extra costs in just over two and a half years.

The California energy efficiency success is largely based on making its buildings more efficient. Its Energy Commission set strong building standards, employing such strategies as better insulation and energy efficient lighting, heating, and cooling. Again, the opportunities are staggering. Research in California found that the average residential air duct leaked 20 to 30 percent of the heated and cooled air it carried. So the new codes required leakage rates below 6 percent.[7]

The state found that, for about 15 percent of outdoor lighting for parking lots and streets, light was directed up, illuminating nothing but the sky. It required that new outdoor lighting cut that to below 6 percent. Regulations required that flat roofs on commercial buildings be white to reflect sunlight and keep the buildings cooler, cutting air-conditioning energy demands. The state subsidized high-efficiency LED traffic lights for cities that lacked the money, ultimately converting the entire state to these dramatically more efficient bulbs.[8]

Increasingly, buildings are constructed to be energy positive: to produce more energy than they use. The Oberlin College Adam Joseph Lewis building[9] and the Bullitt Center in Seattle, Washington,[10] are exemplars of what are now being called "living buildings." Sited to be accessible to transit, the Bullitt building is constructed of non-toxic, recycled, or locally sourced materials.[11] It collects all of the water that it needs, composts its wastes, and uses greywater recycling systems. Built to maximize energy efficiency, it features daylighting and also powers itself with rooftop solar panels. It exemplifies all seven of the Living Building Challenge Petals: Site, Water, Energy, Health, Materials, Equity, and Beauty.[12] Such buildings go a very long way to cut humanity's footprint and deliver higher-quality spaces.

In Europe, EU standards mandate that all buildings constructed after 2020 shall be zero-energy building or nearly so.[13] The Passivhaus Standard[14] is now used in more than 30,000 residential, commercial, industrial, and public buildings around the world. The design features excellent thermal performance and exceptional air-tightness, coupled with mechanical ventilation to ensure plenty of fresh air. Delivering enhanced comfort without much or any external heating or cooling source, the Passivhaus was invented in 1988[15] by Wolfgang Feist in Darmstadt, Germany. Now, however, they have spread across Europe and to Australia, China, Japan, Canada, the US, and South America.[16]

The greenest building is the one that is already standing, retrofitted to use less energy. Doing this was roughly a $90 billion a year business in 2015, projected to increase to $125 billion a year globally by 2020. But to hold global temperature increase to below the Paris

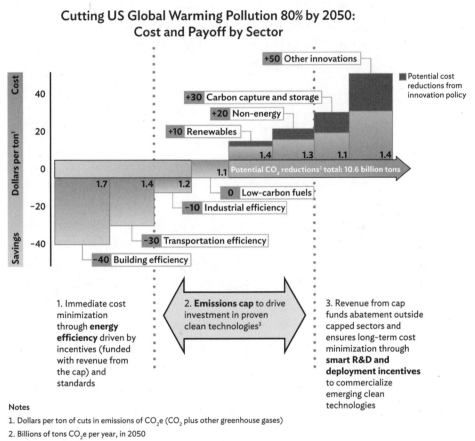

Cutting US Global Warming Pollution 80% by 2050: Cost and Payoff by Sector

1. Immediate cost minimization through **energy efficiency** driven by incentives (funded with revenue from the cap) and standards

2. **Emissions cap** to drive investment in proven clean technologies[3]

3. Revenue from cap funds abatement outside capped sectors and ensures long-term cost minimization through **smart R&D and deployment incentives** to commercialize emerging clean technologies

Notes

1. Dollars per ton of cuts in emissions of CO_2e (CO_2 plus other greenhouse gases)

2. Billions of tons CO_2e per year, in 2050

3. Putting a price on greenhouse gas emissions helps to encourage energy efficiency and innovation but it is sufficient.

The scenario here is based on NRDC analysis, including extrapolations from 2030 cost estimates done by McKinsey & Company. For information about our methodology, visit nrdc.org/globalWarming/blueprint/methodology.asp

Credit: NRDC factsheet: The New Energy Economy, May 2008.

Agreement, an estimated $215 billion will need to be spent on building energy efficiency each year by 2020.[17]

This sounds like a lot, but again, retrofitting just US buildings would save at least $1 trillion this decade and create 3.3 million cumulative job-years of employment.[18] In the US, the built environment comprises almost 78 billion square feet of space, but less than two percent of that is new construction every year. A 2011 survey of commercial building owners found that almost 80 percent intended to implement energy efficiency upgrades within two years.[19]

It's a smart thing to do: the average rate of return on energy efficiency measures in buildings is more than 20 percent.[20]

Funding Efficiency

The inevitable question is how do you pay for such savings? Money is tight and priorities numerous.

The answer is that this is one of the best investments you can make in the entire economy. As a result, there is a growing market in third-party financing for energy efficiency as financiers realize that it has guaranteed returns. When you invest in cutting the energy use of a building, you can be assured that it is not going to get on a boat and go to China. So long as the building stands, the stream of savings will return to investors. Nearly 80,000 emission-reducing projects from 190 Fortune 500 companies reporting data showed almost $3.7 billion in savings in 2016 alone.[21]

As a result, financiers are stepping up with the cash. Aether is a New York company that assembles all of the parties necessary to achieve deep retrofits of commercial real estate. They put owners together with the manufacturers and contractors and provide the financing to generate immediate economic value for the owner. They package disruptive innovations in lighting, controls, power generation, and storage to meet a customer's energy service needs at no up-front cost. Having executed $16 billion in such real estate transactions, they enable cities and large commercial operations to take efficiency to scale.[22]

Another approach was innovated by Sustainable Endowments Institute.[23] Its founder, Mark Orlowski, helps universities and other institutional energy users create Green Revolving Funds (GRFs), using the Green Revolving Investment Tracking System (GRITS).[24] The system enables users to track their returns and share best practices with others. GRITS is now tracking more than $110 million in 350 energy efficiency investments with 75 institutions.

The idea is that savings from efficiency investments are returned to the fund, which then allows the institution to capitalize progressively more ambitious efficiency measures. This defeats the conventional approach in which an energy service company (ESCO) approaches a client, offering to help them cut their energy bills by 10 percent. The ESCO captures the quickest, easiest, cheapest savings, implements those, and leaves with a nice return. But the next round of efficiency looks a bit less attractive, and so on until the institution is locked into high costs and long paybacks to achieve any greater savings. So it quits.

In contrast, Orlowski is helping his organizations achieve less than four-year paybacks and millions of dollars in savings from deep retrofits. Recently Orlowski partnered with the American College and University Presidents' Climate Commitment and APPA to roll GRITS out on a pilot basis to approximately 100 additional universities, and 2,000 after that.[25]

CHAPTER SIX

GOING PLACES:
EFFICIENCY IN VEHICLES

If GM had kept up with technology
like the computer industry has,
we would all be driving $25 cars
that got 1,000 MPG.

BILL GATES[1]

States like California and cities like Fort Collins, Colorado,[2] that have pledged to decarbonize are wise to start with the built environment, but they move quickly to include the transport sector. Moving ourselves around uses about a third of all energy and 75 percent of the oil used in the Western world.[3] Some petroleum is used to heat buildings, but as described above, efficiency and good building design can displace essentially all of that. Substituting the oil used in vehicles seems harder, but here, too, efficiency is taking hold.

In Europe, energy use in transport rose until 2007 but has fallen since then, initially due to economic contraction but increasingly because of a European commitment to energy efficiency in general and to more efficient transport powered by renewable energy in particular.[4] By 2017, there were more than a million electric vehicles on the road globally, growing by a million each year. If these rates continue, by 2030, eight out of every ten (or more) vehicles sold will be electric.[5] There are hundreds of hybrids, electric, fuel-cell, and biofueled cars, with more entering the market.[6]

A similar trend is unfolding in the US. Despite American's love of muscle cars[7] and unlimited driving, since 2007 energy use in vehicles has been declining.[8] The transport sector required 6 percent less energy and 10 percent less oil in 2014 than it did in 2007. A report from the Energy Information Agency found, "as a proportion of transportation fuel, petroleum hasn't been this low since 1954, when coal was still a significant transportation fuel. Petroleum's market share has fallen from 96.5 percent in 2004 to 91.5 percent in 2014."[9] IEA attributed this to the rise in such alternative fuels as ethanol and a growing efficiency in the US auto fleet.[10]

California's efficiency regulations require that more than 15 percent of all vehicles sold in the state by 2025 to be zero-emission vehicles. Nine New England states have indicated that they will join California in this requirement, which means car makers will accept this as the national standard to spread the technology costs across their fleets. Achieving this will require having six to seven million zero-emission (ZEV) or partial zero-emission vehicles (PZEV) by then.[11] Despite the threat of lax federal vehicle efficiency standards, California's standards will require fleets to average 54 miles per gallon by the 2025 vehicle year.[12]

The future of transportation will look very different from the present, as described in chapter 10. As humans urbanize, most transportation will involve multi-modal combinations of more walkable neighborhoods, bicycles, electric light rail, and some very cool innovations. Olli, a 3-D printed, self-driving, electric bus has just started giving rides in Washington, DC.[13] This is only one of many potential solutions to the last-mile problem of how to get people to and from transit stations or around areas where transit services are not cost-effective.[14]

The $20 Is Real

The magnitude of the savings available from the circular economy and from energy efficiency brings to mind the old joke about the classical economist and her son walking down the street. The kid sees a $20 bill lying on the ground and reaches for it. Mom says, "Never mind, if it were real, someone would have picked it up." Our old narrative says that the sorts of savings profiled here are impossible. If the savings numbers were real, someone would have captured them: business as usual acts to capture economic advantage.

But these savings are real, and they are omnipresent.

Andrew Winston, corporate sustainability strategist and author of *The Big Pivot*, tells the story of how the international spirits company Diageo hit the science-based goal of cutting its carbon emissions by 80 percent, but it did that years before climatologists told us the world must achieve it.[15] In 2008, leaders at the company explored becoming entirely carbon free by 2015. Deciding that this exceeded their budget, they set a goal of becoming 50 percent carbon free. They initially thought that achieving this would cost a lot, but low- and no-cost efficiency measures available to them in their North American operations (what Winston calls the "no-brainers") would enable them to hit their target by 2012 with substantial operational savings. Winston writes:

> These projects ranged from easy efficiency efforts like lighting retrofits, boiler upgrades, and installing variable speed drives; to larger, but still economical, changes, such as switching fuels (from oil to natural gas) and cutting back from two boilers to one in a small distillery.

Then Diageo found that a Canadian distillery could contract to be supplied by landfill gas. Burning the methane would help the climate, but the price tag exceeded what that distillery could afford. A senior executive on the company's global sustainability council realized that this was a cheap way to hit the company's global goals, and that the efficiency measures possible at that plant and elsewhere would more than pay the extra cost. By combining the savings from the efficiency already achieved with the opportunity, Diageo was able to become 80 percent carbon-free, in its North American operations, 38 years before the 2050 date of their target.

Rachel Young of the American Council for an Energy Efficient Economy put it this way:

Countries that use energy more efficiently use fewer resources to achieve the same goals, thus reducing costs, preserving valuable natural resources, and gaining a competitive edge over other countries. In the United States, we need to do more on energy efficiency to remain competitive in an increasingly tough global marketplace.[16]

Tell that to the so-called businessman in the White House.

Transformation:
The Plot Thickens

THIS SECTION DETAILS the structural transformations needed to create an economy that works for everyone. It presents the inspiring news of the shifts already underway in finance and in corporate consciousness. It details the shift to regenerative agriculture and the triumph of the sun. It describes how leading institutions in each of these sectors recognize that our survival depends on their behaving responsibly.

The challenges facing humanity are dire and imminent. Using resources—both energy and materials—dramatically more productively can buy us time, but for what?

Unless we fundamentally restructure how we make and deliver the goods and services we desire, unless we shift our economy so that every aspect of how we do business is regenerative of human and natural capital, the odds that modern society will leave a lovely legacy grow very slim.

One book is insufficient to cover all of the transformations necessary and the many inspiring ones that are underway, but the four critical areas identified above must be tackled to build a Finer Future.

> She was unstoppable. Not because she did not have failures or doubts, but because she continued on despite them.
>
> BEAU TAPLIN

The good news is that change *is* underway. We have all of the technologies we need to make a good start at crafting the solutions to the problems facing us.

The sobering news is that we have to implement them.

CHAPTER SEVEN

MOVING MONEY
FROM HARM TO HEALING

Yes, the planet was destroyed.
But for a beautiful moment in time
we created a lot of value for shareholders.

TOM TORO[1]

Financialization

The global economy was created to enable us to meet our needs. Money and banking let people convert bulky assets like sides of beef or bushels of wheat to a tradable form and to store and transfer their wealth safely. When people needed more money than they had stored in a bank, the banker would lend some of the other money on deposit to bring liquidity—finance—to the real economy. This allowed people to build a house or support the growth of a business. So far, so good.

But when was the last time you tried to get a loan from a bank? If you really need the money, your chances of getting it are slim—these days it all tends to go to people who already have a lot of it.

We've always had a conflicted relationship with money. Jesus drove the moneychangers, merchants, and livestock from the temple. From the Bible, Matthew 21:12–13:

> And making a whip of cords, he drove them all out of the temple, with the sheep and oxen. And he poured out the coins of the money-changers and overturned their tables. And he

told those who sold the pigeons, "Take these things away; do not make my Father's house a house of trade."

And Jesus went into the temple of God, and cast out all them that sold and bought in the temple, and overthrew the tables of the moneychangers, and the seats of them that sold doves, And said unto them, It is written, My house shall be called the house of prayer; but ye have made it a den of thieves.

Yet we all use money and seek more of it. The dominant narrative of neoliberalism celebrates this. Milton Friedman, one of its framers, famously said,

There is one and only one social responsibility of business—to use its resources and engage in activities designed to increase its profits so long as it stays within the rules of the game, which is to say, engages in open and free competition without deception or fraud.[2]

That caveat is important, as will be noted below.

In a world of small merchants and yeoman farmers, Friedman's dictum may have had merit. In the era of big banks and Wall Street analysts, it has gone awry.

Management expert Peter Drucker counters Friedman, arguing,

A business cannot be defined or explained in terms of profit. Asked what a business is, the typical businessman is likely to answer, "an organization to make profit." The typical economist is likely to give the same answer. The answer is not only false; it is irrelevant.

The prevailing economic theory of business enterprise and behavior, the maximization of profit—which is simply a complicated way of phrasing the old saw of buying cheap and selling dear—may adequately explain how a particular entrepreneur operates. But it cannot explain how any business enterprise operates, nor how it should operate. The concept of profit maximization is, in fact, meaningless.[3]

Henry Ford is reputed to have said that a business that makes nothing but money is a poor business. Harvard's Professor Clayton Christensen has long argued that the single-minded pursuit of profit and the measurement of success as increased ratios of profit versus assets have stripped America and many other Western countries of their manufacturing capability and thus their capacity to innovate. It has rendered companies, he says, little more than marketing machines dedicated to delivering profits to the financial sector.[4]

Jesus would likely have approved. But he'd be aghast, today, at the success of the moneychangers.

The financial sector (described as FIRE—Finance, Insurance, and Real Estate) was a bit under 3 percent of US GDP in the 1950s. By 2006, it was more than 8 percent.[5] The value of financial assets was five times GDP in 1980. By 2007, it was ten times GDP. Small wonder it all fell apart in 2008. By 2011, six big banks had assets equivalent to 65 percent of GDP.[6]

In 1980, people working in the banking sector made about the same as people in other industries. By 2006, they made 70 percent more.[7]

These numbers are actually understated. Many companies sought to join the party. Harvard's Professor Gautam Mukunda notes,

> Many nonfinancial firms have important financial units. The assets of such units began to increase sharply in the early 1980s. By 2000 they were as large as or larger than nonfinancial corporations' tangible assets. During the early 2000s, for example, Ford made more money by selling loans than by selling cars, while GE Capital generated approximately half of GE's total earnings.[8]

It seems that the entire economy serves as a device to flow money to the financial sector and its bosses. Bruce Bartlett, a senior policy advisor to both the Reagan and Bush administrations in America, argues that this financialization of the economy is the cause of income inequality, falling wages, and the poor performance.[9] David Stockman, Reagan's director of the office of management and budget, agreed, describing our current situation as "corrosive financialization that has turned the economy into a giant casino since the 1970s."[10]

Supporters of finance claim that it brings necessary liquidity to business. If the sector is kept within reasonable bounds, this is true. But at its current size, the opposite is happening. A study by the IMF in 2012 showed that "the marginal effect of financial depth on output growth becomes negative when credit to the private sector reaches 80–100 percent of GDP."[11] At this level, it costs the economy two percent a year in losses to the GDP. In 2012, private sector credit was 184 percent of US GDP.

A key outcome of this financial intensification of the economy is described by Michael Hudson, an economist at Bard College's Levy Center:

> [Companies] are not able to invest in new physical capital equipment or buildings because they are obliged to use their operating revenue to pay their bankers and bondholders, as well as junk-bond holders. This is what I mean when I say that the economy is becoming financialized. Its aim is not to provide tangible capital formation or rising living standards. It exists to generate interest, financial fees from underwriting mergers and acquisitions, and capital gains that accrue mainly to insiders, headed by upper management and large financial institutions. The traditional business cycle has been overshadowed by a secular increase in debt. Instead of labor earning more, hourly earnings have declined in real terms. There has been a drop in net disposable income after paying taxes and withholding "forced saving" for social Security and medical insurance, pension-fund contributions and—most serious of all—debt service on credit cards, bank loans, mortgage loans, student loans, auto loans, home insurance premiums, life insurance, private medical insurance and other FIRE sector charges.... This diverts spending away from goods and services.[12]

Adam Davidson of NPRs *Planet Money* described the behavior of an over-financialized system more simply:

> Generally speaking, businesses earn profits in one of two basic ways. The first is by providing goods and services more productively than others and selling them at a price people are willing to pay. The second is by seeking rents. "Rent," in the economic sense, refers broadly to any excess benefits that people and businesses receive simply because they have power over something that others need.[13]

A study on the causes of the 2008 financial crisis found that from 1980 to 2000 the large banks had moved away from productivity-enhancing activities to rent-seeking.[14] Davidson concluded,

> To fight rent-seeking, we would need banking laws made up of straightforward rules that educated laypeople could understand. They would have to eliminate our maddeningly complex regulatory infrastructure. There would be trade-offs: The financial system might not perform as efficiently, and the economy might not grow as quickly during boom times. But if done right, an overhaul of banking regulations could create a political context in which rent-seeking self-enrichment by banks is no longer the norm. We might even come to call it what it is: corruption.[15]

Davidson was being polite, but his observation makes clear how far the financial system has come from adherence to Milton Friedman's caution that the pursuit of profit must be conducted within the rules. A week before Davidson's article appeared, five big banks—JP Morgan, Citigroup, Barclays, UBS, and RBS—pleaded guilty to criminal misconduct and were fined $6 billion.

But no one went to jail. No bank was closed. No bank was barred from doing the sort of business that crashed the financial system. The ten largest banks in the US are bigger now than they were before the 2008 financial crisis.[16] Could this be because the financial sector spends only slightly less on lobbying than the health care industry? Open Secrets estimates that the securities and investment industries spent $26,088,576 on lobbying in 2015, paying 627 lobbyists, or almost one and a half lobbyists for every member of Congress. Four hundred of these lobbyists are former federal employees.[17] And the scary thing is that, to the financial industry, $26 million is basically zero.

Writing in *Forbes*, financial commentator Steve Dunning suggested that we "re-focus banks primarily on the traditional 'boring' task of making loans for real goods and services to real human beings. It would limit 'hedging' to genuine insurance and ban gambling in derivatives for its own sake." He continued,

> The issue is one of political will to deal with the consequences of blatant, systemic criminality.
>
> How could this political change happen? There are two possibilities.
>
> We could wait for the political will to be generated by another massive financial cataclysm.
>
> Or the change could come from courageous political leadership to call corruption corruption, to recognize felons as felons and to treat organizations responsible for criminal conduct accordingly.
>
> The choice is ours.[18]

Resilience and Efficiency

Shrinking and reforming the finance sector is harder than defusing a bomb. But bombs are safe once the fuse is removed. Powerful vested interests in the finance sector load more explosive material into the system at the same time that other material is being neutralized.[19] Only governments backed by strong public support can bring about the scale of change needed.

Living within planetary boundaries requires, as described in John Fullerton's list of the principles of a Regenerative Economy, a return to economic systems that achieve a balance between efficiency

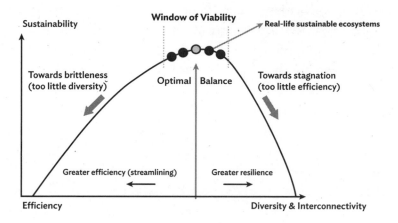

Credit: Bernard Lietaer.

and resilience and are built on principles that mirror those found in healthy natural systems.

Just as sustainable ecosystems must have a balance between efficiency and resilience, economic systems need this as well. Recently our economic systems have aimed only for efficiency—they are extremely good at flowing money into the finance sector—only to have them collapse (e.g., 2008 financial crash and the euro crisis). The result is neither efficient nor resilient.[20]

The New Economics Foundation (NEF) has set out the key parameters for a resilient financial system. Drawing on academic and policy literature and a series of expert interviews and roundtables, it listed seven key factors that build system resilience and that can be measured:

1. Diversity: healthy systems have a diversity of actors who occupy a variety of different niches in the system and employ different strategies to thrive.

2. Interconnectedness and network structure: the way financial institutions are connected to each other affects the way a crisis spreads.

3. Financial system size: financial systems that are large relative to their domestic economy pose a greater threat to economic stability.

4. Asset composition: where banks invest matters, with some types of financial assets particularly prone to boom and bust.

5. Liability composition: the way banks are funded also matters: short-term borrowing from other banks is more fickle and volatile than customer deposits.

6. Complexity and transparency: the growing complexity associated with securitization and the "slicing and dicing" of loans can spread risks around the financial network and make those risks harder to judge, especially during a crisis.

7. Leverage: the ratio between banks' assets and their capital has been a key focus of post-crisis financial regulation.[21]

A Shrunken Finance Sector That Does Not Require Continuous Growth: Reform of the Monetary System and Banking Structures

NEF's publication *Where Does Money Come From*[22] describes how commercial banks create a very large proportion of the money in circulation as new credit—often with no or very limited connection to their deposit base. In the UK, commercial banks create 97 percent of all money in circulation. Banks use the money they have just created either for purchasing assets with secure collateral (e.g., housing) or speculative activity. Well-meaning but "one size fits all" capital requirements, such as the UK's Business, Innovation and Skills regulations,[23] impose a disincentive to create productive credit for small and medium-sized businesses and green infrastructure investments. This is one of the unintended consequences of the understandable regulatory response to the financial crisis. It makes it more profitable for banks to finance existing assets, namely real estate and securities.

This leads to an inflation of asset prices in such areas as housing that have a limited supply or to an increase in demands for very quick returns through speculative investment in certain markets. Countries with highly concentrated banking sectors, where a few large commercial banks dominate, tend to underinvest in the real "green" and job-creating sectors crucial to creating a sustainable economy. As shown in the figure on page 118, Germany has the most diverse and decentralized banking system, while the UK is the most concentrated and centralized system. Local banking networks are much more focused on the sort of traditional high street (credit union) banking of lending to businesses and households than the larger retail or international commercial banks. Local banks devote 66 percent of their balance sheets to community banking and only 15 percent to trading in financial derivatives. In contrast, large commercial banks invest only 37 percent in local lending and 39 percent in derivative trading. If property lending is stripped out, the large commercial banks in the sample lend only 11 percent for productive investment.

It would be fair to conclude that banking sectors in many countries are too focused on investments in non-productive and speculative assets. Capital markets and investors' expectations need to change. Both structural and incentive transformations are critically needed.

Fixing Finance

John Fullerton points out that optimizing single variables such as financial return can no longer be sufficient to investment decision-making in the Era of Regenerative Capitalism:

> Finance's most important practical function in the real economy is the transformation of savings into investment, and the credit-creation process. The flow of real investment is the bridge to, and the steering mechanism for, the Great Transition. The same planetary boundaries that dictate limits to growth also imply limits to investment, a constraint no economic system in the history of civilization has ever before had to contemplate. How much and where large economic actors invest will have critical implications for collective global security and, consequently, must become a central concern of global governance.[24]

The ability of Regenerative Capitalism to emerge, particularly within the present mainstream economy dominated by large-scale

Banks' market shares of deposits by ownership type

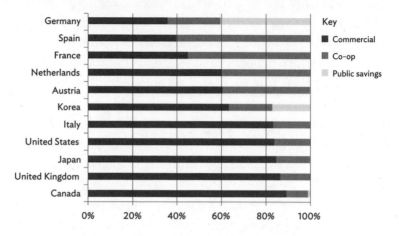

Key
- ■ Commercial
- ■ Co-op
- ■ Public savings

Banks' market shares of deposits by geographic scale

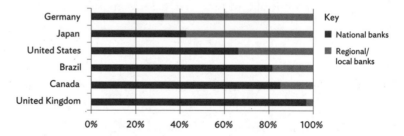

Key
- ■ National banks
- ■ Regional/ local banks

Proportion of balance sheets applied to real economy lending and investment

Real economy assets

Non-property real estate economy assets

Key
- ■ Stakeholder banks
- ■ Large commercial banks

Credit: b.3cdn.net/nefoundation/141039750996d1298f_5km6y1sip.pdf

enterprises and state actors, he argues, will depend upon a fundamental change in finance. He posits Eight Elements of Regenerative Finance,[25] consistent with the shift from a mechanistic to ecological worldview:

1. Means not Ends: finance is a means to a healthy economy, not the "ends" of economic activity.
2. Ethical and in Service: finance must return to being an ethical profession, grounded in a culture of service to clients and service to the emergence of a regenerative economy.
3. The Supremacy of Relationship: we should value relationships over transactions.
4. Transparency: regenerative finance values transparency over complexity, while embracing genuine value-adding innovation.
5. Real Wealth: we should seek to generate long-term wealth creation, harmonizing multiple forms of capital in right relationship, using a fair financial return as a constraint for investment decisions.
6. Right Scale: the system should be appropriately scaled as a system embedded in the economy, which in turn is embedded in culture and the biosphere.
7. Collaborative: there should be values collaboration among values-aligned investors, financial institutions, and enterprises from multiple sectors, mimicking nature's "edge effect."[26]
8. Resilient: the system must balance efficiency with structural resiliency at the system level through decentralization, diversity, and buffers within institutions and even within the money system itself.

Corrective measures to help support a more sustainable financial sector could include
- credit guidance with a bias toward sustainable investment;
- differential reserve requirements with 100 percent reserve requirements for property investments (other than for new-build or socially needed housing) and speculative investments;
- 100 percent reserve requirements/creation of all new sovereign money by central banks;

+ creation of new specialist banks, such as Green Investment Banks or National Investment Banks;

+ creation of new regional or local banks with public interest mandates to serve only a limited geography and to not engage in speculative investment; this could be achieved either through encouraging new entrants or by splitting up large commercial banks;

+ encouragement of diversity of bank forms, including stakeholder banks and public banks, as well as private banks.[27]

None of these items is likely to be sufficient on its own to meet the challenge and size of transformation that is needed, even when matched with a fiscal regime focused on sustainable investment. We need a mixture of these policies to achieve a stable banking sector that supports sustainability.

In the US, Senator Elizabeth Warren, an outspoken critic of big banks and Wall Street, has proposed much the same. In a speech at Bard College's Levy Institute, she set forth an agenda for reining in the excesses:

+ First, financial institutions shouldn't be allowed to cheat people. Markets work only if people can see and understand the products they are buying, only if people can reasonably compare one product to another, only if people can't get fooled into taking on far more risk than they realize just so that some fly-by-night company can turn a quick profit and move on. That's true for families buying mortgages and for pension plans buying complex financial instruments.

+ Second, financial institutions shouldn't be allowed to get the tax-payers to pick up their risks. That's true for using insured deposits for high-risk trading (and the reason we had Glass-Steagall), and it's true for letting too-big-to-fail banks get a wink-and-a-nod guarantee of a government bailout.

+ When small banks break the law, their regulators do not hesitate to shut down the banks, toss their executives in jail, and put their employees out of work. But not so for the biggest financial institutions. The Department of Justice (DOJ) and the Securities and Exchange Commission (SEC) sit by while the same giant financial institutions keep breaking the law—and time after time, the government just says, "Please don't do it again." It's time to stop recidivism in financial crimes and to end the "slap on the wrist" culture that exists at the DOJ and the SEC.[28]

Warren called for policies to

+ change tax policies that encourage excessive risk-taking and financial instability. Close the bonus loophole that allows financial institutions to write off billions in executive bonuses each year;
+ limit highly leveraged financial institutions from fully deducting their interest payments;
+ institute a targeted financial transactions tax;
+ create simple, structural rules for regulating the shadow banking sector. Companies that act just like banks but aren't regulated like banks pose a massive risk to the financial system, and it is time regulators took the threat seriously.[29]

Elizabeth Warren is not alone in her opinions. Former Goldman Sachs banker Neel Kashkari worked with Hank Paulson, former US Secretary of the Treasury, to deal with the toxic assets during the 2008 financial collapse. Now Chair of Federal Reserve Bank of Minneapolis, Kashkari called for

+ breaking up large banks into smaller, less connected, less important entities.
+ turning large banks into public utilities by forcing them to hold so much capital that they virtually can't fail (with regulation akin to that of a nuclear power plant).
+ taxing leverage throughout the financial system to reduce systemic risks wherever they lie.[30]

In the current political climate in the US and the UK, these measures are unlikely. But in the wake of the next financial collapse, it would be worth remembering that some very bright people have real solutions.

And elsewhere, action is beginning. The Global Alliance for Banking on Value (GABV) is a network of almost 50 bankers from around the world who have pledged to serve people first and finance second. They seek to transform the "banking system so that it is more transparent, supports economic, social and environmental sustainability, and is composed of a diverse range of banking institutions serving the real economy." Operating in Asia, Africa, Australia, Latin America, North America, and Europe, GABV members serve more than 41 million customers, hold up to $127 billion in assets under management, and employ 48,000 workers.[31]

Capital Markets Reform

Arguably, a bigger factor than the role of the banks driving financialization is the role of capital markets and the expectations of investors. Andy Haldane, the chief economist of the Bank of England, stated that in the UK there had been a sevenfold increase in the proportion of profit distributed to shareholders in dividends and bought-back shares, over the past 45 years. In 1970, of every £100 in profits earned, roughly £10 went back to shareholders. Now it is an average of £70 out of every £100 in profits. Post World War II, the average share used to be held for six years; now, the average is six months. Similar trends are seen in the US. Haldane put particular emphasis on explaining the fact that British and American law has put the short-term interests of shareholders in the position of primacy.[32]

Too much of what we now call "investment" is nothing more than speculation in the secondary securities markets. Investors blindly follow deeply flawed Modern Portfolio Theory and its simplistic and misleading so-called efficient frontier. But this is efficient only until we experience another hundred-year storm that seems to come every five years or so, or the next financial collapse. Eliminating tax exemptions for debt would also help, since a resilient economy would employ relatively less debt and use more equity capital, even at some cost to the "efficiency" of that equity capital as discussed above.

Relatively simple remedies include giving differential voting rights for shares held for longer periods and heavy taxation of short-term returns. More fundamental reforms would include a shift from a shareholder to a stakeholder economy; major reform of the Private Limited Company/corporation statutes, including regular charter renewal based on environmental performance; and putting major environmental liabilities on company balance sheets. Remember, as stated in the Introduction, the Trucost study found that if environmental costs were properly counted, almost no company on Earth would be profitable.[33]

Evergreen Direct Investment

New investment methods will be needed. Conventional financing relies on debt (taking out a loan) or equity (selling stock in the company). Innovative financing like Evergreen Direct Investment (EDI),[34] as proposed by the Capital Institute, is an appealing option that asks the large superfiduciary asset owners (pension funds and sovereign wealth funds) to fundamentally reimagine what it means to invest.

The core architecture of EDI is a cash-flow-sharing method that already exists in numerous private real estate investment partnerships. In such a deal, investors get priority access to cash flows until their investment is returned. After that, they would get a preferred return of, say, eight percent. Profits that exceed that are split between the investors and the company that holds the brand that the investors "bought."

EDI would be best applied to mature, stable cash flow brands that are often the "cash cows" of public companies. Companies holding such low- or no-growth cash flow generators are often criticized by investors, because with no growth, the brand is seen as an obstacle to getting the stock price higher. In the growth-dependent, speculative valuations market (otherwise known as the stock market), this is the only thing of interest to Wall Street analysts.

Many companies struggle to show new growth opportunities. But these need to be very large in order to "move the needle" relative to the large (but often no longer growing) core business. This is the challenge, for example, that Microsoft faced prior to its "regeneration" with its push into cloud computing in trying to create enterprise growth to contrast with its mature but low-growth domestic Windows and Office brands. Because of this, Microsoft had, stunningly, failed to generate returns for public investors for more than 15 years, despite its extraordinary profitability, until the market got wind of a looming management change in 2014.

To counter this, a pension fund would invest directly into a mature, low-growth brand. An EDI partnership would give the investor, say, a 40 percent ownership of the mature business's cash flows. The business would retain the brand and manage it for sustainable performance. The investors would receive 100 percent of the cash flows attributable to their share until they had their investment back. They would then get, say, 80 percent of the cash flows until they earned a preferred return of 8 percent (IRR). After that, the cash flow split would reverse, with investors getting 20 percent of the remainder (forever), while 80 percent would revert to the parent company (including incentive compensation for good management).

This sort of arrangement would align the interests of the investors and corporate managers. Now, in contrast, management is compensated with stock options. This incentivizes them to pump up the stock price in the short term. With EDI, management has every incentive to manage its beloved mature business units for the long term, rather than sell them off to please stock analysts who would otherwise penalize the parent company with bad reviews.

EDI investments will typically be applied to stable but low- or no-growth businesses, which are valued at five to six times cash flow, far less than hot-growth prospects. Compare that to Tesla stock, which was valued in 2017 at ten times the price earnings ratio of Ford Motor Company, despite Tesla having no profits. Stable businesses should generate a cash-on-cash return in the low- to mid-double digits, essentially forever, hence the name "Evergreen." This would see investors paid back in seven or eight years. In such a situation, management teams need at least a ten-year view and commitment.

Such a time frame would encourage the transition to sustainable, and in fact regenerative, business models.

Reform of the Financial System

Reform of the financial system is needed not only because it's a mess, verging at times on being a criminal enterprise, but because the transition to a regenerative future needs a functional financial sector. The scale of new investment required to avoid collapse is staggering.

A report by the UN Environment Programme (UNEP), *The Coming Financial Climate*,[35] identifies some of the measures that are required globally to develop a sustainable financial system that puts climate security at its heart. It states that, according to the World Bank, the global economy will require $93.1 trillion over the next 15 years in infrastructure investment in cities, energy, and land-use systems. We will also need investment in making the transition to a low-carbon economy if we are to stay within the limit of a 2-degrees Celsius rise in temperature. The report concludes that changes are needed throughout the financial system, as described above, but adds that it will be necessary to properly value natural assets, to put a price on pollution, and to phase out fossil fuel subsidies.

To put the $93 trillion in perspective, the current total value of all global public equity markets combined—the equity value of every public company on Earth—is a mere $60 trillion. When combined with the urgency of transition, the scale of change needed argues for quick and radical financial sector reform.

The scale of infrastructure investment required raises the question of whether it might not be wise to embark on a program of what might be called Strategic Quantitative Easing (QE)[36] to build the necessary infrastructure of a zero-carbon economy. State-owned green banks using QE could take back the power to create new money.

There have been major programs of QE in both the US and the UK. The European Central Bank recently embarked on a similar venture. These programs, used only to buy the toxic assets of large commercial banks, represented a major missed opportunity. If the public borrowing had been used to purchase the assets of institutions focused on developing a sustainable economy instead, then the necessary transformation to such an economy would now be well underway.

For example, the Bank of England purchased £375 billion of major bank assets through its QE program. An estimated £550 billion of investment in new low-carbon infrastructure is required in the UK in the next ten years, but the combined capital in the Green Investment Bank and the British Business Bank totaled only £4 billion in 2013. By contrast, Germany's KfW development bank had capital of £400 billion. Strategic QE could be a very powerful instrument to help build the necessary infrastructure of a zero-carbon economy.[37]

Central bank support for national infrastructure has worked before. For example, the Industrial Development Bank of Canada (which supported Canadian small business from 1946 to 1992) was capitalized entirely by the central bank, with not a penny of taxpayers' money required.

Just as Federal spending built Silicon Valley and the internet, so delivering a renewable future would be a good investment.

Sovereign Money—or 100 Percent Reserve Requirements

The New Economics Foundation[38] proposed an extension of this: use of sovereign (government-created) money to fund the shift to a sustainable economy and/or to fund a "Citizen's Income" that could allow everyone's income levels to be supported and hours of work cut during a recession phase of economic de-growth. This was a reaction to a leading UK economics commentator, the *Financial Times'* Martin Wolf,[39] who argued that the power to create new money should be stripped from private banks and returned to the state.

Wolf's article heavily referenced Positive Money's book *Modernizing Money*, an examination of how reform could be carried out in the UK today—at virtually no cost to the taxpayer. It complements Michael Kumhoff's Chicago Plan,[40] which described how it could be implemented in the United States. The article precipitated an explosion in economics circles, with many expressing concern that sovereign money creation would lead to a drying up of credit. But sovereign money proposes simply that the unit of account, £ sterling, which most British prefer to use for payment transactions (a result of it being the unit in which British must pay their taxes), should not be created by private companies. Such a rule would not stop people from issuing private credit contracts nor stop companies issuing lines of "trade credit" to each other in lieu of sterling for the exchange of goods and services. Many estimates suggest this industry is already a more important source of financing than bank credit. Sovereign money reform might encourage emergence of a range of peer-to-peer and complementary currency systems[41] that would no longer have to compete with heavily subsidized behemoth banks for customers.

More research is needed to explore these approaches. But the sands may be shifting against the current model, once described by Mervyn King as "the worst possible way of organising banking."[42] Martin Wolf's conclusion seems to agree:

> Our financial system is so unstable because the state first allowed it to create almost all the money in the economy and was then forced to insure it when performing that function. This is a giant hole at the heart of our market economies. It could be closed by separating the provision of money, rightly a function of the state, from the provision of finance, a function of the private sector.[43]

Conclusion

The flow of money is the lifeblood of the economy. Efforts by neoliberals to enhance that have created a flood, sweeping through society to deposit its spoils on the shores owned by the one percent. In the process, as more money seeks an ever-greater return, it lays waste to the planet. As John Fullerton puts it, all investment has impact.[44]

The banking sectors in many countries are far too focused on investments in speculative, non-productive assets. Both structural and incentive changes are critically needed. The fixation of Wall Street analysts, the investors they advise, and increasingly corporate leaders to drive continuous high growth is impoverishing people and the Earth. Major reform of the finance sector is necessary.

CHAPTER EIGHT

CORPORATE TRANSFORMATION

*There is no more strategic issue for a company,
or any organization, than its ultimate purpose.
For those who think business exists to make a profit,
I suggest they think again. Business makes a profit to exist.
Surely it must exist for some higher, nobler purpose than that.*

RAY ANDERSON[1]

The neoliberal narrative holds that a company exists solely to make money for its owners. If owners use their profits for philanthropy, that is noble. But it is not the job of the corporate sector, so the story goes, to worry about the woes of the world.

It's an appealingly simple proposition, but that might better be called "Cheater Capitalism." Business as usual has been built on cheap access to the world's resources, especially fossil energy. Access to these has historically been, and today remains, heavily subsidized. The $10 million a minute the world spends in energy subsidies is only the tip of the iceberg of ways that we make resource depletion look cheaper than it really is.

The neoliberal worldview, in which such fraud is celebrated as cleverness, has long believed that companies should "externalize" costs as much as possible. Indeed, companies spend a lot of money to lobby (or corrupt) regulators to ensure that only weak controls are ever imposed on them, arguing that if industry is unduly shackled, it will be unable to deliver the good life its customers want. Activists, in contrast, argue that only by punishing business and imposing draconian regulations can we save nature and our families. And so business and activists have remained in a standoff, the Earth roasts, and collapse looms.

It is perhaps time to recognize that neither narrative is a useful one, and increasingly, neither is true. No one better proved this than industrialist Ray Anderson, who baldly stated, "In the future industrialists like me will be in jail." He rejected the neoliberal narrative outright.

The Radical Industrialist

Ray was a South Georgia high-school football star. After taking his engineering degree at Georgia Tech, he went into the local business: carpets. When he was passed over for a promotion he felt he deserved, Ray, always intensely competitive, founded his own company, Interface. He proceeded to grow it into one of the largest carpet companies in the world.

In 1994, Ray added a European carpet company to his family of brands. Ray's right-hand man, Jim Hartzfelt, reported that the acquired employees asked what Interface's environmental policy was. Ray responded, "Do we have one? Quick, someone get me a book on the environment." Joyce LaValle, Ray's head of human resources, handed him a copy of Paul Hawken's *Ecology of Commerce*, which, among many other things, described the environmental harm being done by businesses, and repeated David Brower's observation that "you can't do business on a dead planet." It was, the book argued, the responsibility of business to solve the crises facing humanity.

In the hundreds of speeches he thereafter gave each year, Ray described lying awake the night before he was to give the speech to his new employees, lamenting, "There is nothing about our company that is sustainable." He described the moment as a "spear in his chest."[2]

And, he pledged, "We are going to be the first company of the Next Industrial Revolution." Ray was a businessman to his core, a fierce defender of capitalism, but in what he described as his "epiphany," he found himself answerable to a new metric that he named "God's currency": non-financial costs and benefits that accrue to the planet and its people.

Ray created what he called his Dream Team, some of the best minds in sustainability, to advise him. Together they remade Interface into the poster child of corporate sustainability.[3]

Ray named the adventure of becoming a regenerative company, the task to which he set Interface, "climbing Mount Sustainability":

> to operate our petro-intensive company (for materials and energy) in a way that takes nothing from Earth that is not naturally and rapidly renewable, and does no harm to Earth's biosphere, e.g., not another fresh drop of oil, no greenhouse gases or other harmful emissions—factories without smoke stacks."[4]

Ray's effort to make Interface the most sustainable company on Earth was far from easy.[5] Investors thought he'd lost his mind, especially in the Y2K scare, as companies bought computers, not carpets. Ray's answer? "It's my job to go round the bend and see what's out there, what most people can't see yet." Because Ray owned 51 percent of the company, he could stay the course.

David Oakey, Interface's lead designer,[6] reacted to Ray's challenge to make a carpet that was recyclable and itself made of recycled materials, by saying, "Boss, it can't be done."

"It has to be possible, Ray replied, "Nature does it."

Interface invested in a largely unknown biologist, Janine Benyus, and the corporate practice of biomimicry[7] was born. Teaming with Oakey, Janine and the Dream Team innovated to close the company's industrial loops and create an early example of the circular economy.

When Oakey reported on his success at a Dream Team meeting, his eyes were big as saucers. "God must be an environmentalist," he marveled. "I said it couldn't be done, but when we did it, it worked better, cost less, had every attribute we wanted and many we hadn't thought to ask for."[8]

When Ray and Mike Bertolucci, Interface's director of research, proudly announced that they had figured out how to make carpet from corn, Hunter Lovins, a Dream Team member replied, "You realize that you're now in the business of sustainable agriculture?" Ray laid his head on his desk and moaned, "Is there never an end?"[9]

But then he picked his head up, turned to Mike and said, "No, that's what it means to be responsible. Let's figure it out." Several years later, the industrial giant Cargill announced that it was selling a line of non-GMO corn precisely to satisfy Interface's demand for sustainable feedstocks.[10]

Interface has not yet summited Mount Sustainability, but the company's achievements are impressive:

- Net GHG emissions down 82 percent in absolute tonnage, 92 percent per pound of product;[11]
- Renewable energy up 84 percent; six of seven manufacturing sites are 100 percent renewable; energy usage down 45 percent per pound of product;[12]
- Waste from facilities reduced 91 percent.[13]

Interface reckons that it is halfway to its Mission Zero goal of zero impact, zero footprint by 2020. And it remains committed to achieving it.[14] Some at Interface are nervous, acutely aware that 2020 is near. Some say it will take a miracle. Jim Hartzfelt dismisses such concerns, "People don't realize that it took five or six miracles to get this far; Interface has always been in the miracle business."[15]

The Right Thing Is Profitable: The Business Case for Sustainability

As impressive as these numbers are, Ray was always clear that unless his commitment to sustainability gave him the means to crush his competition, it would be a valiant effort in vain. He believed that greater sustainability would earn him goodwill and customer loyalty, and it did, but he expected to have to pay for those attributes.

It came as almost as big a surprise to him as it was to David Oakey that their sustainability efforts not only made Interface more effective but dramatically enhanced the company's bottom line. His commitment to behave in more sustainable ways enhanced every aspect of shareholder value.[16] It kept his company alive as several competitors went out of business. It created unprecedented employee engagement and customer loyalty. It also drove his innovation.

Savings from sustainability paid for all of the costs of the transformation and became an enduring source of profit. In the first four years of Interface's work on sustainability, sales increased by two-thirds, profits doubled. Cutting waste 40 percent created $76 million in cost savings. By 2000, annual savings were $185.4 million.[17]

The business case for sustainability began to emerge in the mid-1990s.[18] In 2001, Hunter Lovins coined the term "Integrated Bottom Line," arguing that a corporate commitment to sustainability enhances 13 aspects of shareholder value, including better financial performance, higher stock value, faster-growing stock value, lower risks, better ability to attract and retain employees, better brand equity, better relations with stakeholders, and lower cost of distrust.[19] By the mid-aughts, reports from the big management consulting houses confirmed each aspect of the ways in which companies that led in efficiency, social responsibility, good governance, and other aspects of corporate sustainability outperformed less sustainable peers."[20]

The September 2014 report by Carbon Disclosure Project CDP made the case stronger. Its "Climate Action and Profitability" study showed that companies that integrate sustainability into their business strategies outperform those who fail to show such leadership. Companies that are managing their carbon emissions and are mitigating climate change enjoy 18 percent higher returns on their investment than companies that aren't, and 67 percent higher than companies that refuse to disclose their emissions.[21]

Every three years, Accenture surveys 1,000 CEOs from more than 100 countries. The 2013 report[22] found that while a strong majority believed that a corporate commitment to sustainability is a path to growth and innovation (78 percent), conferring competitive advantage in their industry (79 percent), only 38 percent felt that they could quantify the business value of such programs to their company. Only 15 percent felt that they had made sufficient progress in the prior three years in making their sustainability commitment a must-have asset for customers, and 82 percent saw this as crucial to enabling greater sustainability to transform the economy. Analysts concluded that corporate sustainability had plateaued.[23]

By 2016, attitudes had shifted. Almost 60 percent of CEOs surveyed said that they could accurately quantify the business value of their sustainability program to their company. Ninety-seven percent believed that sustainability is important to the future success of their business, and 53 percent felt that business is making sufficient efforts to address global challenges. Transparency was seen as a critical factor, with 79 percent seeing brand, trust, and reputation as driving action on sustainability.[24]

Corporate social responsibility has come a long way from the days when most companies were what sustainability analyst Bob Willard calls "pre-compliant," getting away with as much as they could and only reluctantly obeying the law. Smart companies discovered that implementing efficiency saved money. Some then moved on to integrating sustainability throughout their operations.[25]

The leaders are now finding, as Ray Anderson did, that when you embed sustainability into your company's core mission, it transforms your business. It moves a company from one focused on serving Wall Street analysts by delivering ever-increasing quarterly profits to one in which enhanced shareholder value is recognized as an outcome of behaving responsibly to people and to planet. When well-managed, a commitment to sustainability creates savings that compound essentially infinitely.

One problem is that after a few years these savings are forgotten, new accounting baselines reset the bar, and normal corporate life goes on. But when calculating whether there is a business case for initiating a sustainability program, remember that the years' worth of costs not incurred, resources no longer needed, and harm not caused ought to be given a place in net present value calculations.

Triple Bottom Line to Integrated Bottom Line to SASB and IIRC

Sustainability is a young discipline. Most of the people creating the field are still alive. Its basic principles and frameworks are still evolving.

The word was first used in *Limits to Growth* but not defined there. In the book *Our Common Future*,[26] then prime minister of Norway, Gro Harlem Bruntland, described "sustainable development" as harmony between economic, social, and environment objectives: "Development that meets the needs of the present without compromising the ability of future generations to meet their own needs."

In 1992, in preparation for the UN's Earth Summit in Rio, a group of business leaders created the World Business Council for Sustainable Development to promote the concept of resource efficiency as the basis of sustainability.

Two years later, John Elkington advanced the concept that businesses should manage to a triple bottom line: profit, of course, but also people and planet.[27] This framing advanced the field significantly, arguing that it was an affirmative obligation of companies to take care of their employees, community stakeholders, and the environment in which they did business. Initially appealing, it turned out to be easy to jettison if the financial bottom line began to suffer.

Randy Hayes, executive director of Foundation Earth, argues[28] that we need a system that transparently counts the costs to the future and to the Earth of the activities of both business and government. Such accounting would reflect the true cost of transactions throughout supply chains. Often described as the problem of how to manage "externalities," solving this system-wide issue requires far more than "make the polluter pay" forms of taxation.

It was not until the introduction of the Integrated Bottom Line[29] in the early aughts that recognition began to grow that behaving responsibly to people and planet were core aspects of delivering superior financial performance.

This begged the question of how to account for the benefit that behaving more sustainably confers on a company, or the cost to it of failing to do so. In the early 2000s, Robert Massie and a team of people from accounting firms, public interest advocacy groups, governments, and companies created the Global Reporting Initiative

(GRI), a protocol to guide companies who wished to report on their sustainability programs.

Harvard's Professor Robert Eccles and accounting expert Michael Krzus reiterated the importance of this approach in their 2010 book, *One Report: Integrated Reporting for a Sustainable Society*.[30] They argued that financial reporting was fatally incomplete, precisely because it was failing to count the value captured by a company from a commitment to sustainability, as well as the risks and costs imposed by failing to have such a program. Such assets and liabilities, they argued, were real and material. Eccles went on to help create the Sustainability Accounting Standards Board (SASB)[31] to establish protocols, industry by industry, setting forth how companies should conduct integrated reporting. SASB recruited Michael Bloomberg, business leader and ex-New York City mayor, to chair the effort.

Based on Eccles' work, and a series of studies[32] showing that the sustainability leaders were financially outperforming companies that rejected this approach, SASB presented the proposition that investors reasonably need credible sustainability reporting to judge the investment merits of a company. This "materiality standard" will, as it is demonstrated, essentially obligate the US Securities and Exchange Commission to require companies to measure, account for, and report on their sustainability performance.

In 2015, Eccles and Krzus published *The Integrated Reporting Movement: Meaning, Momentum, Motives and Materiality*,[33] again arguing that combining financial and sustainability reporting is superior. Several of Eccles's Harvard colleagues and graduate students published a Harvard Business School paper showing that "firms with good performance on material sustainability issues significantly outperform firms with poor performance on these issues, suggesting that investments in sustainability issues are shareholder-value enhancing."[34]

When SASB hit the street in 2017, it began transforming corporate accounting and thus management.

In Europe, a similar effort, the International Integrated Reporting Council[35] provides companies, many of whom already face governmental directives to consider more than short-term investor return, with guidance on how to do integrated reporting. Companies like Puma (and its parent Kering),[36] Novo Nordisk,[37] Baxter Healthcare, and others are already counting the costs and risks of unsustainability in their financial reporting.

The Sustainability Imperative: The New Business as Usual

As more companies embrace various aspects of "sustainability," it has almost become the new normal. A Web search of "The Sustainability Imperative: The New Business as Usual" returns more than 14 million hits.

All businesses, even the most committed ones, have a long way to go, but the momentum has shifted. The 2016 survey of American CEOs, released each year by PricewaterhouseCoopers at the WEF, found that while 85 percent believe that customers make decisions based primarily on cost, convenience, and functionality, they think that by 2020 up to 40 percent will want to do business with companies that manage to a higher purpose, addressing "wider stakeholder needs, like health focus or environmental responsibility or societal consequences."[38]

Almost half of the US Fortune 500 companies have set targets for greenhouse gas emissions reductions, energy efficiency, renewable energy use, or a combination of these three.[39]

More than 8,000 businesses, and 5,000 other stakeholders employing 63 million people in 165 countries, have signed the UN Global Compact Principles. Signatories represent nearly every business sector and size. Derived from the Universal Declaration of Human Rights, the International Labour Organization's Declaration on Fundamental Principles and Rights at Work, the Rio Declaration on Environment and Development, and the United Nations Convention Against Corruption, the ten principles are as follows:

+ Principle 1: Businesses should support and respect the protection of internationally proclaimed human rights; and
+ Principle 2: make sure that they are not complicit in human rights abuses.

+ Principle 3: Businesses should uphold the freedom of association and the effective recognition of the right to collective bargaining;
+ Principle 4: the elimination of all forms of forced and compulsory labor;
+ Principle 5: the effective abolition of child labor; and
+ Principle 6: the elimination of discrimination in respect of employment and occupation.
+ Principle 7: Businesses should support a precautionary approach to environmental challenges;
+ Principle 8: undertake initiatives to promote greater environmental responsibility; and
+ Principle 9: encourage the development and diffusion of environmentally friendly technologies.
+ Principle 10: Businesses should work against corruption in all its forms, including extortion and bribery.[40]

As these become more widely implemented, they will transform business.

Business leaders representing trillions of dollars of revenue were essential to the success of both the UN Sustainable Development Goals and the Paris Climate Agreement, described in chapter 10. CEO Paul Polman of Unilever chaired high-level working groups and summits. At the CEO summit at the Paris COP, business leaders of Fortune 100 companies pleaded with national delegates to give them a binding agreement, promising to unleash trillions of dollars of investment if the deal came through. Following the signing of the Paris Agreement, the Low-Carbon Technology Partnerships Initiative[41] garnered 84 companies committed to work together to find solutions to accelerate low-carbon technology development and scale up the deployment of business solutions to a level and speed that are consistent with the international agreement.

Two business-oriented NGOs, CDP and We Mean Business, issued the *Business End of Climate Change* report.[42] It sets out five initiatives that companies can take to cut carbon emissions. The effort already has 611 companies and investors committed to

+ adopt science-based emission reduction targets
+ put a price on carbon
+ procure 100 percent of electricity from renewable sources
+ implement responsible corporate engagement in climate policy
+ remove commodity-driven deforestation products from all supply chains by 2020
+ remove short-lived (black carbon) climate pollutant emissions
+ commit to improve energy efficiency

We Mean Business and its members work with more than 6 million companies around the world.[43]

The World Green Building Council and its 74 national councils have pledged to retrofit and certify all properties under its members' management (13.5 billion square feet of real estate) to net zero status by 2050.[44] Every day more than two million square feet of building space are certified under LEED green building standards.[45]

The Prince of Wales Corporate Leaders Group enlisted 16 companies to commit to build net zero buildings by 2020 and to retrofit their facilities to this standard by 2030. Signatories include, of course, Interface but also Heathrow Airport, Lloyds Bank, Tesco, Kingfisher, GlaxoSmithKline, and others.

One of the stronger aspects of the sustainability imperative is that if companies wish to attract and retain talent, and drive productivity and profitability, they will implement sustainability throughout their operations. The Economist Intelligence Unit found that "engaging employees on sustainability is a powerful tool for motivating employees, delivering improved customer satisfaction, increased productivity and reduced employee turnover and absenteeism."[46] Gallup's 2015 Employee Engagement report surveyed 82,000 businesses with 1.8 million employees in 73 countries. They found that engaged workforces deliver 20 percent higher productivity and 21 percent higher profitability.[47] Johnson Controls found that 96 percent of young people want to work for a company in which they can find meaning, a company that behaves responsibly to the environment.[48] Monster Track reported that 92 percent of young people would prefer to work for an environmentally friendly company.[49] Fortune found that companies that can authentically tout their environmental credentials will have a competitive advantage in hiring the best of the new generation of talent.[50]

Cone Communications surveys global customers and their attitudes to corporate purpose. Their 2015 survey—of 9,709 consumers in the United States, Canada, Brazil, the United Kingdom, Germany, France, China, India, and Japan (nine of the largest countries in the world by GDP)—found that

- 91 percent of global consumers expect companies to do more than make a profit, that they must also operate responsibly to address social and environmental issues;
- 84 percent say they seek out responsible products whenever possible;
- 90 percent would boycott a company if they learned of irresponsible or deceptive business practices.[51]

Freya Williams is a marketing consultant to Fortune 500 companies. Co-founder of Ogilvy Earth, and previously head of the sustainability practice at Edelman; she now runs the US office of Futerra, the marketing industry's innovative edge. Under her leadership, Edelman studied the role of purpose in enabling a brand to prosper. She found, "[P]urpose is driving consumer preference and loyalty in a world where trust in corporations is low and differentiation between brands is negligible."

In her most recent book, *Green Giants*,[52] she profiled new billion dollar brands that are successful *because* they have sustainability baked into the core of everything that they do.

Freya sets forth six attributes that she sees as critical to future business success:

1. **The iconoclastic leader:** In each of the companies, the sustainability journey can be traced back to one courageous individual who was prepared to stand out from the crowd.
2. **Disruptive innovation:** The companies have not succeeded via

an iterative improvement of existing products but from generating a new mindset that disrupts the status quo.

3. **A higher purpose:** The green giants showcase the paradox that having a clear purpose can naturally lead to financial outperformance. It rarely works the other way around.

4. **Built in, not bolted on:** The companies are driving sustainability into the core of their strategies, ranging from design to finance. A sustainability department operating at the margins of a business will never get the traction needed to drive fundamental change.

5. **Mainstream appeal:** Too many green business initiatives have failed because companies relied on consumers' ethical motives and delivered products that were substandard. The green giants create innovative products that perform better than those of their competitors.

6. **Walking the talk:** Corporate reputation is built through actions and not advertising or PR. Transparency, responsibility, and collaboration are essential ingredients in driving large-scale change.

The green giants find that their purpose-driven brands outperform their brands that have not yet committed to an authentic sustainability mission. Unilever, one of the companies Freya describes, has found that its brands with authentic purpose are growing at double-digit rates, or nearly that—twice the rate of the rest of the company and accounting for half of the company's growth.[53] In addition, the company's efficiency work is saving it €200 million each year.

It's the Right Thing to Do

Ray Anderson began his crusade because it was the right thing to do. Many sustainability frameworks spring from the same instinct. Ray used a Swedish framework, Natural Step, as his model, teaching it to all his senior managers and spending a great deal of money supporting an American division of the organization. The approach,

which has guided various Scandinavian companies, is based on four
system conditions:

> In a sustainable society, nature is not subject to systematically
> increasing
> 1. concentrations of substances from the Earth's crust (such
>   as fossil CO_2 and heavy metals);
> 2. concentrations of substances produced by society (such as
>   antibiotics and endocrine disruptors);
> 3. degradation by physical means (such as deforestation and
>   draining of groundwater tables).
> 4. And in that society, there are no structural obstacles to
>   people's health, influence, competence, impartiality, and
>   meaning.[54]

In practice, however, Ray had a hard time getting the company to
make progress under Natural Step. It helped Ray and some of his
senior managers conceptualize where he believed the company
needed to go, but it was pretty thin on what to do Monday morning.
Ray's efforts to cut Interface's footprint went slowly until he tied personal bonuses to waste reduction. Within a year, eliminating waste
was delivering 30 percent of his operating profits.

Natural Capitalism

As Ray wrestled with how to convey what he was undertaking, he
penned several books: *Mid-Course Correction* and *Confessions of a
Radical Industrialist.*[55] Inadvertently, he helped write a third, *Natural
Capitalism: Creating the Next Industrial Revolution.*[56] Authored by
Paul Hawken, Amory Lovins, and Hunter Lovins, three members
of Ray's Dream Team, *Natural Capitalism* coevolved from the approaches that Ray actually implemented to drive transformation in
Interface. Its principles establish a framework that has been used
since then by thousands of businesses across the world to achieve
greater sustainability and enhance profitability. Ray may have believed that Natural Step guided his thinking, but what he really did

became the principles that now frame the arc of transition to a Regenerative Economy.

The first principle is to buy time, as described in section 2, by using all resources dramatically more productively. Eliminating waste is just good business sense. It cuts costs and improves productivity. Neoclassical economists argue that markets inherently make companies as efficient as is cost-effective, but every engineer knows this is mythology. Every company in the world can improve its resource productivity; most can operate a great deal more efficiently. Natural Capitalist[57] companies save enormous amounts of money. Efficiency helps solve the climate crisis, resource constraints, and many other challenges. The 2012 book *The Way Out: Kickstarting Capitalism to Save Our Economic Ass* showed that pushing the worst challenges facing us off into the future and giving ourselves time to implement more transformational sustainability measures not only avoids collapse, it makes us more money.[58] Efficiency is the cornerstone of any smart resource policy, but is only the beginning.

The second principle of Natural Capitalism is to redesign how we make and deliver everything. Natural Capitalist companies use the financial savings delivered by their efficiency programs to pay for such more sustainable approaches as biomimicry,[59] Cradle to Cradle design,[60] and the circular economy[61] to profitably transform their businesses.[62]

Biomimicry

The discipline of biomimicry is the basis of regenerative practices. In nature, waste is a resource out of place, and a use is found for it. For example, in nature, carbon is not the world's greatest poison: it is the building block of all of life. The Biomimicry Institute, created by Janine Benyus, who, as described above, helped Ray Anderson innovate, has set forth the principles on which nature does business. They are very different than ours.

Nature makes a wide array of products and services running only on sunlight, with no long-lived toxins. It makes everything near to something alive, at ambient temperature, using water-based chemistry, and wasting nothing.[63] Nature also shops locally. Do you?

Nature creates conditions conducive to life. It
- uses only the energy it needs, efficiently,
- fits form to function,
- recycles everything,
- rewards cooperation,
- banks on diversity,
- demands local expertise,
- curbs excesses from within, and
- taps the power of limits.

Nature's big ideas are
- self-assembly
- CO_2 as a feedstock
- solar transformations
- the power of shape
- quenching thirst
- metals without mining
- green chemistry
- timed degradation
- resilience and healing
- sensing and responding — locusts as inspiration for collision-free driverless cars!
- growing fertility
- life creates conditions conducive to life

The Biomimicry Guild, Janine's for-profit company, helps businesses like Interface implement these principles, but she has shared her ideas widely.[64] Because of this, entrepreneurs are using the concept to create whole new companies that embed nature's designs into the core of their operations. For example, rather than use Styrofoam for packaging, Ecovative grows fungi to create crush-resistant, biodegradable product protection. Its Mushroom® Packaging protects

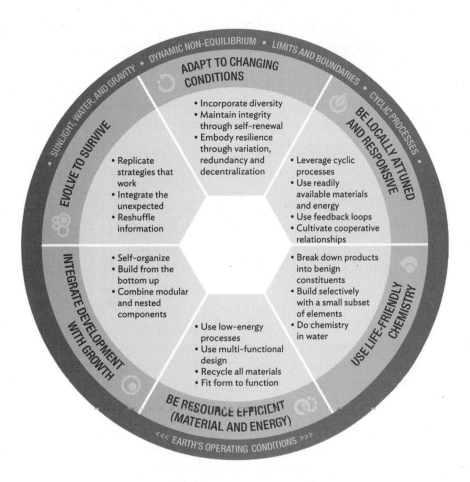

Biomimicry Circle. Credit: Janine Benyus, Biomimicry.net, AskNature.org.

Dell computers. This biomaterials company also uses mycelium to glue together engineered wood products to eliminate formaldehyde. Its Mushroom Insulation provides an array of better acoustics, core materials, and aquatic products.[65]

Biomimetic companies use pollution as a feedstock. Newlight Technologies, for example, produces plastic by combining air with methane-based greenhouse gas emissions. Working with 60 Fortune 500 companies, Newlight supplies cell phone cases, chairs, plastic bags, and other products. Winner of the 2016 EPA Presidential

Green Chemistry Challenge Award, they signed a 20-year contract to supply 19 billion pounds of carbon-based plastic with Paques Holdings.[66]

Lanza Tech, a Chicago-based startup, uses waste carbon monoxide from Chinese steel manufacturers and Indian oil refineries to feed to microbes that produce ethanol.[67] Using more waste and clever biology, the company can make everything from jet fuel to "rubber" for tires.

Regenerative Management

The third principle of Natural Capitalism is to manage all institutions to be regenerative of human and natural capital. Companies, communities, and countries should ensure that they enhance both of these capitals, as well as manufactured and financial capital. A good capitalist will ensure that all forms of capital are enhanced. Anything else is just bad capitalism: liquidating our most important forms of capital to get more money and stuff is a self-defeating practice. Implementing more sustainable measures is a step to creating a Regenerative Economy, but ultimately, nature is sustainable *because* it is regenerative. True sustainability is an outcome of a system that is inherently regenerative of human and natural capital.

Less is known about how to make companies truly regenerative. Use of the term is increasing, with scholarly business articles even talking about "regenerative marketing."[68] But what does it mean to be truly regenerative as a company?

Capital Institute tracks scalable, real-world regenerative projects and enterprises in its *Field Guide to Investing in a Regenerative Economy*.[69] The site profiles companies for whom regenerative principles are the "source code."

For Regenerative Capitalism to sweep the global economy, it will be necessary to apply these principles to large global enterprises. But even here, there is evidence of its presence taking root.

The Next Ray Anderson

Ray Anderson tragically died of cancer in 2011. All who knew Ray have asked themselves many times who will fill his shoes.

Lindsay James, Interface's director of strategic sustainability, answered:

> She (or he) will be the one that completely re-imagines business, its role in our world and its potential. Like Ray, she will know a deeper level of truth that the rest of us are blind to, and she will articulate that truth in a compelling way until we can see it, too. In other words, like Ray, she will question the most basic assumptions that drive our complex systems. She'll be the one that sounds a little crazy to the rest of us, the one that's gone 'round the bend and understood what the future holds, and can map that back to what is needed today.[70]

A year after Ray's death, the editor of *Green Biz* asked a number of people who had known Ray why there weren't more like him, and who the next one might be.[71] Many of those surveyed said Paul Polman, the CEO of Unilever.

Hired to take over a successful, if somewhat stagnant, company, Paul lost no time shaking things up. Shortly after arriving, he announced that he wouldn't report quarterly to Wall Street.

Shareholders freaked. Stocks fell ten percent. Paul reacted that he respected those who had sold as human beings, but if they truly believed that he could best create corporate value in their company by managing on a 90-day rotation, he did not want them as his owners (a statement echoed some years later when a climate-denying shareholder attacked Tim Cook, CEO of Apple, for pledging to go 100 percent renewably powered). When Paul was subsequently asked how he found the courage to take on the financial analysts and his shareholders all at once, he answered, "They'd just hired me. I didn't think they'd fire me."

Nor would they now. Unilever's Sustainable Living Plan guided the company to lower costs, higher profitability, and almost universal acclaim as the next sustainable business poster child.[72] As Paul is fond of saying, he runs the world's largest NGO. Unilever sponsors urban farms in New York[73] and celebrations of the best young entrepreneurs from developing countries at high-level festivals in London.[74]

The company is committed to implement the Unilever Sustainable Living Plan,[75] cutting its environmental impact in half while doubling revenues, sourcing all feedstocks from sustainable agriculture, and improving the lives of a billion people. The company acknowledges that it is doing business at a unique time in human history:

> We are living in a world where temperatures are rising, water shortages are more frequent, food supplies are increasingly scarce and the gap between rich and poor increasing. Populations are growing fast, making basic hygiene and sanitation even more of a challenge. At Unilever we can see how people the world over are already affected by these changes. And the changes will pose new challenges for us too, as commodity costs fluctuate, markets become unstable and raw materials harder to source.
>
> We believe that business must be part of the solution. But to be so, business will have to change; there is not "business as usual anymore." Sustainable, equitable growth is the only acceptable business model. Our vision is to grow our business, whilst reducing our environmental footprint and increasing our positive social impact.[76]

Unilever may soon become the largest global company to go beyond sustainability to commit to becoming "regenerative." It is working through how to behave in a regenerative manner applying Fullerton's principles to its operations.[77]

In early 2017, however, Unilever got what the analysts termed a wake-up call. Kraft Heinz, backed by the corporate raiders 3G, tendered what Warren Buffet thought was a generous and friendly offer of $143 billion to buy out Unilever. The *Financial Times* headline described the reaction: "Hyena Capitalism Receives a Swift Kick from the Unilever Giraffe."[78] Describing Unilever as vulnerable due to its sheer size, and the raiders as "hyenas, which smell weakness a mile off and make a savage living ripping out inefficiencies," the article extoled efficiency, and warned that Unilever had better watch out: "Capitalism needs both giraffes and hyenas. But in a time of modest growth, low productivity and rising inequality, one must keep an especially close eye on the hyenas."

John Fullerton and others rushed to remind Paul Polman about the concept of Evergreen Direct Investment, described earlier in the financial section. It might be precisely the synergistic investment strategy that would allow Unilever to continue transitioning to regenerative management. The company meanwhile doubled down on its sustainability commitments, releasing numbers showing that these are precisely what are driving its profitability.[79]

Getting There from Here: Less Bad Is Good

Some sustainability programs are initiated, as Ray's was, because they are the right thing to do. Many companies, however, implement "corporate social responsibility" as public relations. Such companies then remain trapped in the mud Paul Polman skirted: struggling to reconcile the old narrative that they must deliver ever-increasing quarterly profits while living up to their newfound sense that to be a modern company means you have to appear to be responsible. Without an authentic sense of purpose, deep corporate commitment to sustainability, or strategic sense of why to change, such programs tend to plateau.

As the crises facing the world worsen, as the neoliberal narrative proves hard to dethrone, as short-term fixation on delivering quarterly profits paralyzes companies, it is easy to feel that the corporate sector is simply too ossified to move fast enough.

There is a nasty habit in sustainability, and indeed in many social change movements, to behave like a bucket of crabs: as soon as a crab that has been stuffed into the bucket to be taken home and boiled begins to climb out, the other crabs claw it back down.

The latest self-destructive trend is to declare sustainability dead and to say that corporate social responsibility just means "doing less bad." Unless the listener accedes to whatever proprietary framing the orator is pitching, she is branded as naïve and part of the problem. It is this framing that drove creation of the "ladder up out of the muck" concept described in chapter 3.

One of the better methodologies enabling companies to move from rhetoric to a deep change comes from Andrew Winston, the strategy adviser and business author mentioned earlier. In his book *The Big Pivot*, Winston makes a compelling case that the scale of our collective challenges—what he calls "hotter, scarcer, and more open"—are too large to allow companies to continue on the path they're on. Business must change in fundamental ways.

The big pivot is a move away from seeing business as an exercise in maximizing short-term profits first and addressing shared environmental and social challenges only when there's enough pressure from stakeholders or an investment clears strict hurdle rates.

Instead, Winston advises business to flip that logic: companies should make solving global challenges their core purpose, then, working back from that premise, use the powerful tools of capitalism (like markets and competition) to solve our challenges in ways that drive profitability. Winston has no problem with companies making money—even a lot of money. But he points out, as many others have said, if people and planet aren't thriving, business won't either.

Winston's *Big Pivot* framework is constructed from experience working with the Fortune 100. He outlines ten strategies grouped into three buckets with one key concept to bind them. First, Winston recommends a vision pivot, which starts with fighting short-termism, setting big science-based goals to drive new thinking, and pursuing what he calls "heretical innovation." Ask uncomfortable questions, he says, like "Can we operate without any carbon or water?" Only then will you challenge how the business has always done things and get heretical enough to find much more efficient and innovative ways of producing and delivering goods and services.

The second group of strategies is the valuation pivot, which includes changing incentives to engage employees and execs in larger goals, redefining and rethinking how we make investment decisions (challenging ROI as the dominant metric), and ensuring that natural capital is properly valued.

The third pivot involves inspiring customers to use less (challenging normal models of consumption-led growth), collaborating radically with competitors, and even becoming a lobbyist to encourage governments to implement on pro-climate and pro-people policies.

The Big Pivot is a road map for companies that want to lead in building a thriving world as they create a resilient business for themselves.

Increasingly companies are being built with these values baked in. B Lab was developed to give businesses metrics by which they can compete to be not only the best in the world but the Best for the World®. A non-profit, B Lab certifies companies that have completed its rigorous B Impact Assessment[80] and B Analytics.[81] Certified companies commit to manage their impact—and the impact of the businesses with whom they work—with as much rigor as they pursue profits. More than 2,000 companies in 130 industries in 50 countries have achieved B Corp certification. Together they are leading a growing global movement of people using business as a force for good.™

Taking It Deeper

This may all sound like just saying that all is well with capitalism, that we can go on buying and selling stuff if we just do it a bit more consciously. Nothing could be further from the truth. We cannot consume our way out of our problems.

Does the fact that Walmart drives sustainability concepts four levels deep in its supply chain make it a saintly enterprise? No. They face serious social challenges in paying their associates enough to achieve a decent standard of living, helping host communities retain economic vitality, and sourcing responsibly from developing countries. But when Walmart asked its global supply chain of 60,000 to 90,000 companies to measure their carbon footprint and report it to the Carbon Disclosure Project (CDP),[82] it did more to drive sustainability into even very small companies than years of government regulations. In many ways, hypocrisy is the first step to real change.

It is important to recognize, however, that deeper corporate transformation is needed. Jo Confino,[83] founder of Guardian Sustainable Business and executive editor at Huffington Post, framed it this way

> We face a crisis of leadership in the corporate world which is hampering business from becoming a force for good. Many leaders are stuck in an old paradigm that no longer serves their businesses, wider society or the earth on which we all depend. They need to find the courage to stand up and set their companies on the path to transformation.[84]

The analysts who scrunched their faces in disbelief that Unilever would reject the plump offer the raiders put before them simply have not grasped that their addiction to short-term profits is driving us to collapse and that Polman's leadership is more than just quaint.

When Ray was alive, critics said "Name another sustainability CEO, I'm tired of hearing about Ray Anderson." More recently, Jo Confino began his discussion of corporate leadership by bemoaning

> I would be a very wealthy man if I were given £1 for every time someone mentioned Unilever chief executive Paul Polman. But I may end up in abject poverty if my living were to rely on people naming more than a handful of other sustainability leaders amongst the many thousands of CEOs around the world.[85]

No doubt there are too few such leaders, but their numbers are growing. This sort of leadership is being embedded in innovative business schools[86] and is becoming the management philosophy of a whole new generation of business people.[87]

Paul and Ray are not alone. Emmanuel Faber, CEO of Dannon, is every bit their equal. Yvon Choinard, the legendary founder of Patagonia, is another. Long a leader in more sustainable practices, Patagonia has been growing at 25 to 30 percent a year—even through the recession. One of the first major companies to become certified as a B Corp,[88] it has pledged to minimize its footprint and to implement radical transparency in the impacts it still has. This became the inspiration for the Apparel Coalition's Higg Index[89] that now helps companies across the industry implement sustainability throughout their supply chain.[90] Yvon prides himself on doing the right thing, even—especially—when it seems unreasonable. The first company to commit to 100 percent organic cotton, well before the supply was sufficient or the price right, it famously ran a full-page ad in the *NY Times* telling shoppers, "Don't buy this jacket!" but to buy fewer things that lasted longer. Yvon observed, however

> If all these companies are doing all these great sustainability things, why is the world still going to hell? It's the obsession with growth! Companies that have been in business for 500–1000 years focus on three priorities: quality, innovation, and controlled growth.... There's no difference between a pessimist who says "We're doomed, why bother?" and an optimist who says "We're fine, why bother?" Nothing gets done.... If you want to change government, change business, because business runs government. If you want to change business, change business, change consumers. Make consumption uncool![91]

DNV GL is 150-year-old Norwegian company. In 2013, its then CEO, Henrik Madsen, convened a roundtable of sustainability and regenerative capitalism experts to educate the company on these approaches.[92] Within a year, DNV GL committed itself to creating a regenerative future. Owned by a trust, it is able to take a longer-term view of the company's responsibility than companies "owned" by fractional shareholders seem to believe possible. DNV GL's chief sustainability officer Bjorn Haugland stated that a strategy for change

> should be based on a new narrative of the economy and the purpose of the economy and the corporation, a new conceptualization of wealth and progress, and of the future we want

to see and a new purpose of humanity. It should speak to hearts as well as minds and inspire action and bring hope by communicating positive stories of change.[93]

Their recent report, *A Safe and Sustainable Future: Enabling the Transition*, concluded,

> The overwhelming body of scientific evidence tells us that the physical and biological world is changing rapidly and for the worse. Economic activity is pushing us towards planetary boundaries. The consequences will impact the financial performance of businesses in the short and long term. Take responsibility for managing and mitigating impacts, and start adapting to change. The purpose of business is to generate value across a broad range of capitals, beyond financial, and this should be part of the way in which business is conducted. At the end of the day, business will only thrive in stable, healthy and educated communities. Start seeing sustainability as an opportunity.
>
> The business case is now incontrovertible. The time is ripe for business opportunities with the co-benefits of both generating well-being and taking control of environmental challenges. Be vocal about the needs for predictable and smart regulations. Lobby and support politicians to make regulation an effective instrument to drive the right behaviour.[94]

Massive changes in the way we do business are coming, to the point that what emerges may look little like what we call capitalism today. As section 4 describes, it will be a blend of good policy and enlightened business. The point here is that the smart companies know that they have a long way to go, but they are getting about it.

CHAPTER NINE

GROWING A FINER FUTURE

We think we're here because of our big brain.
We're not. Humans owe our existence to six inches of soil
and the fact that it rains.

JEFF WALLIN[1]

Humans can pick and choose how much and what sort of stuff they want to buy, but every one of us has to eat.

A handful of healthy soil has more living organisms in it than there are people on Earth. A gram of fertile loam can contain up to a billion bacteria.[2] The thin skin covering the biosphere is the living heart upon which all life depends.

Globally, we are losing that soil and the life that is within and upon it. Half of the topsoil on Earth has been lost since the advent of "modern" agriculture.[3] The UN estimates that in the past two centuries, humans have converted 70 percent of the world's grasslands, 50 percent of the savannah, 45 percent of the temperate deciduous forest, and 27 percent of the tropical forest biome to farms and pastures.[4] Throughout history, civilizations that ignored the health of their soils have disappeared. Yet most of us go about our daily lives unconcerned that more than half of the available fertile land capable of producing food on Earth has been degraded[5] and that it is agricultural business as usual that is to blame.

As Wes Jackson of the Land Institute puts it,

Across the farmlands of the US and the world, climate change overshadows an ecological and cultural crisis of unequaled scale: soil erosion, loss of wild biodiversity, poisoned land and water, salinization, expanding dead zones, and the demise of rural communities. The Millennium Ecosystem Assessment (MEA) concludes that agriculture is the "largest threat to biodiversity and ecosystem function of any single human activity."[6]

Treating soil like dirt threatens all life on the planet.

These concerns are not new, and neither are the solutions. Robert Rodale[7] coined the term "regenerative agriculture" in the 1980s: "Regenerative organic agriculture improves the resources it uses, rather than destroying or depleting them. It is a holistic systems approach to agriculture that encourages continual on-farm innovation for environmental, social, economic and spiritual well-being."[8]

Rodale Institute and others demonstrated even then that organic agriculture could be as productive as conventional crop production. Now, however, the need to shift from conventional agriculture to better approaches has become acute.

The word "conventional" is a bit of a misnomer. As author Mark Bittman observed,

> In terms of feeding people, land use and commonality, peasant farming is far more conventional. Peasant farming produces more than two-thirds of the world's food. In its reliance on high tech, fossil fuels, overuse of resources, monocropping, and chemicals, industrial agriculture is, in fact, completely unconventional. It's downright anomalous.[9]

Indeed, the UN Food and Agriculture Organization estimates that still 70 percent of food on Earth is produced by smallholder agriculture.[10] But this is good news: It means we do not have to remake most of agriculture, only help farmers who are still doing things mostly right avoid the mistakes of overdeveloped countries and gain access to the best regenerative practices.

Humanity *will* convert to more sustainable agriculture; it's only a question of how hard we will make it on ourselves before we do.

Carbon-intensive Agriculture

Agriculture as currently practiced is impoverishing the soil and the people who depend on it and putting the climate at risk. Climate change, left unchecked, will, in turn, destroy much of industrial agriculture. Rising temperatures and shifting precipitation levels will affect yields.[11] As the summer of 2010 showed, droughts, desertification, and floods will all worsen our ability to feed people.[12]

For every one-degree Celsius rise in temperature above the norm, yields of wheat, rice, and corn drop 10 percent.[13] This is scary, given that already one in seven people in the world, more than a billion, is food insecure and two to three in seven are malnourished.[14] In 2010, then the hottest year ever (2014 broke that record, 2015 beat it again, and 2016 topped even that, with 2017 close), unprecedented floods on three continents and heat and drought in Russia led to soaring wheat prices and, as food riots ensued across North Africa, the Arab Spring.[15] Soil degradation worsens this, leading the UN to predict a 12 percent decline in global food production over the next 25 years. This would drive a 30 percent increase in world food prices.[16]

Stephen Chu, then US secretary of energy, in a 2009 interview on climate risks, stated,

> You're looking at a scenario where there's no more agriculture in California. When you lose 70 percent of your water in the mountains, I don't see how agriculture can continue. California produces 20 percent of the agriculture in the United States. I don't actually see how they can keep their cities going.[17]

In June 2015, the California mountains had zero snowpack. By midwinter 2017, the state was drowning in massive rainstorms, another climate change phenomenon, but even that did not relieve the threat of drought.[18] In December 2017, California suffered its worst wildfire season and its largest wildfire ever.

Much of the solution to the climate crisis will come from using energy dramatically more productively, as described in section 2, and switching to renewable energy, as described in chapter 10, but it is probably not possible to do either of these at sufficient scale and fast enough to save humanity without regenerative agriculture.[19] A report by PriceWaterhouseCooper's climate change analysts estimated that global economies need to reduce energy-related carbon emissions by more than five times the current rate.[20]

Although three-quarters of the climate crisis results from burning fossil fuels, and to a lesser extent from releases of various industrial gasses, almost one-quarter of the problem derives from agriculture. As described below, regenerative agriculture is probably the only way to soak up carbon fast enough. The world's soil holds as much carbon as is embodied in the biomass above ground[21] and three times as much carbon as the atmosphere. Current production processes are decarbonizing it.[22] But we know how to suck carbon from the air and return it to the soil. We know how to roll climate change backward.

Carbon gets out of the soil in several ways: we dig it up as concentrated fossil fuels and burn it, or we decarbonize the soil through unsustainable agricultural practices. The first is addressed in the energy section below. The second can be fixed only by regenerative agriculture.

The first settlers to plow the American Great Plains unearthed ten feet of dense black soil. That black represented massive carbon reserves; young coal, if you will. The grasslands of the world are the second-largest store of naturally sequestered carbon after the oceans. They coevolved with prehistoric herds of grazing animals, dense-packed because they were pursued by healthy populations of predators. Now, after 150 years of unsustainable agricultural practices, that carbon-rich soil has been reduced to inches.

Soil that has been decarbonized requires the application of intensive amounts of fossil-fuel-based fertilizer before it can grow industrial crops. Producing and using the petrochemicals in fertilizer releases carbon and other greenhouse gases (GHGs), especially nitrous oxide (N_2O), a gas 300 times more potent per ton than CO_2 in causing global warming.[23] The use of these fertilizers and physical disturbances to the soil release even more nitrogen.[24] Both carbon and nitrogen, the building blocks of life in nature, are now out of place, becoming serious threats to the stability of the climate.

It was estimated that in 1995 humans applied more than 6 million tons of artificial nitrogen fertilizer, resulting in human-caused denitrification of between 3 and 8 billion kilograms of N_2O each year.[25] By 2013, 100 million tons of N_2O were being released from farming operations every year.[26] As a result, atmospheric concentrations of N_2O had risen from about 275 parts per billion (ppb) before the industrial era to about 312 ppb in 1994. Synthetic fertilizer use and emissions from manure in confined animal feeding operations and other industrial processes caused most of this.[27]

More nitrogen from fertilizer is lost when soil that has been plowed up and left denuded is eroded by wind and rain. This nitrogen runoff winds up in drinking water, where it poisons farm animals and families, in lakes, where it promotes algal blooms,[28] or in the oceans, where it creates dead zones.[29]

N_2O is also a threat to the ozone layer. Unlike the chlorofluorocarbons regulated by the Montreal Protocol, N_2O is not covered by any regulation, and there is no formal global effort to reduce its emissions.[30]

Vegans provocatively claim that producing red meat, dairy products, chickens, fish, and eggs accounts for 58 percent of food-related emissions.[31] A 2006 UN report concluded that livestock was responsible for 18 percent of global GHGs.[32] In 2010, however, UN scientists acknowledged that claims regarding the impact of meat production were flawed. Analysts had counted emissions common to all industrial activities but neglected to do this when analyzing the impact of other industries.[33] The UN promised a revised report, but none has yet emerged.

Without a doubt, *industrial* meat production drives the emission of significant amounts of climate-destroying gasses. Methane, a particularly potent greenhouse gas, is produced by enteric formation (burping and flatulence) from cattle (1,792 million tonnes CO_2-equivalent each year).[34] But using this argument, as some vegans do, to argue for the elimination of meat and dairy production forgets that cows aren't really adding more methane to the planet so much as cycling compounds already in circulation. Methane emissions from enteric fermentation represent the transformation of carbon already in circulation between the Earth and the atmosphere, and the number of cows roaming the planet today is not significantly larger than the herds of prehistoric bison and other ungulates.[35]

What is different now, however, is that the 95 million conventionally grown cows in the US are taken off the pastures where they were healthy and where methane-loving bacteria in the grass decompose much of their emissions. The animals are "finished" in concentrated animal feeding operations, or CAFOs, with no grass. There they are fed grain and oil crops that require vast amounts of water, energy, and chemical inputs—causing more soil degradation—to fatten the animals for slaughter. As a result, meat animals now consume half of all the oil and grain crops grown in the US and the world.[36] In 2008, 70 to 80 percent of grains grown and acreage farmed was used to feed America's 11 billion meat, milk, and egg-laying animals, 95 percent of which were raised in confinement. This includes nearly 69 million pigs, 300 million commercial laying hens in battery cages, ten billion meat chickens, and half a billion turkeys that live in abusively close quarters. In addition, about 33 million beef cows and 9.7 million dairy cows were confined in crowded feedlots or dairy barns in conditions that foster diseases. But cows and other grazing animals were never designed to eat corn or the industrial byproducts they are increasingly fed. To counter the added tendency to get sick, the animals are fed prophylactic antibiotics, a practice that promotes the evolution of antibiotic-resistant superbugs that now threaten humans.

None of this is good, but perhaps the greatest worry is that modern agriculture worsens climate change. Unchecked, climate change will destroy humankind's already tenuous ability to feed itself.

Regenerative Agriculture: Solving Many Problems at Once

Agriculture's impact, whether from meat production or row crops, depends on the production methods used. There are dramatically more sustainable ways to produce food. One obvious answer is to transition to agriculture that does not rely on unsustainable application of artificial nitrogen fertilizer, that does not decarbonize the soil, and that becomes part of the solution by returning carbon to the soil.

Proponents of regenerative agriculture call for a beyond-modern approach, combining the best of traditional agriculture with the finest science to deliver abundant, sustainable food and high-quality ways of life to all the world's people, even in a time of climate crisis.

Conventional advocates say,

> Without it [artificial fertilizer], human civilization in its current form could not exist. Our planet's soil simply could not grow enough food to provide all seven billion of us our accustomed diet. In fact, almost half of the nitrogen found in our bodies' muscle and organ tissue started out in a fertilizer factory.[37]

The United Nations would beg to disagree. In 2007, the UN Food and Agriculture Organization (FAO) determined that organic agriculture would positively contribute to food security, climate mitigation, water security and quality, agrobiodiversity, nutritional adequacy, and rural development.[38] Both the United Nations Conference on Trade and Development (UNCTAD)[39] in 2013 and the UN FAO in 2015 published reports concluding that only organic smallholder farms could feed the world.[40] The FAO report found that protecting and empowering such bottom-of-the-pyramid growers who produce most of world's food has enabled half of all countries to meet the Millennium Development goal of cutting malnutrition in half.[41]

Given that smallholders are the first to feel the effects of political unrest, climate-related disasters, poverty, and other issues that drive hunger, the UN's focus is a welcome antidote to the "Green Revolution."[42] That hit the developing world by storm in the 1960s and 1970s with an all-out push to "modernize" farming throughout the world. Synthetic inputs and intensive irrigation replaced traditional agriculture methods to increase yields. Many farmers adopted these new practices and, in the short term, told a story of enormous success. Grain production doubled in less than 20 years. Previously famine-stricken regions of rural India became breadbaskets, producing enough wheat and rice to export a surplus. Farmers adopted techniques of monoculture (farmers who had previously grown as many as 30 different crops switched to growing only one cash crop, increasing their short-term profits but dramatically reducing biodiversity). They implemented double-cropping (harvesting twice a year by generating a second "rainy season" through irrigation). All of these increased yields enormously.

It took only a couple of decades for farmers to find that this industrialized approach did not provide a sustainable foundation for their lives. Soil fertility declined; water pollution became rampant; workers suffered health problems including soaring cancer rates from using industrial chemicals often banned in Western countries; and fields could not sustain their peak yields. In addition, because synthetic inputs are heavily reliant on fossil fuel energy, Green Revolution practices made communities dependent on foreign inputs of oil, accompanied by significant exports of cash to pay for it. As water tables fell, farmers bought imported energy to fuel pumps, depleting the water tables ever faster.

This, combined with the impacts of climate change, meant that in 2009, for the first time since the Green Revolution, Indian farmers failed to meet food demand. India announced that it was forced to import food, especially lentils and edible oils. Traditional water sources of local communities failed. In Punjab, aquifers dried up, forcing farmers to dig wells deeper, driving them into a spiral of debt. Widespread applications of insecticides and pesticides caused insects to develop immunity against the chemicals while destroying more and more crops. Farmers bought up to three times as much fertilizer as they did 30 years before to maintain yields. The Punjab State Council for Science and Technology proclaimed that the state's agriculture program "has become unsustainable and unprofitable."

India's once booming agriculture epicenter, Punjab, is now heading for collapse.[43] In 2011, the chairman of the Punjab State Farmers Commission stated, "Farmers are committing ecological and economic suicide." They were also, literally, killing themselves.[44]

"The situation is grim, not just for crop sowing and crop health but also for sustaining animal health, providing drinking water, livelihood and food, particularly for the small and marginal farmers and landless labourers," stated Indian farm minister Sharad Pawar. "Food prices have risen over 10 percent annually."[45]

In contrast, shifting away from the so-called modern practices to refocus on traditional, sustainable agricultural methods has reinvigorated communities. It clearly is critical to ensure sufficient food for the world's population, and it is tempting to say that everyone should farm as intensively as possible.

However, the story of the Green Revolution shows why that's the wrong answer. Remember the principles of Natural Capitalism. First start with efficiency. For every 2 tonnes of food consumed, another tonne is wasted in the supply chain, retail, or manufacturing.[46] Each year 1.3 billion tonnes of food—one-third of all that is produced—goes to waste. Even in poor countries, 5 to 16 percent is thrown away. Globally, 20 percent of dairy and meat, 35 percent of seafood, 30 percent of cereals, and 45 percent of vegetables are wasted. The UN reckons that cutting that loss by just 25 percent would deliver enough food to feed everyone on Earth today.[47]

As with business, we need to reinvent how we make and deliver everything. And again, nature should be the mentor.

In the United States, a bolder vision of sustainable agriculture is emerging at the Land Institute in Salina, Kansas.[48] Wes Jackson led a team to shift agriculture from a single focus on monocultures of annual plants intensively managed to polycultures of perennials, which is the way that nature grows crops.

Jackson observes, "Essentially all of the high-yield crops that feed humanity—including rice, wheat, corn, soybeans, and peanuts—are annuals. With cropping of annuals, alive just part of the year and weakly rooted even then, comes more loss of precious soil, nutrients, and water."

The Institute is developing an agricultural system based on the ecological stability of the prairie but boasting a grain yield comparable to annual crops. Essentially all of the natural land ecosystems, from alpine meadows to rainforests, are mixtures of perennial plants. Annuals, in contract, could be called "opportunists." They sprout, reproduce, throw seeds, and die. Perennials stay in the soil, protecting it, better managing nutrients, and retaining water. The Land Institute's mission is to perennialize several major crops, including wheat, sorghum, and sunflowers, and domesticate a few wild perennial species to produce food just as their annual counterparts do but without the impact. It grows test crops in various mixtures according to what each given landscape requires. With the pre-agricultural ecosystem as the standard, the Institute is bringing as many processes of the wild to the farm as possible, below as well as above the surface.

Such natural systems agriculture should end the days in which "agricultural scientists from industrialized societies deliver agronomic methods and technologies from their fossil fuel-intensive infrastructures into developing countries, thereby saddling them with brittle economies." Wes Jackson writes,

> New perennial crops, like their wild relatives, seem certain to be more resilient to climate change. Without a doubt, they will increase sequestration of carbon. They will reduce the land runoff that is creating coastal dead zones and affecting fisheries and maintain the quality of scarce surface and ground water.

In short, he hopes to save the planet while producing greater economic stability all at the same time.[49]

Regenerative agriculture methods treat the farms, farmers, and customers as holistic systems, where the relationship between all inputs is considered. In best cases, farmers use only what is produced onsite, e.g., manure from livestock, as a fertilizer, supplanting synthetic fertilizer derived from natural gas. Such sustainable practices restore soil structure, build healthy topsoil, nurture soil microbes, and promote biological activity, all of which contribute to long-term productivity and nutritious crops. Water use is optimized, and the best practices in irrigation are applied. Farm worker safety and investment in local businesses sustain farming communities. Additionally, higher soil fertility also sequesters vast amounts of atmospheric CO_2.

Demand for foods produced by sustainable agriculture methods is growing throughout the world.[50] Because more people are needed to do the work that the chemicals previously did, regenerative farming increases employment, helping meet demand for jobs.

The citizen-based Development Research Communication and Services Center (DRCSC) is working in West Bengal and surrounding states in northeastern India to improve the state of agriculture.[51] Focusing on education and capacity building as major strategies for change, the DRCSC supports organic farming as a means to ensure food and livelihood security for India's rural poor. It has built school gardens, organized workshops, created nurseries and seed centers, and even produced a documentary, each emphasizing the benefits of organic farming to community stakeholders. The DRCSC's work has been so successful that some organic farmers are actually producing more than their community needs.

Carbon Farming

Regenerative agriculture (shifting agricultural practices to emit less carbon and engaging in active biosequestration practices that suck carbon out of the air and put it back in the soil where it belongs) may be the only way to save humanity from climate chaos. Ratan Lal, professor of soil science of the Ohio State University's College of Food, Agriculture and Environmental Science, believes that since the beginning of agriculture as much as 486 gigatons of carbon have been lost from the terrestrial biosphere and emitted to the atmosphere. Agricultural lands have lost 80 gigatons, he estimates. "So we have a potential to put back almost 500 gigatons of carbon into the terrestrial biosphere through management and land use conversion and of course through adoption of best management practices."[52]

There are three known ways to put carbon back into the soil.

Biochar

Carbon-based waste in the developed world tends to be burned or thrown away—sent to landfills where it rots, releasing methane, an even more destructive greenhouse gas than the original carbon content. In the developing world, it is sometimes returned to the soil, but typically it piles up, especially in cities. Efforts to compost these flows so that the nutrients can be returned to the soil are beginning, but humanity needs to use the ability of plants to draw carbon from the air, then get it back into the soil on a massive scale. One answer is to convert the wastes into a product called biochar.

Biochar is essentially charcoal. Charcoal is an important energy source; globally nearly three billion people worldwide rely on burning it, along with wood (usually from local forests) for cooking.[53] Charcoal production, however, results in deforestation and is wasteful of the wood and the carbon. Inefficient use of charcoal also contributes to indoor air pollution and greenhouse gas emissions.

Biochar production is quite different. Created through "pyrolysis," the woody material is heated at low temperatures with little oxygen until it is carbonized. This produces energy (heat and power), but unlike fossil fuels, biochar production is a carbon-neutral process; it neither adds nor subtracts carbon from the atmosphere. Done intelligently, it delivers useable energy in the form of charcoal, a bio-oil, and syngas. The syngas can be used much like petroleum-based oil or natural gas to fuel transportation or as another substitute for charcoal.

This approach turns only part of the woody material into fuel. The other 50 percent or more of the biomass's carbon becomes biochar. That carbon, when placed in soil, stays there, representing a near-permanent carbon sink that has actually reduced overall atmospheric CO_2.[54]

In the soil, biochar increases water retention and supports healthy soil, reducing fertilizer requirements and increasing crop yields. Enhancing plant growth, it thus removes even more CO_2 from the atmosphere. Because it can be made in simple homemade devices, and on a small scale, biochar production represents a startup opportunity to create rural jobs.[55]

Tim Flannery, one of Australia's most eminent scientists and author of *The Weathermakers*, states, "Biochar may represent the single most important initiative for humanity's environmental future. Biochar provides a uniquely powerful solution, for it allows us to address food security, the fuel crisis, and the climate problem, and all in an immensely practical manner."[56]

Flannery explains,

> Now if you used these agri-char based technologies and you have your aggressive reaforestation projects for the world's tropics, you could conceivably be drawing down in the order of 10 to 15 gigatonnes of carbon per annum by about 2030. At that rate we could bring ourselves down below the dangerous threshold as early as the middle of this century.

An exciting prospect, but, Flannery warned, "Whether the world can actually get its act together and do that is another matter.[57]

In the future, we will not be afforded the luxury of waste," says Jeff Wallin, co-founder of the Biochar Company, the first company producing commercial biochar. He adds

> The business case is sustainable and profitable without depending on tax subsidies or CO_2 credits, but they will help in finding interested financial partners. The environmental future is upon us and nature does not negotiate.[58]

Despite this, sales of biochar are growing very slowly, and the industry remains an infant. This means that it would take massive government intervention to get biochar production to the scale needed to offset the climate crisis.

Compost-based Organic Agriculture

The second route to return carbon to the soil is organic food production. The Rodale Institute[59] (one of the original centers of scientific research into organic agriculture), the Soil Association of the UK,[60] the Agroecology Lab at UC Davis,[61] and the Leopold Center at Iowa State University are a few of the thousands of organizations around the world building biodiverse systems that can meet the needs of humanity while reintegrating into nature's cycles. Such agriculture takes a longer view of production, seeking not "to maximise yield in an optimum year, but to maximise yield over many years by decreasing the chance of crop failure in an bad year."[62]

Studies conducted over many years by University of California, Davis, the Rodale Institute, and others have shown that compost-based organic production practices increase (not just maintain) the quantity of soil-held carbon through a variety of mechanisms.[63] Farming operations that use more natural agricultural practices that do not rely on chemical inputs like artificial fertilizers, pesticides, and herbicides have higher levels of beneficial soil organisms. Protozoa, bacteria by the billions, algae, and mycorrhizae fungi complement such recognizable species as ants and earthworms, nematodes, and springtails. All of these work together in the soil to build organic (carbon) matter. Operations that do not use chemical pesticides support more diverse habitats. Farms using crop rotations and animal manure deliver better biodiversity than fields farmed with industrial agricultural practices. Organic fields reduce nitrogen runoff and the release of nitrous oxide.[64] Systems that integrate livestock with vegetable production and use perennial pastureland and organic production (e.g., long crop rotations, leguminous crops and cover crops, manure produced by livestock as fertilizer) deliver higher profitability while creating the circular economy of the soil, taking carbon from the air and sequestering it in the soil.[65]

The good news is that, although it is not easy to wait out the three years that it takes to become a certified organic farmer, there is a business case for farmers to convert to organic production. Organic is the fastest-growing food sector. The UK-based Soil Association's Organic Market Report 2016 found

> continued steady growth of 4.9 percent in 2015. This is the third year of consecutive growth for the UK organic sector, now worth £1.95 billion. Sales of organic have continued to outperform the non-organic grocery market which decreased by 0.9 percent in the same period.[66]

The Association's 2017 report announced the fifth consecutive year of increased growth. The 2016 number was 7.1 percent, almost double the growth rate of 2016.[67]

In the US, the growth rate is nearly 11 percent. It has been in double digits nearly every year since the 1990s, when organic sales were $3.6 billion a year. They now top $43 billion a year. In contrast, the general food market is growing at a little over 3 percent each year.[68] Globally the sector is projected to grow at over 9 percent annually, reaching a market of nearly $63 billion by 2020.[69] Organic produce is available in three of every four supermarkets, but the industry remains at only 4 percent of US food sales.[70]

Holistic Management

The practice that might scale sufficiently to be useful is put crisply in the title of Judith Schwartz's book *Cows Save the Planet*.[71] It profiles the work of soil scientists and the increasing number of practitioners around the world who are using grazing animals to repair soil health, reverse desertification, and fight climate change.

The approach Schwartz is touting was developed by Allan Savory. His Savory Institute[72] (SI) seeks to impact a billion hectares by 2025 through the teaching and practice of Holistic Management and Holistic Decision Making. The goal is to enable practitioners to turn deserts into thriving grasslands; restore biodiversity; bring streams, rivers, and water sources back to life; and combat poverty and hunger, all while reversing global climate change.[73] Holistically managed grazing animals are, it claims, one of the best ways to reclaim depleted land. Savory's approach mimics how vast herds of grazing animals coevolved with the world's grasslands: dense-packed because of predators, moving as a herd, eating everything, fertilizing the land, tilling the manure and seeds into the soil with their hooves, and then moving on, not returning until the grass is lush again. This interaction is one of the more important ways to create healthy communities of soil microorganisms. They, in turn recarbonize the soil and restore natural nitrogen cycles.

Savory, in his many writings and a TED talk viewed by four and a half million people, argues that even achieving zero emissions from fossil fuels would not avert major catastrophe from climate change. Grassland and savanna·burning would continue, and desertification would accelerate as soils become increasingly unable to store carbon or water.[74] Averting disaster, he says, will require a global strategy to cut carbon emissions, substitute benign energy sources for fossil fuels, and implement effective livestock management practices to put the carbon already in the atmosphere back into the soils. Profitable Holistic Management is the only way, he argues, to reduce biodiversity loss and biomass burning and reverse the desertification that is not caused by atmospheric carbon buildup.[75]

Awarded the 2010 Buckminster Fuller Challenge prize for decades of work, Savory's Africa Centre for Holistic Management in Zimbabwe and Savory Institute show how to transform degraded grasslands and savannahs into lush pastures with ponds and flowing streams. It shows that this approach to climate protection enhances African agricultural livelihoods. The Challenge celebrates a "comprehensive, anticipatory, design approach to radically advance human wellbeing and the health of our planet's ecosystems."[76] The Fuller award recognized Savory's work to accelerate development and deployment of whole-systems solutions to climate change and sustainable development.

Savory Institute is scaling the approach by creating Hubs[77] around the world to serve as regional centers to teach the approach. SI is using the Hubs as the basis for certifying practitioners as "Regenerative," based not on the processes used but on its Ecological Outcome Verification protocol. Developed with Jason Rountree at Michigan State University, this measures the increases in soil carbon, water retention, and biodiversity and a variety of ecological metrics on each piece of land that is being holistically managed.[78]

Savory Institute offers portfolios of photos showing fence-line contrasts between land that is conventionally managed and land that is holistically ranched, using cattle to mimic the way native herds built up carbon in the soil. In the latter, the land shows increased biodiversity, rebuilt water tables, and enhanced endangered species habitat and greater profitability for the landowners.[79]

Will Harris used Holistic Management to convert White Oak

Pastures,[80] his family's commodity farm in South Georgia, to a successful operation raising, slaughtering, and selling five kinds of poultry and producing five kinds of red meat—all pasture raised—eggs, and vegetables. The products are sold online to high-end restaurants as far away as Miami and to Whole Foods markets across the Eastern US. Will employees 137 residents of the once-decaying town of Bluffton. His commodity farmer neighbor, with the same acreage, employs four.[81] White Oak Pastures features agritourism, a restaurant, and a general store and serves as the Savory Hub for the region.

Will manages his chickens holistically, leaving them free to roam his pastures, cleaning out the bugs left in animal manure. Six years ago he noticed a pair of endangered bald eagles. There are now more than 80 of the raptors who winter with Will, wreaking $1,000 a day in predation on his flocks. Will's response? "You're supposed to give 10 percent to the church, and we don't really do that, but we're giving 10 percent to nature."[82]

More holistic agriculture, with fewer chemicals and better management of the soils and ecosystems, will bring more jobs.[83] It will also reduce consumption of unhealthy foods and reduce damaging emissions from agricultural runoff.

A 2012 study by M+R Strategic Services found that organic agriculture creates 21 percent more jobs than conventional agriculture, with 28,000 jobs for every $1 billion in sales. A similar study in the UK found that the number is 32 percent more jobs than conventional.[84] Studies by the Worldwatch Institute found that organic farming is the only segment of global agriculture that is expanding.[85]

Organic farms need more people to work the operation, tend to be smaller, and trade more locally, increasing the economic multiplier.[86] A study of sustainable agriculture as an economic development strategy in Missouri found that a shift to sustainable farming would create more than 165 additional farm households per county and more than 300 additional farm and non-farm households in total. "Few community leaders," the study stated, "would ignore the potential for creating 165 new self-employment opportunities and the means of supporting 300 new households in total in their counties."[87]

It's Happening

The approach is growing because it works.[88] In the 1990s, Hunter Lovins undertook to rehabilitate almost 1,000 acres of degraded western rangeland. Taken out of cattle production for 20 years, the land had suffered erosion and been overrun by noxious weeds. Its prior owners believed the conventional wisdom that removing grazing animals from land would increase its health. This may be true of intact wilderness, where intact predators still drive native grazing herds to pack up and move across the land. But most of the planet's agricultural land is rapidly releasing stored carbon, nitrogen, and other greenhouse gasses, so the approach that nature is somehow spiritual and will heal itself is clearly wrong.

Working with Allan Savory, Hunter restored cattle to the ground and managed the land based on the principles of Holistic Management. Within two years, the water table rose and wetland plants returned. (The seeds had always been there, just waiting for the right conditions.) Endangered species not seen in two decades returned. Even skeptical government officials acknowledged the evidence of an ecosystem returning to health. The value of the property also rose.

Many others are experiencing the success of Holistic Management. In the Australian desert, SLM Partners has doubled the carrying capacity of cattle on what had historically been desertified rangelands. They achieve superior weight gain while buying no feed, have doubled plant diversity, and restored the grasslands even in a drought. The company is attracting foreign investment to a region of Australia typically struggling to achieve economic development and is rehabilitating the local economy.[89]

From Montana to New Zealand, the company Grasslands LLC[90] has used Savory's approach to heal grazing land and rural communities. This approach enabled conservation buyers to save historic ranches like the charismatic Hana Ranch on Maui from becoming luxury housing.[91]

In 1961, Joel Salatin began farming what he describes as the Shenandoah Valley's most worn-out, eroded, abused property. He used Savory's approach of Holistic Management to turn the destitute farm into a prosperous operation supporting 35 farm-based ventures. Joel speaks often about his success in moving cows daily using portable electric fencing to mimic how predators naturally controlled overgrazing.

Joel is creating what he calls the "Farm of the Future." His system, profiled in the "Meet the Farmer" series,[92] is based on mobile infrastructure instead of stationary facilities. Portable, nimble, and not capital intensive, it allows operators to separate the farm from the infrastructure. It does not even require a user to own the land. Because it is modular, farmers can invest in small components. If successful, they can scale up without borrowing money. Like many regenerative operations, it is management intensive, substituting people and intelligence for capital (concrete, energy, drugs, vehicles). The equity is created in information, management, and customers, not infrastructure. This shifts the economic profile of the farm, giving landless, cashless, equity-less young people the ability to get a start in agriculture.[93] Selling high-end meat, eggs, vegetables, and forest products within a 100-mile radius, Polyface Farm is a profitable enterprise that achieves the Salatin family's mission to develop emotionally, economically, and environmentally balanced agricultural practices that honor nature's cycles.

Meet Gabe Brown.[94] He began farming his 2,000 acres near Bismarck, North Dakota, in 1993. A commodity corn and soybean farmer, he converted to regenerative agriculture to cut costs that were threatening his business. His soil quality was poor, with shallow topsoil that required annual inputs of fertilizer, pesticides, and herbicides to produce a crop. In 1995, Gabe implemented no-till production. In the ensuing years, he diversified into a variety of cash crops and began rotating his fields. In 1997, he added the use of a wide variety of multi-species cover crops. In 2006, he introduced Savory-style grazing practices, adding different livestock species, so that he now raises cows, sheep, broiler hens, and bees as well as corn and soybeans. His system has allowed him to stop using chemical inputs, dramatically cutting his costs and increasing his profitability. For example, in 2014, it cost him $1.35 to produce a bushel of corn,

Management	N lbs.	P lbs. (ppm)	K lbs. (ppm)	WEOC
Organic	2	156 (9)	95 (14)	233
No-till, low diversity	27	244 (14)	136 (19)	239
No-till, MD, high syn.	37	217 (12)	199 (28)	262
No-till, HD, NS, livestock	281	1,006 (56)	1,749 (250)	1,095

Tested by Dr. Rick Haney, ARS, Temple, TX

Note: Gabe Brown, whose ranch is shown in the bottom row of numbers, provided a 2007 soil test from his ranch showing these results: N = 10 lbs. in the top 24 inches, P (Olsen test) = 6 ppm, K = 303 ppm. Gabe says he has not used any fertilizers on his home ranch since 2007. The ppm numbers are a Graze conversion (with help from Gene Schniefer, University of Wisconsin-Extension) from the original lbs. listed in this soil test.

Credit: Gabe Brown: Keys to Building a Healthy Soil.

which he sold for more than $3.50. He cannot keep up with demand for his grass-finished beef and lamb, and his fields have never been healthier.

Gabe has compared the capacity of his acreage to cycle nutrients,[95] including carbon, with neighbors who farm organically but without animal impact on the land and with two no-till operations that use varying amounts of synthetic fertilizers. Soil samples from Gabe's and his neighbors' operations show that he is able, solely through maintaining a healthy soil through animal impact, to increase concentrations of nitrogen (N), phosphorus (P), and potassium (K) dramatically. This drives his productivity and profitability. The water-extractable organic carbon (WEOC) is, however, the most amazing number. Gabe is recarbonizing his soils at a profit.

When he bought his farm in 1993, it had shallow soils with 1.3 percent soil organic matter (soil carbon). By 2013, he had some plots with more than 11 percent soil organic matter. As Gabe puts it, if your soil is healthy you will have clean water, clean air, healthy plants, healthy animals, and healthy people. You will have a healthy ecosystem.

How Much Carbon Can We Sequester?

This approach, now called "carbon farming," has become popular. New articles on it emerge almost daily. [96]

California gives carbon credits for such practices;[97] Australia does as well, and Kenya, through the World Bank's $600,000 Bio-carbon Fund, rewards smallholder farmers for such practices.[98]

But how much carbon can be sequestered in properly managed grasslands and how fast?

In some California experiments, manure from dairy and beef operations is blended with green waste that would otherwise go to landfill, impose costs, rot, and release methane. The mix is composted and spread on pastures. Scientists from the University of California, Berkeley, take annual soil cores a meter deep and test whether that soil has soaked up additional carbon. The answer? One application of compost to rangeland doubled grass growth and increased carbon sequestration by up to 70 percent.[99] Every year the carbon increases. The study found that this can achieve total greenhouse gas (GHG) mitigation rates, over a 30-year time frame, of more than 18 tons of CO_2-equivalents per acre of land treated with organic amendments.[100]

The researchers noted,

> Sequestration of just 1 Mg C ha^{-1} y^{-1} (or one metric ton per hectare—a hectare being 2.2 acres—per year) on half the 23 million hectares of rangeland in California would offset 42 million metric tons of CO_2e, an amount equivalent to all of the annual GHG emissions from energy use for commercial and residential sectors in California.[101]

David Johnson, director of the Institute for Sustainable Agricultural Research at New Mexico State University, has developed a similar approach. His research has shown that[102]

> Promoting beneficial interactions between plants and soil microbes increases farm and rangeland's efficiency for capturing carbon and storing it in soil. These same interactions increase soil microbial carbon-use efficiencies reducing the rate at which soil carbon, as CO_2, is respired from the soil. When this bio-technology is promoted in agroecosystems, it is feasible to capture and sequester an average of >11 metric tons

of CO_2 per hectare per year in rangeland soils[103] and >36.7 metric tons CO_2 per hectare per year in transitioning farmland soils[104] all for less than one-tenth the cost of EPA's recommended Carbon Capture Utilization and Storage (CCUS) technologies.

Can all this roll climate change backwards?

Here are some illustrative calculations. Published, peer-reviewed case studies and projections from Ohio State soil scientist Ratan Lal show that the technical potential for carbon sequestration in the terrestrial biosphere is about five gigatons of carbon per year (GtC/yr).[105] This is in addition to the three GtC/yr that nature already adds to the soil. Humans emit about ten GtC/yr, but if the energy efficiency and renewable energy measures described in Chapter 11 are implemented, this will be substantially reduced.

A team from Tufts University wrote,

> Soil carbon restoration is emerging as a potential strategy to mitigate global warming while also enhancing food and water security. The Paris Agreement, although a laudable achievement for the international community, is insufficient to meet its basic goal of 2°C warming by 2100, while scientists have warned that, in fact, 1.5°C is the maximum that should be permitted to avoid catastrophic impacts. In order to close the emissions gap between nationally determined contributions under the Paris agreement and necessary carbon reductions to avoid the most extreme climate disruptions, extensive sequestration of carbon dioxide from the atmosphere is required. Globally, soils have the potential to sequester up to 3.4 GtC per year, just enough to close the "emissions gap." If combined with other atmospheric CO_2 removal efforts, such as reforestation, yearly additional carbon capture in soils and forests could be as high as 5 GtC per year. When combined with deep cuts in fossil fuel emissions, this could lead to a substantial overall reduction in atmospheric carbon dioxide.[106]

Texas A&M soil scientist Richard Teague, chronicling what he calls Adaptive Multipaddock (AMP) essentially Holistic management grazing in east Texas, has measured sequestration of 3 tons of carbon per hectare per year over a decade (tC/ha/yr).[107]

Soil scientist Megan Machmuller measured the increase in carbon in a conversion from row cropping to management-intensive grazing achieving as high as 8 tons per hectare per year in Georgia, or almost three times the mount measured by Teague.[108]

Put all of these numbers together and what does it add up to? Current emissions from fossil fuels are about 10 GtC/yr. Teague and his colleagues calculated that almost a gigaton could be soaked up just in North American soils.[109]

The world's permanent pasture and fodder lands amount to roughly 3.4 billion hectares. Back-of-the-envelope calculations with Seth Itzkan of Soil4Climate show that multiplying Teague's carbon capture findings of 3 tC/ha/yr (conservative when compared with the 8 tC/ha/yr values Machmuller identified) by the global hectares of pastureland gives 10.2 GtC/yr potential soil carbon capture via grazing. That, alone, would offset all human emissions.[110]

Clearly, it is a big "if" to say that Holistic Management will be practiced on all of the world pastureland, but coupled with the composting approaches of David Johnson, the organic cropping practices of Rodale Institute, the perennial wheat of the Land Institute, and the reductions in carbon emissions profiled in the next chapter. it is clear that we *can* solve the climate crisis and do it in ways that are profitable.

Daniel Riordin, in his book *Averting Global Collapse*, described the numbers necessary to scale this approach. Using current global livestock numbers of 2.24 billion standard animal units, rangeland and crop/pasture land could carry 10.33 billion livestock. Doing this would require a minimum of 2.5 million herders (assuming 1,000 head/herder). Like most sustainable agriculture, Holistic Management is more labor-intensive, not a bad thing in a world needing jobs.[111]

Precisely how much can be sequestered depends exquisitely on the piece of ground, the practices used, climactic conditions, and a host of other variables.[112] As Bill Becker, executive director of the Presidential Climate Action Project, wrote in his series on bio-sequestration,

> Variables like these have resulted in widely different estimates in the past. DOE and several of its national laboratories estimated in 1999 that natural carbon sinks worldwide were removing about 2 gigatons of carbon annually from the atmosphere. The labs concluded that an ambitious international effort could remove five times that much carbon from the atmosphere, more than 10 gigatons each year. "It seems reasonable to assume that advanced science, technology and management can double the capacity (of biological carbon sequestration) at low additional costs," DOE's experts said in another report. "TBCS (terrestrial biological carbon sequestration) offers potential for sequestering more than 50 percent of projected excess CO_2 that will have to be managed over the next century."[113]

In 2016, scientists began to consider these arguments. A very conservative study published in *Nature* showed that soil already holds 2.4 trillion tonnes of carbon. The article felt there is room for only an additional 8 billion tonnes.[114] Given that humans emit at least 40 tonnes annually,[115] that is not a lot. The key, said the scientists, is to ensure that intact ecosystems remain that way. Forests and grasslands store carbon efficiently until disturbed for agriculture. Restoring them and implementing sustainable agriculture, they felt, could soak up four-fifths of annual human emissions of greenhouse gasses from burning fossil fuels and sequester them in the soil.[116]

Carbon farming advocates say that the number could be far higher. Both Carbon Underground[117] and Soil4Climate believe that regenerative agriculture can displace all of the carbon emitted by humans each year and begin rapidly reversing global warming. A wealth of videos on the Soil4Climate site show the extent to which soil can sequester carbon and reverse climate change.[118]

Such claims scare climate change activists, who for years have struggled to get energy efficiency and renewable energy accepted as the way to deal with what they rightly see as the existential crisis of global warming.

In 2015, an *Esquire* article neatly summed up what they're facing:

The physical evidence becomes more dramatic every year: forests retreating, animals moving north, glaciers melting, wildfire seasons getting longer, higher rates of droughts, floods, and storms—five times as many in the 2000s as in the 1970s.... US temperatures have gone up between 1.3 and 1.9 degrees, mostly since 1970—and the change is already affecting "agriculture, water, human health, energy, transportation, forests, and ecosystems."[119] Arctic air temperatures are increasing at twice the rate of the rest of the world—a study by the US Navy says that the Arctic could lose its summer sea ice by next year, eighty-four years ahead of the models—and evidence little more than a year old suggests the West Antarctic Ice Sheet is doomed, which will add between twenty and twenty-five feet to ocean levels. The one hundred million people in Bangladesh will need another place to live, and coastal cities globally will be forced to relocate, a task complicated by economic crisis and famine—with continental interiors drying out, the chief scientist at the US State Department in 2009 predicted a billion people will suffer famine within twenty or thirty years. And yet, despite some encouraging developments in renewable energy and some breakthroughs in international leadership, carbon emissions continue to rise at a steady rate, and for their pains the scientists themselves— the cruelest blow of all—have been the targets of an unrelenting and well-organized attack that includes death threats, summonses from a hostile Congress, attempts to get them fired, legal harassment, and intrusive discovery demands so severe they had to start their own legal-defense fund, all amplified by a relentless propaganda campaign nakedly financed by the fossil-fuel companies.[120]

But it is critical that these legitimate concerns do not destroy the one real shot that we have to counter the climate crisis. According to Allan Savory,

> Global climate change and land degradation have to be put on a war footing internationally—meaning that all nations need to pull together and treat this threat as we would a war.... Only through uniting and diverting all the resources required to deal with climate change and land degradation can we avert unimaginable tragedy. We have all the money we need. All we cannot buy is time.[121]

Perhaps heeding Allan's call, the French government in 2015, in the lead-up to Paris, announced the 4 per 1000 Initiative[122] to demonstrate that agriculture, and agricultural soils in particular, can play a crucial role where food security and climate change are concerned. The Initiative[123] invites all partners to declare or to implement practical programmes for carbon sequestration in soil and the types of farming methods used to promote it (e.g., agroecology, agroforestry, conservation agriculture, and landscape management). It is bringing together willing contributors in public and private sectors (national governments, local and regional government, companies, trade organizations, NGOs, research facilities, and others) under the framework of the Lima-Paris Action Agenda (LPAA).

The goal is to engage stakeholders in a transition toward a productive, resilient agriculture, based on a sustainable soil management and generating jobs and incomes, hence ensuring sustainable development.

Global restoration of grasslands, forests, wetlands, seagrasses, and other biological carbon sinks can reestablish soil integrity and biodiversity as it sequesters massive amounts of carbon. Regenerative agriculture can stabilize local and, eventually, global weather patterns; restore a balanced hydrological cycle; create meaningful jobs, particularly in developing countries; produce high-quality animal protein without synthetic soil supplements and destructive

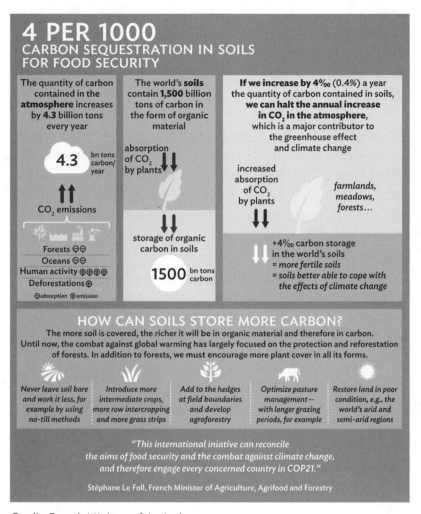

4 PER 1000
CARBON SEQUESTRATION IN SOILS
FOR FOOD SECURITY

The quantity of carbon contained in the **atmosphere** increases by **4.3** billion tons every year

4.3 bn tons carbon/year

CO₂ emissions

Forests ⊖⊖
Oceans ⊖⊖
Human activity ⊕⊕⊕⊕
Deforestations ⊕

⊖ absorption ⊕ emission

The world's **soils** contain **1,500** billion tons of carbon in the form of organic material

absorption of CO₂ by plants

storage of organic carbon in soils

1500 bn tons carbon

If we increase by **4‰** (0.4%) a year the quantity of carbon contained in soils, **we can halt the annual increase in CO₂ in the atmosphere**, which is a major contributor to the greenhouse effect and climate change

increased absorption of CO₂ by plants

farmlands, meadows, forests...

+4‰ carbon storage in the world's soils
= *more fertile soils*
= *soils better able to cope with the effects of climate change*

HOW CAN SOILS STORE MORE CARBON?

The more soil is covered, the richer it will be in organic material and therefore in carbon. Until now, the combat against global warming has largely focused on the protection and reforestation of forests. In addition to forests, we must encourage more plant cover in all its forms.

Never leave soil bare and work it less, for example by using no-till methods

Introduce more intermediate crops, more row intercropping and more grass strips

Add to the hedges at field boundaries and develop agroforestry

Optimize pasture management— with longer grazing periods, for example

Restore land in poor condition, e.g., the world's arid and semi-arid regions

"This international iniative can reconcile the aims of food security and the combat against climate change, and therefore engage every concerned country in COP21."

Stéphane Le Foll, French Minister of Agriculture, Agrifood and Forestry

Credit: French Ministry of Agriculture.

factory farming; and support local communities worldwide in sustainable living.

Not a bad idea.

Savory's approach to land management contradicts accepted practice and theories of removing animals from land. The vitriol leveled against him is daunting.[124] Despite this, Holistic Management is now successfully practiced on more than 40 million acres around the world, growing rapidly because it works. Reestablish-ing the symbiotic balance between plant growth and herd animals is helping land managers bioremediate barren land back to thriving grasslands. It is increasing crop yields and ensuring food security for millions of people.[125]

To anyone who realizes how dire the climate crisis is, regenera-tive agriculture is exciting. The possibility that respecting and using the services of intact ecosystems might save us is almost a miracle.

In his book *Gardeners of Eden: Rediscovering Our Importance to Nature*,[126] Dan Daggett profiles a dozen small grazing operations that are reclaiming land by managing cattle in harmony with the ecology that is there, not against it. He shows that while humans have come to behave as an alien species in recent years, rapaciously taking from the land what they want, for most of our history, we lived on land as natives, working with place and the natural cycles in ways that enhanced our homes, and us. As Daggett argues, we all need to become native again in the places that support us.

CHAPTER TEN

TRIUMPH OF THE SUN: THE MOTHER OF ALL DISRUPTIONS

*We are like tenant farmers chopping down the fence
around our house for fuel when we should be using
Nature's inexhaustible source of energy—sun, wind, and tide.
I'd put my money on the sun and solar energy.
What a source of power! I hope we don't have to wait
until oil and coal run out before we tackle that.*

THOMAS EDISON[1]

Jeremy Leggett started his profession conducting research on shale oil as an Earth scientist funded by British Petroleum and Royal Dutch Shell. What he learned convinced him to pivot and became a renewable energy entrepreneur. Now chair of Carbon Tracker, a financial-sector think tank that warns investors of the risk that investments in carbon-fuel assets will be stranded, he is also a great storyteller. His most recent book, *The Winning of the Carbon War*, reads like a thriller as it chronicles the transition from the recent past, when a fossil future seemed inevitable, to the cusp of the greatest energy transformation in history. Jeremy writes,

> A Saudi Prince talks of his nation's "dangerous addiction" to oil, and sets out a plan to kick dependency within just a few years. A Bloomberg guru talks of renewables "crushing" fossil fuels around the world. Arguably the most successful entrepreneur ever turns the unveiling of an electric car not

183

due to be delivered for 18 months into the most successful product launch in history. A revered Silicon Valley futurist ponders the seven doublings of the global solar market since 2000—one roughly every two years—and advises doubters in the technology not to ignore the arithmetic of exponential growth: six more doublings over the next 12 years would mean 100 percent of global energy from the sun.[2]

Official energy prognosticators aren't worried. The International Renewable Energy Agency predicts that solar will comprise, at most, 13 percent of global electricity by 2030.

Bloomberg New Energy Finance disagrees:

> The best minds in energy keep underestimating what solar and wind can do. Since 2000, the International Energy Agency has raised its long-term solar forecast 14 times and its wind forecast five times. Every time global wind power doubles, there's a 19 percent drop in cost, and every time solar power doubles, costs fall 24 percent.[3]

Leggett is not alone in calling 2014 the year of the shift. Paul Gilding, an Australian corporate consultant, in his paper "The Fossil Fuel Industry Is Now Entering Terminal Decline," writes,

> It's time to make the call—fossil fuels are finished.… The rest is detail…and once everyone wakes up to that reality, it will die faster because the market will discount it, taking away capital and shifting it to the future winners. This process will drive scale deployment and innovation of renewables while denying capital to fossil fuels, constraining their options.… The fossil fuel energy industry…will be all but gone within 15–30 years. The key driver is not what most see as their greatest threat—future climate change policy. It's that competing energy products of renewables and batteries, in a system with electric vehicles, will behave as a disruptive technology always does, delivering ever lower prices and ever higher quality in

a decades' long period of innovation and deployment, which fossil fuels can't match.[4]

Jeremy Leggett worries, in fact, that the transition is happening so rapidly that the fossil industries may implode before the ascendency of renewables is ready.[5] He cites the Chinese retreat from coal, the divestment movement, the bankruptcies of coal and oil companies around the planet, and the fall of Venezuela. At the same time that the price of oil falls, the cost of extraction rises. This, he fears, will result in what Carbon Tracker is now calling a "disorderly transition."[6]

The economic slowdown after 2008 worsened the fundamental dynamic that it now costs more to pull resources from the ground than they are worth. This puts banks holding debt paper of extractive industries at risk. The 2008 economic collapse was triggered in part by high oil prices.[7] The next banking emergency may be triggered by low prices. An analyst writing in *Forbes* concluded,

> Persistently low oil prices represent a risk on par with the housing bust. And in recent days we're seeing the signs of another global financial and economic crisis creeping uncomfortably closer to a "round two." As we've said, this time would be much worse because governments and central banks have exhausted the resources to bail out failing banks, companies and countries. But central banks, namely the Bank of Japan and/or the European Central Bank, do have the opportunity to step in here, become an outright buyer of commodities (particularly oil), as part of their QE programs, to avert disaster. But time is the oil industry's worst enemy and therefore a big threat to the global economy. The longer policymakers drag their feet, the closer we get to the edge of global crisis—a crisis manufactured by OPEC's price war.[8]

The global economy remains dependent on the dwindling supply of fossil energy. In 1955, the Paley Commission in the US urged an immediate transition to renewable energy as a matter of national security.[9] Had we done it, the transition would already have been achieved. We have left it until essentially the last moment, and so concerns about resource security, the issue that motivated the Paley Commission, are more acute.

This is not to say that we are running out of oil. A Shell Oil geophysicist named M. King Hubbert, writing in the mid-1950s, pointed out that if you have a finite resource—and it is a corollary of the round Earth theory that oil is finite—and exponential demand for a resource, which human desire for petroleum has certainly been since the 1950s, then you fall off the production curve as steeply as you went up when you have exhausted half of the resource. Peak oil, named for what was called "Hubbert's needle" or "peak," has many adherents, who herald every run up in oil prices as the beginning of the end.[10] It is more likely, however, that we are facing peak demand. It is true that new oil discoveries are at a 70-year low and declining,[11] and the costs of extraction are rising, but the cost of oil continues to fall, because demand is falling and alternatives emerging. The success of US shale oil extraction from hydrofracturing swamped the world market with cheap oil and gas. And this is only the latest example of a durable phenomenon of oil price volatility.

Daniel Yergin[12] has long been an advocate of the position that oil is effectively economically infinite: as soon as shortages begin to bite, the price rises, and the enormous overhang of efficiency brings demand back down. If this dynamic exhausts itself, then the substitutions (electric cars, renewables) become attractive as soon as prices get much above $50 a barrel.[13] The trouble with the belief that we are on the verge of running out of oil is that at higher prices other alternatives become attractive, too, most especially energy efficiency and now the various renewables.

Rising costs of extracting more of the ever-scarcer fossil resources[14] depress demand. Investor Jeremy Grantham warns that, because of this, the era of economic growth may be over, entirely.[15] He argues that the years of low economic growth are not an aberration but the durable result of exhaustion of productivity gains that cheap energy, and the entry of women into the workforce, had made possible, as well as the rising capital expenditures needed to extract ever-scarcer ore bodies, oil, and gas. Before the recent fall in oil prices, Grantham stated, "Resource prices are now rising, and in the last eight years have undone, remarkably, the effects of the last 100-year decline!"[16]

This projection may seem at odds with predictions of low prices for oil and gas, and to some extent it is, but it is precisely the volatility phenomenon discussed above.

The price of oil, and to some extent gas, is a function not only of supply and demand but of the political forces at work. Can OPEC keep prices high by constraining its members' desires to meet their budgets by extracting more?[17] Are the Saudis cashing out of oil and investing in renewable energy?[18] They built up a huge war chest to enable themselves to weather extended low oil prices, but even with this, they will run out of money in five years.[19] To meet current accounts,[20] they need oil to be at more than $100 a barrel. Countries like the Emirates can make it on $50 a barrel oil, but Venezuela requires a price of almost $150 a barrel to break even and has collapsed into a failed state.[21]

What matters, however, are the long-term dynamics. If the costs of extracting more resources, particularly fossil energy and minerals, are higher than the revenues derived from selling the resulting oil, coal, or metals, they will stay in the ground. Which is a very good thing, because if fossil energy continues to fuel the economy, we truly are lost.

The Climate Crisis

Scientists agree that to avoid total system collapse it is essential to cap global warming at no higher than 2° Celsius (C) above pre-industrial levels. Our current trajectory will result in a world that has warmed 5° to 6°C or more.

The International Energy Agency's (IEA) *World Energy Outlook*[22] calculated various scenarios that would result in a world able to hold warming to 2°C Scenario (2DS). This approach, the focus of the IEA's *Energy Technology Perspectives*, "sets the target of cutting energy-related CO_2 emissions by more than half in 2050 (compared

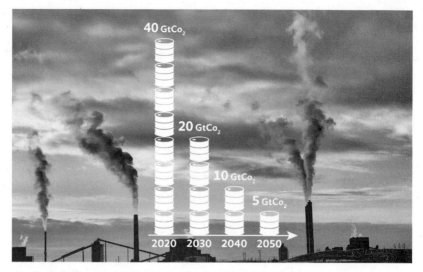

Credit: J. Lokrantz, Azote Images for Stockholm Resilience Centre

with 2009) and ensuring that they continue to fall thereafter." The 2DS acknowledges that transforming the energy sector is vital but not the sole solution. The goal can be achieved, in this scenario, only

> provided that CO_2 and GHG emissions in non-energy sectors (agriculture, waste disposal, industrial activities) are also reduced. The 2DS is broadly consistent with the *World Energy Outlook* 450 Scenario through 2035. This is consistent with an emissions trajectory that climate science indicates would give an 80 percent chance of limiting average global temperature increase to 2°C.[23]

In contrast, a middle scenario would see the world warm by 4°C. This is where the world is likely to get to if no greater action is taken than the voluntary pledges made by countries to cut emissions and improve energy efficiency prior to the Paris Climate Summit in December of 2015. That may seem easy, but it is a relatively ambitious scenario compared to the emissions reductions achieved to date and will require significant changes in policy and technologies over current practice.

Worse, a 4°C world, says World Bank President Jim Yong Kim, is still a "doomsday scenario."[24] The Bank's report, *Turn Down the Heat,* shows that a 4-degree increase in temperature would drive extensive crop failures and malnutrition. Rising seas would inundate vast areas, dislocating large numbers of people.

The 6°C scenario, an extension of current trends, is the nightmare. By 2050, energy use almost doubles (compared with 2009), and total GHG emissions rise even more. This scenario is pronounced by many scientists as unsurvivable.[25]

Bear in mind that IEA is an intergovernmental organization whose board is composed of delegates from OECD (the rich countries). There is reason to question strongly whether their scenarios are bold enough. Leading climate scientists like Johan Rockström, Malte Meinshausen, and John Schellnhuber believe they are far too inadequate, and they call for rapid decarbonization.[26] They state that "although the Paris Agreement's goals are aligned with science and can, in principle, be technically and economically achieved, alarming inconsistencies remain between science-based targets and national commitments." They fear that long-term goals will be trumped by political short-termism.

The Paris goals, they say, must translate into a finite planetary carbon budget:

> A 50 percent chance of limiting warming to 1.5° C by 2100 and a 66 percent probability of meeting the 2°C target imply that global CO_2 emissions peak no later than 2020, and gross emissions decline from roughly 40 gigatons (metric) CO2/year in 2020 to roughly 5 gigatons/year in 2050.[27]

To make this happen, Rockström et al. introduce a global roadmap based on a simple heuristic—a "carbon law"—of cutting gross anthropogenic carbon dioxide emissions in half every decade. If such a reduction pathway is combined with carbon removal and efforts to cut land-use emissions, "this can lead to net-zero emissions around mid-century, the path necessary to limit warming to well below 2°C."

The roadmap affects all sectors and suggests much more rapid action than hitherto discussed. Fossil fuel subsidies have to be abolished no later than 2020. Coal has to exit the energy mix no later than 2030. A carbon levy of, at minimum, $50/ton must be imposed. Combustion engines should no longer be sold after 2030. After 2030, all building construction must be carbon-neutral or carbon-negative—a daunting task. Agro-industries must develop sustainable food strategies, and massive reforestation programs must be launched. Removal of CO_2 from the atmosphere will have to complement efficiency in the form of biosequestration (BECSS) and/or direct air carbon capture and storage (DACCS). Direct carbon capture, however, remains an expensive proposition.[28] As described in chapter 9, using smarter agriculture to take carbon out of the air and return it to the soil makes great sense.

But what really is needed is a new energy economy.

The Chronology of Change Over the Past Four Years Is Inspiring

In June 2014, Citi Group released its *Energy Darwinism* report, warning of the "alarming fall in the price of solar." Alarming to whom?

Citi stated that this was now the Era of Renewables, predicting that within ten years solar, even without subsidies, would be the cheapest way to generate electricity.[29] Actually, in much of the world, it already is.[30]

And if we did the economics honestly, it already would be everywhere.

Subsidies are a two-edged sword. They have been instrumental in the shift to clean energy, but we also subsidize the continued use of fossil fuel. Free marketeers would prefer eliminating *all* subsidies and letting the technologies fight it out in the market. This isn't going to happen. But the magnitude of the subsidies makes clear the economic advantage of eliminating them. In 2015, the International Monetary Fund reported that fossil subsidies had reached $5.3 trillion a year, or $10 million every minute, more than all spending in the world for health care.[31] The IEA has repeatedly called for an end to such market distortions.

Such economies as Egypt, India, Indonesia, Malaysia, Mexico, Thailand, and the United Arab Emirates are doing just that: cutting or abolishing fuel consumption subsidies. It's not easy. These hold prices of fossil fuels lower on the argument that poor people cannot afford higher prices, and from China to Indonesia to Iran to Africa, efforts to cut such subsidies have resulted in riots.[32]

It would at least be better to eliminate the worst subsidies and use the money to make poor people less poor.

In January 2015, Deutsche Bank analyst Vishal Shah predicted that rooftop solar would be the cheapest electricity option for everyone in the US by 2016.[33] In April 2016, the average cost of rooftop solar was 12.2¢ per kilowatt-hour (kWh). The average cost of grid electricity was 12¢ kWh.[34]

- 1 kilowatt (1kW) is about the amount of power used by a hairdryer. A typical middle-class home uses somewhat under 10 kW on average.[35]
- 1 megawatt (1MW) is about enough to power 164 homes from solar photovoltaics. The actual amount depends on where you are (how much sun you get) and how efficient the solar panels are.[36]
- 1 gigawatt (1GW) is a billion watts, roughly the amount of power produced by a nuclear plant.

1 kilowatt-hour (1 kWh) is the energy to run a hairdryer for an hour. Typical electric rates in the US are 11¢ kWh. Energy efficiency in well-run programs costs ½¢ kWh. Running a natural gas plant costs 4¢ to 6¢ kWh. Building a new nuclear plant can cost upwards of 20¢ kWh.[37]

Only one month later, Agora Energiewende, a German think tank, reported that solar electricity was already a low-cost renewable energy technology in many regions of the world.[38] It stated that by 2025 solar will be the cheapest form of electricity everywhere. The report described how large-scale photovoltaic installations in Germany fell from over 40¢ kWh in 2005 to 9¢ kWh in 2014, with even lower prices reported in sunnier regions of the world.

Even with no technological breakthroughs, the report concluded, there is no end to cost reduction, with costs of 4 to 6 ¢ kWh (competitive with just the running cost of a natural gas plant, heretofore the cheapest option) expected by 2025, and 2 to 4 ¢ kWh by 2050. In spring 2016, a consortium of solar developers led by Abu Dhabi committed to build the 800 MW Mohammed bin Rashid Al Maktoum Solar Park at an unsubsidized price of 2.99 ¢ kWh.[39] At that price, solar competes with energy efficiency. The German study warned, "Most scenarios underestimate the role of solar power in future energy systems."

The National Bank of Abu Dhabi now says that, even at $10 a barrel, oil no longer competes with solar.[40] Wind is even cheaper. DONG Energy's latest unsubsidized offshore wind farm is bid at less than the running cost of a natural gas plant.[41] The report's projected 2025 price was achieved for utility-scale solar four months later when Austin, Texas, announced that its utility had received offers for 7,976 megawatts of projects after issuing a request for bids in April. Out of those bids, 1,295 megawatts of projects were priced below 4 cents per kilowatt-hour.[42]

Change rolled on. In March 2015, Bloomberg Business reported that, from 2013 to 2014, California went from utility-scale solar installations supplying 1.9 percent of its electricity to 5 percent.[43] And that number is not even counting the private rooftop solar, which would increase the figure by almost half again.[44] The National Bank of Abu Dhabi report stated that solar energy is on track to achieve grid parity in 80 percent of countries by 2017.

In April 2015, Michael Liebreich of Bloomberg New Energy called the time of death, saying, "Fossil fuel just lost the race with renewables.... The world is now adding more capacity for renewable power each year than coal, natural gas, and oil combined. And there's no going back."[45] By late 2016, he had declared that solar was now cheaper than coal and, even more surprising, cheaper than wind.[46]

In late 2016, the CFO of Royal Dutch Shell stated that the company expects demand for oil to peak by 2020.[47]

In 2017, the amount of electricity generated by nuclear in the US fell below that generated by renewable energy.

Solar and wind are now cheaper in most of the world than the cost of running an existing coal, gas, or nuclear plant. Nuclear is dying; solar, wind, and the other renewables are increasing. It's only a matter of time before the old nuclear, coal, and gas plants are shut down and a brighter future dawns.[48]

If humanity is in a horse race with catastrophe, we may just be witnessing the winning move.

The Rest of the World

In June 2015, the Institute for Energy Economics and Financial Analysis (IEEFA) reported slowing demand globally for coal and rapidly rising investment in renewables. Tim Buckley, the Institute's director of energy finance stated,

> Globally, 2014 was the year of the renewable energy installation juggernaut.... Wherever you look around the globe, be it China, India, Europe, or the US, the trend of a rapidly expanding renewable energy industry is the same. 2015 will inevitably see this gather pace.[49]

He was right. In 2014, South Africa began using solar and wind to meet its capacity shortfalls because doing this was cheaper and faster than building new coal or nuclear facilities.[50] This saved the country $69 million that year[51] and created jobs[52] and local industrial capacity. With proposed coal plants on hold because of soaring costs,[53] South Africa then commissioned 79 renewable energy projects, totaling more than 1 GW. A gigawatt is roughly a nuclear-power-plant–sized chunk of capacity, but a new nuclear plant would take ten years to build and cost $6 per watt, according to one recent estimate.[54] Coal, long thought of as dirt cheap, comes at $2.30 per watt. Top Chinese manufacturers were producing solar panels for 42 cents per watt.[55]

South Africa's renewable capacity hit 5.24 GW in 2015 and 7 GW by 2016,[56] up from nothing in 2012.[57] Another 6.3 GW is already commissioned.[58] No fossil technology can scale this quickly.

Across the Atlantic, Brazil's commitment to biofuels and hydroelectricity made it independent of imported oil in 2006.[59] Since

2009, Brazil has added solar and wind energy, contracting 14 GW of wind at prices below any other option. In 2014, at prices only a bit higher, it also brought on almost 1 GW of solar energy. As a severe drought drives Brazil's electricity prices higher, industries eager for access to reliable and affordable power are turning to renewables that do not require dams and abundant rainfall.[60]

The biggest user of energy, China, is becoming the world's renewable energy powerhouse.[61]

As described in section 2, China is coupling energy efficiency with renewable energy to shift away from fossil fuels. The IEEFA study agrees: "While real economic growth in China exceeded seven percent, electricity demand grew by less than four percent." Rapid supply diversification saw China's coal consumption drop by 2 percent and coal imports fall by 11 percent in 2014. China's coal demand may have permanently peaked in 2016 and will decline thereafter, the report predicted.[62]

Growing its installed solar capacity by twentyfold within only four years, China went from a capacity of 0.3 GW in 2009 to 13 GW by 2013[63] and added 30.5 GW of renewable energy in 2015, 16.5 GW of that solar. It planned to grow its renewables by 21 percent in 2016.[64]

The transformation has only begun. The "China 2050 High Renewable Energy Penetration Scenario and Roadmap Study," released in 2015, found that renewable energy could economically provide China the majority of its energy by 2050.[65] Wang Yimin, representing the State Grid Corporation of China, told the United Nations Global Compact meeting on pricing carbon in June 2015 that by 2050 China would be 80 percent renewable.[66]

Even India, the world's fourth-largest emitter of greenhouse gasses, and long seen by the coal industry as their last great hope, is entering the solar age.[67] As described in chapter 4, it pledged to cut the energy intensity of its economy by up to 35 percent by 2030 and get 40 percent of its electricity from non-fossil sources by then.[68] India's Power Minister, R.K. Singh, observed, "This is a matter of worry for those who produce coal or oil. But, this [growing use of renewable energy] cannot be stopped as it makes economic sense."[69]

At the Paris Climate Summit in 2015, Indian President Narendra Modi joined French President Hollande in launching the International Solar Alliance, a union of countries with abundant sun.[70] India, like Pakistan, has long declared that it has every right to burn coal or build nuclear plants (the latter clearly for military purposes in both cases) to deal with energy poverty. International energy experts have, however, pointed out for years that the fastest, cheapest way to reduce energy poverty is to enable villagers to use the biomass they now burn (dung or wood) far more efficiently in better cookstoves, or in biogas plants, and to leapfrog to renewable energy as soon as possible.[71]

President Modi pledged to enable India to exceed its 2016–17 target of 30 GW of renewable energy to 175 GW of renewables, most of it solar, by 2022. To achieve this, India increased its subsidy for rooftop solar fivefold to $3.7 billion in late 2017.[72] If successful, it would cut 326.22 million tonnes of carbon dioxide equivalent per year. States such as Punjab and Karnatatka are shuttering coal plants and building solar instead.[73] India also has a significant wind resources, estimated at 70 percent of India's renewable potential.[74]

Companies like SELCO (the Solar Electric Light Company)[75] are delivering this future today. It sells solar electric panels that provide lighting and electricity to poor villagers at monthly prices comparable to what they would pay to use traditional, less-effective sources. Through its network of 25 centers across India, SELCO provides solar lighting and electricity, clean water, and wireless communications to underserved households and businesses with advanced but inexpensive lighting, electricity, water pumping, water heating, communications, computing, and entertainment. The systems do not require connection to a larger network. SELCO meets its customers where they live, partnering with rural banks, leasing companies, and microfinance organizations to provide necessary credit. It has brought reliable, environmentally sustainable electricity to 200,000 homes and businesses since 1995. It empowers its customers by providing complete packages of products, services, and consumer financing.

With solar electricity comes communication technology, clean drinking water, refrigeration, power for clinics, and other development technologies. Lighting even one bulb enables villagers to provide light for silkworms, looms, and moveable lights that can go room to room as needed. This gives them an income source to power sustainable development.

SELCO's market-based system, requiring no government subsidies, lifts thousands of people from poverty vastly more effectively than many aid programs. The company's founder, Harish Hande, suggests that development experts rethink their definition of what poor people can afford. He argues that the poor actually spend a great deal of money on kerosene lamps, diesel for generators, and batteries for flashlights. With fair financing, they are capable of paying for a solar installation to displace the more wasteful options. If people are told that the solar installation will cost them $30 a month, they tend to say that it is too expensive. But if asked to pay $1 a day, they agree, "Yes, we can do that." In the SELCO model, the purchaser pays 20 percent down. SELCO provides financing that enables the buyer to pay off the system in 4 years at $10 to $20 per month. The financing matches a person's ability to pay.

President Modi has realized that conventional Western grid-based systems will never meet the needs of the 360 million people in India without electricity. Only distributed renewables can meet his goal of electricity in every household. According to the Climate Group and Goldman Sachs, this approach can overcome projections that, business as usual, only 10 percent more households will get power over the next ten years.[76]

The Profound Transformation

Massive change is coming to the energy sector. Entrepreneur Elon Musk created a car company that now threatens the car, oil, gas, coal, nuclear, and utility industries.

In early 2016, Tesla's market capitalization was $30 billion, compared to $47.7 billion for GM,[77] despite selling 300 times fewer cars. By spring 2017, the company's market cap exceeded $52.7 billion, beating both Ford Motor Company and General Motors.[78]

Tesla also pulled off the entrepreneuring coup of the century, selling $10 billion worth of orders in one day for cars that would not be built for at least a year.[79] And when cash ran short, Elon sold Tesla-branded flamethrowers, netting the company $10 million in four days.[80]

OK, it's a market darling, but what makes it such a threat? Because Tesla, as its "Master Plan, Part Deux," released July 2016, makes clear, is not a car company; it's a battery company. More than that, it's an integrated energy company. In 2016, Tesla bought Solar City to integrate all of the energy solutions customers want. Combining rooftop solar with home battery storage with electric cars[81] will eliminate pretty much any rationale to dig up and burn ancient sunlight in ways that are dirty and dangerous. If battery costs come down as they have been—dropping 70 percent since 2009[82]—then the game really is over for the fossils.

Advocates of last century's energy options think this is nuts. OPEC believes that in 2040, electric vehicles will make up just one percent of all vehicles.

They'd best watch out: Bloomberg New Energy Finance sees 2025 as the peak year for oil, coal, and gas.[83] In 2009, there were essentially no electric cars on American roads, compared to nearly one billion gasoline cars. Today there are more than 2 million cars with a plug, and electric car sales are increasing ten times faster than purchases of fossil fueled vehicles.[84] China, representing one-quarter of the world automobile market, mandated that eight percent of cars sold there be electrics by 2018.[85] In 2017, it announced that it would begin phasing out sales of internal combustion vehicles.[86] In 2018, there were 500 electric car companies in China.[87]

Cheaper oil prices in 2017 engendered one last American explosion of sales of urban assault vehicles. But by fall 2017, EVs sales regained their American momentum, increasing almost 50 percent over 2016.[88] Globally, sales rose 63 percent in the third quarter of 2017 over the year before, with China representing half of the increase.[89] By mid-2018, with oil prices edging upward of $70 a barrel on fears of Middle Eastern instability, EV sales increased again.

Such numbers are impressive, but the increases are over a very small base. EVs have only just reached the one million sold per year mark, one percent of global car sales. Like many new technologies, they are also very sensitive to policy shifts. But globally, policy seems to be going in the right direction: like China, countries from the UK to France, India, and the Netherlands say they will ban sales of fossil-fueled cars, with California likely to follow suit.[90]

In Norway, a combination of tax relief, free parking, and ability to drive free on toll roads brought electric vehicles to almost half of all new car sales. Almost 40 percent of Norway's cars are now electrics, and they expect that to be 100 percent within eight years.[91] And they are cheaper to operate: a grid charge costs the Norwegian equivalent of a couple of dollars. A fill-up of gasoline would cost $6.[92] In the US, the money you spend on monthly payments for a Nissan Leaf is what you would have paid in gasoline. In effect, the company has given you a free car.[93]

Bloomberg believes that EVs will constitute half the cars on the road by 2040. But long before this, by 2023, it predicts, reduction in demand for gasoline will cause another oil price collapse.[94] With transportation responsible for 30 percent of carbon pollution, soon a bigger problem than power plants,[95] displacing oil for vehicles will be as big a deal for climate protection as bankrupting coal, but it will be a far bigger deal economically.

Whole new business models are emerging. One of Solar City's co-founders believes that, well before 2020, there will be a "sharing economy for electricity."[96] Battery costs will have come down so much that houses will all have battery banks like the Tesla Wall, capable of powering them through the night from the solar energy stored during the day. These smart storage units will be able to trade power with electric cars and share electricity across the grid, earning their owners extra cash every time they do and further stabilizing a renewable grid.[97]

This means that traditional utility companies face the "Death Spiral."[98] Their old business model of building large fossil plants is no longer viable. Former Energy Secretary Stephen Chu warned, "The utilities are in danger of getting 'Fed-Exed' just like the Post Office got 'Fed-Exed' as rooftop solar modules drop in price."[99]

In Europe, where feed-in tariffs allow farmers, cooperatives, communities, and citizens to make money from installing renewable energy, RWE and Eon, two of the biggest European utilities, lost 60 percent and 91 percent of their profits respectively in the first nine months of 2014. Declaring themselves to be distributed renewables companies, they divested of ownership in fossil and nuclear facilities.[100]

Most utilities, however, still fight the transition. All things equal, they claim, gas is cheaper than renewables and battery storage, and gas is the transition fuel to a renewable future.

They're wrong. A report from Lazard proves it:

> The levelized cost of utility-scale solar power with storage is $92 per megawatt-hour (MWh). This means that solar-plus-storage can be highly competitive, even after dark, with natural gas peaking plants, which have levelized costs ranging from $165 to $217 per MWh. It is even competitive to a degree with gas-powered reciprocating engines, whose costs are from $68 to $101 per MWh.... Both onshore wind and solar PV have seen insane drops in cost over the past eight years—66 and 85 percent, respectively.... And, in...emerging nations...electricity demand [is] rising quickly. They need new electricity generation, and when one surveys the options for new power plants, renewables look really good.[101]

In Australia that became true in 2016: storage plus solar is cheaper than gas-fired generation.[102]

In late 2017, the coal-dependent Public Service Company of Colorado released the numbers from its request for bids to supply energy for its utility customers. Thousands of MW of wind, solar, and solar with battery storage were offered at prices far below competing fossil options:

+ Median wind price below 2 cents/kwh

+ Median solar below 3 cents/kwh
+ Median solar and storage median price at 3.6 cents/kwh[103]

The future has arrived.

In late 2016, the *Financial Times* reported that Fitch Ratings agreed that gas plants were unlikely to have much of a future but warned that utilities are not the only ones at risk:

> Widespread adoption of battery-powered vehicles is a serious threat to the oil industry.... The oil sector would not be the only industry affected. Big electricity utilities burning fossil fuels such as gas or coal face the risk of batteries solving the intermittency problem of wind or solar plants that cannot generate on windless days or at night.
>
> Utilities with a lot of gas "peaker" plants that deliver power quickly at times of peak demand, when prices are generally high, could be more at risk. If batteries start supplying this peaking power, prices could eventually fall to the point where "traditional peakers can no longer compete.... But the impact of batteries on the oil industry may be profound.... [T]ransportation accounted for 55 per cent of total oil use in 2014.... An acceleration of the electrification of transport infrastructure would be resoundingly negative for the oil sector's credit profile.... In an extreme scenario where electric cars gained a 50 percent market share over 10 years about a quarter of European gasoline demand could disappear.[104]

It endangers the banks, as well: a quarter of all corporate debt, perhaps as much as $3.4 trillion, is related to utility and car company bonds that are tied to fossil fuel use.[105] Fitch Ratings warned that low-cost batteries could

> tip the oil market from growth to contraction earlier than anticipated. The narrative of oil's decline is well rehearsed—and if it starts to play out there is a risk that capital will act long before and in the worst case result in an "investor death spiral."

Tesla and other battery companies are working hard to make it so. In 2016, Tesla teamed with four other battery companies to set the world record for fast installation of utility-scale battery storage.

The speed was driven by crisis. In 2015, the natural gas well and storage facility at Aliso Canyon operated by Southern California Gas Company failed. For 119 days, gas spewed out, forcing thousands of nearby residents to evacuate, hospitalizing many, and emitting as much climate damage as a year's worth of 2 million cars, the burning of a billion gallons of gasoline, or the corporate emission of 9 million tons of CO_2.[106] This loss of gas cast into doubt utilities' ability to meet summer peak demand. Southern California Edison and San Diego Gas and Electric companies commissioned Tesla, Samsung, AES, and others to meet the shortfall with the largest utility-scale battery storage facility ever built.

In early 2017, six months later, 20 megawatts of battery storage went live, capable of delivering 80 megawatt hours.[107] In contrast, competing gas peaking plants would have taken years to build and required far more land. The exercise was driven by need, but soon such facilities will simply be cheaper.[108]

Tesla immediately bet that it could install 100 MW of storage in South Australia, creating the world's largest battery, in 100 days or the rig would be free. It won that bet, proving that grid-scale storage is not only faster but now cheaper than any other option.[109]

Elon then signed a deal with South Australia to give 50,000 low-income households solar panels and Tesla Wall battery packs, creating a 250-megawatt virtual power plant, the world's largest. Smart meters will dispatch the power from the distributed renewable and battery storage systems, giving the utility the ability to react to load fluctuations instantly and reliably, giving the residents a 30 percent discount on power.[110] South Australia plans to greatly expand the system in the coming years.

Battery technology continues to improve, and prices fall. They've dropped by almost half since 2014. In Ojai, California, SimpliPhi Power is producing lithium ferrous phosphate batteries for the US forward operating bases in Afghanistan[111] as well as for homes in the US and aid operations in Africa.[112] Unlike the lithium cobalt batteries produced by Tesla and most other battery companies, SimpliPhi's product is non-toxic (cobalt, a conflict mineral, is highly toxic).[113] The military likes them because they do not get hot, and without a heat signature they are far less likely to attract a heat-seeking missile. In home applications, they are far less likely to catch fire. They don't care if they get cold, hot, or are deployed in inhospitable conditions.

Organic flow batteries of the sort now being prototyped are safer, cheaper, and capable of being scaled to back up renewable technologies.[114] Similarly, vanadium flow batteries are safe and scalable for utility applications. Vanadium is an abundant material, and because of the nature of the system, the batteries do not degrade over time or develop "memory."[115]

Lithium air batteries being developed in the lab use far less lithium and can store five times as much energy as today's lithium-ion batteries.[116]

Going All the Way

With cheap ubiquitous batteries, solar and wind become firm power and replace all fossil power plants. Already a growing number of companies and cities are committing to become 100 percent renewably powered.

Launched during Climate Week in 2014, the RE100 is a consortium of more than 119 companies who have pledged to go 100 percent,[117] including Unilever, Walmart, Google, Goldman Sachs, Coca Cola, BMW, and Apple. Most of these companies that pledge to go entirely renewable have set target dates of 2020, but commitment dates ranged from "soon" to 2016, in the case of Microsoft and Pearson, to 2050, the date set by the world's scientists as needed for decarbonization. Alstria, a large real estate company in Germany, has committed to power all of its portfolio buildings with renewables by 2025.

Google became 100 percent renewable in 2017 through purchasing energy from installations in five countries on three continents.[118] Unilever, promising to be 100 percent renewable by 2020, has also pledged to be energy positive by 2030—making more renewable energy than it needs and giving power to the communities where it does business.[119] Corporate buyers make up 50 percent of the purchases for renewable energy in the US, now representing more than six nuclear plants' worth of capacity, even in the face of historically low prices for grid electricity (from the natural gas bubble). The second-biggest buyer is the US military, which has found that renewable energy enhances its war-fighting ability.[120]

In the wake of the late 2015 historic agreement by all of the world's nations in Paris to cut carbon emissions and drive the transition to renewable energy, more than 1,000 cities have committed to become 100 percent renewably powered. Since the US announcement that it will not honor its Paris commitments, this movement has gained strength.

Author and technology investor Ramez Naam agrees. Asking how cheap solar can get,[121] he reviewed the falling prices for solar, wind,[122] battery storage,[123] and electric vehicles[124] to predict that renewables can provide at least 90 percent of American energy by 2030. His answer: very cheap indeed.

Naam believes that three changes to the current electricity supply system will make this possible: increasing capacity factors for solar and wind, far lower prices for battery storage, and grids that span continents.[125]

Entrepreneur and financier Jigar Shah believes that the only thing stopping all of this is a lack of effective business models and financial innovation. His book *Creating Climate Wealth*[126] issued the 100 × 100 = 10 challenge: a worldwide challenge to solve climate change by unleashing the equivalent of 100,000 companies each selling $100 million worth of climate change solutions by 2020, creating a new $10 trillion economy.[127]

> Solving big challenges have always resulted in wealth creation. Think about the challenges of transportation, and then the economic and societal impact of the railroad, automobile and airlines. Or think about any other industry like telecommunications. Then let's think about big goals we have had like

curing polio, or landing a man on the moon. Addressing all of these issues had much more of an impact on our society and our lives than just solving the problem or taking on the challenge. Each changed our lives, created jobs, and made life better. We have always been able to make problems into opportunities. So, I look at climate change as the biggest opportunity in our lifetime, in fact the largest wealth creation opportunity on the planet.[128]

Shah's business model innovation of "no-money-down solar installations" is one of the three reasons that solar is now adding more new energy-generating capacity each year than coal, oil, and natural gas combined. He believes that 50 percent of greenhouse gas emissions will always be profitable to eliminate due to continuous technology innovation.

The shift is already creating wealth where it is being implemented. In California, which, as described above, has committed to cut its

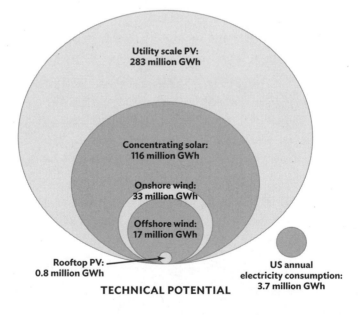

Credit: Jigar Shah.

carbon emissions 80 percent below its 1990 levels by 2050, there are already more people employed in the solar industry (64,000 people) than in the electric utilities. Manufacturing is expanding in the state, and the economy is booming, with state gross income increasing 17 percent from 2003 to 2013, while greenhouse gas emissions fell by 5.5 percent.[129]

In his early article declaring the end of fossil fuels, Paul Gilding wrote,

> With renewables already competitive today without subsidy in some markets and the above trends playing out, it is inevitable that before long—maybe a decade—virtually all new electricity generation will be from renewables. Add in the need to be clean—not just for climate change reasons but for local air quality—and the choice developing countries will face will be between large, old, dirty, hard to finance infrastructure that requires heavy government support or small scale, easy to finance, more convenient, popular and clean energy and transport that will get even cheaper over time. Tough choice?
>
> So the very thing that the fossil fuel industry had relied on for its growth—the rapidly expanding need for energy in the developing world—is the very thing that will drive the competition to wipe them out.[130]

Change will not come easily. President Jimmy Carter once stated that energy was not a commodity but the entity on which the entire economy depends. Thus, he said, any attempt to limit America's supply of it was "the moral equivalent of war." Such beliefs derive from extremely powerful forces and will not cede global power gracefully. The Union of Concerned Scientists study, *The Climate Deception Dossiers*, showed that for decades the fossil industry conducted a coordinated campaign to spread climate disinformation and block climate action to protect its profits.[131]

A common way of arguing for the continuation of the status quo is to claim that renewables cannot possibly meet our energy needs until after said fossil company executive, or incentivized legislator, has safely retired. Despite the evidence listed above, they can find plenty of analysts like the US Energy Information Administration to say that coal will provide a third of the world's electricity by 2040, and renewables only 17 percent.[132]

If that is true, say fossil advocates, and if climate change is a threat, then it will be essential to make all that coal clean, using carbon capture and sequestration (CCS). It is tempting to say that, well, China will burn a lot of coal, regardless, and therefore perhaps we *should* invest in this technology. Sure, it has never worked on a commercial scale, but shouldn't we put more research dollars into one more go....?

No. We shouldn't. The trouble is that, like nuclear power, it will take a *lot* of dollars, assuming you can ever get it to work.

Bill Becker, executive director of the Presidential Climate Action Project, described why carbon capture can never deliver:

> Despite the years of research and spending, CCS is not yet ready for large-scale commercialization. So, part of the price is further delays in the urgent job of cutting emissions. Electric customers will pay a significant price: Researchers say that CCS would add between 35 percent and 80 percent to consumer electric bills initially, and only slightly less in the long term.
>
> Power plants equipped with CCS would increase water withdrawals by 83 percent to 91 percent depending on the type of technology used to generate electricity. That makes CCS problematic in arid and drought-affected places and in places where power production must compete with agriculture and city water consumption.[133]

It's time to stop nibbling at this bullet and invest in the triumph of the sun.[134] This change can happen fast. Globally renewables have been increasing dramatically. In Chile[135] and Germany[136] recently, so much renewable energy was produced that the utility gave it away for free. Germany has pledged to be 80 percent renewable by 2050,

Scotland 100 percent by 2020. In the US, since 2009, solar costs have dropped 80 percent and installations increased twentyfold[137] to more than 42 GW in service. In 2016, annual installations grew 95 percent over the previous year.[138]

Is It Enough? Is It Too Much?

Some predictions say that all this is just the beginning. As described in chapter 1, Stanford's Professor Tony Seba believes that by 2030 the entire world will run on renewable energy—not just for electricity, but for all forms of energy. If this is true, oil companies; gas, coal, uranium extractors; the nuclear industry; utilities; and the auto industry will either become part of the solution or they won't be a problem, because they won't exist.

Seba's book *Clean Disruption* describes why he believes the transformation will come so fast.[139] He credits the convergence of disruptive technologies and business models, especially four factors—the fall in the cost of solar, the fall in the cost of storage (batteries), the electric car, and the driverless car—to make a renewable world inevitable.

This will have profound implications for, well, everything. But particularly for transportation. Transportation as a service using autonomous electric vehicles will be ten times cheaper than current private ownership of internal combustion cars. Seba points out that whenever in history a new technology has enabled tenfold savings, it has driven disruption of the dominant industry.[140]

He reminds doubters that experts totally underestimated sales of mobile phones. In the 1990s, McKinsey told AT&T to expect 900,000 mobile subscribers by 2000. They were only off by 108 million.[141] By 2014, there were more mobile phones on Earth than the seven billion people, increasing five times faster than humans.[142]

Seba cites what is called Swanson's law[143] (named for Richard Swanson, founder of the solar company Sun Power), which holds that for every doubling of solar photovoltaics made and shipped, the price declines 20 percent.

Seba's colleague at Singularity University, Ray Kurzweil, calculates that it would take only *six* more doublings to power the entire world with solar:

> In 2012, solar panels were producing 0.5 percent of the world's energy supply. Some people dismissed it, saying, "It's a nice thing to do, but at a half percent, it's a fringe player. That's not going to solve the problem." They were ignoring the exponential growth just as they ignored the exponential growth of the internet and genome project. Half a percent is only eight doublings away from 100 percent.
>
> Now it is four years later, [and solar] has doubled twice again. Now solar panels produce 2 percent of the world's energy, right on schedule. People dismiss it, "2 percent. Nice, but a fringe player." That ignores the exponential growth, which means it is only six doublings or [12] years from 100 percent.
>
> It's not true we're running out of energy. We're only running out of resources if we stick with 19th century technologies.[144]

That's fast. And it's possible. Mark Jacobson of Stanford demonstrated in 2009 that renewables could power the world by 2030.[145] His Solutions Project has shown how to do that for every US state.[146] More recently, scholars like Christian Breyer have shown how to do this with photovoltaics alone.[147]

Seba warns that falling costs will see solar achieving not only global grid parity by 2018 but soon what he calls "God parity—generation on demand." This means that the cost to put solar on your roof is cheaper than just having the utility ship power to you and maintain its lines. In this scenario, which he believes could come as early as 2020, even free electricity at any central station would be more expensive than distributed solar. Tony writes,[148] "Don't believe in the Clean Disruption? The IEA wants you to invest $40 trillion in conventional energy (nuclear, oil, gas, coal) and conventional utilities. It's their Kodak moment. It's your money."[149]

OK, a new solar array goes up in the US every 150 seconds,[150] but can the whole world be renewable by 2030? No way, you say....

Or will it?

In August 2017, China announced that it had already eclipsed its 2020 goal in solar installations. It now adds 45 GW of solar (more than the entire installed solar capacity of Germany) every year.[151] California predicted it will hit its declared 2030 target of getting 50 percent of its power from renewable energy by 2020—ten years early[152]—and, as described earlier, is debating resetting the goal to 100 percent renewable power.

In April 2017, an industry journal predicted that solar power would fall below 2¢ per kilowatt hour (kWh) that year.[153] In October, Saudi Arabia announced the new world record low price: 1.7 c/kWh.[154] When the Kentucky Coal Museum puts solar on its roof rather than plug into the coal-fired electric grid at its doorstep,[155] you know that the fossil era is over.

Well, OK, we *can* run our society on solar energy, but what if the sun isn't shining or the wind blowing?

Storage technology to make renewable energy available 24/7 is only in its infancy as an industry, but as described above, it is coming on fast, and its prices are collapsing, too.[156] Combinations of renewable energy and storage are now cheaper than the fossil alternatives.[157]

Then there are electric vehicles. Two days after Jerry Brown, governor of California, announced that he intended to follow China's lead to ban internal combustion engines, General Motors, which had reclaimed its coveted status of the world's leading automobile manufacturer on the strength of its Bolt electric car, announced that its future is electric. Meanwhile, Daimler, Volkswagen, and Volvo had already committed to electrifying their entire product portfolios.[158]

Within a month, Elon released an all-electric long-haul truck, and China announced the launch of the world's first all-electric cargo ship.

Hmmm, that looks like three for three. But in Seba's scenario, it's the driverless, autonomous electric vehicle (AEV) that drives the real reduction in cost he claims will make the disruption inevitable. Are AEVs more than just science fiction? Didn't Tesla's self-driving car kill a guy?

To get the straight story, let's talk to Tom Chi,[159] the brilliant head of product experience at Google X and one of the designers of the self-driving Google car. Is what Tony's saying possible?

"Within ten years?" asked Tom. "Easy." Tesla, he said, released its driverless vehicle when it was as safe as a human-driven car. Remember, hundreds of thousands of people die every year in car crashes. Teslas have driven more than 5 billion miles in autonomous mode[160] en route to the company's 10 billion mile safety proof point. In fact, all Teslas are now capable of full autonomous mode. The Tesla Autopilot car fatal crash, one of several accidents now accumulated, was caused by a flaw in the detection system: the car failed to distinguish a white tractor-trailer rig pulling out in front of it while driving into a brightly lit sky. Even so, the Tesla car is far safer than human driving. This fatality came after 130 million miles of testing. Humans crash once every 60 million miles.[161]

In a second fatality, a woman stepped in front of an autonomous Uber when the human co-pilot was looking down. Neither car nor human saw that. But in 2017, more than 6,000 pedestrians were killed by human-piloted vehicles.[162] The Google car has driven 4 million real miles, and 2.5 billion simulated miles.[163] Waymo, Google's spinoff, threatens to have its service on the road very soon.

It had better. GM just announced that it is pivoting its business model to offer autonomous electric vehicle transit as a service by 2019.[164]

Does that make it four for four? Is Tony right?

You decide.

But realize that if the evidence laid out here is true, it will mean the dissolution in value, likely complete loss, of the oil, gas, coal, uranium, nuclear, utility, and auto industries; the banks that hold the loan paper for all of these companies; and the pension funds and insurance companies that are invested in them. Just the self-driving cars will drive significant changes. The war between taxi and ride-sharing drivers will be over soon. Both will lose.[165] That's 4.1 driving million jobs, alone.

Unless managed well, the changes that are already upon us will mean an economic collapse on a scale you've never seen, coming at us within about ten years.

So, let's get serious about managing the transition well. Contrary to popular belief, switching to the regenerative economy would create millions of jobs. It is obvious to anyone with empathy that the shift needs to give people time to adapt. Millions of people working in "dirty" sectors will lose their jobs, especially those working in the fossil fuel business today. But those numbers are not as big as many think. By early 2017, you were twice as likely to have a job in solar as in coal.[166] That's right, solar employs twice the number of people as the coal industry.[167] These are well-paying jobs that cannot be outsourced to machines or offshoring. The workforce is diverse, featuring women and minorities, and spread across the country. Massachusetts has more solar installers than Texas, despite being a lot less sunny.

In 2015, only 184,500 Americans worked in oil and gas extraction, a number 17,000 fewer than a year before. The number of US mining jobs had decreased to 191,000 from the 203,700 in 2014. Coal extraction actually increased between 1980 and 2015, but coal jobs fell 60 percent because of automation.[168]

The International Renewable Energy Agency (IRENA) stated that, in the US,

> Solar employment continued its rapid expansion—growing by almost 22 percent to reach 209,000 in 2015. Jobs in the solar industry grew 12 times as fast as overall job creation in the US economy, and surpassed those in oil and gas extraction (187,200) or coal mining (67,929). Most solar jobs (194,200) are in solar PV.[169]

By 2017, American clean energy jobs exceeded 4 million.[170]

IRENA noted in mid-2016 that renewable jobs were growing at five percent a year globally, then exceeding 8 million. By 2015, China alone had created 3.5 million renewable jobs. By 2017, there were more than two and a half times more clean energy jobs than fossil employment,[171] and almost 10 million people employed in renewable energy industries globally, with the number expected to grow to 24 million by 2030.[172]

Bob Keefe, executive director of Environmental Entrepreneurs, cited the obvious:

> In a short amount of time, clean energy has become a huge part of our workforce and our economy. Smart policies helped jump-start this industry, and smart policies will keep these made-in-America jobs growing—and help our environment along the way.[173]

Dan Smolen, managing director of The Green Suits echoed, "Clean energy is no longer a niche business—it's a big-time job creator. Our lawmakers need to realize that—and put policies in place, right now, to help the sector grow even more."[174]

The jobs are also more satisfying than many today. This fact is not lost on young people, who want a greener and more responsible world. Johnson Controls found that 96 percent of workers aged 18 to 35 want to work for a responsible and green-minded company.[175]

Interestingly, it appears that if the renewable energy projects are locally owned, they create twice the number of jobs and deliver up to three times the economic value to the community.[176]

These figures focus on jobs in renewable energy, but the principles apply even more to the transition to a regenerative economy. More sustainable approaches create more, not fewer, jobs.[177] A greener economy could create between 15 and 60 million jobs worldwide over the next two decades. Achim Steiner, director of the UN Development Programme, estimates that by 2030 at least half of the global workforce will be in the green economy.[178] The discussion earlier in the section on the speed with which the transformation in energy is coming suggests that the UN's numbers are conservative.

Stranded Assets

Carbon Tracker neatly summed up the situation facing the fossil companies:

A trend in US coal risk disclosures:
1. Assume no new technology & policy
2. Go bankrupt[179]

In 2011, Mark Campanale and his colleagues at Carbon Tracker published the first of its series of reports, *Unburnable Carbon: Are the World's Financial Markets Carrying a Carbon Bubble?*[180] Carbon Tracker calculated that at least 80 percent of the fossil deposits still in the ground would have to stay there if the world is to avoid warming beyond 2 degrees C more that pre-industrial levels.

On the basis of that, John Fullerton published an article titled "Big Choice," describing the financial implication of Carbon Tracker's numbers.[181] Given that those fossil assets are on the balance sheets of some of the world's wealthiest companies and sovereign wealth funds of the nations of the world, Fullerton estimated, this implied a write-off of at least $20 trillion dollars. In contrast, he warned, the 2008 financial collapse was triggered by the stranding of only $2.7 trillion in mortgage assets. We're looking at an order of magnitude more dislocation.

A year later, Bill McKibben, founder of the climate activist group 350.org, popularized the math in a *Rolling Stone* article titled "Global Warming's Terrifying New Math."[182] Bill was less concerned about the financial health of the fossil companies but alarmed that to keep that much carbon in the ground would require instant and massive mobilization. By his numbers, we can burn 565 gigatons more carbon. Period. Ever. That's our carbon budget.

But the companies have five times that: 2,795 gigatons of fossil assets in reserve, and it is their business model to dig them up and burn them. If they do, the scientists warn, we roast. Between 60 to 80 percent of all coal, oil, and gas reserves of publicly listed fossil companies are unburnable if we are to keep within the 2°C limit. And yet the companies spend enormous amounts of money continuing to search for more. This is somewhat puzzling, as the rising threat of climate change means that they will not be able to

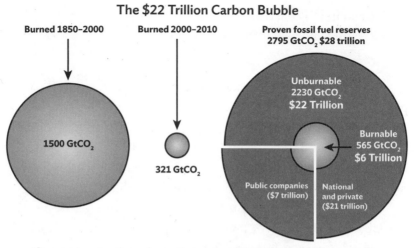

The $22 Trillion Carbon Bubble

Burned 1850–2000

Burned 2000–2010

Proven fossil fuel reserves
2795 GtCO$_2$ $28 trillion

1500 GtCO$_2$

321 GtCO$_2$

Unburnable
2230 GtCO$_2$
$22 Trillion

Burnable
565 GtCO$_2$
$6 Trillion

Public companies
($7 trillion)

National
and private
($21 trillion)

On our present pathway, humanity is expected to burn through proven fossil
fuel reserves by 2050, with global warming greater than 5°C (9°F) likely. To
have an 80 percent chance of keeping warming below 2°C, 80 percent of
proven reserves need to stay unburned. The present estimated value of these
civilization-threatening reserves is approximately $22 trillion.
Credit: Think Progress. https: thinkprogress.org/infographic-the-22-trillion
-carbon-bubble-d15a0887295f/

burn what they already have on hand, let alone more of it—Carbon
Tracker estimates that such companies as Royal Dutch Shell, Pemex,
Exxon Mobil, Peabody Energy, Coal India, and Glencore are wast-
ing $2.2 trillion of investment—old habits obviously die hard.

John Fullerton described the risk of carbon bubbles and stranded
assets, and he set forth fundamentals that should guide investors in
the age of climate crisis.[183] Short answer: fossil energy is no longer a
safe place to put your money.

In 2014, Bloomberg New Energy Finance estimated that coal
stocks had lost 50 to 90 percent of their value since 2005.[184]

This sobering conclusion was joined by the 2015 report by Mercer,
analyzing the portfolio risk to investors who hold stocks of fossil
companies. It found,

Average annual returns from the coal sub-sector could fall by
anywhere between 18 percent and 74 percent over the next
35 years, with effects more pronounced over the coming dec-

ade (eroding between 26 percent and 138 percent of average annual returns). Conversely, the renewables sub-sector could see average annual returns increase by between 6 percent and 54 percent over a 35-year time horizon (or between 4 percent and 97 percent over a 10-year period).[185]

Bank of America stated in May 2015 that coal mining companies pose an increasingly risky investment.

> "Going forward, Bank of America will continue to reduce our credit exposure to coal extraction companies." It also committed to increasing lending to renewable energy, energy efficiency, and carbon capture and storage. The spokeswoman said the bank's renewable energy portfolio was currently more than three times as large as its coal extraction portfolio.[186]

"Coal companies' underperformance against the global equity market is unprecedented," said IEEFA's Tim Buckley.

> A more than 50 percent decline in coal prices has seen most listed coal companies globally lose 80–90 percent of their equity market value in the last four years. While the sun will undoubtedly rise for renewable energy in 2015, for coal, there remains a lot further to fall.[187]

Change came fast. By February 2015, an analyst observed, "Shares in Peabody, the world's biggest private-sector coal company, have sunk 84 percent since 2010. Its debt has slipped to three rungs below investment grade. The company lost $525 million in 2013 and hemorrhaged $787 million in 2014."[188]

Peabody Coal's 2015 filing with the SEC signaled this, warning, "Divestment could significantly affect demand for our product."

This turned out to be a bit of an understatement. By July 1, 2015, Peabody Coal, which had traded at $60 a share in 2011, fell to $1.68.

In August 2015, Hunter Lovins called out the behavior of Peabody Coal and its marketing muscle, Berson Marsteller,[189] for mounting a campaign to get Bill Gates and Bjorn Lomborg to trumpet that coal was the answer to energy poverty.[190] It was thus gratifying to watch on April 13, 2016, as Peabody Coal, once the world's largest private sector coal company, filed for bankruptcy.[191]

In covering Peabody's demise, Bloomberg noted, "Recovery prospects for unsecured notes are poor."[192] This turned out to be true when the judge approving Peabody's exit from bankruptcy rewrote many longstanding legal provisions, including requirements that all classes of creditors be treated alike.[193] The deal, being challenged by investors left holding the sack, means that the CEO will net an estimated $15 million in stock bonuses, with $3 to $5 million each going to five other executives.[194]

As stated above, oil is not much safer. A *Financial Times* article from 2013 described the performance of international oil and gas companies as "lamentable from a shareholder perspective" over the past decade. Since June 2014, big oil has lost $200 billion.[195] According to Tom Sanzillo, who served as deputy comptroller of New York State, Exxon was, until the fall 2017 run-up in oil prices, borrowing to pay dividends.[196]

Goldman Sachs warned that nearly $1 trillion worth of oil projects in the US were effectively stranded, costing more to continue operation than any oil that might be recovered would be worth.[197] The study, which found that $930 billion worth of projects (more than two-thirds) would be unprofitable at Brent crude prices below $70, was conducted when oil prices were at $70 a barrel. Through much of 2017, they hung around $50. They will go up. It would surprise no one to see an attack on oil facilities that drive prices over $200 a barrel. Or sudden claims of oil curtailment. Day traders now make the same arguments that they did about coal before that crashed. But if the dynamics laid out above are at all right, it's not a market for amateur investors—like most of the people now owning oil stocks in their mutual funds.

Early in 2016, the consulting company Deloitte predicted that more than 35 percent of independent oil companies would go bankrupt, with another 30 percent to follow in 2017. This came on the heels of 50 North American extractors bankrupted in late 2015.[198]

Ernst and Young warned that 64 percent of the 365 oil and gas megaprojects they surveyed were over budget, with 74 percent behind schedule.[199]

The International Energy Agency, generally very conservative in such matters, warned the oil industry that more than $1.3 trillion in oil assets and another $300 billion in natural gas were at risk of being stranded as companies and countries move to clean energy.[200]

Mark Campanale recently warned that it's even worse: an October 2017 CitiGroup report calculated that if you count the foregone revenues from not digging up, selling, and burning all that fossil fuel, the looming loss is $100 trillion, or more than global GDP.[201]

It is essential that a just transition be found for the mining communities and all of the working people abandoned by fossil energy companies. In addition, resource extraction has massive impacts on the environment, but because of the complicity of regulators for decades, the companies have typically been allowed to self-bond for cleanup costs. Who will pay those, if the companies are gone? Peabody Coal, previously the world's biggest coal miner, is expected to default on its environmental obligations and on lease payments to various governments. Peabody was the fourth such company to crash, but it will not be the last.

Fossil companies are highly leveraged (which means that they owe a lot of debt). The high and rising costs of extraction mean that they borrow to punch new holes in the ground to find ever more oil, gas, and coal. If oil prices rise, it all works out, but if they don't...?

Nafeez Ahmed, in an article titled "This Could Be the Death of the Fossil Fuel Industry: Will the Rest of the Economy Go With It?" wrote,

> Oil and gas companies most at risk are those with the largest debt burden. And that burden is huge—as much as $2.5 trillion, according to *The Economist*. The real figure is probably higher.
>
> At a speech at the London School of Economics in February, Jaime Caruana of the Bank for International Settlements

said that outstanding loans and bonds for the oil and gas industry had almost tripled between 2006 and 2014 to a total
of $3 trillion.

This massive debt burden, he explained, has put the industry in a double-bind: In order to service the debt, they are
continuing to produce more oil for sale, but that only contributes to lower market prices. Decreased oil revenues means
less capacity to repay the debt, thus increasing the likelihood
of default.

This $3 trillion of debt is at risk because it was supposed
to generate a 3-to-1 increase in value, but instead—thanks to
the oil price decline—represents a value of less than half of
this.[202]

Ahmed concludes that, if oil company projects are rendered unprofitable, it would cut oil and gas extraction by eight percent of current
world demand, posing the risk of crashing the global economy. He
also shares the belief supported by an article in the journal *Applied
Energy* from a team at Oxford University's Institute for New Economic Thinking, "that the 'stranded assets' concept applies not just
to unburnable fossil fuel reserves, but also to a vast global carbon-
intensive electricity infrastructure, which could be rendered as defunct as the fossil fuels it burns and supplies to market."[203] This is
precisely the fate that befell the two big European utilities RWE and
Eon, described above.

Of course, the costs of continued fossil use are even higher. A
variety of studies going back to the *Stern Review* in 2006[204] found
that unmitigated climate change poses financial risks. Lord Nicolas
Stern, previously the chief economist of the World Bank, was commissioned by the government of the UK to consider the economic
impact of global warming on the global economy. In a data-rich
tome of 700 pages, Stern showed that approximately one percent
of global GDP will need to be invested to hold warming to below
4°C but that costs of failing to limit climate change would rise to

between 5 and 10 percent of world GDP. Clearly, he argued, there's a business case to act.

Deutsche Bank's 2013 study supported Stern. Following the release of the Intergovernmental Panel on Climate Change's Fifth Scientific Assessment, it observed,

> If governments do not implement policies that sufficiently reduce GHG emissions, this could reduce economic growth and increase volatility.... More and more potential investors now consider companies' sustainability risk management as part of their investment decisions. Sustainability rating used by investors are starting to ask questions about whether banks' own lending and financing leads to higher greenhouse gas emissions. Over the next two years, the financial sector will develop new tools to measure the emissions that arise from bank business activities.[205]

This is of particular concern to insurance companies, for several reasons. One, they are, at root, investment companies, seeking sufficient returns to pay claims from their policyholders over time. Insurance companies own large fossil holdings. With the risk to the solvency of these companies, this is of questionable wisdom.

Second, climate change worsens the risk of fire, floods, extreme weather, crop failure, and many other risks against which these companies insure. Bloomberg Briefs reported that insurance companies' refusal to consider these risks threatened the financial system.[206] A report from the Asset Owners Disclosure Project (AODP)[207] showed that only 14 of the 116 insurance companies surveyed are taking action to screen climate risk from their portfolios. Quoting the AODP chief executive Julien Poulter, Bloomberg reported,

> "Investors in insurance companies must start to care" about climate risk in insurers' investment portfolios, Poulter said. "I don't think it's any accident that [Bank of England governor] Mark Carney gave his speech last year on climate risk to the

insurance sector at the Lloyds of London event. If the insurance sector gets climate risk wrong, there is a financial stability problem for everybody."[208]

The Global Risk Institute agrees. Their 2016 report, *Climate Change: Why Financial Institutions Should Take Note*, warns that insurers now face annual losses of $50 billion from climate-change-driven weather events (increased from $10 billion a year over the past decade) as well as "transition risk" from a lower-carbon economy. It also urged banks to cut exposure from "high carbon industries" and other assets that may suffer from efforts to curb climate change, and "pursue new green opportunities in commercial and investment banking."[209]

A case in point is the recent fires in California. Severe drought, record winds, and high temperatures fanned the biggest wildfires ever in state history. Several appear to have been caused by failing utility company infrastructure. The California Public Utility Commission ruled that the utility at fault could not recover its costs, and liability for the fire, from its ratepayers. The CEO of San Diego Gas and Electric stated, "If these wildfires become the new normal, if these wildfires become endemic and part of the effects of climate change day in and day out, I don't think it's sustainable for utilities to afford that on a long-term basis."[210]

A month prior, that is precisely what Governor Jerry Brown said, calling California's fire situation "the new normal. California is burning up. The fire season is not a couple of months in the summer; it's virtually year-round."

The year 2017 was only the third-hottest on record, but climate-change–driven impacts set a new record for devastating, and expensive, "natural" disasters, with almost a third of a trillion dollars in damages.[211]

Investing in a Finer Future

Milton Friedman famously admonished that the "social responsibility of business is to increase its profits."[212] Throughout history, there have been corporate leaders who have rejected this fixation on profit maximization, but they have been a minority. In the late days of the presidency of George W. Bush, the US Department of Labor issued a guidance to discourage investors managing employee pension funds from considering environmental and social factors in the companies and funds in which they invest.[213]

Churches and other moral leaders ignored this. In the 1960s, they had begun to refuse to own so-called sin stocks: weapons, tobacco, alcohol, and what they saw as companies producing degenerate products. Even they believed that such a philosophy, while noble, was going to result in lower returns on investment. Professional investors just thought it was foolish. Why mix the work of making money with Sunday school?

But a funny thing happened on the way to the counting house: investors who blended money and morality outperformed the market. It turns out that companies that fail to respect people and the planet are a risky business.

Early in the 21st century, a group of investors and sustainability experts convened Bottomline 2001 in San Francisco. They invited several of the largest institutional investors to consider whether there might be a business case for shifting their investments to more sustainable options.[214]

Pension funds have substantial resources. OECD estimates that in 2013 institutional investors held $92.6 trillion in assets. In contrast, the 34 countries that comprise OECD have $47.3 trillion in GDP. Exxon-Mobil's capitalization was only $334 billion.[215] Traditionally, pension funds invested their money without any particular concern for social and environmental criteria, despite the fact that the invested money came from constituencies such as workers, teachers, churches, charitable organizations, and educational institutions who often are value-driven.

The neoliberal belief held that portfolios screened to exclude any class of investments must underperform financially, because they, by definition, are not playing with a full deck. Adherents say that trustees have a fiduciary duty to earn the highest possible return over the short term; therefore, it would be irresponsible to limit their investment options.

But what if it's not true that screened investments always under-perform? What if they often outperform less socially conscious companies? When presented with the business case for behaving more sustainably, the pension fund managers and state and munici-pal treasurers who attended Bottomline 2001 began to redefine their fiduciary responsibility and, as a result, reorient their portfolios.

Such speakers as the treasurer of California, the chair of Califor-nia Public Employees Retirement System, one of the world's largest pension funds, and many other representatives from institutional investors generally agreed that their funds must, by definition, be invested for the long-term success and overall sustained upturn of the entire economy. They agreed that it matters little to a pension fund if one company does well in the short term, especially if it does so at the expense of natural and human capital, the health of which underlies the health of the economy. Pension funds are so large that they are invested in essentially every large company in the economy. Further, unlike day traders, next quarter's profits do them little good. What matters to them is ensuring that the whole of the economy is healthy in 20 years, when they will be paying out the pensions for which they are investing the money today. These investors realized that they may turn out to be the institutions with the greatest vested interest in sustainability.[216]

They were right. The US Forum for Sustainable and Responsible Investment (US SIF) now states,

> The past 25 years have shown that environmental, social and governance (ESG) factors can affect shareholder value and corporate and investment portfolio risk and return, discredit-ing the longstanding perception that fiduciary duty precludes consideration of ESG criteria in institutional investment decisions. In 2005, international law firm Freshfields, Bruck-haus, Deringer found, after examining fiduciary law in nine developed markets, including the United States, that, "the links between ESG factors and financial performance are in-creasingly being recognized. On that basis, integrating ESG

considerations into an investment analysis so as to more reliably predict financial performance is clearly permissible and is arguably required in all jurisdictions."[217]

Two years later, Bob Massie, founder of Ceres, one of the most effective groups working to get institutional investors to become active in countering climate change, created the Investor Network on Climate Risk.[218] Mindy Lubber, his successor at Ceres, has worked tirelessly to engage 120 institutional investors (with assets of more than $14 trillion) in countering climate change and all other forms of unsustainability. Her Clean Trillion initiative seeks to close the investment gap between what is spent on clean energy and what is needed to protect the climate.

In 2007, Mindy and former California Public Employees' Retirement System chief investment officer Russell Read organized investors with $1.2 trillion in assets to petition the Securities and Exchange Commission (SEC) to issue guidance on how companies should report their risks from climate change.[219] More than 100 investors with $7.6 trillion supported the effort. In 2010, the SEC issued such a guidance, and climate reporting became mainstream.

In 2016, the Department of Labor repealed its anti-responsibility bulletin, stating,

> Environmental, social, and governance issues may have a direct relationship to the economic value of the plan's investment. In these instances, such issues are not merely collateral considerations or tie-breakers, but rather are proper components of the fiduciary's primary analysis of the economic merits of competing investment choices.[220]

This happened in part because socially responsible impact investing (SRI) is the fastest-growing investment field. The US SIF reported,

> Assets managed using strategies that consider environmental, social and governance (ESG) issues in investment analysis, portfolio selection or shareholder engagement totaled $6.57

trillion at the start of 2014. This represented one out of every six dollars under professional management in the United States and growth of 76 percent over 2012.[221]

By early 2016, global sustainable investment assets had reached $22.89 trillion, a 25 percent increase from 2014.[222] This shift is itself changing how business is done. The US SIF found that SRI investors have created four key impacts. They have

+ changed the investment industry and investors
+ influenced companies through active ownership and engagement strategies
+ assisted communities
+ achieved progress on various environmental, social, and governance issues by influencing public policy and by supporting the development of US and global organizations to promote sustainable investment[223]

The importance of SRI is reflected in the statistic that 73 percent of all investment managers globally use ESG criteria for making investment decisions.[224]

The stranded assets discussion above brings even greater urgency for investors to ensure that the companies in which they are placing their faith and their money are taking sustainability seriously.

As Chris Davis, the senior program director at the sustainability consultancy Ceres, puts it, "If climate trashes the economy, they're not going to be able to meet their pension-fund obligations."[225]

Ellen Dorsey, the executive director of the Wallace Global Foundation, created the "Divest–Invest" movement to enable investors to begin voting with their dollars.[226] Asking what she could do after the 2009 failure of the UNFCCC Climate Summit in Copenhagen, Dorsey shifted her foundation's endowment away from fossil fuels and into clean investments, pointing out, "If you own fossil, you own climate change."

In the cold and rain in November 2012, Bill McKibben, who had helped call global attention to the issue of stranded assets, boarded a bus to tour the US on what he called the "Do the Math Tour."[227]

Using his *Rolling Stone* article, he toured almost every corner of the country, speaking at sold-out shows on college campuses, calling on students to protect their future by demanding that their college endowments divest of ownership of fossil companies.

No one gave him a prayer of success.[228]

But a funny thing happened on the way to the bank. Thousands of people started calling for a fossil-free future. Divestment started to catch on. The University of Oxford's Stranded Assets Programme's report concluded, "Divestment outflows, even when relatively meagre in the first wave of divestment, can significantly and permanently depress stock price of a target firm if they trigger a change in market norms."[229]

In early 2015, the movement got international support from Alan Rusbridger, the courageous and visionary chief editor of the *Guardian*. Alan called an array of advisors to his office overlooking the Regent's Canal and asked how the newspaper might be most effective in the fight against climate catastrophe in the run-up to the Paris Summit. After extensive consultations, he launched a Guardian campaign to Keep It In the Ground, calling for divestment by such entities as the Gates Foundation and the Wellcome Trust.[230]

Values-oriented investors heard the call and began pulling their money out of the fossil industry. Ordinary investors began to realize that the economic fundamentals of the fossil industry had turned against them.

Fossil fuel divestment scaled rapidly. In September, organizations with $2.6 trillion in assets under management had joined the divestment movement.

Prior to the 2016 Paris Summit, activists announced that holders of $3.4 trillion in assets had pledged to divest from coal or other fossil fuels. Shortly after, 70 new institutions joined. By the end of 2016, Arabella Advisors reported,[231]

> To date, 688 institutions and 58,399 individuals across 76 countries have committed to divest from fossil fuel companies, doubling the value of assets represented in the last 15 months. Pension funds and insurance companies now represent the

largest sectors committing to divestment, reflecting increased financial and fiduciary risks of holding fossil fuels in a world committed to stay below 2°Celsius warming.[232]

The increase comes, in part, from evidence that fossil-free portfolios have outperformed fossil-heavy ones.[233] FTSE's North American fossil-fuel–free index has consistently outperformed the conventional benchmark index.[234] MSCI, a stock market index company, found that fossil-free funds have earned a higher return than conventional ones over five years.[235]

Norway recently announced that it is considering divesting of ownership in fossil industries.[236] BNP Paribas, the large French bank, sold its holdings in a tar sands pipeline.[237]

On November 7, 2017, the little company Change Finance[238] rang the opening bell in the New York Stock Exchange on Wall Street as 3.5 million eyeballs watched the launch of the first truly fossil-free exchange traded fund.[239] For the price of a pizza, ordinary individuals can now invest in companies that are not subject to the looming fossil risk.

The death knell of fossil investing came a bit more than a month later when the governor of New York and the city comptroller of New York City both announced a freeze on fossil investments and proposals to divest their collective $390 billion from fossil fuel companies and reinvest in renewable energy. Bill McKibben wrote,

> The dam has broken: after years of great activism, New York has taken a massive step towards divesting from fossil fuels. Coming from the capital of world finance, this will resonate loud and clear all over the planet. It's a crucial sign of how fast the financial pendulum is swinging away from fossil fuels.[240]

Funding the New Energy Economy

Christiana Figueres is the wickedly bright, inspirational leader of the UN's Framework Convention on Climate Change who masterminded the success in delivering an internationally binding accord to limit global warming in Paris in 2015. Now head of Mission 2020,[241] she has stated, "Where capital goes over the next 15 years is going to decide whether we're actually able to address climate change and what kind of a century we are going to have."[242]

How money is invested—whether by companies, by colleges, or by you—determines whether we trash the planet or save it. What you do with your money *does* make a difference.

In 2015, investors from around the world poured $348 billion into clean energy, a new record,[243] up from $60 billion a year in 2004.[244] The amount invested fell 18 percent in 2016, in part because falling costs of renewables meant that more could be built for less money. Acquisition of clean energy companies rose, however, to $117 billion, up from $97 billion in 2015.[245]

The report *Carbon Clean 200: Investing in a Clean Energy Future*[246] declared that the 200 leading clean energy companies returned triple the profits of fossil fuel companies in the last ten years.[247]

Again, new business models are being created. Green bonds (debt instruments offered to raise money to finance clean energy and other green initiatives) more than doubled from $93.4 billion in 2016 to an expected $208 billion in 2017, according to the rating firm Moody's doubling the record set in 2016.[248] China was responsible for a third of this, an amount that is expected to rise as the country seeks to fund a proposed $308 billion in projects to cut air pollution, meet its climate targets, and ensure abundant energy for prosperity.

The market has grown by 163 percent a year since 2011, with consecutive issuance records every year from 2013 to 2017. Created initially by the European Investment Bank in 2007, they are now being used by a variety of nations[249] and such states as Connecticut and New York, who have created green banks. Apple issued a billion dollar green bond to finance its efficiency and renewable projects after the US announced its withdrawal from the Paris Accord.[250] The bonds are being joined by such green money-market securities as short-term commercial paper and preferred stock, structured as securitized transactions.

As impressive as this is, it represents a small part of the $6.7 trillion a year global debt market. And it is miniscule compared to $44 trillion that the International Energy Agency projects needs to be spent on energy deployment by 2040.[251]

Still, remember the logic of exponential growth that Kurzweil described above. The green bonds market grew by 42 percent in the first quarter of 2017, with more than $20 billion offered in the first three months. This is almost seven times the amount offered in the entire year in 2012.[252]

What Can You Do?

For starters, figure out where *your* money is. It appears unwise to have any of your assets in the industries that will be disrupted. Bevis Longstreth, former Securities and Exchange Commissioner, observed, "It is entirely plausible, even predictable, that continuing to hold equities in fossil fuel companies will be ruled negligence."[253]

Think about where your energy comes from. Are you dependent on an industry that is at risk? Are you part of the millions of people, communities, and cities that are implementing renewables?

Is your job at risk? Companies either will become part of the solution or they will face stiff headwinds. The emerging industries are creating millions of jobs, but millions are at risk. Figuring out how to deal with this is discussed more in section 4, but it's time to begin discussing it in your community. Will we "entrepreneur" our way to a well-being economy? Will we substitute a universal basic income? Will we descend into unimaginable darkness? Or will we create a Finer Future?[254]

What is increasingly clear is that we will totally transform the global economy. The crises we face, and the inevitabilities of change described here, *will* drive change.

The change is here. How will you change to deal with it?

Standing at the bottom of any S curve of adoption of a new technology, it may seem impossible to get there from here.

When change comes, however, looking back, it will seem inevitable and incredibly rapid.

The speed with which renewable energy, especially solar, is grow-ing means we have a shot at solving the climate crisis, creating jobs, reinvigorating manufacturing, and buying the time needed to do the more fundamental work of implementing a Regenerative Economy. Let's return the energy sector to nature's principles. Nature runs on sunlight, not huge flows of fossil energy. We can too.

Systemic Change: Policies to Get Us Out of the Mess

Now the hard work begins. We know that a different world is possible. It's emergent in many communities, initiatives, and struggles around the world.

We know the basic shape of the regenerative principles that must guide the world we want to create. To get there, however, institutions around the world must commit to the three outcomes:

1. Enable all people to achieve a flourishing life within ecological limits;
2. Deliver universal well-being as we meet the basic needs of all humans; and
3. Deliver sufficient equality to maintain social stability and provide the basis for genuine security.[2]

This section addresses the policy changes that can implement these three. It takes the conversation from technical possibilities into the political transformations necessary to ensure that the tectonic changes coming at us are managed in ways that deliver well-being and ecological integrity for everyone. It starts with policies that nations can implement to address inequality and provide

> Until you dig a hole, you plant a tree, you water it and make it survive, you haven't done a thing. You are just talking.
>
> WANGARI MAATHAI[1]

lives of dignity within planetary boundaries. It shifts, then, to policies that can be implemented at the regional, state, and local levels. It concludes with actions that you can take yourself.

The solutions described can move us deliberately back below the planetary boundaries and begin to meet the needs of everyone on Earth. All are feasible. All have been or are being implemented somewhere on Earth. Achieving them universally, however, will require communities, companies, and governments to act in ways not often seen.

In a pre-collapse situation, foresight and focus on global common good seem utopian. But in the post-collapse scenario, the pessimists are predicting, it may not be possible. The time to act is now, however daunting the odds.

Concerted pressure by informed citizens asserting a compelling new story about how we can live better lives that don't cost the Earth is the first step. But citizens alone cannot implement the necessary changes. We are going to have to rededicate ourselves to creating functional institutions of government.

The three goals above will not be achieved by a minor change of course. If we are going to move to a better economic system, it will require a shift in values, incentives, institutions, and the distribution of power on this planet.

We must rebuild trust in government. The neoliberal narrative that tells us that markets are perfect and government intervention always drives bad outcomes is precisely the view that has created the challenges chronicled in chapter 1. In the decades to come, humanity will have to grapple with climate change, migration, joblessness, and inequality. The market has demonstrated that it cannot fix these problems alone.

It is beyond debate that market forces are powerful. That said, how should they be managed? Market forces can play a vital role in bringing about the new economic system for which humanity hungers. There is a strong business case for companies to behave more responsibly. But markets will need to operate within a different set of values and incentives than advocated by those who prefer unfettered free trade. A Finer Future requires intelligent public intervention.

Neoliberal mythology aside, there *are* no free markets. Classical economists identified at least 18 aspects that they say characterize free markets. None are present in what we call markets today.[3] For example, market theory assumes that all actors have perfect information. Was this ever true? There are assumed to be no barriers to entry or to exit. There must be equitable access to capital. Few assumptions could be further from the truth today.

Power imbalances determine whether economic access is equitable or not. Players who enter markets with more power than the others tend to emerge with more economic gain. In *The Wealth of Nations* and again in *The Theory of Moral Sentiments*, Adam Smith was clear that markets serve the common good only when no buyers or sellers have enough power to affect market outcomes and when all players are moral actors. Seriously?! In most markets, neither of these conditions exists. Antitrust policies, however poorly implemented by nations, are nonexistent at the international level. Digital platforms like Facebook, Apple, Amazon, Netflix, and Google (called FAANG) are creating powerful new international monopolies that drive "winner takes all" outcomes, economically and, increasingly, politically.[4]

Market ideologues argue that even policies to address monopolies constitute interference with the free operation of the market. But without them, markets cease to be anything but a cruel fraud. When companies become more powerful than most nations, change is urgently needed. Those who believe in the future of capitalism need the policies below. Unless we reduce national and international inequality, control monopolies and oligopolies, and ensure that we live within the Earth's means, capitalism itself is at risk.

Zealotry about the evil of regulations serves us badly. What one set of players labels burdensome regulations are precisely what another, typically less powerful, set calls "protection."

Regulations to ensure the fair operation of markets are particularly important when vital public services are at stake. Industries like public health and air traffic control should be managed strategically through incentives, ownership structure, and/or regulation to ensure that companies serve the public interest. Ball bearing factories and local restaurant operation, by contrast, need little management outside of rules to ensure fair employment and health and safety.

It is important to remember that markets are a human construct, not economic black boxes. We built them; therefore, it is not out of order to ask that markets serve us all. The fight over this has raged for years and is in no danger of ending any time soon, but the prior chapters make two things clear:

- Unfettered markets have not served the interests of anyone but the richest one percent of people.
- Markets can be overseen effectively to benefit both people and the planet.

Well-managed markets will empower the new narrative of an economy in service to life, but we should recognize that our creations of the past are no longer fit for purpose.

The best businesses already operate on this basis. When Paul Polman, CEO of Unilever, rejected a lucrative offer from corporate raiders to take over his company, he replied that his obligation was not to owners but to the world as a whole.[5] "Do you run this for society or not?" Paul queried, answering, "The real purpose of business has always been to come up with solutions."[6] It is urgent that citizens demand the same responsibility from their governments.

This section discusses many of the policies needed and gives examples of where they are being implemented. Chapter 11 discusses the growing disparities in wealth and income that must be reversed. Chapter 12 describes how we can ensure that every person has enough to sustain basic health and dignity. Thirteen confronts the myth of growth. Fourteen looks at how we can shift the values that underlie the economic system. Chapter 15 discusses the need to reform national and international governance. Finally, 16 discusses what cities and local government can do, with or without national and international governance reform. It hands the reins to you.

CHAPTER ELEVEN

LEVEL THE PLAYING FIELD

*I am influenced more than ever before
by the conviction that social equality
is the only basis for human happiness.*

NELSON MANDELA[1]

What You Need to Know About Inequality

Income Inequality (in country)

The basic numbers on inequality make clear the threat that it poses. But inequality is both a global phenomenon and often a very local one.

Inequality is measured in the international system by what are called Gini coefficients.[2] Zero shows perfect equality, and 1 shows perfect inequality. In less equal regions, the Gini ratio ranges between 0.45 and 0.60. In 2010, the Gini coefficients for the UK and US were 0.36 and 0.37 respectively. Relatively equal countries such as Denmark, Sweden, and Norway have Gini coefficients of around 0.25.[3]

Data for 141 countries shows that income inequality, again measured by the Gini coefficient, has increased since 1990 most in Eastern Europe and the former Soviet Union, as well as Asia and Africa. Sub-Saharan Africa remains highly unequal: its Gini ratio has worsened almost five points on average. It declined significantly in Latin America after 2000. Driven by the spread of the neoliberal agenda and the global influence of its proponents like Ronald Reagan and Margaret Thatcher, approximately two-thirds of countries for which there is available Gini data experienced an increase in income inequality between 1990 and 2005. The income gap between the wealthiest and poorest 10 percent of income earners increased in 70 percent of countries.

Levels of wealth inequality inside of countries are harder to decipher because of a combination of tax avoidance by those at the top of the wealth spectrum and the lack of comprehensive tax systems in some developing countries. However, where data is available, it is clear that wealth is far less equally distributed than income. For example, in Vietnam, while the income Gini coefficient is 0.37, the wealth Gini is 0.68.

Even in the US, one of the richest nations on Earth, the top 1 percent now owns half of all assets,[4] while the bottom 40 percent have essentially no net worth.[5] More than half of Americans have less than $1,000 in savings and checking accounts. Almost a quarter have less than $100.[6] This situation was created by 30 years of neoliberal policies to cut taxes for the rich "to increase economic growth." Instead it redistributed $2 trillion annually from the bottom 99 percent to the 1 percent.[7]

The situation is worsened by a tax system that allows the rich to hire accountants and lawyers to dodge obligations. In 2012, the US top 400 earners paid an average tax rate of 17 percent on average incomes of $336 million.[8] The 2017 tax law will deliver 90 percent of the gains to the richest 20 percent.[9] Such financial power also enables these individuals to have disproportionate political influence. In the first nine months of the 2016 US presidential election, 158 families donated one-half of the money given to candidates for president. The *New York Times* identified them as "overwhelmingly white, rich, older and male."[10]

Global Inequality (across all countries)

The top one percent of the world's population enjoys more than half of global income.[11] But who are the one percent? Actually, you are, if you make a bit more than $32,000 a year (30,250 euros, 2 million Indian rupees, or 223,000 Chinese yuan). That's because so much of the world lives on essentially no income at all.

In terms of total wealth, though, not just income equality, you'd have to own $770,000 to be in the one percent. That's because the uber-rich really do have one hell of a lot of wealth.[12]

There has been some good news. Total global wealth rose 6.4 percent in 2017, considerably better than the 3.9 percent growth of wealth in 2016. On top of that, rising levels of income and falling poverty in China helped create what looks like a convergence in global incomes. However, if the data is not weighted by population (China, which has so many people, makes any gain in reducing income inequality seem large statistically), any reduction in disparity between rich and poor countries vanishes. And almost all of the income and wealth increases went to the richest. In 2017, the wealthiest of the world got $1 trillion richer, four times the increase the year before.[13]

Overall, estimates suggest a current global Gini coefficient (among all people in the world) of 0.65, with 85 percent of this amount due to differences among countries. Remember, the goal is to get closer to zero than to one.

It is hard to be specific about a level of equality that would be needed in order to deliver social stability. However, an economy that enables people to thrive within planetary limits should at least aim for a level of global income equality equal to that currently achieved by the US or UK (0.36 and 0.37, respectively). Even there, the perception of worsening disparities in both countries is blamed for both Brexit and Trump. Obviously, Nordic levels of under 0.30 is a better target.[14]

Again, the HANDY study made clear that tackling inequality is not just "good to have." It is necessary to avoid collapse. Expert consensus could not be clearer: economic inequality has a corrosive effect on health, social cohesion, economic growth, education, and crime. Without narrowing the gap between the richest and poorest in our societies, other attempts to fight poverty and stabilize the environment will be fatally undermined. The report *Reducing Economic Inequality as a Sustainable Development Goal*,[15] by Faiza Shaheen of the UK's New Economics Foundation, showed that tackling economic inequality is not a by-product of fighting poverty and climate change—it is key to achieving them.

Only by creating a more equal world by 2030, can we hope to

+ maintain social stability;
+ have societies resilient enough to adapt to climate and other environmental shocks without collapse;
+ address extreme poverty and meet the basic needs of humankind without requiring unstable levels of growth, and
+ avoid excessive and unstable consumption, fueled by debt, which is caused by status competition in unequal societies.

Living within planetary boundaries will almost certainly result in a lower overall global growth rate. The trouble with this prescription is that, so far in human history, the only way to reduce poverty has entailed economic growth.[16] Work by Peter Edward and Andy Sumner shows that extreme poverty could be significantly reduced by 2030, but, they argue, current inequality trends coupled with low growth would lock 1.3 billion people into extreme poverty (according to the metric of earning less than US $1.25 a day).[17] Even more shocking, low growth combined with current inequality levels would

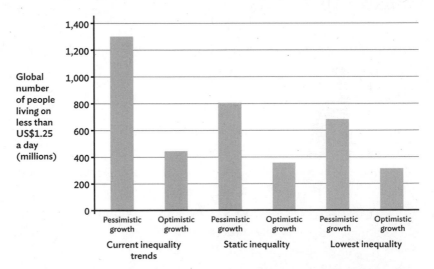

Credit: NEF report b.3cdn.net/nefoundation/226c9ea56ee0c9e510_gqm6b 9zpz.pdf

imply locking 2.5 billion people on the planet—more than today—into living on less than $2.00 per day.

Conversely, low growth combined with low inequality could halve extreme poverty levels. Redistribution is thus vital to achieve poverty reduction in the low-growth world, which is vital to human survival.

Perversely, inequality also drives excess consumption. The New Economics Foundation argues that economic inequality is a driver of resource depletion through the way it encourages unnecessary consumption. Economist Robert Frank from Cornell University and others have observed that, in an unequal society, individuals feel increasingly drawn to purchase goods and, in particular, luxury items to signal their status in society. Frank has written extensively about how income and wealth at the top have set off "expenditure cascades" that cause overconsumption and rising levels of household debt. According to one Nobel prize-winning economist, "Trickle-down economics may be a chimera, but trickle-down behaviourism is very real."[18]

Addressing Inequality

If analysts like Jeremy Grantham, whose assertion, described above, that the era of economic growth is over, are correct, it is unlikely that the world will see dramatic economic growth with large surpluses to distribute. Without this, redistribution is the only way to reduce inequality within the rich world and from the rich world to the poor world. Unless the rich world helps poorer countries meet the basic needs of their citizens, major social unrest/conflict will ensue.

A recent report by the New Economics Foundation showed that economic inequality is corroding both society and democracy. It described both the vicious cycle that causes inequality and the virtuous cycle that can reduce it. The report focused on inequality in a rich country (the UK), but its principles apply across most countries.

The report identified five critical intervention areas:

+ Access to education, health services, and other vital public services as well as access to childcare, particularly for women.

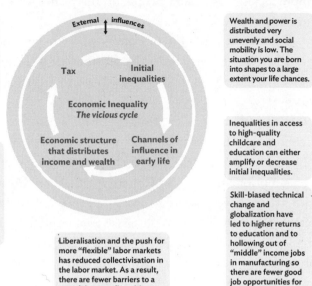

Currently taxation does little to mitigate the unequal outcomes of the economic system and feeds into initial inequalities of the next generation.

Together, skill-biased technical change, globalisation, financialisation and liberalisation have led to a falling wage share, fewer decent jobs and growing wealth accumulation at the top.

External ↕ influences

Tax

Initial inequalities

Economic Inequality
The vicious cycle

Economic structure that distributes income and wealth

Channels of influence in early life

Wealth and power is distributed very unevenly and social mobility is low. The situation you are born into shapes to a large extent your life chances.

Inequalities in access to high-quality childcare and education can either amplify or decrease initial inequalities.

Skill-biased technical change and globalization have led to higher returns to education and to hollowing out of "middle" income jobs in manufacturing so there are fewer good job opportunities for those with vocational skills in high-income countries.

Liberalisation and the push for more "flexible" labor markets has reduced collectivisation in the labor market. As a result, there are fewer barriers to a growth in wage disparities.

The vicious cycle of economic inequality: *Addressing Economic Inequality at Root*. Credit: NEF, b.3cdn.net/nefoundation/95d3ace05149504890_vcm6i wxrv.pdf

+ Increasing wage shares and building skills.
+ Provision of good jobs/livelihoods.
+ Progressive, fair, and unavoidable taxation schemes that support productive activity and a fair distribution of economic power.
+ Providing a basic income to those who need it most, like maybe all of us.[19]

The first three address what is called "*pre*-distribution" (enabling poorer people to meet their needs without spending their limited money, or enabling them to get more money through wages), while the fourth area is a classic redistribution strategy (shifting money to the poor from the rich). The need for the fifth is becoming increasingly obvious.

Tax
A tax system which is progressive, fair and unavoidable and which supports productive activity and a fair distribution of economic power.

A target to reduce inequality, with publication of semi-annual inequality indicators alongside Gross Domestic Product estimates.

Good jobs strategy
Realisation of the right to a good job for everyone economy-wide that pays enough to live on, that has decent terms and conditions and that contributes to local economies and society in a sustainable way.

Public funding is committed to a full employment guarantee assuring well-designed jobs training opportunities.

Fair, efficient taxation of income and wealth

INSTITUTIONS
Social partnership
Department of Labour
State investment bank
Local governance
HMRC

Good jobs strategy

High-quality universal childcare

Decent wages and working conditions

Childcare
Universal provision of high-quality childcare that ensures availability to all children and their families on an equal basis regardless of location, employment or income status.

Wages and working conditions
Increase in the wage share of Gross Domestic Product and narrowing of the distribution of earnings across the workforce to avoid excess at the top and insufficient wages at the bottom.

Building skills and progression pathways with access to valued careers, not just jobs, via vocational as well as graduate routes, with a balance of responsibility for lifelong formal, informal and on-the-job skills development between individuals, employers and the state.

The virtuous cycle of action for tackling economic inequality at root. Credit. NEF, b.3cdn.net/nefoundation/95d3ace05149504890_vcm6iwxrv.pdf

The virtuous cycle that these interventions would create is shown above.

Universal Provision of High-quality Childcare That Is Affordable for All

High-quality childcare can create life opportunities for children and help to address unequal starting points. Making it equally available and affordable to all families also gives parents more choices about balancing their working lives and families' needs.

Policy priorities should include public funding supporting the supply of childcare in order to cap family childcare expenditure at 15 percent of income; increased standards of training and qualifications to ensure that childcare is always high-quality; and better working conditions for childcare workers, including a living wage, stable contract hours, and career and pay progression opportunities.

In Boulder, Colorado, the non-profit Bringing School Home works with the local public housing authority and the school system to ensure that children living in public housing get the educational advantages that children in wealthier homes get. By creating extended day and weekend schooling in the public housing, they have enabled 93 percent of participants to graduate from high school, compared to 63 percent of their public housing peers who lack the program. This breaks the cycle of poverty into which lower-income children are often locked.[20]

Such programs are common in Europe, with Finland now recognized as a world leader in education reform.[21]

Narrow the Difference Between Top-to-bottom Earnings and Rebuild the Link Between Economic Prosperity and Wages

Over time, the proportion of economic prosperity shared out as wages in countries like the UK and the US has shrunk in favor of shareholder profits. Within this smaller share of money going as salaries, wages for ordinary workers have fallen while pay at the top has sky-rocketed.

Recent studies have shown that executives in the US earn 204 times what an average worker makes.[22] One found that average CEO pay across all companies was $13.8 million. Average median pay for workers was under $78,000. Obviously minimum wage workers make far less. The highest pay ratio was 1,951 to one. Concerted action to restore wages and shrink the income gap would create a healthier economy and address the needs of the working poor.

A striking example of cutting inequality through pre-distribution is the effect on inequality of increasing the minimum wage. Brazil's minimum wage rose by nearly 50 percent in real terms between 1993 and 2011, in line with a decline in poverty and inequality.

To shrink the income gap, workers need to have a real voice in workplace decision-making. Departments of labor need to be tasked with restoring wages in the economy, improving working conditions, and ensuring workers' rights to organize. A stronger wage floor should eliminate in-work poverty. Pay ratio reporting to make wage differentials transparent needs to be enforced.

Access to Valued Careers for All with
Opportunities for Progression and Skills Development

Everyone should have the right to a well-paid, secure, and meaningful job, if they want one.

Young people without a degree are often funneled into low-paid, dead-end jobs with little or no prospects of future progression. Addressing the lack of investment in training and development for staff and managers would broaden opportunities for purposeful and rewarding work.

Neoliberals believe that Homo economicus works simply because man (and such treatises generally refer only to men) must earn a living.

Anyone who has ever lost a job, however, knows that work means far more than just earning our keep.

The utility-maximization theory of work ignores what the psychologists, social psychologists, and sociologists tell us about the real reasons we all get up in the morning and go to work.[23] The book *Man Enough* explains:

> Work keeps us busy. It gives us structure, it defines us as functioning, contributing, worthwhile citizens. It makes us part of the team, a community of fellow workers—even if we do our work in isolation. If we feel work bringing us closer to our fellow workers or to the human community, we can feel pride and joy in our work, feel mutual emulation with all other workers, and feel ourselves the equal to any man.[24]

A regenerative economy will enable all people to create meaningful purpose, as well as sufficient livelihoods.

Companies and governments should combine training investments by sector. They should invest in incentive structures to improve high-quality management skills at different levels. Government support is needed to ensure that apprenticeship schemes lead to progression at work across more industries. Obviously, there is a need for better education, training, and employment links at the local level, especially in jobs that are not vulnerable to automation.

National industrial strategies are essential to guide policy in how to deal with this challenge. The digital economy will require schemes to ensure lifelong learning. A government investment bank with a regional focus can provide funding for better jobs and training to support full employment. Companies will need to ensure that workers have a collective voice in such programs.

Most jobs are created by startups.

Ashok Khosla's[25] Development Alternatives has demonstrated an alternative to job creation by conventional capital-intensive approaches. These entail raising finance, often from foreign investors, and producing goods to be sold elsewhere, while destroying local jobs and eroding the environmental resource base. In 1991, the government of India bought the neoliberal argument that socialist ideas led to balance of payments issues. They "liberalized" the economy by privatizing many sectors and opening the borders for trade, hoping to accelerate growth rates above the previous one to two percent. But such a system led to elimination of jobs, increasing disparities, and growing corruption.

From 1991 to 2011, the number of jobs created by formal industry went down from 10.5 million to 9.5 million per year. The big companies were net job destroyers. Most jobs, up to 80 percent in some economies, are created and sustained by small companies and startups.

This, by the way, is true in most places. In the US, the Kauffman Foundation found that, in every year from 1977 until 2013, the large companies were net job destroyers. Only small companies and startups were net job creators.[26]

Ashok explains this by observing that big companies do not like people: people make demands and increase costs. So these companies de-create jobs. Even if big companies wanted to be part of the job creation solution, he argues, the capital investment needed in big industry to create a workplace is prohibitive. The cost of creating one job in 2010 ranged from $600,000 in India to $900,000 in the US to over $1 million in Japan. In India, he says, creating the jobs needed would require capital that exceeds the nation's GDP many times over.

In fairness, figures for job creation are all over the map. One estimate of job creation cost for the Obama-era stimulus package was $90,000 per job.[27] The American Enterprise Institute estimated the cost for the same job created at $4.1 million.[28]

Ashok argues that we need to create jobs much more affordably and ensure that they last. Smaller companies do this because they avoid the costly use of capital.

Development Alternatives is creating jobs that require investments as low as $1,000 to $5,000 by developing labor-intensive mini-industries in villages and small towns that produce goods and services for the basic needs of local consumers. They design industries to respond to needs and set up local companies to do this, each employing 5 to 50 people, who now have jobs with dignity. The total investment for an industrial plant ranges from $20,000 to $80,000. Each industry is profitable, so the jobs endure.

Jobs created in low-cost-of-living communities at, say, an investment of $2,000, Ashok says, deliver a greater increase in economic and social well-being than a job created at three times the cost in a big city where they also pay a heavy toll in loss of identity, relationships, and culture. Development Alternatives has impacted the lives of millions of people in many ways, including enabling—empowering—them to gain livelihoods and jobs, improve lives, and create opportunities. As reported by an independent evaluation by a British government-supported project to empower households, the numbers and scale of impact on the ground can be very significant.

The current jobs market is unbalanced, both in terms of geography and job quality. We need to invest in good, environmentally sustainable jobs in all countries of the world. Entrepreneur Gunther Pauli's book, *Blue Economy*, profiles the work he has done to "shift society from scarcity to abundance 'with what is locally available,' by tackling issues that cause environmental and related problems in new ways." He cites 200 innovations creating 3 million jobs out of $4 billion in profitable investments.[29]

Similarly, Unreasonable Impact offers accelerators for early-stage entrepreneurs. In their first year, they have worked with 46 ventures with almost $430 million in revenues, almost a trillion in financing, to impact more than 100 million lives.[30]

Unless we succeed at job creation, some form of universal basic income or jobs guarantee will be essential.

A Fairer, More Progressive Tax System

When direct and indirect taxes are taken into account, those with low incomes are hit too hard, while billions of dollars each year are lost through tax avoidance and evasion at the top.[31] Progressive tax reform would help to address inequality at its root. It would also give governments the means to redistribute economic power.

Effective tax and transfer systems are important tools for redistribution, as shown by the effect of taxation and investment by governments in 40 countries in the OECD and Latin America/Caribbean. Finland and Austria, for instance, halved income inequality, using market mechanisms, thanks to progressive and effective taxation accompanied by wise social spending.

Legislation and resources will be needed to abolish tax avoidance and evasion. The Panama Papers showed that billions of dollars are being shielded from national taxation, not only by Mafia figures and organized criminals but by 12 national leaders and 143 politicians, so far.[32] In the wake of the scandal, thousands of tax evasion cases are working their way through the courts, including investigations of several heads of state.[33]

Countries that wish to avoid inequality-driven collapse will have to implement and co-ordinate more progressive income and wealth taxes. A land value tax would also help. Finally, as mentioned above, governments should shift the tax burden onto environmentally unfriendly activities through green taxes, cutting taxes on income and employment and increasing them on resource extraction and pollution.

Providing a Basic Income to Those Who Need It Most

Buckminster Fuller famously said,

> We should do away with the absolutely specious notion that everybody has to earn a living. It is a fact today that one in ten thousand of us can make a technological breakthrough capable of supporting all the rest. The youth of today are absolutely right in recognizing this nonsense of earning a living. We keep inventing jobs because of this false idea that everybody has to be employed at some kind of drudgery because, according to Malthusian Darwinian theory he must justify his right to exist. So we have inspectors of inspectors and people making instruments for inspectors to inspect inspectors. The true business of people should be to go back to school and think about whatever it was they were thinking about before somebody came along and told them they had to earn a living.[34]

None of the options mentioned above will solve the challenges of technological unemployment: when robots replace humans. Nor will they reverse inequality and poverty in both the rich and the poor worlds.

Until now, economic development has been seen as an undifferentiated process that should be implemented identically in every community. This has left billions in poverty and a world hurtling toward ecological and climate disaster.[35]

Solutions need to be crafted appropriately in different places and economic circumstances and designed with real input from those who live in each area.

But thinkers as diverse as Robert Reich and Elon Musk agree that some form of a universal basic income (UBI)[36] is likely to become inevitable if the world is to avoid collapse from rising automation. Preserving the benefits of 200 years of industrial development will require enabling those already unable to meet their needs as well as those who lose employment from climate change, industrial shifts, or the march of technology to survive and thrive.

Many countries are experimenting with variants of guaranteed incomes. Several Nordic countries provide basic financial support, at about one-third of the national average salary, to enable the sick, the elderly, and the unemployed to provide for themselves. They managed to pass these without a revolt from the rich.

A bipartisan agreement has a Finnish municipality testing the grant of €560 ($678) a month to 2,000 unemployed citizens who are at least 25 years old and younger than 58. The money is unconditional. If you find work, you still get the UBI. The goal is to eliminate the disincentive to work created by most welfare programs that stop paying if you become employed, and which do not help entrepreneurs start new companies.[37] The experiment elicited fierce reactions even before it ended, with both sides claiming victory.[38]

In the Netherlands, four cities are giving selected welfare recipients $1,000 a month. In Utrecht, payments are given to four randomly selected groups: those who get the money outright, those who agree to do volunteer services with the risk of losing money for nonperformance, those who get even more money if they volunteer, and those who get the money but are not allowed to work (essentially the current welfare system).[39]

In Oakland, California, Y Combinator Research proposes to give 100 families $1,500 a month to study UBI as a solution to technological unemployment.[40] The study's framers are keeping their methodology under wraps to "preserve scientific integrity." Critics claim that the study should be transparent, that changes in economic behavior resulting from UBI can impact a whole community.[41]

The OECD modeled the impact of a UBI that would replace welfare payments among UK, France, Finland, and Italy.[42] The authors observed the obvious, that it would require higher taxes, but concluded it would do little to reduce poverty, while producing more losers than the current systems targeted at the poor.[43] They found, however, that in both Italy and Finland, UBI would result in budget savings.

Providing a UBI for everyone immediately is politically divisive, especially in countries most wedded to the current neoliberal economic model. Voters in Switzerland overwhelmingly rejected a proposed UBI (an estimated 78 percent voted no) in 2016 that would have given every Swiss citizen and person who had lived there more than five years about $2,000 a year.

Critics call such programs "paid slothfulness" and believe they will lead to the ruin of prosperity.[44] But this ignores actual experience that when people have their basic needs met, they don't become couch potatoes; they engage in creating whatever they are passionate about, and poverty decreases, especially the number of children who are poor.[45]

In Kenya, in Bando Province, the aid group GiveDirectly is conducting an experiment to give 26,000 dirt-poor villagers $22 a month for 12 years. This is close to what people with jobs make there each month. The free money is distributed through M-Pesa, the nearly universal mobile money app. Although the pilot is in its early days, results show that the poor spend their new money well. Perhaps the most significant finding to date is that UBI gives people dignity. The freedom to decide how they will spend their own money relieves the stigma of begging for aid.[46]

Now the Indian government is studying the concept,[47] as are the governments of Ontario, Canada; Glasgow, Scotland; and Iceland.[48]

Even if critics are right, the prospect of a growing number of countries with bored, jobless youths turning to extreme politics or religious violence for lack of anything better to do is equally daunting. The anticipated wave of robotization is predicted to eliminate more than 800 million jobs globally.[49] Population growth and longer life expectancies mean that many millions of people need a job or some form of safety net during a transition to a healthier economic system. Payments to reduce inequality and social tension could take the steam out of today's socially divisive kettle before it blows.

Companies should welcome the idea of UBI because it will boost consumption in the short term and make it easier for them to boost efficiency through mechanization, without the backlash that would otherwise arise from people made redundant in the process.

Most proposals would substitute UBI for current welfare schemes, diverting unemployment and social security payments to pay for it. Businesses and the wealthy would have to pay higher taxes on their earnings, but smart ones will see the benefit over total societal meltdown.

The European Union recently considered, but rejected, a plan to tax the owners of robots to pay for retraining of displaced employees.[50] This concept, supported by Bill Gates, advocates that the benefits arising from automation be widely shared. Gates, like the EU proposal, argues that revenues could train people to take care of the elderly or work with children, tasks for which humans are best suited.[51]

A more fundamental question might be "Who owns the robots?" Is it right to assume that because they were invented by a person or a company (also assumed to be a person) then ownership automatically belongs to them? Neoliberals assume that any innovation is the property of the person who conceives and implements it. Mariana Mazzacuto sets out in her recent book, *Rethinking Capitalism*, that businesses ought to focus on solving humanity's most pressing problems through true public–private partnerships.[52] She contends that state investment banks have a crucial part to play and argues that there should be a return to the state from successful technological breakthroughs. This would more fairly represent the state's contribution in education and funding of both theoretical and applied research and could help pay for those rendered unemployable.

Guaranteed Jobs

An alternative to a universal basic income is the jobs guarantee (JG) program proposed by Randall Wray and colleagues.[53] Randy writes,

> The JG would pay a living wage (a national minimum wage would be $15 per hour) with free Medicare-style healthcare. It would provide free childcare to enable parents to participate in the program. This itself would greatly expand childcare provisioning, as many JG workers could be employed to provide childcare to underserved communities and to JG workers.
>
> Congress (or equivalent national legislative body) would appropriate the necessary funds to pay program expenses.

The JG would be universal—providing paid work to anyone ready and willing to work. It should also serve every community, offering jobs where people live and providing real benefits to their communities. The JG's wage and benefits would then set the minimum standard nationwide. This would provide a boost to communities across the nation, with relatively greater benefits where they are needed most: where jobs are scarce, where pay is lowest, and where markets suffer the most from lack of income to support buying power. Given the projected size of the program, it would be phased in over several years. Current proposals for the $15 minimum wage envision a complete phase-in by 2022; the JG program might follow the same time-line.

The JG should not devolve to either workfare or welfare. The social safety net should not be dismantled; no existing social services should be eliminated. Individuals should be able to continue to receive existing benefits if they do not want to work in the JG program. At the same time, the JG should not provide income support to those that do not work in the program. The JG should be seen as an employment program in which workers are paid for work. The program should have visible benefits to communities so that the workers in the program are recognized as making positive contributions in return for their wages. The program's purpose is to provide paid work, not welfare. Workers can be fired for cause—with grievance procedures established to protect their rights, and with conditions on rehiring into the program.

However, there should be room in the JG for time-limited training and education. While on-the-job training should be a part of every project, proposals can be solicited for specific training and basic education programs that will prepare workers for jobs in the JG—and, eventually, for work outside the JG. It is important that these are time-limited and that the training is for jobs that actually exist.

Project implementation and management should be decentralized. There should be diversity of types of employments and employers—to help ensure there are projects that appeal to workers and their communities. Projects should go through several layers of approval before implementation (local, state or regional, federal) and evaluated at these levels once in progress. Decentralization helps to protect the program from whatever political winds emanate from the du jour occupant of the White House (or equivalent residence).

Where possible, proposals should scale-up existing projects with proven track records and with adequate administrative capacity to add JG workers. Making use of existing capacity will minimize additional overhead. Program funds should be focused on paying wages and benefits to JG employees. Federal spending should not subsidize administrative expenses.

The JG should not be used to subsidize wages of workers employed by for-profit firms. This distorts markets and is not likely to generate substantial new employment. Private business is already heavily subsidized by all levels of government. The JG should not be used as yet another corporate welfare program. However, private firms will benefit indirectly (and greatly) from the program as it provides a pool of hirable labor and as it contributes to economic growth that improves markets for firms.

Direct employment by the federal government for the JG should not dominate the program. Most employment should be administered at the local level—where the workers are, in the communities where they will work. The JG program will probably need to create 15 million new jobs in the US—six times greater than the number of federal employees today. Federal supervision of all these new workers would, alone, require hiring a large number of federal employees if all of them were to become federal employees. This would be politically difficult even if the massive scaling-up of the federal workforce were administratively possible. The federal government's role in direct provision of jobs should be focused on providing projects to underserved communities and workers—after not-for-profits and state and local governments have employed as many as they can.

Inclusivity and experimentation should be encouraged. The federal government should solicit proposals for novel approaches to job creation. For example, workers' co-ops could be formed to propose projects in which wages, benefits, and limited materials costs would be covered by the federal government for a specified time period.

Consistent with experimentation, project proposals put forth should not be summarily dismissed simply due to political bias. The JG program should welcome diversity. We should entertain the notion that even our political enemies might have good ideas for projects. Determination of organizations eligible to submit projects would be similar to the process the IRS uses for designation of tax-exempt status, although the standards for keeping politics and religion out of the projects should be higher since federal government money will be spent directly for employment in the program.

With decentralization, the types of projects permitted would take account of local laws and rules, include prevailing wage laws and union wage rates. With the JG paying $15 per hour, this means that in many states and localities, rules and laws will prohibit various types of work including construction. In those areas, JG workers will not build infrastructure—for example. It is possible that limited term training or apprentice projects could be funded in those areas, instead. However, in many states construction by JG workers paid $15 per hour would be permissible. Decentralization helps to ensure conformity with local laws and rules, while maintaining a uniform JG wage.

Exceptions to the uniform wage should be considered, but this should not become the norm. For example, state or local governments might want to subsidize (at their own costs) the federally-paid wage of $15 per hour in order to increase wages to some higher level. This might be because of locally high living costs. Or some JG employers might want to offer additional benefits (at their own cost) to workers, including housing allowances for high rent areas.[54]

Other Solutions

The Oxfam report *Even It Up* includes a detailed set of recommendations for tackling inequality, both globally and in the poorest countries on the planet.[55]

The rich world could provide much of the poor world with a financial safety net at relatively low cost. The money that a person in the rich world routinely spends on a Starbucks caramel latte is enough to feed several people in the poor world for a day.

Modern society is incredibly wealthy, but much of that money is spent on things we don't really need. The world spends $1.5 trillion a year on weapons systems. Over $1 trillion flows to luxury items each year, growing at three to eight percent annually.[56]

In comparison, the UN has estimated that meeting the Sustainable Development Goals agreed to by the nations of the world will cost $3 trillion to $5 trillion each year.[57] This is a lot of money, but unlike weapons or cosmetics, it is an investment in a Finer Future.

It is controversial to talk about North–South redistribution: the transfer of income and wealth from the richest billion people to the 6.5 billion poorest, but many companies now realize that enabling the poor to be less poor is the fastest way to create new customers.

The links between inequality and sustainability run deeper than just the issue of growth. Resource wars are not just the basis of dramatic movie scripts—they are already happening. Given the existing links between inequality and conflict, resource shortages add fuel to the fire.[58] There is a double injustice when it comes to global carbon emissions. Those emitting the least tend to be those who face the brunt of climate change impacts. If we remain unequal, ongoing climate change will worsen the vulnerabilities driven by high levels of preexisting inequality. However, cutting emissions in a way that limits those further down the socioeconomic scale from accessing goods and amenities with which the rich will continue to be privileged without addressing economic inequality will worsen social exclusion. This may cause further ill feeling and widen class divides.

One way to structure a wealth transfer would be to give everyone on the planet an equal right to burn a certain amount of carbon. Although humanity needs to transition to a carbon-free world, this will take time. During the transition, a global carbon market could allow those in the poor world, if they had the same right to burn carbon as those in the rich world but less need to do so, to sell that right to companies, North or South, who still wished to burn carbon. This would drive a North–South funds transfer that would rebalance global wealth at the same time that it was drove the decarbonization process.

The redistribution of income would provide a disincentive for those in the rich world to use so much fossil energy if they had to buy the right to burn it. As carbon consumption declines, the cost of burning more carbon could increase, providing a rising disincentive as it maintained a steady flow income to the poor world. Over 20 years, this would improve living standards in the poor world and generate funds for the development of locally owned infrastructure there. It would also create millions of jobs as the South leapfrogged from inadequate energy to abundant renewables. This logic, developed in the 1990s by Anil Agarwal and Sunita Narain, was echoed in the UN's Clean Development Mechanism (CDM).[59] At that time, it would have worked splendidly. Today, when China is already far above the global limit per capita, it is difficult to see how it could work. CDM also fell far short of giving every citizen of the world the ability to participate and, at least initially, was rife with corruption. Developing uncorruptible mechanisms to allow every person to account for and transfer her carbon credits would clearly take some clever accounting.

CHAPTER TWELVE

MEET BASIC NEEDS FOR ALL

The fight is never about grapes or lettuce.
It is always about people.

CESAR CHAVEZ[1]

Redistribution from the rich to poor worlds is a critical part of addressing this challenge, but other policies are also needed. These would

+ tax resource use and wealth not work
+ reform agriculture
+ use trade barriers
+ offer a minimum wage
+ create cooperatives, not lending
+ reform the legal system
+ cancel national debts
+ invest in clean energy, water, and sanitation
+ encourage worker cooperatives
+ ensure population stability

Tax Resources and Wealth Not Work

The economic incentives embedded throughout the present system were structured for a time in history—the first industrial revolution—in which nature was abundant and people scarce. Now, with 10,000 more people arriving on Earth every hour and every major ecosystem in decline, we still tax what we want more of, income and employment, and subsidize what we do not, pollution and depletion

The Social Foundation and It's Indicators of Shortfall .

Dimension	Illustrative Indicators*	%	Year
Food	Population undernourished	11	2014–16
Health	Population living in countries with under-five mortality rate exceeding 25 per 1,000 live births	46	2015
	Population living in countries with life expectancy at birth of less than 70 years	39	2013
Education	Adult population (aged 15+) who are illiterate	15	2013
	Children aged 12–15 out of school	17	2013
Income and work	Population living on less than the international poverty line of $3.10 a day	29	2012
	Proportion of young people (aged 15–24) seeking but not able to find work	13	2014
Water and sanitation	Population without access to improved drinking water	9	2015
	Population without access to improved sanitation	32	2015
Energy	Population lacking access to electricity	17	2013
	Population lacking access to clean cooking facilities	38	2013
Networks	Population stating that they are without someone to count on for help in times of trouble	24	2015
	Population without access to the Internet	57	2015
Housing	Global urban population living in slum housing in developing countries	24	2012
Gender equality	Representation gap between women and men in national parliaments	56	2014
	Worldwide earnings gap between women and men	23	2009
Social equity	Population living in countries with a Palma ratio of 2 or more (the ratio of the income share of the top 10% of people to that of the bottom 40%)	39	1995–2012
Political voice	Population living in countries scoring 0.5 or less out of 1.0 in the Voice and Accountability Index	52	2013
Peace and justice	Population living in countries scoring 50 or less out of 100 in the Corruption Perceptions Index	85	2014
Resilience	Population living in countries with a homicide rate of 10 or more per 100,000	13	2008–13

Sources: FAO, world Bank, WHO, UNDP, UNESCO, UNICEF, OECD, IEA, Gallup, ITU, UN, Cobham and Summer, ILO, UNODC, and Transparency International. All percentages are rounded to the nearest integer.
*Percent of global population unless otherwise stated

UN Sustainable Development Goals. Credit: un.org/sustainabledevelopment
/news/communications-material/

of resources. As Randy Hayes, executive director of Foundation Earth says, "We need full cost accounting, and honest economics."[2]

As described earlier, shifts in tax policy can drive greater employment as they slow depletion and pollution. Employing people should not cost more in taxes than the wages they are paid. Government policies can promote jobs in the poor world and the rich if taxes are shifted to that which is undesirable (resource use, pollution, and waste) and away from what we want more of (employment).

The problem is that, while this has been a good idea for decades, it is largely ignored in policy circles. In Europe, where the idea has adherents, the 2013 EU's Environment Action Programme called on member states to consider "fiscal measures in support of sustainable resource use such as shifting taxation away from labour towards pollution." But a report in late 2017 found essentially no action had been taken.[3] One exception appears to be Germany, whose 1999 Ecological Tax Reform seems to have cut carbon emissions, while 90 percent of the money gained from the green taxes went to "offset payroll contributions from employers and employees with much of the remainder going towards the funding of renewable energy schemes."[4]

In the developing world, the number of people who pay income tax is very small. Thus, the impact of this proposal will be lower than it will be in rich countries. It still delivers an important signal. Poor countries that focus on taxing excess wealth—and some of it is excessive indeed—will find plenty of money for development. The challenge, of course, is political. The gap between rich and poor in the developing world is often far wider than in the rich world. Many poor countries are also corrupt. (Rich countries are corrupt, too, just in different ways.[5]) This is why reform of the legal system is essential. It is likely, indeed, that this will have to happen before fairer wealth taxes can be introduced.

Reform Agriculture

As described in chapter 9, in both the rich and the poor worlds, sustainable farming practices should become the norm, not just because this will better protect soils and vital ecosystems but because it creates far more jobs and local resilience. As both the UNFAO and UNCTAD now recognize, smallholder organic agriculture is likely also the only way to feed the world. This should be prioritized over investments of big multinational agricultural firms. The hundreds of millions of people employed in small-scale agriculture produce some 70 percent to 80 percent of global food now. The belief that we can shift from this to industrial agriculture is not only fantasy, it would create a job loss disaster difficult for many countries to manage. It would also collapse global food production. Will Harris of White Oak Pastures, described earlier, profitably provides 30 times as much employment using regenerative agriculture as his commodity-farmer neighbor. The Business and Sustainable Development Commission found that "meeting the challenges of the food and agriculture sectors sustainably could unlock 14 major business opportunities worth US$2.3 trillion annually, generating 80 million jobs by 2030." An annual investment of $320 billion would deliver a sevenfold return and address the needs of the 1.5 billion smallholder farmers and the 800 million undernourished people in the world. Most of the opportunities are in developing countries.[6]

Use Trade Barriers

Poor countries should introduce trade protection measures when this is in their interests. The neoliberal dogma that openness to trade is always good for the developing world is simply wrong. The results are in; they are visibly one-sided and are not in favor of the poor. The push for free trade has meant that many developing countries have become little more than colony sources of raw materials and cheap labor as well as growing markets for the rich world's products. This makes it almost impossible for poor countries to develop, to become more than sources of whatever can be logged, mined, or extracted from their territory at low wages.

Because they are unable to compete, due to a lack of economies of scale, they find it impossible to climb the economic development ladder and to become able to make goods with added value. Only China and South Korea, and before them Japan and Taiwan, successfully made the transition to become more developed economies in the past 50 years, and none of these countries encouraged fully open trade. Rather the opposite; they closed their markets until they

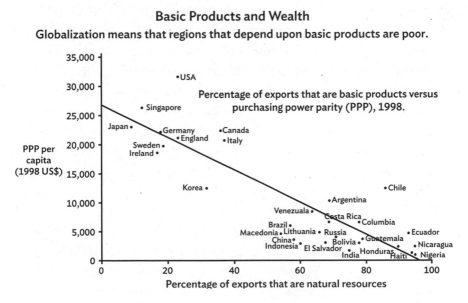

Basic Products and Wealth

Globalization means that regions that depend upon basic products are poor.

Percentage of exports that are basic products versus purchasing power parity (PPP), 1998.

Credit: On The Frontier Group.

were able to compete. This earned them the political wrath of the rich world, but what the policy did worked and should be copied by all developing nations.

Conversely, countries that depend most on exporting commodity raw resources are trapped in a race to the bottom.

Offer a Minimum Wage

Paying people decently boosts morale, improves customer service, and reduces staff turnover. It boosts social well-being and economic activity because it increases spending. It also creates a level playing field for companies and leads to higher average living standards across society. If the goal is to boost living standards and not just help big investors and their shareholders, a guaranteed minimum wage is an efficient tool and a good first step until a universal basic income or job guarantee is practical. (See the earlier section on UBI.) It also slows the descent into slavery that happens in a world where the supply of labor greatly outweighs the demand.

Neoliberal ideologues claim that the imposition of a minimum wage increases joblessness because it raises the costs of doing business.[7] Companies, they say, will turn more to automation, and this will eliminate jobs. The evidence shows the opposite. In the US, every state that imposed minimum wages saw increased employment.[8] A study by the Center for Economic and Policy Research showed that the 13 states that raised the minimum wage have enjoyed faster employment creation, not job losses. The study cautioned that its simple analysis "can't establish causality, it does provide evidence against theoretical negative employment effects of minimum-wage increases."[9]

Create Cooperative Finance Options, Not Lending

Another idea that has fallen from fashion because it is not as profitable for big business is the cooperative movement. It could be especially helpful in providing more equitable access to capital. For several decades now, many of the poor of the world have been enticed to take out loans from microlenders to enable them to invest in their businesses and grow. If this stimulates the jobs market through this process, development experts say, better still.

Unfortunately, because the loans are usually small and the administrative costs are comparatively large, the interest rates charged on these borrowings are often shockingly high. Consequently, the poor become saddled with mounting debts they cannot pay, forcing them to sell their land or their companies. The big banks and other lenders boost their earnings, but the poor lose. To encourage investment and savings in a sustainable way, it is better to form lending and savings cooperatives, where the rewards and costs stay within manageable communities and there is no incentive for anyone to rake off excess profits. Studies by development agencies have found that these structures reach more families and do a better job of poverty reduction.[10] Worker co-ops are similar and are described in more detail below.

Reform the Legal System

Very high levels of corruption blight much of the poor world. "Rolex and relax" is the way some put it, referring to the rewards and lifestyle that accrue to those who extract what they can from others in a system built on payoffs. Reducing levels of inequality and providing a better standard of living for most people will be much simpler to achieve if the system can be made less corrupt. Few of us, however, voluntarily give up privilege.

In many areas, the judicial system is the only way to force change on those with money and power. It is essential that elected officials become more accountable to those who vote for them. This sets the ground for greater equality and a fairer economic approach. It will, in the long run, deliver a wide range of social dividends for the majority of people, as well as more jobs. It is certainly preferable to the violence that some now predict will result from the failure to reduce inequality.[11]

Take the example of Kenya. "We found a judiciary that was designed to fail," said Willy Mutunga, Kenya's new chief justice, in a speech four months after his June 2011 confirmation to the post. "We found an institution so frail in its structures; so thin on resources; so low on its confidence; so deficient in integrity; so weak in its public support that to have expected it to deliver justice was to be wildly optimistic."[12] Many Kenyans doubtless agreed with Mutunga's assessment. A popular joke, "Why hire a lawyer when you can buy a judge?" summed up many Kenyans' views of their country's judicial system. In 2011, Kenya had only 53 judges and 330 magistrates for a population of 41.4 million. There was a massive backlog of almost one million cases. Litigants often bribed staff to get earlier court dates or to "lose" case files and prevent hearings altogether. In 2010, 43 percent of Kenyans who sought services from the judiciary reported paying bribes, according to Transparency International.

With the help of the international community, Kenya embarked on a major judicial reform programme, which has achieved concrete, measurable successes. The judiciary hired more than 200 new judges and magistrates and established 25 new court stations since 2011 in an effort to increase capacity and access to the judiciary in remote areas. This, along with greater institutional pressure and streamlined procedures, helped begin to clear the massive backlog of cases, which stood at 311,800 as of 2014, from estimates of nearly a million only three years earlier. "We've recorded tremendous progress, especially on lost files," said Duncan Okello, chief of staff to the chief justice. "I think that, institutionally, knowing that somebody was paying attention put people on their best behavior."[13]

Cancel National Debts

The ratio of debts owed by governments in much of the poor world to governments and banks in the US and Europe comes as a shock to those new to the field. Over decades, many developing countries have been encouraged to borrow from the rich world, typically at commercial rates of interest. As they grew indentured to the banks in the North, they became unable to invest in their own development, in infrastructure, health systems, or education. Most of any tax revenue they bring in is passed on to the rich world to pay the interest on the loans.

This phenomenon is not limited to the Global South. Greece is only the latest sordid example.[14] Banks in New York did the same to the American territory Puerto Rico, extracting more in debt payments than the entire GDP of the commonwealth.[15]

It will not be possible to write off all debts. But the capacity of the rich countries to create money when they want to is enormous. According to the IMF, the cost of providing full or partial debt relief to the 39 countries most in need would be around $75 billion in 2014 terms.[16] This is roughly the amount of money the US Federal Reserve printed each month that year after the financial crisis and called "quantitative easing." The rich world has the capacity to stimulate development, and create jobs, simply by reducing numbers on computers. Call it "quantitative development." This would benefit the rich world, as it would cut long-term migration from South to North, much of which is driven by inequality and a lack of jobs. By allowing more orderly development, and much greater local investment, it would improve living standards and even reduce the rate of population growth in many poor countries.

For example, the HIPC (Heavily Indebted Poor Countries) Initiative and the MDRI (Multilateral Debt Relief Initiative) organized by the World Bank and IMF led to a 97 percent reduction in the debt stock of the 36 countries involved by writing off $42 billion of debt. They reduced their debt service levels from 22 percent of government revenues to 9 percent.[17] The initiatives freed considerable revenue that could now be used for health and education expenditure and to strengthen development.

Invest in Clean Energy, Water, and Sanitation

Small changes can make a big difference in improving basic living standards. The provision of power as well as water and sanitation can quickly lift people from extreme hardship and put them on a better path. As described in chapter 10, developing and maintaining the infrastructure for clean energy is already creating millions of jobs and higher levels of economic development. It speeds industrialization and empowers sensible urbanisation, making it possible for many millions of people to stop living in the slums that characterize much of the poor world today. Doing this does not have to be a handout. Most of the best innovations for urban development are being created in slums around the globe by the people who live there, understand the problems, and have every incentive to innovate simple, cheap solutions.[18] It is well past time that international development experts listen to them instead of the high-priced consultants.[19]

Developing clean power and sustainable water infrastructure also reduces pollution. It is imperative that this process employs the best technologies, as opposed to allowing Northern companies to dump unwanted and obsolete equipment on the developing world.[20] To give billions of people access to energy from fossil-derived power would be shortsighted, would accelerate climate change, and as stated above, is no longer the cheapest option.[21] Rather, the rich world should ensure that the poor world develops its own distributed, renewable power network. Arguably, the South should be paid by the rich world to switch to clean energy because the rich countries are the ones who created most of the climate problem in the first place. It is unlikely that the North will be so magnanimous, but given the enormous market for energy in the South, investors are increasingly looking at such options. In 2015, more money was invested in renewable energy in developing countries than in the rich ones, with renewable investments in India increasing 22 percent and those in South Africa up 329 percent.[22] In 2016, China alone invested $32 billion in overseas renewable energy. It is investing additional billions in the New Development Bank that it created with India, Brazil, and Russia.[23]

Encourage Worker Cooperatives

Cooperatives are worker-owned businesses in which each owner has a vote to determine management of the company. Advocates such as Gar Alperowitz[24] call worker ownership in cooperative structures the best way to build living wages and create equitable communities. Cooperatives deliver workplace democracy and help lift people from poverty.

One of the best-known co-ops is the Mondragon Group of Co-operatives, in Spanish Basque country. A €15 billion corporation, it is a parent of more than 250 smaller co-ops.[25] Following the 2008 global financial collapse, Spain's economy fell almost two percent a year. Youth unemployment neared 50 percent, and millions of Spaniards were laid off.[26] At Mondragon, where managers' salaries can be no more than eight times the lowest-paid worker, wages fell by an average of five percent across the board, but almost none of its 100,000 employees lost their job. Mondragon was operating not to maximize returns to distant shareholders but to deliver quality lives to its more intimately involved owners, the workers.

Critics point to the fact that, to survive competition from companies with factories in lower wage countries, Mondragon has bought production facilities in developing countries with nonowner workers.[27] This is true, although Mondragon answers that it treats the workers far better than traditional corporate owners and offers membership to those who want it.

Critics also claim that it's a one-off, that Mondragon was founded in the 1950s but the idea seems not to have gone much beyond Spain. This is not actually true. The International Cooperative Alliance publishes a periodic survey of the world's 300 largest co-ops. Collectively these have revenues of $1.6 trillion, equal to the GDP of Spain, the world's ninth-largest country.[28] Globally more than one billion people are members of co-ops.

In Germany, co-ops enable citizens to own half of the country's renewable energy production.[29] The cooperative movement has not grown as fast in the US, with an estimated 320 co-ops employing only 5,000 people. However, New York City recently decided to triple the number of co-ops, awarding a $1.2 million Worker Cooperative Business Development Initiative grant to encourage co-op creation.[30]

Cleveland's Evergreen Cooperatives[31] secured agreements with several hospitals to serve as anchor partners to buy $3 billion worth of services from three co-ops. Created to bring economic development to an African American neighborhood in that rust-belt city,

Evergreen has created almost 100 jobs providing laundry services, solar energy installation, and fresh vegetable production from the largest urban greenhouse in the US. Providing a living wage to inner-city residents, the Evergreen model seeks to reverse urban decline. Gar Alperowitz, one of its founders, stated,

> Cleveland was once home to more Fortune 500 corporation headquarters than perhaps any city other than New York. Today, almost all of them are gone. The city's population has gone from 900,000 to under 400,000, all because the economic decision-making power was left to corporations, leaving the city vulnerable. It's a wasteland now—we've thrown away the houses, schools, and local businesses for 500,000 people.[32]

Barely a decade old, Evergreen has become a model for similar ventures as far away as the UK. From co-op banks and credit unions with more than a trillion in assets to agricultural marketing to industrial facilities, co-ops are increasingly being recognized as a viable model to conventional capitalism.[33] The United Nations, recognizing co-ops as one of the fastest growing forms of business, stated,

> [They] promote the fullest possible participation in the economic and social development of all people, including women, youth, older persons, persons with disabilities and indigenous peoples, are becoming a major factor of economic and social development and contribute to the eradication of poverty.[34]

Ensuring Population Stability

The topic of population is controversial, but the impact of human population more than doubling over the past 50 years is clear. This problem will eventually be resolved. Either we find ways to evolve toward a population sized for the carrying capacity of the planet and reduce our ecological impact, or nature will fix the problem for us.[35]

The latest estimates from the UN[36] are that the global population will rise from 7.3 billion in 2015 to 9.4 to 10 billion in 2050, then to between 10 and 12.5 billion by 2100.

The population aged between 15 and 59 is estimated to grow from 4.5 billion in 2015 to 5.5 billion in 2050, suggesting an increase in working-age people of a billion over the next 35 years, or 30 million people per year.

But trend is not destiny. We know how to achieve population stability and do so humanely: ensure that we meet the basic needs of all humankind. Dr. Malcolm Potts, University of Berkeley School of Public Health, has shown that if five conditions are met, population goes to zero population growth and stays there. These are

+ end hunger
+ reform land tenure so that squatters have a deed to the land they are on and can enter the capital system
+ educate especially women
+ provide information about contraception
+ access to contraception

Although much work remains to be done before all women have real choice, because of the measures listed above, the fertility rate—the number of kids each woman bears—has been falling globally for decades. Also, as economies grow and people move to the cities, the fertility rate declines. There are fewer advantages to having lots of children when people live in urban areas. Already more than half the world lives in cities or towns, and the trend toward greater migration to cities is expected to continue.

Steady improvements in education, especially of women, and in the availability of contraception have also played a large role in the declining fertility rate, and there is every reason to believe that these trends will continue.

A study published in 2014 by Wolfgang Lutz, director of the Vienna Institute of Demography, highlights why women's education is so important. In Ghana, for example, women without education have an average of 5.7 children, while those with secondary education have 3.2 and those with tertiary education, only 1.5.[37]

Better health care is also important. When the first-born and second-born are more likely to survive into adulthood and be around to take care of their parents in old age, there is less reason for women to have a third or a fourth child. If the first- and second-born children are properly educated and have higher earnings potential, which is again more likely in an urban environment, fertility rates fall further.

Similarly, the livelihood creation work of Development Alternatives (DA) has demonstrated how lifting people, particularly women, out of poverty reduces birth rates and brings prosperity to communities through enterprise.[38] Giving living-wage work to women, DA enables them to delay having children until they are financially able to support them, thus reducing family size in India far more cost-effectively than any government program of incentives or coercion. In one of DA's factories over 21 years, 24 women (who were employed after they already had a small family) produced, among them, a total of two additional births. In a similar cohort of women without work, there were 23 births. DA employs people delivering sustainable solutions to the problems facing their villages.[39] This approach regenerates human as well as natural capital.

It is vital to spread such successes for many reasons. The moral argument is undeniable: it's the right thing to do. But more, these cycles are self-reinforcing. There is a high correlation between birth rate decline and women having access to education and to a secure livelihood with income levels above $2.50 a day or higher. We could have between 500 million and one billion fewer humans on the planet by the end of this century if we took the goal of population stabilization seriously.[40]

Most projections of population growth are extrapolative estimates based on the current trend in the headline numbers. A declining fertility rate would change all this. It is likely that the global population will peak earlier and at a lower level than the UN suggests, at just over 8 billion people.

Obviously, it will be far easier to meet the basic needs of all humankind if the policies described above are used to reduce levels of global inequality. The good news is that all of these changes are possible and are being implemented by companies and communities on different continents. As Einstein said, "Whatever exists is possible."

CHAPTER THIRTEEN

CONFRONT THE MYTH OF GROWTH

*Anyone who believes exponential growth
can go on forever on a finite planet
is either a madman or an economist.*

KEN BOULDING[1]

The current economic system is built on growth of stuff and money. The goal of growing the economy has been embraced by both conservative and progressive economists, on the presumption that growth is the proven path to prosperity. It turns out, this is not true. Research has well documented the decoupling of growth from prosperity in the developed economics. GDP is rising, but human happiness, well-being, and environmental health are all declining.[2]

Gallup-Healthways has conducted annual well-being surveys since 2008.[3] Interviewing 500 adults each day, they have conducted 2.5 million surveys around the world of people's perceptions of their purpose (whether they like what they do each day), their social well-being (strength of relationships), financial status (level of stress about money), community (whether people like where they live), and physical (health and energy levels). Aimed particularly at encouraging corporate well-being programs, the surveys also allow governments to track progress against these categories. As described in chapter 3, people are less happy than ever.

Communities are beginning to question whether more growth does deliver greater happiness and a higher quality of life. The maxim has always been "If you are not growing, you are dying." But how big can a community grow and still be a place in which people want to live? In most areas, the growth that developers and builders advocate does not deliver sufficient revenue to the community to pay for the increased costs that the growth imposes on the town.[4]

But growth is so central to our way of life that economists, from neoliberals like Milton Friedman to Keynesians like Paul Krugman, shriek in unison at the prospect of less of it. Proponents of what has come to be called "degrowth," putting the economy in reverse, are told by almost all "serious" economists that this would destabilize the system uncontrollably.

Growth in the flow through the economy of money and stuff is *the* sacred cow of our times. It is assumed that without growth, our quality of life will decline. How on Earth could anything be a higher-priority goal than keeping the economy flowing?

There is no doubt that people in poorer countries need more energy to use, more food to eat, even more things to possess.

The real problem with growth as conventionally conducted is not the increase in productivity or wealth it has delivered, both of which are good, but rather the attendant ecological footprint and social degeneration. As described in chapter 1, what must be reduced is overall resource throughput—the use of materials unsustainably extracted from the Earth—and human misery.

But any attempt to curtail negative impacts on the environment or people is met, first, by the stubborn insistence that growth is essential to job creation.

Now, even growth may not be enough to achieve these imperatives. According to the authors of *The Second Machine Age*, the almost perfect correlation that used to exist in the US between growth—productivity gains in the private sector—and the creation of new jobs has now been broken.[5] Economic growth, historically the job creation engine, has now become a direct threat to employment. The faster the economy grows, the more that companies tend to invest in automation and robotization. New jobs are created in this process, of course, but far fewer and lower paying than those being lost.

We need a different logic and a transition to get to a better system.

The question ought to be not "How can we grow?" but "Growth of what?"

Many things should grow: human happiness, health, education, well-being, restoration of damaged ecosystems, renewable energy, innovation....

The materialist addiction to consume ever more stuff is threatening our life-support systems. It sacrifices the happiness that people find in the sense of belonging that comes from family and community to the loneliness of urban affluenza.[6] The new narrative that this book addresses argues that what people truly want is happiness, not wealth.

A widespread shift in values to prefer fewer consumer goods, as some claim that the Millennial Generation favors,[7] would significantly shift, and initially slow, a global economy now largely dependent on discretionary spending. But even that, as discussed in the context of energy, would be very tricky to manage.

It has long been thought that capitalism has an inherent "growth imperative" that arises from the creation of money as interest-bearing debt by the bank. However, a recent paper by Tim Jackson and Peter Victor[8] casts doubt on this assumption. Their analysis, which they call the "Falstaff model," finds that neither credit creation nor the charging of interest on debt creates a growth imperative by itself.

The real driver of the need for continuous growth and, hence, ecological overshoot, they say, is "quarterly capitalism"—the insistence by Wall Street analysts that companies report an increase in profitability every quarter. This mentality, described more in chapter 7, also fueled the financial collapse as the banks took on too much debt in their quest for ever higher returns.

Jackson and Victor argue it is possible to move from this destructive growth path toward a stationary state without crashing the economy or dismantling the system.

Victor uses this "lowgrow" model to detail the types of policies that will be necessary to set forth an attractive low-/no-growth scenario through 2035 in Canada.[9] In this approach, GDP per capita stabilizes at well above the level in 2005, while unemployment, poverty, the debt-to-GDP ratio, and greenhouse gas emissions are all substantially reduced. This scenario comes from a combination of initiatives including expanded anti-poverty programs, a revenue-neutral carbon tax, a stable population and labor force, a reduced work year, reduced net investment, and balanced trade. Additional, complementary changes in policies, values, and institutions, including a switch from measuring and maximizing GDP to measuring and maximizing human well-being, all support the scenario.

Many analysts feel that moving toward much shorter hours of paid work offers a route out of the multiple crises we face. Many of us consume well beyond our economic means and beyond the limits of the natural environment but fail to improve our well-being by this consumption. At the same time, others suffer poverty and hunger because they cannot get sufficient work to earn enough to support themselves and their families. Continued economic growth of the traditional sort in high-income countries worsens these and will make it essentially impossible to achieve urgent carbon reduction targets. Widening inequalities, a failing global economy, critically depleted natural resources, and accelerating climate change pose grave threats to the future of human civilization.

A "normal" working week of 21 hours[10] would enable more people to achieve purpose and income. It would succeed, however, only if productivity gains are shared. At present, any increase in work accrues only to the uber-wealthy owners of financial capital. Many people work several jobs to make their meager ends meet and would regard the prospect of shorter hours as a recipe for bankruptcy.

The challenge is greater in the poorer countries. Many of the measures described here will be needed, but with rising populations and existing or growing poverty rates, the challenges are massive. As described above, a redistribution of wealth from richer countries to poorer ones will be required if we are to meet basic needs for all.

With Victor's measures, however, the world could begin to address such urgent, interlinked problems as overwork, unemployment, overconsumption, high carbon emissions, low well-being, entrenched inequalities, and the lack of time to care for each other. We could begin to live sustainably and simply enjoy life more.

Well-being, Not GDP, Needs to Be Measured and Maximized

Kate Raworth's *Doughnut Economics: Seven Ways to Think Like a 21st-Century Economist* suggests we seek the sweet spot of a safe and just operating space for humanity. Key to this is shifting our focus from growing our economy, as measured by gross domestic product, to ensuring shared well-being on a healthy planet.

It is easy to measure wealth as dollars and Simon Kuznets' metric of gross domestic product (GDP) as the hallmark of success.[11] The only flaw is, as Kuznets himself warned, his metric ought not to be used as a measure of aggregate well-being. GDP is useful as an indication of the speed with which money and stuff flow through the economy. But this utterly fails to tell us if we are any better off. Thus, a divorcing cancer patient who gets in a car wreck adds nicely to the GDP. Is she any better off? Clearly not. But her misery adds far more to the economic metric than the choice of her mother to stay out of the workforce to care for her child after the crash.[12]

GDP has retained its status as a sacred cow because it has, in the past, mapped closely to the creation of jobs. If this is no longer going to be true, there is even less reason to keep the increase in GDP as the prime directive.

Herman Daly, the great ecological economist, advised that we stop confusing speed with whether we are getting to where we want to be. Counting consumption of anything as a metric of progress is questionable, but counting use of natural capital as income is particularly perverse, he wrote.[13]

Income, he pointed out, equals the maximum amount that a society can consume this year and consume the same next year. Balance-of-payments accounting by most developing countries, however, counts export of depleted natural capital: oil drilled or timber cut beyond sustainable yield, as income, and enters it as such in the ledger in current accounts. This, Daly argued, is a basic accounting error.

We should, instead, maximize the productivity of natural capital in the short run and invest in increasing its supply in the long run. Daly believes that we should move away from the ideology of global economic integration by free trade, free capital mobility, and export-led growth and, instead, seek domestic production for internal markets, local job creation, and maximization of human well-being as the first option.

Nothing here is meant to suggest that intelligent development should not remain a primary driver for economic prosperity, especially in the poorer economies. What's new is to recognize the distinction between liquidating vital resources, whether human or natural, that a nation will need to deliver a high quality of life and saying it is richer because it has more money. As economies mature out of adolescence, the quality of their growth *must* adapt if the entire system is to be sustainable over long periods of time. This will require that we

+ commit to long-term thinking and investment;
+ ensure strong, democratic economic governance and diverse and equitable ownership of resources; and
+ build a strong non-market economy within which a viable market economy can prosper.

It will also be key to prioritize full and stable employment or provide secure livelihoods, as described above. Macroeconomic instability and job insecurity both reduce well-being. Recent research proved that secure employment and the absence of recessions matter much more to people's well-being than the growth rate.[14] Thus, measuring and maximizing well-being rather than GDP and ensuring employment are critical to living within planetary boundaries. This means that all people must have access to a job that affords them dignity, a minimum livelihood, and a decent standard of living, as we address the global challenges. For too long, these have been seen as contradictory priorities. They are not, and solving such crises as climate change and implementing regenerative agriculture create more jobs, better jobs.

The Dynamic Model of Well-being

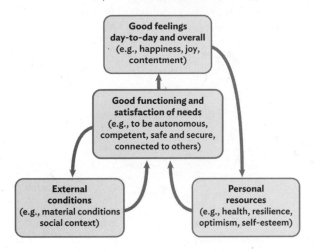

The dynamic model of well-being, developed by the New Economics Foundation (NEF). Also NEF report, b.3cdn.net/nefoundation/db3d5f02f6e2f328e8 _k1m6bv6on.pdf

Maximizing subjective well-being (defined as both feeling well on a day-to-day basis and functioning well in society over the long term) is also key to enabling people not to substitute the use of "stuff" that stresses the planet's resources and an individual's finances as a substitute for genuine happiness.

Various alternative measurements of well-being to replace GDP have been suggested. One of the first was the Calvert-Henderson Quality of Life Indicators.[15] Coordinated by new economics pioneer, Hazel Henderson, and published by the Calvert Group, one of the first socially responsible investment houses, it went far beyond GDP to measure whether national trends in education, employment, energy, environment, health, human rights, income, infrastructure, national security, public safety, recreation, and shelter were improving or lagging.

In 2010, the New Economics Foundation set forth what it called the Happy Planet Index (HPI).[16]

HPI plots every country's "happy life years" (left-hand vertical access) against ecological footprint (bottom horizontal axis). Just

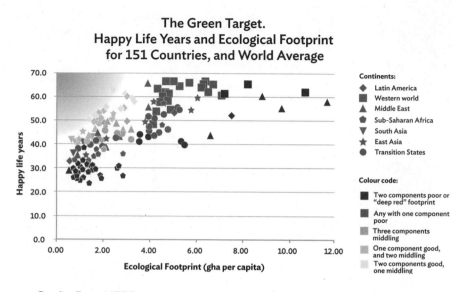

The Green Target.
Happy Life Years and Ecological Footprint
for 151 Countries, and World Average

Credit: From NEF Report.

under 2.00 on the horizontal axis represents one–planet living (as described in the discussion of ecological footprints in chapter 1). If humanity is to survive, all countries need to move to the top left-hand side of the graph to stay within planetary boundaries and achieve long and happy lives for everyone.

The HPI is not a strict measurement tool but a graphic example. It demonstrates the direction in which humanity needs to move.[17] Across the planet, people see that conventional economies, although efficient at providing stuff, are not delivering what we really want:[18] prosperity, healthy environments, and well-being.[19] The current narrative extols the virtues of life to the right, and many countries are working hard to move rightward. Some are even dropping on the left-hand axis, doing worse at meeting basic needs. Both are recipes for misery and collapse.

At the international level, the OECD Statistics Directorate has established the Better Life Index.[20] Its goal is to supplant GDP as the measure of national progress, tracking what matters most to people across 361 regions worldwide. With more than 100,000 users, this highly interactive, graphical interface enables individuals,

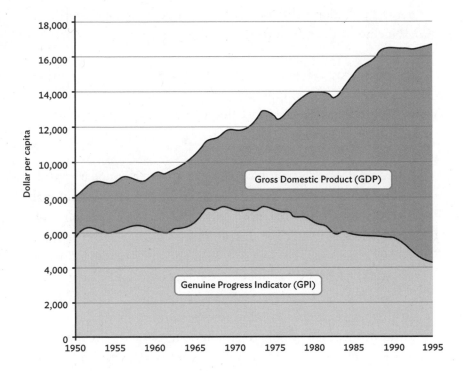

"Why a GPI Should Replace the GDP," Sustainability Advantage, 2011, sustainabilityadvantage.com/2011/03/08/5-reasons-why-a-gpi-should -replace-the-gdp/

communities, companies, and countries to customize their own index, putting in their own weights on what they want measured. Users can then generate the results immediately. It also ranks member countries on housing, income, jobs, community, education, environment, civic engagement, health, life satisfaction, safety, and work-life balance. Are you better off than you were last year? Check it out.

The Index of Sustainable Economic Welfare (ISEW) was first developed by Herman Daly and John Cobb.[21] Later modified and renamed the Genuine Progress Indicator (GPI),[22] it counts Personal Consumption Expenditures (a major component of GDP) but adjusts these using 24 different components, including income distribution, environmental costs, and negative activities such as crime and pollution. GPI also adds positive components ignored by GDP, including the benefit to society of volunteering and household work.[23]

By separating activities that diminish welfare from those that enhance it, GPI better approximates true economic welfare.[24] Remember, GDP measures velocity, not welfare. It can tell you whether more money is flowing in the economy but not whether you are better off.

There are decreasing marginal returns to income. A dollar's worth of additional income to a poor person produces a lot of additional welfare to that person. One more dollar given to a rich person adds little to their well-being. The distribution of income within a country and whether a range of social problems are present also influence overall well-being.[25] GPI counts these effects of income distribution and thus better approximates real well-being.

With these examples in mind, there is undeniable opportunity to confront the myth of growth and in doing so, shift our practices to reward conditions that matter. As discussed in *Cents and Sustainability*, this is essential for securing "our common future."[26]

CHAPTER FOURTEEN

A VALUES SHIFT

*The moment you give up
your principles, and your values,
you are dead, your culture is dead,
your civilisation is dead. Period.*

ORIANA FALLACI[1]

Crafting our new narrative requires asking what is the purpose of the economy. Is it to make people in the one percent even richer? Or is it to create, as Buckminster Fuller put it, "a world that works for 100 percent of humanity."[2] What is the purpose of human life? Are we profit-maximizing automatons, or do we aspire to a higher meaning? Who are we as humans?

People seek a way of living that brings meaning to their lives and is worth the struggle. Impact investor Donna Morton said,

> I don't believe humans are destined to be a destructive virus; we are reflections of the universe; we are light; we are the beauty of a child. We are destruction and regeneration; we choose every day to create or destroy. Align with the forces of regeneration (grow food; make energy; put your money and life in alignment with the world you want)—it is that easy.[3]

What values should guide us? Are values always culturally determined? Or are there core or absolute values that can give us direction?

Some values transcend our narrow frameworks and prejudices. The WEF Global Agenda Council on Values has studied these issues over many years and determined that some values transcend religion, nationality, and politics. Most faiths and enlightened civilizations subscribe to these core values:

+ The concept of **human dignity**, encompassing human rights and responsibilities;
+ The **common good**, the idea that all institutions should be pursuing the common good; and
+ **Stewardship**, the recognition that it is our responsibility to steward the planet and its resources for future generations.

Creating a Future Where All Are Valuable

> Humans don't mind hardship; in fact, they thrive on it; what they mind is not feeling necessary. Modern society has perfected the art of making people not feel necessary. It's time for that to end.
> — Sebastian Junger, *Tribe: On Homecoming and Belonging*[4]

There is widespread agreement, even in the richer countries, that what has been called the "social contract" is broken. This is the belief that if you work hard and play by the rules, the system will reward and ensure your security. Now, instead, many people fear the loss of their jobs, insecurity in old age, and the destruction of their dreams and cultural norms. They feel they have no voice and are of no value.

In the developing world, globalization has brought great benefits to some but failed to protect many others. Rapid technological advances, while bringing many positive benefits, threaten to destroy jobs worldwide. We urgently need a new shared vision of how to live together.

What this book seeks to set forth is a story of a new type of economy. It will be open, dynamic, and entrepreneurial while also being fair. It will be locally rooted and enable everybody to feel valued. It will keep the best features of globalization while directly addressing globalization's key problems.

Is this combination achievable?

Yes. But achieving it will require a radical shift in economic thinking and, above all, basing our economies on a new/old set of values. At the heart of the new economy must be the same values and characteristics as those to which well-functioning families and households aspire.

The neoliberal belief that if everybody pursues their own selfish goals, the well-being of society is maximized, if applied to families, drives divorce and loneliness. Its assertion that we are independent, rational individuals motivated only by wealth and success is not only a gross simplification of who we are as humans. It is clearly wrong.

A WEF survey of 140,000 business people and policy-makers in 2009 found that 75 percent thought the world was facing not just an economic crisis but a values crisis as well. Respondents stated that they wished they could practice the same values at work as they do at home.[5] This is what a new economy must make possible.

An economy based on the values of well-functioning families and households would be

- rooted
- fair
- secure
- flourishing
- sustainable
- welcoming
- creative[6]

Rooted

People need to feel in control of their lives. This requires strong local democracy and strong local organizations. Energy and food need to be locally produced wherever possible; local businesses ought to be supported; rules should prevent undue competition from national and international businesses; banks dedicated to serving the local population; and cultural norms and customs should flourish (provided they respect universal human rights and democratically agreed laws).

Fair

This means not only reducing inequality but restoring trust in the major institutions of society—government, businesses, public bodies, media, banks, and nongovernmental organizations. People have to believe that organizations are ethical and serving the public interest rather than that individuals within them are looking after their own interests at the expense of everybody else.

Secure

It is going to be increasingly difficult for governments to ensure that there is full-time employment for everybody. Just as universal education and health provision have been the norm for many years in many rich countries, economic security for all throughout life needs to become a new norm. This will require exploring the basic income provisions described above, amongst other options. The cost of providing economic security for all would almost certainly require higher taxes but would also inject new purchasing power into economies and greatly reduce the risk to people starting up small businesses or projects. It would reduce the risks to people moving between jobs and let businesses change the size of their workforces.

Flourishing

Providing lifelong economic security will make people less vulnerable but will not make them feel necessary. The norm must be that everybody contributes to society by doing something worthwhile and that this is recognized and valued, whether financially or otherwise. This would include effective nurturing of children, making useful products, providing needed services, promoting artistic creation, improving the natural world, caring for others, and undertaking research (to name just a few areas). Encouraging and enabling everybody to contribute, and to be recognized for the contributions with real value, is the key to a flourishing society and economy.

Sustainable

The health and well-being of all of us as well as other living things depends on a healthy planet. Not only have we got to look after the planet much better but we need to heal the harm we have already done. This requires a major focus on regeneration of the natural world.

Welcoming

A locally rooted economy can also be an open one. An economy in which people feel valued and economically secure will be more welcoming to people from other nations and much less fearful about global trade and immigration. Knowledge transfer, sharing, and international cooperation to tackle global issues can become the norm.

Creative

Enterprise, innovation, and creativity would be valued, facilitated, and rewarded in all areas. This will require not just healthy competition but also collaboration. Businesses of all sizes and types will have a key part to play, but they will need to have clear societal purposes. They will need to make money to achieve these purposes, rather than their purpose being to make money.

Such values may seem idealistic, but they have characterized human societies for millennia. They are not utopian; we've just forgotten that they work better than the values imposed on us since the neoliberal takeover.

Strategic Management of the Commons

Scarce resources were not always managed only by markets. Throughout history, people created mutually agreed-upon societal regulations. From first days of human settlements, resources needed by all were held in what came to be called "commons." In the 1960s, Garret Hardin succumbed to the neoliberal mindset to make famous a conundrum he called "the tragedy of the commons."[7] He argued that humans always over-appropriate any free good, whether it be shared grazing rights on a commons or clean air. Shared resources, he argued, will always be over-stripped by rapacious individuals who can gain personal advantage by, say, putting more cows out on the commons than their allocation.

Elinor Ostrom showed that, actually, "primitive" commons are exactingly managed by cultural norms that prevent precisely the sort of neoclassical greed Hardin feared. She answers the tragedy of the commons:

> I don't see the human as hopeless. There's a general tendency to presume people just act for short-term profit. But anyone

who knows about small-town businesses and how people in a community relate to one another realizes that many of those decisions are not just for profit and that humans do try to organize and solve problems.

If you are in a fishery or have a pasture and you know your family's long-term benefit is that you don't destroy it, and if you can talk with the other people who use that resource, then you may well figure out rules that fit that local setting and organize to enforce them. But if the community doesn't have a good way of communicating with each other or the costs of self-organization are too high, then they won't organize, and there will be failures.[8]

Studying groundwater management in California and irrigation management in Nepal, Ostrom described how people cooperate to manage critical shared resources. Her Workshop in Political Theory and Policy Analysis at Indiana University produced hundreds of studies of the conditions in which communities self-organize to solve common problems.

Ostrom set forth eight core design principles that people evolved in successful commons management systems:
  1. Clearly defined boundaries
  2. Proportional equivalence between benefits and costs
  3. Collective choice arrangements
  4. Monitoring
  5. Graduated sanctions
  6. Fast and fair conflict resolution
  7. Local autonomy
  8. Appropriate relations with other tiers of rule-making authority (polycentric governance)[9]

Following Ostrom's receipt of the Nobel Prize for Economics,[10] interest in the concept of the commons enjoyed an upswing. An international team formed to establish the commons as a third way of organizing society, evolving beyond what they consider the failures of both central planning and the "market state." They propose a system based on the practices and needs of civil society and the environment each society inhabits at the local, regional, national, and global levels. They established the Commons Transition[11] as a database of case studies and policies to achieve "a more humane and environmentally grounded mode of societal organization." The group believes that a society based on collaborative stewardship of shared resources would deliver a more egalitarian, just, and environmentally stable society.

Author David Bollier, one of the group's founders, describes the commons as

- A social system for the long-term stewardship of resources that preserves shared values and community identity.
- A self-organized system by which communities manage resources (both depletable and replenishable) with minimal or no reliance on the Market or State.
- The wealth that we inherit or create together and must pass on, undiminished or enhanced, to our children. Our collective wealth includes the gifts of nature, civic infrastructure, cultural works and traditions, and knowledge.
- A sector of the economy (and life!) that generates value in ways that are often taken for granted—and often jeopardized by the Market-State.
- The protection and enablement of existing Commons, along with the creation of new ones, are at the core of our Commons Transition policy proposals.[12]

Proponents of this approach believe that commons requires a community with the requisite protocols, values, and norms sufficient to managing the resource. They consider such resources as the atmosphere, oceans, genetic knowledge, and biodiversity as commons, and sharply criticize what they call "the enclosure of the commons," the expropriation, privatization, and commoditization by private owners of resources that should serve all humanity. This includes patenting of genes and other life-forms, copyrights, the closure of the internet, and the looming threat in the US by the administration to sell off public lands and national parks. This, they say, "dismantles a commons-based culture (egalitarian co-production and co-governance) with a market order (money-based producer/consumer relationships and hierarchies). Markets, they say, have thin commitments to localities, cultures, and ways of life; for any commons, however, these are indispensable."[13]

Is it possible to go back to such simpler, more consensus-based decision-making? Michel Bauwens, another founder of the Commons Transition, has set forth a Commons Transition Plan[14] to achieve what he calls a social knowledge economy. He argues, "There is no commons without communing—the social practices and norms for managing a resource for collective benefit.... A commons must be animated by bottom-up participation, personal responsibility, transparency and self-policing accountability."

Globally, two billion people still depend for their livelihoods on shared forests, fisheries, water, and wildlife. Commons Transition proposes a federation among "commoners" and different tiers of commons. It proposes the creation of "innovations in law, public policy, commons-based governance, social practice and culture" to enable those dependent on commons to maintain their ways of life. "These," they say, "will manifest a very different worldview than now prevails in established governance systems, particularly those of the State and Market."[15]

Entrepreneurs, branding experts, and activists came together in 2011 to launch Common, the world's first collaborative brand. One part community, one part incubator, and one part collaborative brand, Common is the brain child of marketing genius Alex Bogusky, impact investor Rob Shuham, collaborative facilitator Mark Eckhardt, and others. It has brought together entrepreneurs wishing to unleash their creativity and rapidly prototype and launch hundreds of mutually supportive businesses under a brand that is community owned and community directed. It enables small social entrepreneurs in any corner of the world the ability to launch with the immediate global awareness of a brand that represents shared purpose, goals, means, and values. The brand Common represents products, businesses, and the ideals of its community.[16]

Others are answering this call. In Australia, Robert Costanza is using Peter Barnes's idea of a Sky Trust[17] to propose that we "claim the sky"[18] as a common asset that belongs to us all. Under this approach, activists would assert property rights on behalf of all humanity and use legal institutions to protect that right. This would require any who would pollute to pay for the right to do so under a public trust doctrine.

American lawyer Mary Wood asserts that the ancient doctrine of public trust can be used in this way. Its purpose has been to force the government, as a trustee, to protect the public's asset and serve the public good. She proposes to establish an Earth Atmospheric Trust to charge for damages to the atmospheric commons and to qualify regeneration projects (projects that achieve carbon drawdown through soil sequestration and reforestation, or that promote transition to a renewable energy infrastructure).[19]

In late 2016, a federal judge in Oregon ruled that a lawsuit filed by Wood for Our Children's Trust, on behalf of 21 young plaintiffs, 9 to 20 years old, could proceed to trial using this theory.[20]

The plaintiffs argue that the federal government is violating their constitutional rights to life, liberty, and property because it is failing to prevent climate change despite knowing well the dangers posed. They allege that the government has failed in its legal obligation to protect public trust resources. The suit asks the court to compel federal agencies to regulate emissions and stop further climate change.[21]

Perhaps creation of common values and open, participatory conversation across society, prioritizing the needs of those people and environments affected by policy decisions over market or bureaucratic considerations, might not be such a bad idea.

Could we make these narratives come true?

Yes, if enough of us want it and are prepared to work together to make it happen. We need to stop being paralyzed by what economists tell us is not possible or by the popular myths and false paradoxes of economics.

For example, the myth that giving everybody economic security means that people won't work, or that an economy can't be local and global at the same time. As described throughout this book, the evidence is clear that these are simply not true. We know what we want in our families and households. It is time to demand the same for our economies.

CHAPTER FIFTEEN

REINVENTING GOVERNANCE

Once social change begins it cannot be reversed.
You cannot un-educate the person who has learned to read.
You cannot humiliate the person who feels pride.
You cannot oppress the people who are not afraid anymore.
We have seen the future and the future is ours.

CESAR CHAVEZ[1]

Humans have been creating governance structures as long as we have lived in organized groups, which, as shown in chapter 3, is what enabled us to survive.

Ostrom's work on the commons showed that markets are not the only way to apportion scarce resources. Wherever people share a required resource, they create governance structures, which tend to do a better job of ensuring that everyone gets what they need than do "expert systems" introduced from the outside.[2]

Like markets, governments are human creations. If they aren't working, we can and should fix them. But politics is broken. From the UK's Brexit vote, where proponents admitted afterwards that they lied, to the 2016 campaign in the US where "post-truth" assertions and an arcane electoral system gave the presidency to the loser of the popular vote, now under investigation for collusion with the Russian government that hacked the opposition, politics as usual is forcing people to lose faith in government. There is even evidence that citizen confidence in government integrity is essential to personal generosity. Where confidence is undermined, people become meaner, more selfish.[3]

Such systems are unlikely to take the bold steps necessary to facilitate the transition to a Regenerative Economy and to forestall the twin drivers of collapse outlined in the HANDY Study discussed in chapter 1. Certainly, neither the US nor the UK is likely to implement legislation to reduce inequality, protect the climate, or implement regenerative policies.

This situation is not an accident. The neoliberal narrative has been extraordinarily successful in convincing us that our governments are inefficient, ineffective, and unnecessary.

Edelman, the PR agency that annually surveys more than 33,000 respondents in 28 countries, has found the lowest levels of public trust in the institutions of government, business, media, and NGOs since the surveys began in 2001.[4] This is particularly true among the less well-educated members of society. More than half of people trust NGOs, but fewer than 42 percent trust governments, and only 29 percent believe government officials are credible. A survey of seven European countries in 2012 found that more than half of the voters "had no trust in government" whatsoever. A YouGov opinion poll of British voters in the same year found that 62 percent of those polled agreed that "politicians tell lies all the time." Only in Singapore, Indonesia, India, UAE, and China do more than two-thirds of people trust their governments. This is an all-time low globally. The Edelman report titles this a crisis of trust, pointing out that without trust, belief in the system fails.

The resulting alienation leads to perverse results. In the UK, 70 percent of people voted, but because only a slim majority decided that Britain should leave the EU, 36 percent of the population determined the outcome—the rest either voted no or abstained. The result will impact the entire continent.

In the 2016 US election, only 55% of voting age citizens cast a ballot—a 20-year-low voter turnout.[5] An election night count revealed that the presidency was decided by a quarter of Americans—hardly a mandate.

Such cultural tensions began to develop decades ago with the emergence of what have been called "post-materialist values." The culture wars of the 1960s celebrated sex, drugs, and rock and roll. Since then, the rise of self-expression and issue politics focused to gender, race, and the environment, in the words of author and television commentator Fareed Zakharia, traumatized "the older generation, particularly men, [with] an assault on the civilization and values it cherished."[6] These people looked for candidates to hold at bay these forces of cultural and social change.

George Monbiot writes that he doesn't blame people for voting as they did:

> These are responses to a twisted, distrusted system. Elections captured by money, lobbyists and the media; policy convergence among the major parties, crushing real choice; the hollowing out of parliaments and other political institutions and the transfer of their powers to unaccountable bodies: these are a perfect formula for disenfranchisement and disillusion. The global rise of demagogues and outright liars suggests that a system nominally built on consent and participation is imploding.[7]

In Europe, people are showing their dislike of politics in an increasing number of countries, criticizing national governments but, increasingly, the European Union, as well. The nationalistic parties— UKIP in the UK, the National Front in France, the Law and Justice Party in Poland, Fidecz in Hungary, Erdogan's AKP in Turkey—are gaining adherents. Brexit voters resonated with the claim that too much of decision-making was taking place in distant Brussels, that migrants from other European countries were a threat to jobs, and that the only winners in the EU were financial and political elites.

On top of that, political ideologies are broken. Professor Eban Goodstein, founder of the Bard MBA, diagnosed the situation well:

> For much of the twentieth century, the globe wrestled with two competing, and at the time, compelling political visions. The left stood for self-determination: every woman and man deserved freedom from poverty, disease and ignorance, in

order to realize their potential as human beings. The right stood for absolute personal liberty: every man and his property deserved to be left as far alone as possible from an intrusive government.

The left demonized capitalism as the source of oppression and fought for the expansion of democracy—both political and economic—as the way to tame, or overthrow, the power of big business. The right demonized government and sought to shrink it to a size it could be stuffed into a bathtub, as Grover Norquist put it, and drowned.

At its best, tension between these two perspectives was creative. When neither side had the upper hand, compromises were made, progress was possible, and not infrequently achieved. However, when one side or the other triumphed, the results were generally not good. The left was betrayed by totalitarian politicians, who, rather than expanding political and economic democracy, used the military and police to crush opposition and enriched political elites. The right was betrayed by crony capitalists, who, rather than creating truly competitive markets, rewrote market rules in their favor, used the military and police to crush opposition, and enriched economic elites.

Behind this ideological struggle loomed, and still looms, the powerful pull of tribalism—religious, ethnic, national. The political left made use of tribalism in its appeal to class division and nationalism; the political right in its alliances with religion, racism, and nationalism. In failed or failing states—where post-colonial elites tried without success to pursue development models advocated by the left or right—tribalism has reemerged as the dominant ideology.

At the beginning of the 21st century, the left's utopian vision has been tamed. European social democrats and American and Asian liberals no longer view politics as a savior but rather as a necessary, imperfect, compromised, and compromising counterbalance to the power of business. Very few retain faith in worker control of the means of production as a guiding principle, and the expansion of political democracy is just another box to check on the list of liberal social and economic concerns.

Free-market ideology in anything approaching a pure form (for example the American politician Rand Paul) has also lost whatever mass political appeal it might have had in its Milton Friedman heyday. IMF and World Bank economists have wandered beyond the neoliberal Washington Consensus to a mushier middle of policy advising. Globally, conservatism has embraced xenophobic, social-issue, right-wing populism, hanging on, primarily in the US, to unpopular, billionaire-backed bits and pieces of a libertarian economics.

To be sure, the two grand traditions of 20th century political economy do still lumber on. They wake every few years in ever-diminished form, to battle through national election cycles over a set of issues. In the US, the battles are around inequality and poverty (tax cuts for the middle class versus tax cuts for the rich); social security and health care (single payers versus privatizers); climate change (clean energy promoting climate realists versus regulation-hating climate deniers); widened democracy (campaign finance reform versus voter suppression); education (teachers' unions versus voucher advocates). In European countries government intervention to secure basic welfare services (such as free health care and education and unemployment protection) is accepted by the vast majority of the population. Here the battles presently are around the degree of government support—and hence the level of taxation—and the quality of government services. In addition, migration has emerged as a major issue, putting at risk the support for further policy integration within the EU.

Both the centre-right and the centre-left have run out of any general or lasting idealistic appeal. The US candidates most identified with neo-liberal economics, Jeb Bush and Marco Rubio, got no traction with voters in 2016. On the left,

Bernie Sanders is doing surprisingly well but still failing to break out beyond the liberal quarter of the engaged electorate. For most people, and in spite of the high and rising stakes in all of these areas, politics outside of presidential campaigns has become the acknowledged and tedious arena of interest groups. Cynicism and nihilism have replaced idealism among the politically aware, the young in particular.

In the EU far-right political groups are gaining increasing support in a majority of the member-states—at the expense of both the social democrats and centre-right. The strange thing is that none of the traditional parties seem to realize the need to rethink their policies. Although the arguments against the neo-liberal agenda are overwhelming—and one of the reasons behind the rise of the far-right—there is almost no indication for real soul-searching among the political elite.[8]

Political parties have two essential functions: to link society to the state, and to articulate social demands so that they can be turned into state policies. In the US, Europe, and other parts of the world, this system has become little more than a debating society for the elite.

Governance assumes that politics functions and that nations protect the interests of their people. But most of the really serious challenges today have no respect for borders. But global governance is nowhere on the horizon. After World War II, institutions like the United Nations were formed on a wave on internationalism to move in this direction. The modern incarnation of the UN, which can barely pay for itself, has legitimacy issues and has become a ponderous bureaucracy.

Globalization changed national politics profoundly. National politicians have surrendered power, for example, over trade and financial flows, to global markets and supranational bodies, such as the International Monetary Fund, the World Trade Organization, and the European Union. Economic elites think of the world as one system. But it is not. We do not even have an embryo of democratic decision-making at the global level. Local politicians are unable to keep promises—or even make them—to voters.

Globalization benefits corporations and the wealthy who run them, as it strips jobs and community security from ordinary people. The main winners are the one percent at the top, as income gaps widen, jobs are outsourced, and wages have been suppressed. This is true in the US and in most OECD countries as well. Robotization and automation will accentuate this trend.

The European Union was launched as a peace project. The first step was a common market for steel and coal; France and Germany, enemies in two devastating wars, became partners in peacetime in industry and trade. "You do not shoot at your customers" is a premise that has worked well for many decades. The enlargement in 2004—when ten new member states were adopted—was a highlight and major achievement.

But cooperation has not been without problems. The EU project suffers a lack of legitimacy and has no model of democracy. The elections of the European Parliament normally attract less than 50 percent of the public—normal in the US but considered in Europe a clear democratic deficit. The selection of the main officeholders of the EU Commission, not least its president, is done behind closed doors. The decision to introduce the euro in 1999 was taken largely by technocrats; only two countries, Denmark and Sweden, held referendums on the matter (both said they rejected the idea). Efforts to win popular approval for the Lisbon Treaty, which consolidated power in Brussels, were abandoned when people started voting the wrong way. During the darkest days of the euro crisis, the euro-elite forced Italy and Greece to replace democratically elected leaders with technocrats. The EU's treatment of Greece since the crisis in that country begun is scandalous. The social implications have been devastating.

Partly as a consequence of Brexit, but not only, there is increasing criticism about the handling of the euro and about migration. The financial crisis exposed structural flaws in the European Union itself. The euro imposed a common monetary policy and a fixed exchange rate but without fiscal integration among countries. As Randall Wray and the Modern Monetary Theorists demonstrate,[9] this is a recipe for disaster. It clearly has hampered Europe's response to the economic crisis and caused serious drops in employment.

There is intense dialogue among member states as to what the next phase of cooperation should be: moving toward increasing cooperation—including fiscal integration—or at the other extreme, giving back authority to member states in some policy areas?

The central thesis of this book is that we need a new narrative—for politics as surely as for the economy. A new narrative is of particular importance for the EU. For the young generation, peace is not a sufficiently concrete and attractive story.

Even those lucky enough to live in mature democracies, like in Scandinavia, that work pretty well need to pay close attention to the architecture of their political systems. The combination of globalization and the digital revolution has made some of democracy's most cherished institutions appear outdated.

We no longer live in the industrial society. We live in a digital economy. The logic is different, in terms of employment, the way the economy will function, the business models, and many other aspects. To address the problems of "overshoot"—our overuse of ecosystems, resource depletion, and pollution of the atmosphere—we need new institutions and policy frameworks. The trading system needs to be rethought in a situation where trade rules seriously clash with social and ecological objectives. Established democracies need to update their political systems and rethink all institutions.

Very few Western democratic politicians actually demonstrate real leadership. They spend a great deal of time and money with focus groups and pollsters trying to figure out what will resonate enough to get them elected in two years' time. They then tailor a marketing strategy to reflect back upon the public what the pollsters say are the voters' wishes and desires. Once elected, they spend most of their time preparing for the next election, especially in America, with its two-year terms in the House of Representatives.

Political parties are in deep trouble. Party membership is declining across the developed world: just over 1 percent of Britons are now members of a political party, compared with 20 percent in 1950. The picture is similar in most OECD countries. Although substantially higher than in the US, voter turnout is falling in Europe, too. It was around 85 percent in the 1970s. Today it is on average 70 percent, driven in large part by the crisis of trust, described above.

Political scientists have analyzed the decreasing interest in party membership and participation in elections, and they propose several theories. One blames de-politicization: people are less interested in politics because other interests take precedence and because they would rather dwell in their private lives. That was the main thesis of Robert Putnam's book, *Bowling Alone*.[10] That said, 2017 saw an upsurge from a very low political engagement in the UK, due to many young people joining the Labour, Green, and Scottish Nationalist Parties. In the US, there is an unprecedented increase in young people, women, and minorities running for local, state, and national office.[11]

Another approach, the cognitive mobilization hypothesis, says that people are better educated and are less interested in belonging to parties that tend to be more top-down than before, and where the possibilities of influencing policy are miniscule. According to this theory, political parties must make more serious efforts to engage people and offer them a real chance to influence policy. With modern information and communication technologies this would be easy to do.

Politics is full of engaged and committed people. So the reason politics does not work is, in general, not the people in it. It is the system.

What could then be done?

Here are ten suggestions:

1. Reach out and engage citizens in the work of political parties. Many people are interested in politics, not least the young. But they are not attracted by the way political parties work and function. Use new technology to engage people.

2. Reduce the role of lobbying and big money in politics. This is crucial. Money talks louder than ever, especially in American politics. Thousands of lobbyists (more than 20 for every member

of the US Congress) add to the length and complexity of legislation, if they do not write it entirely.[12] As shown by a Princeton
study on oligarchy, American democracy is for sale, and the rich
therefore can afford more power than the poor, particularly now
that the Supreme Court held that political spending is an exercise of free speech.[13]

3. Make both the political and economic systems more long-term
   in their orientation.
4. Incorporate the narrative of this book, with a focus on people's
   well-being while respecting the planetary boundaries, into politics worldwide. The new US president, having run on a platform opposing much of the neoliberal narrative, on entering the
   White House gratefully accepted the playbook handed him by
   the Heritage Foundation, the first of the think tanks created by
   the massive cash support of neoliberalism engendered by the
   Powell Memorandum, described in chapter 2. As a result, he appointed the most neoliberal cabinet since Ronald Reagan, and
   set an agenda classically cut from the Mont Pelerin School: small
   government and strong military.
5. Policy frameworks must also be reformed to take into account
   the major changes that disruptive technologies, like IT, will
   imply. Jobs are threatened, and this must be met by policies like
   the guaranteed income described above, offering support for all
   those who will lose their jobs, and education and training to obtain the skills necessary in the digital economy.
6. Political parties, both to the right and the left, must realize that
   the way globalization has been implemented has made a lot of
   people worse off. There are benefits to trade, but social and environmental concerns must be respected, and the race to the bottom must be reversed. The idea of totally free financial markets
   has made a travesty of the trade principles introduced by Adam
   Smith and David Ricardo. Ricardo, in particular, extolled the
   benefits of trading to comparative advantage but was explicit that
   if capital is mobile but people are not, then trade creates only
   absolute advantage and very real winners and losers. It was, of

course, inconceivable to him that capital could become as mobile as it is today, where trillions of dollars zip about the planet every second, at the speed of a keystroke.

7. The financial sector must be reined in—not only in relation to trade. As described in chapter 7, the financial sector does not primarily serve the real economy any longer. Its fixation with maximum short-term profits from different forms of asset speculation is crippling communities and the natural world. The utter failure of politics to even acknowledge the fault of the finance sector for the 2008 collapse has driven a loss of legitimacy in the system.

8. Politics at all levels must become more transparent and democratic. The austerity policies must be scrapped. The EU, in particular, must do this. It must also decide whether to keep the euro. If it does, financial integration will then become a must.

9. Countries, first and foremost in Europe, must develop policies to improve the assimilation of migrants and asylum seekers. The migration witnessed so far is only the beginning.

10. Politics must celebrate and ensure a free and independent media but also insist that it function responsibly, with severe penalties for deliberate dissemination of false news. The corporatization of the media must be countered with fairness doctrines that guarantee access to dissenting views. Journalism must assume its responsibility in the recent elections. Its preference for sensationalism over responsibility to inform and educate the public means it is culpable in helping to create and feed the phenomenon that has now taken over in both the US and the UK.

Media made the personality who would become the 45th president of the US. The entertainment industry started him, but news media picked up where reality TV left off. As he became their most entertaining asset, they earned fortunes on him. In what must be one of the most cynical—but honest—comments of the 2016 campaign, Les Moonves, the CEO of the US national broadcaster CBS, said of the election debacle: "It may not be good for America, but it's damn good for CBS."[14]

Neil Postman's 1985 book, *Amusing Ourselves to Death,*[15] warns about the disinclination in communications media to share serious ideas—turning complex issues into superficial images, less about ideas and thoughts and more about entertainment.

Social media played a key role, as well, distributing fake news— primarily bad things about Secretary Clinton—via Facebook and Twitter. In the words of the *Washington Post* executive director, "If you have a society where people can't agree on basic facts, how do you have a functioning democracy?"[16]

These ten prescriptions are only a start. Ultimately people get the politics they deserve. An active citizenry will take the steps to ensure that its politicians are answerable to the needs of the public. Whatever legitimate criticisms can be leveled against the 2016 US election, it has energized citizens on both the right and the left to reengage with politics.[17] Jeremy Corbin's surprise gains in the 2017 snap election called in the UK also show a sharp increase in citizen participation.

This is the first step to reversing the pervasive, and perhaps perceptive, sense that the system is out of control. Governments used to run things. In today's world, however, more than half of the largest economic entities are not countries but companies. And in an internet-empowered world, a small group of people can delegitimize any country or company. So who's in charge here?

Perhaps people are awakening to the recognition that when the people lead, the leaders will follow.

CHAPTER SIXTEEN

BRINGING IT HOME

*The Key to the future of the world
is finding the optimistic stories
and letting them be known.*

PETE SEEGER[1]

The old order is fighting to sustain itself and the privilege it confers on the richest one percent on the planet. To the privileged, this is a fight to the death. As it is for the rest of us, as well: if they win, they take us all down. To save ourselves, and them, will require creating a formidable new power base and wise policies to provide the right incentives.

This last part of this section discusses what we can do as citizens in cities, and at the state or provincial level, as we create the political will to recognize that it is, after all, only a little planet. It's time for us all to work together to save it.

Is it possible to imagine "healthy communities" that embrace the new narrative of shared well-being on a healthy planet? Can we create cities free of poverty, disease, and ignorance that are also creative supporters of entrepreneurship and risk-taking, free of corruption and arbitrary political coercion?

The key may be to start not with the nation but at a more local level. Imagine what might be called the Just City.[2] In such a place, every person has both the right to live in a healthy environment and the responsibility to work for the health of their community. The Just City provides freedom for all to pursue their individual vision—

including business enterprise—and also freedom for all from economic oppression and lack of opportunity.

Such political jurisdictions would be geographically distinct, economically interconnected, politically defined regions of up to, say, twenty million people. For example, Shanghai[3] or California's Bay Area.[4] Or Singapore,[5] Denmark,[6] Oregon,[7] and Costa Rica.[8] These small regions, countries, and states are each made up of smaller communities, yet are defined in many ways by the success of their leading cities: Copenhagen, Portland, and San Francisco. To borrow a phrase, the Just City is change we can believe in for three reasons: economy, politics, and identity.

Jane Jacobs pointed out in the 1970s that cities are the natural units of both economic activity and progress.[9] Each city (or, to lesser extent, town) contains within itself the capability to grow its own way out of poverty and to promote the material well-being, education, and health of its citizens.

Jacobs described how economic development is and should be rooted in the city. Development proceeds through cycles as cities go through waves of import replacement, leading to the development of export industry, financing more imports, leading to a further round of import replacement.

Jacobs spoke against today's preferred economic determinants of trade and investment: increasingly mobile capital and economies of scale. She saw how these factors were wreaking havoc on small- and medium-scale manufacturing in the cities of developed countries, the sector that Jacobs placed at the heart of her story. Simultaneously, emergent information technology was enabling the globalization of formerly local systems of finance, food, retail, and other medium-scale enterprise. This was the backdrop for Margaret Thatcher's TINA, the repeated insistence that "There Is No Alternative" to an increasingly liberalized and privatized world economy, subject to the whims of global capital.

But of course, local economies did not disappear, and many cities and city-regions on the decline in the 1980s have recovered. Dying and abandoned downtowns have been reclaimed, small and medium import-replacing businesses have sprung up. Homegrown export industries, increasingly tech-related, have transformed cities from Seattle to Bangalore. Globally, rural to urban migration continues, with 55 percent of the global population now in cities, a number expected to grow to 66 percent by 2050.[10] Jacobs's fundamental observation that the city is the natural unit of economic progress (or decline) remains sound, even in a world of low transport costs and very low information costs.

The neoliberals' fixation on global free trade enabled a wave of offshoring, but maturing information technology is now providing the foundation for innovative new business models to regrow local energy, food, finance, retail, and even manufacturing systems. Steep declines in solar panel prices combined with smart-grid upgrades are enabling homeowners and small businesses to become energy producers.[11] Internet connections supporting direct-to-consumer sales have sparked the growth of organic family farms. Locally owned banks and credit unions now offer remote banking services similar to global chains and are seeing a resurgence. Local networks are promoting local retail stores and restaurants. Etsy.com hosts one and a half million small-scale producers, while 3-D printing is dramatically reducing the costs of design and prototyping. The advent of blockchain-enabled systems will disintermediate many of globalization's monopoly institutions.[12]

Local economy expert Michael Shuman points out that the strategy that currently dominates US economic development agencies is to "attract and retain" multinational exporters.[13] This completely ignores *existing* local business, local entrepreneurial potential, and all of Jacobs's insights into the real way cities develop. Shuman provides extensive evidence that successful local development policy should follow four principles, three of which echo Jacobs: maximize local ownership, maximize local self-reliance (through import replacement), and create entrepreneurial ecosystems. His fourth principle is to help existing and emerging local business maximize social and environmental benefits to the community as they grow and to spread the stories of their success. Shuman's work, documenting the effectiveness of local economy strategies, provides a contemporary outline for how to grow a Just City. The Natural Capitalism

Solutions manual, *Local Action for Sustainable Economic Renewal*, from which much of Shuman's framing was drawn, provides a step-by-step guide to implementing these ideas.[14]

None of this is to dismiss the challenges of relocalization in a world of mobile capital. Large businesses will continue to whipsaw communities by threatening to relocate if tax cuts and other subsidies are not forthcoming. Innovation will continue to replace people with machines. Many large manufacturing sectors, particularly in durable goods, will continue to be dominated through globally sourced multinational corporations. Nevertheless, 30 years on from Thatcher's TINA, there is an alternative: to grow locally and side-step both the neoliberal prescription of chasing mobile capital and the left wing model of dependence on national programs. Just Cities can develop—as all cities ultimately can only develop—primarily from the resources they find and cultivate close to home.

Some cities progress down this path, developing diverse eco-systems of productive capacity. Jacobs was clear, however, that not all cities naturally progress through the development cycle of import replacement leading to exports, and continued diversification through ongoing import replacement. Some become dependent on one lucrative export industry and historically fail to engage in the process of import substitution: for example, Detroit or Lagos.[15] These cities faced rapid decline when competition for their exports arose or commodity prices fell. Some such cities stagnate, some decline. And then some, like these two, rise again.[16]

Success depends on creating entrepreneurial culture, particularly for cities that emerged primarily as raw material export platforms. Jacobs co-discovered what is now known as the resource curse—that resource-rich regions become mired in colonial extraction, an idea that first gained currency around the time she was writing.[17] Jacobs focused on the answer to this: replacement of imported manufacturing—bicycles, for example, in late 19th-century Tokyo. There, a network of small manufacturers that evolved first to produce bicycles later created the vehicles that become the foundation for Japanese industrial corporations. She noted, as argued above, that, historically, success has depended on strategic use of tariffs and, prior to that, currency independence.

In the 1980s she was prescient enough to see in Boston the emergence of high technology as one new basis for a city to develop an export economy. She noted the role of private capital in seeding local ventures to foster an entrepreneurial regional cycle of import replacement, export emergence, greater imports, and then more import replacement.

How does a city do this? Jacobs celebrated what she called a culture of "improvisation"—today called entrepreneurship. At the end of her book, she pointed toward private investors supporting the nascent tech industry in Boston.[18] Now there are hundreds of examples of cities that have used policy and public-private partnerships to support the growth of small and medium-sized businesses. Shuman discusses the role of business development agencies in particular, but many policies can grow import-replacing enterprise clusters with export potential, while also achieving other local policy goals related to quality of life, climate protection, education, environmental enhancement, or affordable housing.

This is the second reason that the city or community is the right locus for a 21st-century story. City regions are small enough places for democratic participation, transparency, and accountability to flourish. Overcoming vested interests is not easy, but it is possible. Politics is local. Issues are sufficiently contained and meaningful to voters. This makes it possible to replace abstract philosophical difference—right, left, demonization of government or big business—with pragmatic problem solving. When this is achieved, a positive political economic feedback cycle develops.

Businesses can support the Just City vision. "Mission-driven businesses," if successful locally, give political leaders sufficient private-sector support to establish policies that support the growth of further mission-driven businesses.[19] City regions like Portland, Oregon,[20] or Vauban, Germany,[21] or Austin, Texas,[22] illustrate this dynamic. Curitiba, Brazil, under Mayor Jaime Lerner, became a global model.[23] Similarly Mayor Enrique Penalosa has reformed

Bogota, Columbia, into a people-friendly city.[24] In a world weary of politics, the city represents a realm where good governance and policy reform is possible.

None of this is to dismiss the importance, discussed above, of reforming national politics and policy. It is not OK that such critical national and global issues as inequality, climate, campaign finance, and human rights have descended from inspiring political vision into bitter, partisan trench warfare. At some point, and perhaps through a growing belief in the Just City, the stalemate will break. In the meantime, the story of the Just City is one that sidesteps the big business versus big government narrative, and in so doing can engage a new generation in a constructive politics.

Any compelling narrative features a heroic protagonist. The heroes of 20th-century ideology were universal, beyond city or nation: socialist man (Joe Hill) on the left, and on the right Ayn Rand's self-made man, John Galt. At the end of the day, however, neither character was sufficiently complex or flesh and blood, nor their tribes real enough, to engage the hearts and minds of a political movement. And so the left and right hitched their heroes to the service of traditional tribal allegiances (race, class, religion, nation). This is proving their undoing, and left unattended will undo us all.

The heroine of the Just City is the social entrepreneur. Like Jane Jacobs, she uses ingenuity in the service of building a healthy community. She can be a business person, a neighbor, a politician, an educator, an NGO worker, a health professional. She is tackling many of society's worst challenges with new business models and entrepreneurial NGOs. And she will be an intrapreneur, who, like Paul Polman at Unilever,[25] transforms a major company from the inside.

She is a visionary who marshals support and resources to build lasting institutions that promote the progress of *her* Just City.

Beyond heroes, successful social movements understand that people do carry strong tribal instincts. We are hardwired via evolution to divide others into insider and outsider categories. But as shown in chapter 3, we are also hardwired to bond and to be curious. The essence of human moral progress is a hard-fought, culturally reinforced widening of the insider category, from white male property holders to white men to white heterosexual men and women to all men and women. The progress has been tenuous, and subject to reversal. But the rise of the #MeToo signals that progress continues and that institutions that lose legitimacy can crumble amazingly quickly.

The Just City is grounded, uniquely, in people's identification with place. Despite increased global mobility, the vast majority of people, unless driven by catastrophe, seldom relocate far from family. It's natural for most people to identify in a deep way with their region and their city. This is the essence of sports loyalties. In this way, civic pride and a sense of belonging can reinforce the story of the progress of the Just City. It is not a bolt-on identity, like the national, ethnic, or religious tribalism used to support rightist or leftist political movements.

A challenge to this story is the risk of parochial focus. "Think global, act local" risks falling into tangled politics of local concerns and ignoring the ambitious global-scale solutions necessary to meet the very real global challenges. Critics will say that the existential threats to democratic societies of runaway inequality and runaway climate change require doubling down on a national social and political movement—a Bernie Sanders strategy. Wouldn't shifting focus to Just Cities distract from state and national politics and cede ground there?

The evidence suggests not. Just Cities, as they succeed, tend to strengthen state and national progressive politics.

What about the global refugee crisis and immigration? Do Just Cities have an obligation to accept immigrants? Since the focus is on promoting entrepreneurship and diversity in the economy, Just Cities have strong grounds for embracing immigration as part of a positive development strategy. The Sanctuary Cities movement in the US is evidence of this.[26]

Every city region has deep, untapped potential and the capability to begin to create well-being for all of its people. City regions are small enough, in principle, to create and sustain the good governance required for economic development. The Just City could be a crucial part of the engaging 21st-century narrative we need. In a world weary of partisan gridlock at the national level, it is a realistic vision that promises both social justice and a dynamic economy. The work is local, grounded in solid and easy-to-understand economic reasoning. It can be supported by accountable, relatively accessible, local politics. It speaks to an underlying human desire to belong: natural instincts toward loyalty and affection can easily attach to a city region.

There are also larger regions and states acting responsibly. California, long an innovator, implemented a cap on carbon emissions proposed and brought to fruition by the Republican governor Arnold Schwarzenegger. As described in chapters 5 and 10, the state's commitment to energy efficiency and renewable energy has created prosperity helping to lift the state to the world's sixth-largest economy. Jobs in solar electricity generation (152,947) are nearly ten times those in natural gas electricity generation employment (16,960).[27]

In the wake of the US federal decision to exit the Paris Accord, Governor Jerry Brown of California, Governor Jay Inslee of Washington, and Governor Andrew Cuomo of New York committed their states to abide by the Paris Agreement. Forming We Are Still In,[28] they quickly gathered seven other states, 125 cities (211 adopted the Paris Agreement), 902 businesses (more than 20 of them Fortune 500 companies), investors, and 183 colleges and universities. Within a week, the coalition represented 120 million Americans and $6.2 trillion of the US economy.[29] An additional 13 governors created the bipartisan US Climate Alliance, and 17 governors released statements standing by Paris. Several of the governors initiated conversations with the leaders of Germany and China.

The Paris Agreement on Climate[30] is worth saving. Even if critics warn that it only gets us to the starting line of action to save a stable climate, it is a major achievement that the nations of the world, which usually have a hard time agreeing to go to lunch, agreed to act to save humanity.[31]

For the Paris Agreement to have a chance, it must be complemented by more ambitious emissions-reduction targets by governments worldwide, but as chapter 10 outlines, this may happen with or without government action.

Nations are beginning to make significant commitments to a Finer Future. In 1991, Norway, 20 percent dependent economically on oil extraction, decided to become carbon neutral by 2050. It imposed a rising tax for all fossil fuels burned.[32] The money gained helps pay for a transition to a sustainable future.[33]

Perhaps the most amazing is Saudi Arabia, which recently announced that it was beginning a transition away from oil to a more sustainable economy. In analyzing this move, investment expert Patrick Doherty writes,

> The owner of the world's largest oil company is, in effect, divesting a portion of its interest (five percent, initially) and preparing to invest the proceeds in a cleaner, greener, more resilient economic hypothesis.... With extreme weather events occurring more frequently than scientists predicted, and no meaningful transition plan, a devastating storm, flood or drought could trigger a series of policy reactions that preclude an orderly transition to sustainability, leaving the oil-revenue-dependent government vulnerable.[34]

In the past two years, other hopeful signs have emerged: just weeks before the world agreed to the Paris Agreement, the nations enacted the Kigali Amendment to the Montreal Protocol to protect the ozone layer. They also unanimously agreed to the Sustainable Development Goals (SDGs) to end poverty, protect the planet, and ensure prosperity for all.[35] Implementation of the SDGs can move the world to a much Finer Future. The devil is in the details. The SDG goals should neither be pursued one by one, nor within the framework of conventional economic growth policies. If so, the ecological and social goals would be crushed. An integrated approach must be developed and the pursuit of GDP growth replaced by welfare and well-being priorities and metrics.

Still the emerging numbers show that it's worth the struggle. Achieving the SDGs in the four sectors of food and agriculture, energy and materials, cities, and health care and well-being would create 380 million jobs by 2030. Nearly 90 percent of these would be in developing countries.[36] The *Better Business, Better World* report found that implementing the Sustainable Development Goals would unleash $17 trillion in profit.[37]

Quoting Gandhi, an Indian representative to the UN said of the agreement on SDGs,

> I will give you a talisman. Whenever you are in doubt, or when the self becomes too much with you, apply the following test. Recall the face of the poorest and the weakest man/woman whom you may have seen, and ask yourself, if the step you contemplate is going to be of any use to him/her. Will he/she gain anything by it? Will it restore him/her to a control over his/her own life and destiny? In other words, will it lead to swaraj [freedom] for the hungry and spiritually starving millions? Then you will find your doubts and your self melt away.[38]

What Can You Do?

If the idea of a Just City or a sustainable nation inspires you, get engaged. Your city is a good place to start. Get to know your local politicians. Attend city council meetings. Join a citizens' committee. Run for local office.

Get active politically. Although the dramatic progress in renewable energy has been built by entrepreneurs and companies working in the private sector, good public policy is essential if we are to implement what we know how to do in energy efficiency, renewable energy, climate protection, and regenerative agriculture fast enough to escape the worst ravages of climate change. Reducing inequality and the transformations needed in finance and corporations all require good public policy.

On January 21, 2017, one day after the somewhat anemically attended US inauguration, half a million people, three times as many people, flooded Washington, DC, to protest the new administration.[39] The Women's March became the largest protest in US history, with more than five million people on every continent across the globe calling for change.[40] Comprised mostly, but far from exclusively, of women, the crowds were peaceful, joyful even, but stern. Signs warned, "The Resistance begins now."

If this seems like too much, begin the conversation with your neighbors about what matters to you. Become neighborly. Invite those who live around you over for coffee and conversation.

Your daily choices are the real representation of your values. Do you buy from companies that are making a commitment to create a Finer Future? Seek out B Corporations and support them. Do you buy your food locally? Is there a farmers' market near you? Talk to the growers. Come to understand what it takes to create a sustainable food production system in your region.

Have you weatherstripped your home? Have you invested in solar for your home? Companies from Solar City to Independent Power Systems will install solar on your home—no money down. Or if you have the ability to finance it, buy your own electricity system. Then power your electric car from your own solar panels. Write to your politicians and ask that they support increases in renewable energy.

Germany, hardly the country you would first think of to be a leader in solar energy, became so because advocates like Hermann Sheer and politicians like Ernst Ulrich von Weizsäcker formulated and implemented Germany's feed-in tariff and Energiewende. Without such policy, Germany, at the same latitude as Labrador, would not now regularly get up to half of its energy from the sun.[41] In 2017, it got as much as 85 percent from renewables. Similarly, the Chinese clean energy surge is driven by the government's concern that public anger over air pollution is delegitimizing the party. Once they began installing renewable energy, they realized that this commitment to clean its air not only delivers abundant, affordable energy for development, it is the best way to support domestic industry and create jobs.[42]

Many of the best renewables programs in the United States are run by municipal utilities,[43] while the investor-owned utilities have to be dragged kicking and screaming into the solar age. In Boulder,

Colorado, the citizens voted to create their own utility so that they could move away from Xcel Energy's commitment to coal and implement 100 percent renewable power.[44]

More than 12 cities around the world[45] are replicating the success of Vauban, the German city mentioned above, which went car-free in 2006. Oslo just announced that it will ban cars from the city center by 2019. The 350,000 cars will have to find somewhere else to go, as investment shifts to bike lanes and public transport. Madrid plans to do the same by 2020.[46] Such policies resulted from engaged citizens demanding that their politicians implement programs to serve them.

How can you fight entrenched power and money? You can take yours out. Perhaps the most powerful thing that an individual can do personally is to divest from investments that they don't like.[47]

The policies needed to enable humanity to avoid total system collapse are clear. What is lacking is the political will.

Whatever you do, understand that getting involved is key to crafting a Finer Future. The International Energy Agency (IEA) reported in early 2015 that the world's efforts to limit carbon emissions has begun to work: for the first time in 40 years, global carbon emissions from the energy sector stalled and began to decline.[48] In March 2017, IEA reaffirmed this. For the third straight year, emissions were holding flat. The increase in renewable energy generation, the shift away from coal power, energy efficiency, and structural changes in the economy favoring services had kept emissions from rising, even as the economy grew more than three percent.[49] Progress stalled later that year, however, as global emissions rose again. American emissions declined, but Chinese coal burning increased.[50] In the first quarter of 2018, however, the Chinese brought on ten nuclear plants' worth of solar: ten gigawatts in three months' time.[51]

We *can* save the planet from the threat of collapse, but only if we act.

What will you do?

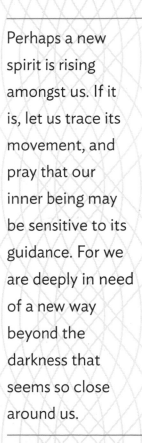

A Finer Future Is Possible

D AVID BROWER, founder of the modern environmental movement, once said, "What do we want the earth to be like fifty years from now? Let's do a little dreaming. Aim high. Navigators have aimed at the stars for centuries. They haven't hit one yet, but because they aimed high they found their way."

Humanity can avoid collapse. We have the technologies, we have the knowledge.

Do we have the wisdom?

Do we have the courage to change course?

Shared Well-being on a Healthy Planet

The ideas presented in this book should seem like common sense to most people. Rest assured that they do not come across that way to proponents of neoliberalism. If you've made it this far and are wondering why it seems so hard to create a world that works for most people, remember that since 1947 a small group of people have worked very hard to make the world just the way it is now. They mobilized massive amounts of money to drive their agenda, and they are benefitting enormously.[2]

Perhaps a new spirit is rising amongst us. If it is, let us trace its movement, and pray that our inner being may be sensitive to its guidance. For we are deeply in need of a new way beyond the darkness that seems so close around us.

MARTIN LUTHER KING, JR.[1]

315

Perhaps it will require the prospect of collapse under the neoliberal approach to convince those calling the shots to try another course. Or it could just take you deciding that we have a better way.

Regardless, we need to act, and soon. The global economy rests on a knife edge, based on unsustainable business practices. We suffer

+ growing inequity and the prospect of social and biophysical collapse;
+ rising levels of anger, fear, and intolerance; and
+ a growing thirst for meaning and connection.

We have left it too late to save many species or to avoid massive impacts of climate chaos. But we do have time to save humanity and many of the marvelous life-forms with whom we share this little planet, the only place in all the universe where we know that there is life.

If we act now.

Many priorities clamor for your attention. We believe that the opportunities set forth in this book merit your attention.

If we're to survive, the minimum requirement is to craft an economic system that respects the planet's capacity to regenerate itself. This means that economic activities cannot exceed any of the nine planetary limits set out by the scientists at Stockholm Resilience Centre described in chapter 1.

The next requirement is that we create a system that has sufficient equality to maintain social stability. High levels of inequality make it difficult for humanity to maintain a basic standard of living. If the nine planetary boundaries form the ceiling below which the human economy must operate, Kate Raworth's *Doughnut Economics* sets the foundation. We must provide these minimums to ensure that the economy ensures human dignity.

Living within planetary boundaries, avoiding the worst of climate change, dramatically reducing inequality, and meeting the basic needs of humankind will require tectonic changes in our economic system. It will require a fundamental shift in values, incentives, institutions, and the distribution of power on this planet.

But most of all, it requires stitching together the story of what it is we want and how to achieve it. In this time of profound disruption, our task is to create a compelling narrative and a powerful movement for a new economy based on the core values of human dignity, the common good, and stewardship.

It is time to distinguish between "ideal" and "better." But some elements are crucial. Our new system must have as its goals the equitable distribution of resources to maximize well-being for all within planetary ecological limits. The principles of this new narrative must be regenerative of natural and human systems—not striving just to sustain them. We must commit to long-term thinking and investment and ensure strong, democratic governance of our economy. Diverse and equitable ownership of resources will be essential if we are to preserve a strong non-market economy on which a real market economy can rest. From these principles, we will construct the compelling New Story needed to drive change.

The foundation for the new narrative is *well-being*. We must deliver dignity and a high quality of life for all. These outcomes are not negotiable. One cannot be traded off to achieve the other. Our goal, then, must not be a system that is efficient at funneling money to the already wealthy but the well-being of all. The economy is the toolbox to achieve this purpose of shared well-being. It is not the end in itself. The new narrative is about WEAll.

If humanity is to survive, it will be because we reconnect to the natural world that sustains us, and to each other. Ban Ki-moon said,

> Saving our planet, lifting people out of poverty, advancing economic growth…. These are one and the same fight. We must connect the dots between climate change, water scarcity, energy shortages, global health, food security and women's empowerment. Solutions to one problem must be solutions for all.[3]

In an age of "Me first," we need a new ethic, like the one shared by astronauts, that from space there are no border lines drawn across the globe.

A New Story

The neoliberals created and disseminated a message that rested on four principles: small government, free markets, freedom of the individual, and strong defense. Solutions exist, but requisite actors are not implementing them because the neoliberal narrative tells us,

+ The goal of the economy and business is to generate financial wealth only.
+ The only legitimate economic actor is the individual (person or corporation).
+ Freedom means disconnection from others and limited societal or government structures.
+ If we just let the market sort things out, all will be well.

These are continually repeated and have embedded themselves into our thinking and subconscious. As David Brooks argued,

> Up until now, America's story [And that story has been sold to the rest of the world, even into the heart of communist China] has been some version of the rags-to-riches story, the lone individual who rises from the bottom through pluck and work. But that story isn't working for people anymore, especially for people who think the system is rigged.

This book proposes a new story of shared well-being on a healthy planet. Those who care about having a future must now disseminate it. This is neither a left wing nor right wing exercise. It reaches for a transpartisan consensus on approaches that will deliver superior outcomes for all. It rejects neither the value of market mechanisms nor cooperative action for shared prosperity. It distills the best of both approaches into a new narrative of an economy in service to life.

Every chapter of this book makes clear that the new story rests on a very different mental model. It will require us to rethink every aspect of conventional economics:

+ GDP is not the same as well-being;
+ Natural capital and ecosystem services need to be accounted for;
+ We must distinguish between weak sustainability that comes

from checklists and strong sustainability that is the outcome of regenerative practices;

+ The system must address nonlinearity and tipping points;
+ We must prepare for far greater damage than climate models anticipate;
+ Financial systems must account for the value of sustainability;
+ They must write off stranded assets and many financial debts;
+ The debts to intact nature will be harder to repay;
+ We will shift from maximizing shareholder value to stakeholder value;
+ Inequalities must begin decreasing, not increasing;
+ Jobless growth will be replaced by meaningful contributions and livelihoods.

It is instructive to compare the old narrative with the new:[4]

Current economy	New, inclusive economy
GDP growth: more economic activity is the goal	"Beyond GDP": flourishing of all life is the aim
Short-termism: quarterly profits	Long-termism: durable prosperity
Maximization of return	Safeguarding of long-term opportunity
Shareholder value	Stakeholder value: benefit to society
Extraction of natural resources	Management of ecosystem integrity
Linear production systems	Circular production systems
Short-life products for sale	Long-life services
Efficiency measured in monetary terms (CBA)	Multidimensional resilience (e.g., multi-criterion analysis, MCA)

Credit: Eva Alfredsson and Anders Wijkman, "The Inclusive Green Economy," MISTRA 2014, mistra.org/download/18.2f9de4b14592a1589d172e2/140076556 1079/Mistra_Prestudy_TheInclusiveGreenEconomy_April2014+(1).pdf

This new way of seeing the world is more complex than the old one. It needs the storytellers and artists to weave it into a compelling narrative.

There is a business case, a personal case, and a global case for reframing these diverse conversations around an economy in service to life, a world in which the goal is universal well-being. It will enhance corporate effectiveness, bring a more fruitful framing to policy, unite activist efforts that have seen themselves as isolated, use a rich body of research, and create a community of learning that offers the promise of delivering solutions to some of the world's worst threats.

Work is needed across society but especially at the individual level, as Chris Laszlo,[5] faculty director for research and outreach at the Fowler Center at Case Western Reserve University, puts it: changing who leaders are, not just what they are doing. Change agents will adopt deep practices of engaged connectedness, from meditation to devoted gardening, time spent in nature, or any other practices that connect a person deeply to herself and to a purpose greater than herself. Each of us must find our path to internal wholeness and well-being in order to bring this to the larger world.

Much of the work must be done at the community level, at the national level, and globally. The art is to identify the scale at which any given action is needed to match the challenge, and then align your capabilities to the task. There is honor at every rung of the ladder. The graphic below seeks to outline how a few of the approaches discussed throughout the book fit into this spectrum. One of the tasks needed is to map the diversity of change agents and organizations and to ensure that they become a self-aware, supportive community. We haven't time, anymore, to be that bucket of crabs described earlier.

Change Is Possible

Some argue that the sort of societal transformation needed is impossible. Remember, though, massive transformations in society are occurring all around us. The music business has gone from vinyl to streaming. Kodak learned to its regret that it is better to disrupt your own business than to allow others to do it to you. Autonomous vehicles and renewable energy now threaten the oil, gas, coal, uranium, utility, automobile, and transportation industries—and all those invested in them. The possibility of block chain offers a free, secure, citizen-driven alternative to the financial services industry that could do more to destroy banking than Occupy ever dreamed possible.

Alternative Frames

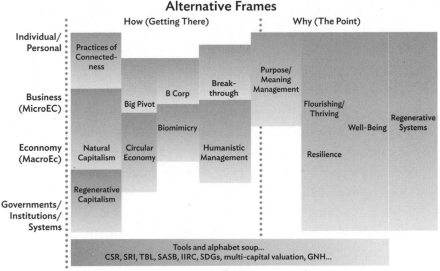

Note: Horizontal is not an axis—no meaning on left-right besides the two buckets.

Illustrative perspectives and tools to enable us to transition from a failing economy to a Finer Future. The measures on the left are foundational principles. The boxes in the middle are illustrative practices. The columns on the right are examples of what we seek to achieve. These are only a few of the thousands of useful frameworks, practices, and definitions of what success will be when we get there. Pick the ones that you resonate with. But pick something. Achieving change requires a set of core principles/values that will guide you in the arc of transition, clarify what you will do differently to achieve that new world, and provide a vision of where you want to get to.

Change of the magnitude we need *is* possible. The 20th century saw two major economic transformations. From the 1930s to the late 1970s, Keynesianism, with its emphasis on the management of markets, and social safety nets replaced the Gilded Era of the 1920s.

Then in the late 1970s, neoliberalism, with its focus on individualism and markets, answered that the common good required the freeing of markets and getting governments "off the backs" of the people. It became the dominant global economic narrative.

Each of these shifts occurred because advocates discredited the existing story, created a new narrative, weakened existing power bases, and constructed new ones.

If we combine what is known about how transformations occur with the best science of what is necessary, the outline of the way to avoid collapse emerges.

Teilhard de Chardin said that the future belongs to those who give hope to the next generation.[6] But hope is not a strategy.

For our new narrative, an economy in service to life, now emerging in the Wellbeing Economy Alliance and around the world, to replicate what the framers of the neoliberal paradigm did at Mont Pelerin and thereafter, its advocates must settle on a theory of change and then a strategy of change, as Lewis Powell did in 1971.

This book sets forth one such theory of change, the Meadows Memorandum, and a strategy: the transformation of finance, corporations, agriculture, energy. It sets forth the policy initiatives needed.

We don't have all the solutions. But we have the beginnings.

Our job, now, yours and mine, is to create a powerful movement for a new economy based on the core human values of human dignity, the common good, and stewardship. These values are resonant with the ancient wisdom we have forgotten.

We're changing stories. We're giving people a place to stand, a place to hold on to.

We have a powerful new story, one that tells how we want to live. If we are to avoid collapse, enough people must live this story and demand that their governments change policies and practices. We need courage to commit to the entrepreneurial experiments that can help us regain safety, respect for the sacred, and a sense of home again.

The poet Wendell Berry put it more elegantly in ending his "Poem on Hope":

> Because we have not made our lives to fit
> Our places, the forests are ruined, the fields eroded,
> The streams polluted, the mountains overturned. Hope
> Then to belong to your place by your own knowledge
> Of what it is that no other pace is, and by

Your caring for it as you care for no other place, this
Place that you belong to though it is not yours,
For it was from the beginning and will be to the end.[7]

Our new story tells of ways of being that are truer representations of who we really are than the neoliberal narrative. As described in chapter 3, the best science shows that many of the underlying assumptions of that old narrative are wrong. Most people are not the greedy, rugged individualists we've been told we all are. Rather, we seek goodness, caring, and connection first. All people need basic material support, but few of us are motivated primarily to acquire wealth. We seek to live lives that mean something, to leave the world a little better than we found it. And we long to bond with others who do the same. This is why organizations that respect dignity and implement more sustainable practices better engage workers, and all stakeholders, increasing productivity. These purpose-driven, sustainable brands deliver higher profitability.

For change to happen, people throughout society must demand it. Politicians, by nature of the electoral cycle, follow what people articulate as their demands. They are concerned mostly about whether they can persuade enough voters to fund them and reelect them in two years. Politicians won't lead us. But perhaps we can.

Our work is to empower this growing movement to create an economy resonant with the ancient wisdom we have forgotten. The work is internal as we, each of us, find our way. But it is also external. It will require you and me and all who would craft a finer future to get our hands dirty in the contract sport of politics.

The creation of new power bases or movements operating at all levels is needed—local, national, regional, and global. Such movements will be collaborating networks that draw on civil society, research and policy communities, business, multifaith groups, cultural icons, and new economics practitioners. They will operate at the level of values and principles and articulate a compelling story of possibility.

Dana Meadows wrote in her book *Beyond the Limits*:

Can the world actually ease down below the limits and avoid collapse? Is there time? Is there enough money, technology, freedom, vision, community, responsibility, foresight, discipline, and love on a global scale?

We think a transition to a sustainable world is technically and economically possible, but we know it is psychologically and politically daunting.

The sustainability revolution, if it happens, will be organic and evolutionary. It will arise from the visions, insights, experiments, and actions of billions of people.

It will require every human quality and skill, from technical ingenuity, economic entrepreneurism, and political leadership to honesty, compassion and love.

The world faces not a preordained future, but a choice. The choice is between mental models. One model says that this finite world for all practical purposes has no limits. Choosing that model will take us even further beyond the limits, and, we believe, to collapse within the next half century.

Another model says that the limits are real and close and that there is not enough time and that people cannot be moderate or responsible or compassionate. That model is self-fulfilling. If we choose to believe it, we will get to be right.

A third model says that the limits are real and close and there is just exactly enough time, with no time to waste. There is just exactly enough energy, enough material, enough money, enough environmental resilience, and enough human virtue to bring about a revolution to a better world.

That model might be wrong. All the evidence we have seen, however, from the world data to the global computer models suggests that it might be right. There is no way of knowing for sure, other than to do it.[8]

However difficult, across the globe, engaged groups *are* reimagining the economy and the society in which it resides. There are even the beginnings of a movement of seven nations who have met to form an alternative to the G7, perhaps called the WE-7: The Group of Well-being Economies. Nicola Sturgeon, the first minister of Scotland, has even begun referring to this in her speeches.

Traditional political parties are stuck in the logic of the industrial society and in the pockets of big business. We're in a crisis of politics. How can we entice the right people to become active?

People who think deeply about the future tend to focus on the proximate challenges. It's good that somebody does. But there is a risk that, if all you do is deal with crises every day, you fall prey to the view that they will, in the end, overcome our puny attempts to counter them. We can rattle off evidence of trends leading to collapse: that the parts per million level of carbon dioxide in the atmosphere continue to rise, that this is again going to be the hottest year on record since records have been kept, that we are losing every major ecosystem on the planet.

It's all true. But this fixation leaves no time to craft a vision of what it would mean to win, to build that Finer Future. Our movies are all apocalyptic. We know in detail how to battle zombies. We've put a man on the moon. We have no idea how men and women can walk in happiness on Earth.

What would, in Buckminster Fuller's words, "a world that works for 100 percent of humanity" look like? What would it feel like to live there?

Winning the Story Wars[9]

Alex Steffen, an extraordinary change agent and brilliant author of *World Changing*,[10] gave one answer in a speech to the 2015 Nature Conservancy Annual Trustee Meeting:[11]

A Talk Given at a Conservation Meeting a Hundred Years from Now....

We meet today to speak of great ancestors.

Here in 2115, we may find it hard to understand that a century ago, many people actually believed there was nothing we could do to stave off the planetary crisis we faced. Many had given up. Many did too little. Some even lived in denial of increasingly loud warnings from the world's scientists, or refused on ideological grounds to even consider change.

Humanity made calamitous mistakes in the Twentieth and early Twenty-first centuries, sometimes in the name of progress, but more often springing from inattention, ignorance or simple shortsighted greed.

The losses were staggering.

We live today surround by the legacy of those mistakes, that carelessness. The missing ice and rising seas, the burnt forests, the growing deserts, the toxic places, the tens of thousands of vanished plants and animals, the weather chaos we all experience, the conflicts over water and food and the refugees they've created. We've lost so much. We came far too close to losing nearly everything. If things went on as they were, we might have.

Instead, we live today on a healing planet. Yes, much has been lost, but much was saved or restored or reinvented, and what was saved and healed and made anew has become a powerful legacy.

Those gifts became the seedbeds from which sprouted our new world. That we have so much left from which to coax a long and bountiful tomorrow is no accident. Those seeds of hope were saved and planted and tended to by people who made the decision that they would live as if the future mattered. As if nature mattered. As if we mattered.

These were visionary people. Responsible people. Courageous people. All around the world, our best ancestors took up the challenge of leaving a different, bolder legacy, one not of error and loss, but of leadership, stewardship, innovation.

On every continent and in every sea, some of our most important wild places were made safe. Ecological restoration was begun. Species were saved. In the face of planetary catastrophe, the tide was turned.

Forests have begun once again to cover the Earth. The oceans teem with renewed life. In every community, people and nature are being reconnected. We live, again, in a world of whales, tall trees and awestruck children.

Our prosperity has found its rightful role within that living planetary fabric. Our great cities, our global industries, our science and our inventiveness have all grown past their destructive adolescence. They've matured within the boundaries of our single, small world. We've discovered, of course, that living within our limits has made us more inventive than we were when we believed there were no limits. Science, engineering, design, technology: all have grown more creative when faced with constraints. We are richer now than we were then, in every sense of wealth.

Our cities have become the engines of a bright green prosperity. Our ancestors began by planning and building ecological cities for billions more people. That work made possible innovative leaps in development and transportation. It helped rebuild slums into great neighborhoods, and develop entirely new districts that redefined the limits of urban ecology. Walkable neighborhoods, green buildings and low-carbon infrastructure have made our cities more livable, but they've also made our cities far lighter on the planet. Though more than eight billion people now live in cities, their footprint is tiny compared to people a century ago.

Our cities now, like cities then, depend on their interconnection with nature. Now, however, we recognize the value of the natural systems that support our lives, and we safeguard it. The rivers that give us our water have been protected and restored. On the farms that feed us, soil is conserved and biodiversity woven into our fields and orchards. Well-tended forests give us wood and fiber. Wetlands guard our cities from rising waters.

Our world, of course, is powered wholly by clean energy now. Near every city can be found longs rows of wind turbines, blades spinning slowly in the breeze, or fields of solar panels glittering in the sun. Carbon dioxide, meanwhile, is now being drawn back down out of the air, as forests regrow and carbon capturing crops are plowed back into our soil. The chemistry of the atmosphere is beginning, very slowly, to return to balance. We suffer tremendous disasters from the climate change already set in motion, of course, but restoring our climate is beginning to feel less like a dream than a plan of action.

Our common humanity and shared world has continued to inspire us to do better by one another and our own descendants. These are still tough times for many, and we still must to struggle [sic] to make our societies rugged in the face of chaos and erosion. Yet, we do not live in the apocalyptic hell many once seemed to think was our destiny. We have grappled with tremendous poverty, inequality, poor health, tyranny, failed states, ignorance and despair—and if haven't [sic] yet succeeded in making a world where everyone's basic needs are well-met, the intent to do so no longer seems utopian. When you have met great challenges, and won, you become less willing to accept the idea that some problems can never be overcome. Our ancestors gave us the early victories that today give us the strength to keep striving for not just a better world, but a fairer one.

If today, in the twenty-second century, we live in an era of optimism and hope, it is because some of our ancestors, in the dawn of the twenty-first, lived in a time of clarity and commitment.

When they understood the planetary crisis they faced, their answer was not cynicism or surrender, but to seek out others and together meet that crisis with action.

When they rose in the morning, they put their hands to not only the common tasks of providing for their families and communities, but the exceptional work of honoring their kinship with those who would live in generations to come, and laboring on our behalf to leave a bright green world.

When they sat to eat together, they not only nourished their bodies, they nourished their connection to Earth itself, and reminded themselves that humanity lives within this planet, not apart from it.

When they looked at the world, they taught themselves to see with fresh eyes, eyes that saw the world not as a thing, but as a vast, intricate dance of flows and systems, seasons and cycles. They understood that we are only a small part of all that. They understood that we're all in this together.

When they dreamt, they dreamt of rain and forests, rivers and prairies, oceans and reefs; of fishing and farming and lives lived outdoors. They dreamt of stewardship and healing, wonder and discovery. They dreamt of humanity coming home again.

When they took council together, they felt the hopes of their childrens' childrens' children keeping them company. They made ambitious plans.

When they rose to speak, they spoke not for themselves, but for human possibility and the renewed bounty of life on Earth. They spoke for bold action. They got to work, knowing time was short.

Where these ancestors gathered, heroes gathered.

And when they departed, they had given us back our future.

— Alex Steffen, November 3, 2015

It *is* possible for humanity to avoid total system collapse. It is possible to create a Finer Future. Attaining it is the challenge for every human alive today. It is our great work, and, as Buckminster Fuller also said, this is humanity's final exam.

Join us.

Notes

Acknowledgments

1. This gathering, sponsored by the KR Foundation, Natural Capitalism Solutions, and the Club of Rome, was held at Thomas Bjorkman's Ekskaret Conference Center. Facilitated by Huffington Post's Jo Confino, it was the genesis of this book.
2. Alliance for Sustainability and Prosperity, asap4all.com/
3. Leading For Wellbeing, leading4wellbeing.org/
4. Leading for Wellbeing Video, vimeo.com/161271346
5. Wellbeing Economy Alliance, wellbeingeconomy.org
6. WE-Africa, we-africa.org/

Introduction: Welcome to the Anthropocene

1. William Gibson, The Future Has Arrived—It's Just Not Evenly Distributed Yet," 24 January 2012, quoteinvestigator.com/2012/01/24/future-has-arrived/
2. Will Steffen et al., "The Trajectory of the Anthropocene," favaretoufabc.files.wordpress.com/2013/06/2015-steffen-et-al-the-great-acceleration-1.pdf
3. Berrien Moore, "Sustaining Earth's Life Support System," Global Change Newsletter, May 2000, igbp.net/download/18.316f1832132347017758000 1401/1376383088452/NL41.pdf
4. Paul Voosen, "Atomic Bombs and Oil Addiction Herald Earth's New Epoch: The Anthropocene," Science, August 24, 2016.
5. Adam Vaughn, "Human Impact Has Pushed Earth into the Anthropocene, Scientists Say," The Guardian, January 7, 2016.
6. Colin N. Waters et al., "The Anthropocene Is Functionally and Stratigraphically Distinct from the Holocene," Science, January 8, 2016.
7. Nathaniel Rich, "The Lawyer Who Became DuPont's Worst Nightmare," New York Times, January 6, 2016.
8. "Up to 90% of Seabirds Have Plastic in Their Guts, Study Finds," Associated Press, The Guardian, September 1, 2015,
9. Lynn Hasselverger, "22 Facts About Plastic Pollution (And 10 Things You Can Do About It)," EcoWatch, August 7, 2014, ecowatch.com/2014/04/07/22-facts-plastic-pollution-10-things-can-do-about-it/

10. BP Statistical Review of World Energy 2006.

11. *Natural Capital at Risk*, trucost.com/_uploads/publishedResearch/TEEB%20Final%20Report%20-%20web%20SPv2.pdf

12. Simon Kuznets, 1934. *National Income 1929–1932*. A report to the US Senate 73rd Congress, 2nd Session, Washington, DC, US Government Printing Office, pp. 3–5.

13. clubofrome.org/activities/reports/

14. earth-policy.org/publications/

15. George Monbiot, "Neoliberalism: The Ideology at the Root of All Our Problems," *The Guardian*, April 15, 2016.

16. Safa Motesharrei et al., "'Human And Nature DYnamical' Study: HANDY: Human and Nature Dynamics: Modeling Inequality and Use of Resources in the Collapse or Sustainability of Societies," *Ecological Economics*, Vol. 101, May 2014, pp. 90–102.

Section 1: It'll Do Til the Mess Arrives

1. Tommy Lee Jones, actor in *No Country for Old Men*, Miramax, 2007.

2. Dark Mountain, dark-mountain.net/

3. Robert Krulwich, "How Human Beings Almost Vanished from Earth in 70,000 BC," *Krulwich Wonders*, National Public Radio, October 22, 2012, npr.org/sections/krulwich/2012/10/22/163397584/how-human-beings-almost-vanished-from-earth-in-70-000-b-c

4. Anne Minard, "Early Humans Were Prey, Not Predators, Experts Say," *National Geographic News*, March 7, 2006, news.nationalgeographic.com/news/2006/03/0307_060307_human_prey.html

5. John Fullerton, *Regenerative Capitalism*, Capital Institute, 2015, capitalinstitute.org/wp-content/uploads/2015/04/2015-Regenerative-Capitalism-4-20-15-final.pdf

Chapter 1: Imagine

1. Dana Meadows, "Envisioning a Sustainable World," Academy for Systems Change, October 24–28, 1994, donellameadows.org/archives/envisioning-a-sustainable-world/

2. Rumah Minimilis, 2015, blog.arsitekonline.com/2010/02/rumah-cohousing-perumahan-berkonsep.html

3. Mohammad A. Alshenaifi, "High Performance Homes in Saudi Arabia," Philadelphia University, May 2015, philau.edu/sustainability/inc/documents/theses/MohammadAlshenaifiFinalThesis.pdf

4. Warm and Humid Climates, Passivhaus UK, passivhaus.org.uk/page.jsp?id=19

5. Safa Motesharrei et al., "'Human And Nature DYnamical' Study: HANDY: Human and Nature Dynamics: Modeling Inequality and Use of Resources in the Collapse or Sustainability of Societies," *Ecological Economics*, Vol. 101, May 2014, pp. 90–102.

6. E.g., Ian Angus, "What Did That 'NASA-funded Collapse Study' Really Say?" *Climate and Capitalism*, March 31, 2015, climateandcapitalism.com /2014/03/31/nasa-collapse-study/

7. Steve Melia, "On the Road to Sustainability: Transport and Car-free Living in Freiburg," UWE Bristol, carfree.com/papers/freiburg.pdf

8. Kevin Drum, "The Future of Mass Transit Is Driverless," December 31, 2016, *Mother Jones*.

9. Jeevan Yasagar, "Indonesia Toxic Haze Kills 100,000 in One Year," *Financial Times*, September 20, 2016, p. 4.

10. George Ogleby, "Palm Oil Sector Agrees on Unified 'No Deforestation' Approach," *Edie*, November 10, 2016, edie.net/news/7/Palm-oil-sector -agrees--no-deforestation--approach/?utm_source=dailynewsletter,%20 edie%20daily%20newsletter&utm_medium=email,%20email&utm_con tent=news&utm_campaign=dailynewsletter,%208e02e572e9-dailynews letter

11. Sustainable soy, rapeseed, and sunflower oils, unilever.com/sustainable -living/reducing-environmental-impact/sustainable-sourcing/our -approach-to-sustainable-sourcing/sustainable-soy-rapeseed-and -sunflower-oils/

12. Transforming the palm oil industry, unilever.com/sustainable-living /reducing-environmental-impact/sustainable-sourcing/transforming -the-palm-oil-industry/#244-423980

13. Indonesia Ecotourism Network, indecon.or.id/en/

14. *Economic Benefit of Palm Oil to Indonesia*, World Growth, 2011, worldgrowth.org/site/wp-content/uploads/2012/06/WG_Indonesian _Palm_Oil_Benefits_Report-2_11.pdf

15. *Unilever Extends Agreement on Sustainable Algal Oil*, March 15, 2016, worldgrowth.org/site/wp-content/uploads/2012/06/WG_Indonesian _Palm_Oil_Benefits_Report-2_11.pdf

16. Tomas Friedman, "What If?" *New York Times*, January 20, 2016.

17. John Wong, "China's Economy 2016, How 'Scary' Is Its Sustained Slow-down?" *Straits Times*, January 9, 2016, straitstimes.com/opinion/chinas -economy-2016-how-scary-is-its-sustained-slowdown

18. Nick Cunningham, "The Oil Rally Is Running Out of Steam," *Business Insider*, 13, January 2017, markets.businessinsider.com/commodities /news/oil-prices-running-out-of-reasons-to-rally-2017-1-1001664179

19. Anders Borg, "How Will the Fourth Industrial Revolution Affect Economic Policy?" World Economic Forum, January 28, 2016, weforum .org/agenda/2016/01/how-will-the-fourth-industrial-revolution-affect -economic-policy?utm_content=bufferee98e&utm_medium=social &utm_source=twitter.com&utm_campaign=buffer

20. Nagaire Woods, "Populism Is Spreading: This Is What Is Driving It," World Economic Forum, December 9, 2016, weforum.org/agenda/2016 /12/populism-is-spreading-this-is-whats-driving-it

21. Lucify, "A Novel Visualisation of the Refugee Crisis," *Medium*, October 21, 2015, medium.com/@lucify/a-novel-visualisation-of-the-refugee-crisis-565e40ab5a50#.jio3odbco

22. Steven Levitsky and Daniel Ziblatt, "Is Donald Trump a Threat to Democracy?" *New York Times*, December 16, 2016.

23. "Central Banks Can't Save the Markets from a Crash. They Shouldn't Even Try," *The Guardian*, August 30, 2015.

24. Jenna Orkin, *The Moron's Guide to Global Collapse*, 2012.

25. Fernando Aguirre, "What to Expect from the Government After Collapse," The Shift Network, December 23, 2011, shtfplan.com/emergency-preparedness/what-to-expect-from-the-government-after-the-collapse_12232011

26. Economic Collapse 2016, Google, google.com/webhp?sourceid=chrome-instant&ion=1&espv=2&ie=UTF-8#q=economic%20collapse%202016

27. Dominique Mosbergen, "Air Pollution Causes 4,400 Deaths in China Every Single Day: Study," *Huffington Post*, August 14, 2015, huffingtonpost.com/entry/air-pollution-china-deaths_us_55cd9a62e4b0ab468d9cefa9

28. Reuters, "More Indians Than Chinese Will Die from Air Pollution: Researcher," *Financial Express*, August 18, 2016, financialexpress.com/economy/india-air-pollution-death-rate-to-outpace-china-researcher/351209/

29. *Sin Luz: Life Without Power*, Hernández, Arelis R., Leaming, Whitney, and Murphy, Zoeann, *Washington Post*, video, December 14, 2017, washingtonpost.com/graphics/2017/national/puerto-rico-life-without-power/?tid=sm_tw&utm_term=.1b326a1dce72

30. Mark Fishetti, "Climate Change Hastened Syria's Civil War," *Scientific American*, March 2, 2015.

31. John Vidal, "Global Warming Could Create 150 Million 'Climate Refugees' by 2050," *The Guardian*, November 2, 2009.

32. "A Global Crisis: Life in Fragile States and the Effects of Mass Migration," *Global Washington*, 2016, globalwa.org/issues/2016-2/fragile-states-mass-migration/

33. Aryn Baker, "How Climate Change Is Behind the Surge of Migrants to Europe, *Time Magazine*, September 7, 2015.

34. Daniel Bilefsky and Alison Smale, "Dozens of Migrants Drown as European Refugee Crisis Continues," *New York Times*, January 22, 2016.

35. Nagaire Woods, "Populism Is Spreading: This Is What Is Driving It," World Economic Forum, December 9, 2016, weforum.org/agenda/2016/12/populism-is-spreading-this-is-whats-driving-it

36. *Report of the High Level Panel on Humanitarian Financing*, January 12, 2016, worldhumanitariansummit.org/whs_finance/HLPhumanitarian financing

37. Mark Anderson, "$1.4tn a Year Needed to Reach Global Goals for World's Poorest," *The Guardian*, November 18, 2015.
38. Gregor Aisch, Adam Pearce, and Bryant Rousseau, "How Far Is Europe Swinging to the Right?" *New York Times*, July 5, 2016.
39. Christiana Figueres, "Restoring Hope," *Huffington Post*, July 14, 2016, huffingtonpost.com/christiana-figueres/restoring-hope_b_10974734 .html
40. "The State of Homelessness in America 2012–2016, National Alliance to End Homelessness, April 1, 2015, endhomelessness.org/library/entry /the-state-of-homelessness-in-america-2015
41. Jordan Golson, "It's Time to Fix America's Infrastructure," *Wired Magazine*, January 23, 2015, wired.com/2015/01/time-fix-americas -infrastructure-heres-start/
42. Matthew Dolan, "Flint Crisis Could Cost U.S. a $300B Lead Pipe Overhaul, Agency Warns," *Detroit Free Press*, March 5, 2016, freep.com/story /news/local/michigan/flint-water-crisis/2016/03/04/flint-crisis-could -cost-us-300b-lead-pipe-overhaul-agency-warns/81316860/
43. Gayle McDonald, "Youth Anxiety on the Rise Amid Changing Climate," *Globe and Mail*, May 1, 2014, updated March 25, 2017.
44. Mark Hay, "Can Big Data Help Us Fight Rising Suicide Rates?" *Good Magazine*, September 6, 2015, magazine.good.is/articles/suicide -prevention-week-data-driven-efforts
45. nydailynews.com/life-style/health/1-12-teens-attempted-suicide-report -article-1.1092622
46. Marcus Gilmer, "Forgotten Twitter Password Comes at a Real Awkward Time for Hawaii's Governor," *Mashable*, January 23, 2018, mashable.com /2018/01/23/hawaii-governor-missile-alert-twitter-password/#wLLPh VPpkmqi
47. Johan Rockström et al., "A Safe Operating Space for Humanity," *Nature*, September 23, 2007.
48. John H. Richardson, "When the End of Human Civilization Is Your Day Job," *Esquire Magazine*, July 7, 2015.
49. "Growing Roots Program Seeks to Improve Fresh Food Access and Education in City Communities," Unilever, February 16, 2016, unileverusa.com/news/news-and-features/2016/growing-roots -program-seeks-to-improve-fresh-food-access.html
50. Bard MBA, bard.edu/mba/
51. Wellbeing-Africa, we-africa.org/the-network/
52. Daniel Kammen, Kamal Kapadia, and Mattias Fripp, "Putting Renewables to Work: How Many Jobs Can the Clean Energy Industry Generate?" Energy and Resources Group, Goldman School of Public Policy, April 13, 2004 rael.berkeley.edu/old_drupal/sites/default/files /old-site-files/2004/Kammen-Renewable-Jobs-2004.pdf
53. Nur Energie, nurenergie.com/

54. Helena Smith, "A Year After the Crisis Was Declared Over, Greece Is Still Spiraling Down," *The Guardian*, August 13, 2016.

55. Tony Seba, Clean Disruption of Energy and Transportation, 2014, Tony Seba Beta Edition, 2014, tonyseba.com/portfolio-item/clean-disruption -of-energy-transportation/

56. "Commit To 100% Renewable Power," We Mean Business, wemean businesscoalition.org/take-action/commit-100-renewable-power

57. Lord Nicholas Stern and Dimitri Zenghelis, "The Importance of Looking Forward to Manage Risks: Submission to the Task Force on Climate-Related Financial Disclosures," Grantham Research Institute, June 2016, lse.ac.uk/GranthamInstitute/wp-content/uploads/2016/06 /Zenghelis-and-Stern-policy-paper-June-2016.pdf

58. "Energy in Scotland: Get the Facts," Scottish Government, gov.scot /Topics/Business-Industry/Energy/Facts

59. Maria Gallucci, "Costa Rica Barely Used Any Fossil Fuels in 2016," *Mashable*, January 1, 2017, mashable.com/2017/01/01/costa-rica-renewable -energy-2016/?utm_content=buffere40ce&utm_medium=social&utm _source=twitter.com&utm_campaign=buffer#1b4KEyFgMmqJ

60. Cassie Werber, "Where in the World Have We Achieved 100% Renewable Power?" *Quartz*, December 18, 2015, qz.com/576437/which-places -have-achieved-100-renewable-power/

61. "Study to Find Out If the UAE Can Use 100% Renewable Energy by 2050," November 16, 2016, dubaieye1038.com/study-find-out-if-the-uae -can-use-100-renewable-energy-by-2025/

62. Fiona Harvey, "Saudi Arabia Reveals Plans to be Powered Entirely by Renewable Energy," *The Guardian*, May 29, 2015.

63. "List of Cities to Go 100% Renewable Continues to Grow," *Engerati*, January 29, 2016, engerati.com/article/list-cities-go-100-renewable -continues-grow; Jan Lee, "1200+ Businesses, Cities and States Tell World 'We're Still In,'" *Triple Pundit*, June 12, 2017, triplepundit.com/2017 /06/still-paris-businesses-tell-trump/; Andrea Reimer, "100% Renewable Energy: The New Normal?" *Huffington Post*, April 24, 2015, huffingtonpost.com/andrea-reimer/100-renewable-energy-the-new -normal_b_7126906.html

64. Dimbangombe Center, africacentreforholisticmanagement.org /dimbangombe-learning-centre.html

65. Johan Rockström and Pavan Sukhdev, "How Food Connects All the SDGs," Stockholm Resilience Center, December 2016, stockholm resilience.org/research/research-news/2016-06-14-how-food-connects -all-the-sdgs.html

66. "The Sustainable Development Agenda," United Nations, January 1, 2016, un.org/sustainabledevelopment/development-agenda/

67. Dana Meadows et al., *The Limits to Growth*, Club of Rome, 1972, clubof-rome.org/report/the-limits-to-growth/

68. Dana Meadows et al., *Beyond the Limits*, Chelsea Green, 1992.

69. Mark Strauss, "Looking Back on Limits to Growth," *Smithsonian Magazine*, April 2012.

70. Graham Turner, "Is Global Collapse Imminent?" August 4, 2014, sustainable.unimelb.edu.au/sites/default/files/docs/MSSI-Research Paper-4_Turner_2014.pdf

71. Johan Rockström et al., "A Safe Operating Space for Humanity," *Nature*, Vol. 461, September 24, 2009. The systems include climate change, novel entities, stratospheric ozone depletion, atmospheric aerosol loading, ocean acidification, biochemical flows, freshwater use, land-system change, and biosphere integrity.

72. Johan Rockström et al., "Planetary Boundaries 2.0," new and improved, stockholmresilience.org/21/research/research-news/1-15-2015-planetary -boundaries-2.0---new-and-improved.html

73. Rockström et al., "A Safe Operating Space for Humanity."

74. Global Footprint Network: footprintnetwork.org/en/index.php/GFN /page/world_footprint/

75. William Rees, "Why Degrowth," Part 1 of 3, The Extraenviromentalist, YouTube, April 17, 2014, youtube.com/watch?v=zJQdVCwOZiY

76. Boris Worm, Edward B. Barbier, et al., "Impacts of Biodiversity Loss on Ocean Ecosystem Services," *Science*, 314, 2006, pp. 787-790.

77. Global Footprint Network, footprintnetwork.org/en/index.php/GFN /page/methodology/

78. For a discussion of how the calculations are made, see Charlotte McDonald, "How Many Earths Do We Need," *BBC News Magazine*, June 16, 2015, bbc.com/news/magazine-33133712

79. Edward O. Wilson, *Half Earth*, Norton, 2016.

80. "Global Biodiversity Outlook 3," Secretariat of the UN Convention on Biodiversity, 2010, cbd.int/doc/publication s/gbo/gbo3-final-en.pdf

81. Yadigar Sekerci and Sergei Petrovskii, "Mathematical Modeling of Plankton–Oxygen Dynamics Under the Climate Change," *Bulletin of Mathematical Biology*, Vol. 77, Issue 12, December 2015, pp. 2325–2353.

82. *The Global Risks Report*, World Economic Forum, 2016, www3.weforum .org/docs/Media/TheGlobalRisksReport2016.pdf

83. Bishop Desmond Tutu, "Desmond Tutu: We Fought Apartheid; Now Climate Change Is Our Global Enemy," *The Guardian*, September 20, 2014.

84. *Warming World: Impacts by Degree*, based on the National Research Council report, *Climate Stabilization Targets: Emissions, Concentrations, and Impacts over Decades to Millennia*, 2011, dels.nas.edu/materials /booklets/warming-world

85. Alex Renton, "More Fatal Earthquakes to Come, Warn Geologists," *Newsweek*, April 28, 2015, europe.newsweek.com/nepal-earthquake -could-have-been-manmade-disaster-climate-change-brings-326017. This thesis is also supported by the Migration Policy Institute, migration policy.org/article/top-10-2015-issue-7-climate-change-and-natural -disasters-displace-millions-affect

86. Pope Francis, *Laudato Si*, w2.vatican.va/content/dam/francesco/pdf/encyclicals/documents/papa-francesco_20150524_enciclica-laudato-si_en.pdf

87. Suzanne Goldenberg, "Climate Change: The Poor Will Suffer Most," *The Guardian*, March 31, 2014.

88. Full text of President Obama's Glacier Conference Speech, August 31, 2015, ktuu.com/news/news/full-text-of-president-obamas-speech/35027560

89. Lester Brown, *Full Planet, Empty Plates*, Earth Policy Institute, W.W. Norton, 2012.

90. Marco Springman et al., "Global and Regional Health Effects of Future Food Production Under Climate Change," *The Lancet*, March 2, 2016.

91. William J. Ripple et al., and 15,364 scientist signatories from 184 countries, "World Scientists' Warning to Humanity: A Second Notice," *Bioscience*, November 13, 2017, academic.oup.com/bioscience/advance-article/doi/10.1093/biosci/bix125/4605229

92. Christiana Figueres et al., "Three Years to Safeguard Our Climate," *Nature*, June 28, 2017, nature.com/news/three-years-to-safeguard-our-climate-1.22201

93. Safa Motesharrei et al., "'Human And Nature Dynamical' Study: HANDY: Human and Nature Dynamics: Modeling Inequality and Use of Resources in the Collapse or Sustainability of Societies," sciencedirect.com/science/article/pii/S0921800914000615

94. "An Economy for the 99 Percent," Oxfam, January 2017, oxfamamerica.org/static/media/files/bp-economy-for-99-percent-160117-en.pdf

95. Ibid.

96. Kim Hjelmgaard, "Study: 8 People Have Same Wealth As World's Poorest Half," *USA Today*, January 15, 2017.

97. "#OWS VICTORY: The People Have Prevailed, Gear Up for Global Day of Action," October 14, 2011, occupywallst.org/article/ows-victory-people-have-prevailed-gear-global-day-/

98. OccupyWallStreet, "We Are the 99%," occupywallst.org/about/

99. *62 People Own the Same As Half the World, Reveals Oxfam Davos Report*, January 18, 2016, oxfam.org/en/pressroom/pressreleases/2016-01-18/62-people-own-same-half-world-reveals-oxfam-davos-report

100. Richard Wilkinson and Kate Pickett, *The Spirit Level*, Bloomsbury Press, 2010.

101. The Equality Trust, equalitytrust.org.uk/

102. Richard Wilkinson and Kate Pickett, "A Convenient Truth," Fabian Ideas 638, Fabian Society, 2014, community-wealth.org/content/convenient-truth-better-society-us-and-planet

103. "Off the Deep End: The Wall St. Bonus Pool and Low-wage Workers," Institute for Policy Studies, 2016, ips-dc.org/wp-content/uploads/2016/03/Wall-Street-bonuses-v-minimum-wage-2016-FINAL.pdf

104. Sam Becker, "The $70,000 Minimum Wage Experiment Reveals a Dark Truth," CheatSheet, January 4, 2017, cheatsheet.com/money -career/the-70000-minimum-wage-experiment-reveals-a-dark-truth .html/?a=viewall

105. For a rigorous discussion of this, see Neva Goodwin, usbig.net/ papers/GoodwinNhouseholdBIG.doc

106. Kate McFarland, "Finland: Basic Income Experiment Authorized by Parliament," Basic Income Earth Network, December 18, 2016, basicincome.org/news/2016/12/finland-basic-income-experiment -authorized-parliament/

107. Scott Santens, "Minimum Wages vs. Universal Basic Income," *Huffington Post*, August 11, 2015, updated December 6, 2017, huffington post.com/scott-santens/minimum-wages-vs-universal-basic-income _b_7957850.html

108. Safa Motesharrei et al., "Human and Nature Dynamics: Modeling Inequality and Resources in the Collapse or Sustainability of Societies," *Ecological Economics*, May 2014, pp. 90–102.

109. Nell Greenfieldboyce, "2016 Was the Hottest Year Yet, Scientists Declare," National Public Radio, January 18, 2017, npr.org/sections /thetwo-way/2017/01/18/510405739/2016-was-the-hottest-year-yet -scientists-declare

110. Bilal Pervez, "This Map Shows the Incredible Growth of Megacities," *World Economic Forum*, July 12, 2016, weforum.org/agenda/2016/07/this -map-shows-the-incredible-growth-of-megacities/

111. "Lagos Population 2018," World Population Review, worldpopulationreview.com/world-cities/lagos-population/

112. Fiona Harvey, "Seven Things We Learned from Lord Stern's New Climate Economy Report," *The Guardian*, September 16, 2014.

113. John Fullerton, "City States Rising," Capital Institute, December 29, 2016, capitalinstitute.org/blog/category/city-states/

114. Kate Gorden, *Risky Business: The Economic Risks of Climate Change in the United States*, Risky Business Project, June 2014, riskybusiness.org /site/assets/uploads/2015/09/RiskyBusiness_Report_WEB_09_08_14 .pdf

115. Nicholas Stern, "The Economics of Climate Change," Chancellor of the Exchequer, October 30, 2006, mudancasclimaticas.cptec.inpe .br/~rmclima/pdfs/destaques/sternreview_report_complete.pdf

116. Marshall Burke, Matthew Davis, and Noah Diffenbaugh, *Nature*, May 23, 2018.

117. "A Strategic Approach to Climate Action in Cities: Focused Accel-eration," McKinsey Center for Business and Environment, November 2017, mckinsey.com/business-functions/sustainability-and-resource -productivity/our-insights/a-strategic-approach-to-climate-action-in -cities-focused-acceleration

118. Robert Walton, "How Fort Collins Colorado Plans to Reach Zero Carbon Emissions by 2050," *Utility Dive*, April 29, 2015, utilitydive.com /news/how-fort-collins-co-plans-to-reach-zero-carbon-emissions-by -2050/392118/

119. We Mean Business Coalition, wemeanbusinesscoalition.org/

120. Marc Engel, "Local Sourcing Is the Future," *This Is Africa*, May 31, 2013, thisisafricaonline.com/Analysis/Local-sourcing-is-the-future ?ct=true

121. "Seattle's Carbon Neutrality Initiative Achieving a Carbon Neutral Food System," Food Systems Working Group, City of Seattle, 2010, clerk.ci.seattle.wa.us/~public/meetingrecords/2010/spun c20100914_6b_pm.pdf

122. Anna-Maria Renner, "Solar Energy Can Change Greece," Greenpeace International, March 1, 2016, greenpeace.org/international /en/news/Blogs/makingwaves/solar-energy-greece-debt-rhodes -renewables/blog/55692/

123. "Special Memorial Edition for Donella 'Dana' Meadows, 1941– 2001," *Balaton Bulletin*, Newsletter of the Balaton Group, April 2001, donellameadows.org/archives/the-balaton-bulletin/

124. Dana Meadows, "Beyond the Limits: Executive Summary," 1992, natcapsolutions.org/natcaptest2/beyond-the-limits-executive-summary/

125. Dana Meadows, "Envisioning a Sustainable World," Donella Meadows Archives, October 24-28, 1994, donellameadows.org/archives /envisioning-a-sustainable-world/

Chapter 2: The Story That Got Us In Trouble

1. "Nelson Mandela Speech at Trafalgar Square," YouTube, youtube.com /watch?v=tevKVIcHscw

2. Peter Salonius, "Agriculture: Unsustainable Resource Depletion Began 10,000 Years Ago," *The Oil Drum*, October 20, 2008, planetthoughts.org /?pg=pt/Whole&qid=2542

3. Jamie Weiss, "'Solution-caused Problems' and How to Prevent Them," *Manufacturing Net*, January 4, 2012, manufacturing.net/article/2012/01 /solution-caused-problems-and-how-prevent-them

4. Milton Friedman, *Capitalism and Freedom*, Fortieth Anniversary Edition, University of Chicago Press, 2002.

5. Philip Mirowski, *The Road from Mont Pelerin*, Harvard University Press, June 2009.

6. Jonathan Catalan, "Government Spending Is Bad Economics," *Mises Daily*, March 31, 2011, mises.org/library/government-spending-bad -economics

7. Ibid.

8. Murray Rothbard, "Freedom, Inequality, Primitivism, and the Division of Labor," *Mises Daily*, Mises Institute, August 9, 2008, mises.org/library /freedom-inequality-primitivism-and-division-labor

9. Quoted in Beatrix Campbell, "Neoliberal Neopatriarchy: The Case for Gender Revolution," 50.50 inclusive democracy, January 6, 2014, open democracy.net/5050/beatrix-campbell/neoliberal-neopatriarchy-case -for-gender-revolution

10. Jim Clayton, "A Nation of Wimps and Sheep," CDN, July 4, 2015, conservativedailynews.com/2015/07/a-nation-of-wimps-and-sheep/

11. Leland Ryken, "The Puritans and Money," A Puritan's Mind, apuritansmind.com/stewardship/rykenlelandpuritansandmoney/

12. Genesis, The Bible, King James Edition.

13. This derived from the adaptation of agency theory by Michael Jensen, who was trained at Friedman's Chicago School of Economics.

14. Milton Friedman, "The Social Responsibility of Business Is to Increase Its Profits," New York Times, September 13, 1970.

15. David Moore, "GOP Tax Cuts Will Strengthen Our Economy and Drive Democrats Nuts," Fox News, December 13, 2017, foxnews.com /opinion/2017/12/13/gop-tax-cuts-will-strengthen-our-economy-and -drive-democrats-crazy.html

16. George Monbiot, "How Ayn Rand Became the New Right's Version of Marx," The Guardian, March 5, 2012.

17. Lewis Powell, "Attack on American Free Enterprise System," Reclaim Democracy, August 23, 1971, reclaimdemocracy.org/powell_memo _lewis/

18. Lewis Powell, "Confidential Memorandum: Attack on the Free Enterprise System," August 23, 1971, quoted in Kim Phelps-Fein, Invisible Hands: The Making of the Conservative Movement from the New Deal to Reagan, New York: Norton, 2009, pp. 158, 160.

19. Sally Covington, "How Conservative Philanthropies and Think Tanks Transform US Policy," Covert Action Quarterly, mediafilter.org/CAQ /caq63/caq63thinktank.html

20. People for the American Way, "Buying a Movement," 1995, pfaw.org/sites /default/files/buyingamovement.pdf

21. Ben Tarnoff, "Donald Trump, Peter Thiel and the Death of Democracy," The Guardian, July 21, 2016.

22. George Monbiot, "Our Democracy Is Broken, Debased and Distrusted, But There Are Ways to Fix It." The Guardian, January 25, 2017.

23. Personal communication, E. Von Weizsäcker to Hunter Lovins, April 17, 2016.

24. Michael Fleming and Weiling Liu, "Near Failure of Long-term Capital Management," Federal Reserve Bank of New York, September 1998, federalreservehistory.org/Events/DetailView/52

25. "Timeline: A Chronology of Enron Corp." New York Times, January 18, 2006.

26. Simon Romero and Riva Atlas, "Worldcom's Collapse: The Overview; Worldcom Files for Bankruptcy; Largest Case," New York Times, July 22, 2002.

27. Thomas I. Palley, "Financialization: What It Is and Why It Matters," Levy Economics Institute and Economics for Democratic and Open Societies, December 2007, levyinstitute.org/pubs/wp_525.pdf

28. Zaid Jilani, "CHART: Top 'U.S.' Corporations Outsourced More Than 2.4 Million American Jobs Over the Last Decade," *Think Progress*, April 19, 2011, thinkprogress.org/chart-top-u-s-corporations-outsourced-more -than-2-4-million-american-jobs-over-the-last-decade-2ea66dfc0e35# .vy5uwbm86

29. Sean Wilentz, "A Scandal for Our Time, *The American Prospect*, January 31, 2002, prospect.org/article/scandal-our-time

30. Pia Lee-Brago, "ILO: Recession, Massive Job Loss Threaten Global Economy," *Philippine Star*, November 2, 2011, philstar.com/Article.aspx ?articleId=743718&publicationSubCategoryId=

31. Paul Krugman, "Why We're in a New Gilded Age," *New York Review of Books*, May 8, 2014.

32. Annie Lowrey, "For Two Economists, the Buffett Rule Is Just a Start," *New York Times*, April 16, 2012.

33. Ezra Klein, "In 2010, 93 Percent of Income Gains Went to the Top 1 Per-cent," *Washington Post*, March 5, 2010.

34. "An Economy for the 1%," Oxfam, 2016, oxfam.org/sites/www.oxfam.org /files/file_attachments/bp210-economy-one-percent-tax-havens-180116 -en_0.pdf

35. "Before House and Senate Vote, Here's 13 Worst Things in Trump-GOP Tax Scam," *Common Dreams*, December 19, 2017, commondreams.org /news/2017/12/19/house-and-senate-vote-heres-13-worst-things-trump -gop-tax-scam?

36. Thomas Piketty, *Capital in the 21st Century*, Belknap Press, 2014.

37. Nicholas Kristof, "An Idiot's Guide to Inequality," *New York Times*, July 23, 2014.

38. Thomas Piketty and Emanuel Saez, "Top 1% Fiscal Income Share, USA, 1913-2015," World Wealth and Income Database, 2018, wid.world /share/#0/countrytimeseries/sfiinc_p99p100_z/US/2015/eu/k/p /yearly/s/false/7.476000000000002/25/curve/false

39. Joseph Stiglitz, *The Price of Inequality*, W.W. Norton and Co., 2012, p. 7.

40. Joseph Stiglitz, "Of the 1%, by the 1%, for the 1%," *Vanity Fair*, May 2011.

41. Evan Osnos, "Doomsday Prep for the Super-rich," *New Yorker*, January 30, 2017.

42. Nick Hanauer, "The Pitchforks Are Coming…for Us Plutocrats," *Politico Magazine*, July/August 2014, politico.com/magazine/story/2014/06/the -pitchforks-are-coming-for-us-plutocrats-108014

43. Paul Krugman, "The Case for Cuts Was a Lie. Why Does Britain Still Believe It? The Austerity Delusion." *The Guardian*, April 29, 2015.

44. Carmen Reinhart and Kenneth Rogoff, *Growth in a Time of Debt*, Harvard University, 2010.

45. Paul Krugman, "The Excel Depression, *New York Times*, April 18, 2013.

46. Paul Krugman, "Austerity and Growth, Again," *New York Times*, April 24, 2012.

47. Laurence Ball et al., *The Distributional Effects of Fiscal Consolidation*, IMF Working Paper, IMF Research Department, 2013, imf.org/external/pubs/ft/wp/2013/wp13151.pdf

48. Ibid.

49. "The True Cost of Austerity and Inequality: Norway Case Study," Oxfam, September 2013, oxfam.org/sites/www.oxfam.org/files/cs-true-cost-austerity-inequality-norway-120913-en.pdf

50. Niraj Chokshi, "Norway Is No. 1 in Happiness. The U.S., Sadly, Is No. 14," *New York Times*, March 20, 2017.

51. "The True Cost of Austerity and Inequality."

52. Ibid.

53. Facundo Alvaredo, "Inequality Over the Past Century," *Finance and Development*, 48, 3, IMF, 2011, imf.org/external/pubs/ft/fandd/2011/09/picture.htm

54. Edmund Andrews, "Greenspan Concedes Error on Regulation," *New York Times*, October 23, 2008.

55. Dan Kopf, "Data Show That the World's Poor Have Still Not Recovered from the 2008 Financial Crisis," *Quartz*, January 10, 2017, qz.com/881666/data-show-that-the-worlds-poor-have-still-not-recovered-from-the-great-recession/

56. Graeme Wearden and Ben Quinn, "Eurogroup Head Says Cyprus Shows Future of Bank Rescues: As It Happened," Eurozone Crisis Live, *The Guardian*, March 25, 2013.

57. "Sergei Magnitsky Uncovered Russia-to-Cyprus Money Laundering, and Look What Happened to Him," *Mafia Today*, March 22, 2013, mafiatoday.com/tag/russian-president-vladimir-putin/

58. "The Inside Track on Cyprus," *Princeton Asset Management*, May 2013, princetonam.com/may2013/

59. Chris Giles, "Central Bankers Say They Are Flying Blind," *Financial Times*, April 17, 2013.

60. Alan Greenspan, Testimony before House Committee on Government Oversight and Reform, 23 October 2008, quoted in Heroes and Zeros: Zero Alan Greenspan, *CNN Money*, money.cnn.com/galleries/2008/news/0812/gallery.heroes_zeros_2008/8.html

61. Jeff Cox, "Too Big to Fail Banks Just Keep Getting Bigger," CNBC NETNET, March 5, 2015, cnbc.com/2015/03/05/too-big-to-fail-banks-just-keep-getting-bigger.html

62. Danielle Douglas, "Risky Trading Comes Roaring Back," *Washington Post*, June 21, 2013.

63. Stephen Roach, "How Zombie US Consumers Menace the World Economy," *Financial Times*, June 21, 2011.

64. Frank Pellegrini, "The Bush Speech: How to Rally a Nation," *Time Magazine*, September 21, 2001; see also, "Bush: Go Shopping," YouTube, youtube.com/watch?v=fxk9PW83VCY

65. Ann Pettifor, "I Was One of the Only Economists Who Predicted the Financial Crash of 2008: In 2017 We Need to Make Urgent Changes," *The Independent*, January 9, 2017, independent.co.uk/voices/brexit -economy-economists-predict-financial-crash-recession-2008-michael -fish-austerity-cant-solve-a7513416.html

66. Nick Hanauer, "The Pitchforks Are Coming…for Us Plutocrats," *Politico Magazine*, July/August 2014, politico.com/magazine/story/2014/06/the -pitchforks-are-coming-for-us-plutocrats-108014

67. Jonathan Ostry, Prakash Loungani, and Davide Furceri, "Neoliberalism: Oversold?" *Finance & Development*, International Monetary Fund, Vol. 53, No. 2, June 2016, imf.org/external/pubs/ft/fandd/2016/06/ostry.htm

Chapter 3: Tell Me A Better Story: Regenerative Economics

1. Buckminster Fuller, quoted in Sieden, Steve, *A Fuller View: Buckminster Fuller's Vision of Hope and Abundance*, Divine Arts, 2012, buckyfuller now.com/a-fuller-view---buckminster-fullers-vision-of-hope-and -abundance-for-all.html

2. Thomas Berry, "The New Story," *Teilhard Studies*, No. 1, Winter 1978.

3. Colin Grabow, "If You Think Communism Is Bad for People, Check Out What It Did to the Environment," *The Federalist*, January 13, 2014, thefederalist.com/2014/01/13/if-you-think-communism-is-bad-for -people-check-out-what-it-did-to-the-environment/

4. John J. Walters, "Communism Killed 94M in the 20th Century, Feels Need to Kill Again," *Reason Magazine*, March 13, 2013, reason.com/blog /2013/03/13/communism-killed-94m-in-20th-century

5. Anamarie Mann and Jim Harter, "Worldwide Employee Engagement Crisis," *Gallup Business Journal*, January 7, 2016, gallup.com/business journal/188033/worldwide-employee-engagement-crisis.aspx?g_source =employee%20engagement&g_medium=search&g_campaign=tiles; see also, *State of the Global Workforce*, Gallup, 2017, news.gallup.com /reports/220313/state-global-workplace-2017.aspx#formheader

6. Adam Epstein, "Half of US Workers Have Left a Job Because They Hated Their Boss," *Quartz*, April 2, 2015, qz.com/375353/half-of-us -workers-have-left-a-job-because-they-hated-their-boss/

7. Catherine Clifford, "Unhappy Workers Cost the U.S. up to $550 Billion a Year," Infographic, *Entrepreneur*, May 10, 2015, entrepreneur.com /article/246036, see also good.co/contact/

8. J. D. Vance, *Hillbilly Elegy*, Harper Collins, 2016.

9. David Brooks, "If Not Trump, What?" *New York Times*, April 29, 2016.

10. Dana Meadows, "Envisioning a Sustainable World," Third Biennial Meeting of the International Society for Ecological Economics, Octo-

ber 24–28, 1994, San Jose, Costa Rica, linkedin.com/pulse/envisioning
-sharing-wisdom-donella-meadows-all-refresh-huma-beg/

11. Pippa Norris, "Trump, Brexit, and the Rise of Populism: Economic
Have-nots and Cultural Backlash," Harvard Kennedy School, August
2016, research.hks.harvard.edu/publications/workingpapers/citation
.aspx?PubId=11325

12. Allen Furst, *Midnight in Europe*, Simon and Schuster, 2014.

13. Peter Turchin, "Social Instability Lies Ahead, Researcher Says," *UConn
Today*, December 27, 2016, today.uconn.edu/2016/12/using-social-science
-to-predict-the-future/

14. John Maynard Keynes, *The General Theory of Employment, Interest and
Money*, Palgrave Macmillan, UK, 1936.

15. For a fuller critique of the failings of economics, see, Robert Nadeau,
"Brother, Can You Spare Me a Planet?" *Scientific American*, 2008. See also,
The Wealth of Nature: How Mainstream Economics Failed the Environment,
Columbia University Press, New York; *The Environmental Endgame:
Mainstream Economics, Ecological Disaster, and Human Survival*, Rutgers
University Press.

16. Thomas Piketty, *Capital in the Twenty-first Century*, Harvard University
Press, 2013, p. 974.

17. Stewart Wallis, "A New Economic System Based on Core Human
Values," in Sherto Gill and David Cadman, eds., *Why Love Matters:
Values in Governance*, Peter Lang, Inc., 2015.

18. Humanistic Management Network, humanetwork.org/

19. R.D. Hare, *Without Conscience: The Disturbing World of the Psychopaths
Among Us*, New York, Guilford Press, 1999, p. xi.

20. John Harvey, "Five Reasons You Should Blame the Economics Discipline for Today's Problems," *Forbes Magazine*, October 31, 2016.

21. Ellen Goodman, quoted in John de Graaf, David Wann, Thomas H.
Naylor, *Affluenza: The All-Consuming Epidemic*, Berrett-Koehler Publishers, 2005.

22. Pope Francis, *Laudato Si*, w2.vatican.va/content/dam/francesco/pdf
/encyclicals/documents/papa-francesco_20150524_enciclica-laudato
-si_en.pdf

23. The Earth Charter, earthcharter.org/

24. Elinor Ostrom, "Beyond Markets and States: Polycentric Governance
of Complex Economic Systems," Sveriges Riksbank Prize in Economic
Sciences in Memory of Alfred Nobel, Prize Lecture, 2009, nobelprize.org
/nobel_prizes/economic-sciences/laureates/2009/ostrom-lecture.html

25. David Sloan Wilson, "The Woman Who Saved Economics from Disaster: Who Is Elinor Ostrom?" *Evonomics*, February 1, 2016, evonomics
.com/the-woman-who-saved-economics-from-disaster/

26. Paul Mason, "Thomas Piketty's Capital: Everything You Need to Know
About the Surprise Bestseller," *The Guardian*, April 28, 2014.

27. "Impossible Hamster," YouTube, January 24, 2010, youtube.com/watch ?v=Sqwd_u6HkMo

28. Security is defined by *Webster's Dictionary* as "freedom from fear of privation or attack." Privation is defined as "lack of basic necessities or comforts of life."

29. https://regencommunities.net

30. Bernard Lietaer, quoted in Hallsmith, et al., *Local Action for Sustainable Economic Renewal*, natcapsolutions.org/tools/laser-local-action-for-sustainable-economic-renewal/

31. Lidia Brito and Stafford Smith, "State of the Planet Declaration," Planet Under Pressure, March 26–29, 2012, planetunderpressure2012.net/pdf/state_of_planet_declaration.pdf

32. Nature Specials, Planetary Boundaries, nature.com/news/specials/planetaryboundaries/index.html

33. Jeremy Grantham, "Be Persuasive, Be Brave. Be Arrested (If Necessary)," *Nature*, November 14, 2014.

34. Bill McKibben, author, educator, environmentalist, billmckibben.com/

35. Idle No More, Canada, idlenomore.ca/

36. Sarah Jaffee, "Standing Firm at Standing Rock: Why the Struggle Is Bigger Than One Pipeline," Moyers and Company, September 28, 2016, billmoyers.com/story/standing-firm-standing-rock-pipeline-protesters-will-not-moved/

37. 350.org, We're Building A Global Climate Movement, 350.org/

38. International Labor Rights Forum, laborrights.org/creating-a-sweatfree-world/sweatshops

39. Vandana Shiva, India, navdanya.org/

40. Wilderness Society, wilderness.org/

41. European Environment Agency, eea.europa.eu/

42. World Business Council for Sustainable Development, wbcsd.org/Overview/About-us

43. International Labour Organization, ilo.org/global/about-the-ilo/lang--en/index.htm

44. CDP, cdp.net/en

45. GRI, globalreporting.org/Pages/default.aspx

46. International Integrated Reporting Council, integratedreporting.org/the-iirc-2/

47. Sustainability Accounting Standards Board, sasb.org/

48. Sustainable Development Knowledge Platform, sustainabledevelopment.un.org/sdgs

49. US Green Building Council, usgbc.org/articles/leed-dynamic-plaque-diaries-alliance-center

50. International Living Future Institute, living-future.org/lbc

51. International WELL Building Institute, wellcertified.com/

52. Peter Dreier, "Today's Environmental Activists Stand on David Brower's

Shoulders," *Huffington Post*, June 20, 2012, huffingtonpost.com/peter
-dreier/todays-environmental-acti_b_1613782.html

53. Personal communication, Jo Confino, Conference on Beyond Business
As Usual, DNV-GL, Copenhagen, November 16, 2013.

54. Kate Wolf, "Brother Warrior," katewolf.com/

55. Capital Institute Mission Statement.

56. John Fullerton, "Regenerative Capitalism: How Universal Principles
and Patterns Will Shape the New Economy," Capital Institute, 2015,
capitalinstitute.org/wp-content/uploads/2015/04/2015-Regenerative
-Capitalism-4-20-15-final.pdf

57. Eric J. Chaisson, *Cosmic Evolution: The Rise of Complexity in Nature*,
Harvard University Press, 2002.

58. "Right Relationship by Peter G. Brown and Geoffry Garver," YouTube,
November 19, 2008, youtube.com/watch?v=Tjfx7diJ-ug

59. "The Wealth of Nature: A Three-part Series Profiling Ecological
Economists," *Grist Magazine*, April 2003, grist.org/series/the-wealth
-of-nature/

60. Douglas H. Boucher, *The Biology of Mutualism, Ecology and Evolution*,
Oxford University Press, 1985.

61. David Despain, "Early Humans Used Brain Power, Innovation and
Teamwork to Dominate the Planet," *Scientific American*, February 27,
2010.

62. David Myers, "Wealth, Well-being, and the New American Dream,"
davidmyers.org/Brix?pageID=49

63. Frances Moore Lappe and Adam Eichen, "Dare for Democracy: Three
Essential Steps," Moyers and Company, December 13, 2016, billmoyers
.com/story/dare-democracy-three-essential-steps/

64. quotefancy.com/quote/1130134/Pierre-Teilhard-de-Chardin-There-is
-almost-a-sensual-longing-for-communion-with-others

65. Ellen MacArthur Foundation, "What Is a Circular Economy?"
ellenmacarthurfoundation.org/circular-economy

66. N.J. Turner, I.J. Davidson-Hunt, and M. O'Flaherty, "Living on the
Edge: Ecological and Cultural Edges as Sources of Diversity for Social-
Ecological Resilience," *Human Ecology*, Vol. 31, Issue 3, September 2003,
pp. 439–461.

67. Bernard Lietaer et al., "Options for Managing a Systemic Bank Crisis,"
Sapiens, Vol. 1, Issue 2, April 6, 2009.

68. Robert Costanza and Michael Mageau, "What Is a Healthy Ecosystem?"
Aquatic Ecology, 33, January 27, 1999, pp. 105–115.

69. Sarah Leonard, "Nature as an Ally: An Interview with Wendell Berry,"
Dissent, Spring 2012, dissentmagazine.org/article/nature-as-an-ally-an
-interview-with-wendell-berry

70. Janine Benyus, "A Biomimicry Primer," *Biomimicry 3.8*, 2016, biomimicry
.net/b38files/A_Biomimicry_Primer_Janine_Benyus.pdf

71. Christopher Peterson, "What Is Positive Psychology and What Is It Not?" *Psychology Today*, May 16, 2008.

72. Robert Costanza, "Flourishing on Earth," YouTube, June 24, 2010, youtube.com/watch?v=PZkTlVPgqG4&feature=relmfu

73. Edward O. Wilson, *The Social Conquest of Earth*, Liveright, 2013.

74. Small Planet Institute, smallplanet.org/about/mission

75. Michael Pirson, *From Capitalistic to Humanistic Business*, Palgrave, UK, 2014.

76. David Sloan Wilson, "The Tragedy of the Commons: How Elinor Ostrom Solved One of Life's Greatest Dilemmas," *Evonomics*, October 29, 2016, evonomics.com/tragedy-of-the-commons-elinor-ostrom/

77. C. Darwin, *The Descent of Man and Selection in Relation to Sex*, New York, Appleton and Company, 1909, p. 101.

78. Ibid., p. 50.

79. Robert McFarlane, "The Secrets of the Wood Wide Web," *New Yorker*, August 7, 2016.

80. Paul Lawrence, *Driven to Lead: Good, Bad, and Misguided Leadership*, Jossey-Bass, 2010.

81. Anne Minard, "Early Humans Were Prey, Not Predators," *National Geographic News*, March 7, 2006, news.nationalgeographic.com/news/2006/03/0307_060307_human_prey.html

82. Chad Huff et al., "Mobile Elements Reveal Small Population Size in the Ancient Ancestors of Homo Sapiens," December 18, 2009, Proceedings of the National Academy of Sciences, pnas.org/content/107/5/2147.full.pdf?sid=d523fbf4-43de-4dff-b8a4-66a59a1cd843

83. David Despain, "Early Humans Used Brain Power, Innovation and Teamwork to Dominate the Planet," *Scientific American*, February 27, 2010.

84. Natalie Angier, "Edward O. Wilson's New Take on Human Nature," *Smithsonian Magazine*, April 2012.

85. Edward O. Wilson, *The Social Conquest of Earth*, Liveright, 2013.

86. Edward O. Wilson, *On Human Nature*, Harvard University Press, 2012.

87. Edward O. Wilson, *The Social Conquest of Earth*, W.W. Norton & Company, 2012.

88. Humanistic Management Network, humanetwork.org/

89. Michael Pirson, *Humanistic Management*, Cambridge University Press, 2017.

90. Introductory video, Humanistic Management Network, humanetwork.org/

91. Christopher Peterson, "What Is Positive Psychology and What Is It Not," *Psychology Today*, May 16, 2008.

92. Martin Seligman, "The New Era of Positive Psychology," TED Talk, February 2004, ted.com/talks/martin_seligman_on_the_state_of_psychology

93. Chris Laszlo, *Flourishing Enterprise*, Stanford University Press, 2014.

94. John Mackey and Raj Sisodia, *Conscious Capitalism*, Harvard Business Review Press, 2013.

95. Natural Capitalism Solutions, www.natcapsolutions.org

96. John Fullerton, "Regenerative Capitalism," Capital Institute, 2015, capitalinstitute.org/wp-content/uploads/2015/04/2015-Regenerative -Capitalism-4-20-15-final.pdf

97. "Andrew Winston: The Big Pivot," TED@Unilever, September 17, 2014, ted.com/watch/ted-institute/ted-unilever/andrew-winston-the-big -pivot; and Andrew Winston, *The Big Pivot*, Harvard Business Review Press, 2014.

98. Janine Benyus, Biomimicry Institute, 2016, ben.biomimicry.net/coolbio /2012/welcome-to-the-wood-wide-web/

99. OECD, Better Life Index, 2016, oecdbetterlifeindex.org/

100. Robert Costanza et al., "Development: Time to Leave GDP Behind, *Nature*, January 15, 2014.

101. The New Economics Foundation collected surveys from around the world on what makes people happy. From this, it developed the Happy Planet Index (HPI), a combination of material sufficiency and expressed satisfaction with one's life. happyplanetindex.org/

102. David Brooks, "The Future of the American Center," *New York Times*, November 29, 2016.

103. Wellbeing Economy Alliance, www.wellbeingeconomy.org

104. Ibid.; see also: vimeo.com/161271346

105. Nic Marks, "The Happy Planet Index," TED Talk, ted.com/talks /nic_marks_the_happy_planet_index?language=en

106. Donella Meadows Project, Academy of Systems Change, donellameadows.org/

107. Jonathan Friedland, "The New Age of Ayn Rand: How She Won Over Trump and Silicon Valley," *The Guardian*, April 10, 2017.

108. Kate Raworth, *Doughnut Economics*, Chelsea Green 2017.

109. Kate Raworth, kateraworth.com/doughnut/

110. For tutorial videos see kateraworth.com/videos/

111. Ibid.

112. kateraworth.com/animations/

113. Humanistic Management Network, humanetwork.org/

114. Melvin Konner, "The Evolutionary Roots of Altruism," *American Prospect*, May 22, 2015, prospect.org/article/evolutionary-roots -altruism

115. "Martin Seligman," The Pursuit of Happiness, pursuit-of-happiness .org/history-of-happiness/martin-seligman-psychology/

116. David Sloan Wilson, "The Road to Ideology: How Friedrich Hayek Became a Monster," *Evonomics*, October 28, 2015, evonomics.com/the -road-to-ideology-how-friedrich-hayek-became-a-monster/

117. Jeanette McMurtry, "The Purpose-Driven Brand," *Target Marketing*, April 16, 2015, targetmarketingmag.com/post/the-purpose-driven-brand -why-it-matters-more-than-ever/all/

118. Jo Confino, "Sustainable Corporations Perform Better Financially, Report Finds," *The Guardian*, September 23, 2014.

119. Robert Macfarlane, "The Secrets of the Wood Wide Web," *New Yorker*, August 7, 2016.

120. Brian Cox, *The Quantum Universe (and Why Anything That Can Happen, Does)*, Da Capo Press, January 31, 2012.

121. George Bernard Shaw, "Epistle Dedicatory to Arthur Bingham Walkley," *Man and Superman*, 1903, bartleby.com/157/100.html

Section 2: Buying Time to Fix the Mess

1. Zachary Shahan, "Cleantech Revolution," YouTube, March 20, 2016, youtube.com/watch?v=iVo8YiO6uW4

Chapter 4: Everyone Wins: The Circular Economy

1. Arthur, C. Clarke, cited in Sir Arthur's Quotations, clarkefoundation .org/about-sir-arthur/sir-arthurs-quotations/

2. Paul Ekins and Nick Hughes, *Resource Efficiency: Potential and Economic Implications, Summary for Policy Makers*, UN Environment Programme, 2016, env.go.jp/press/files/jp/102839.pdf

3. "Growth Within: A Circular Economy Vision for a Competitive Europe," Ellen MacArthur Foundation and McKinsey Center for Business and Environment, 2015, ellenmacarthurfoundation.org/assets/downloads /publications/EllenMacArthurFoundation_Growth-Within_July15.pdf

4. P. R. Himasree et al., "Bamboo As a Substitute for Steel in Reinforced Concrete Wall Panels," IOP Conference Series: Earth and Environmental Sciences, 80 01204, 2017, iopscience.iop.org/article/10.1088/1755 -1315/80/1/012041/pdf

5. L. Hunter Lovins et al., *The Future of Industry in Asia*, UNIDO, 2009, natcapsolutions.org/the-future-of-industry-in-asia-for-unido/

6. Ernst von Weizsäcker et al., *Factor Four: Doubling Wealth, Halving Resource Use, A Report to the Club of Rome*, Earthscan, 1998.

7. Ernst von Weizsäcker et al., *Factor Five: Transforming the Global Economy Through 80% Improvements in Resource Productivity*, Routledge, 2009.

8. Product Life Institute, product-life.org/

9. James Rainey, "California Lawmakers Fail to Approve 100 Percent Renewable Energy Goal," *NBC News*, September 16, 2017, nbcnews.com /science/environment/california-lawmakers-fail-approve-100-percent -renewable-energy-goal-n801991

10. "Chinese Leaders Join Lawmakers, Political Advisors in Panel Discussions," March 8, 2012, newyork.china-consulate.org/eng/xw/t912428 .htm, chinadaily.com.cn/china/2007-01/18/content_786230.htm

11. "A European Strategy for Plastics in a Circular Economy, European Commission," January 16, 2018, eur-lex.europa.eu/legal-content/EN /TXT/?qid=1516265440535&uri=COM:2018:28:FIN

12. "Communication on the Implementation of the Circular Economy Package: Options to Address the Interface Between Chemical, Product and Waste Legislation," European Commission, January 16, 2018, ec.europa .eu/docsroom/documents/27321

13. *Monitoring Framework for the Circular Economy*, January 16, 2018, ec.europa.eu/environment/circular-economy/pdf/monitoring -framework.pdf

14. *Report on Critical Raw Materials and the Circular Economy*, European Commission, January 16, 2018, ec.europa.eu/docsroom/documents /27327

15. *Towards a Circular Economy*, ellenmacarthurfoundation.org/about /circular-economy/towards-the-circular-economy

16. Anders Wijkman, *The Circular Economy and Benefits for Society*, Club of Rome, March 7, 2017, clubofrome.org/wp-content/uploads/2016/03 /The-Circular-Economy-and-Benefits-for-Society.pdf

17. Anders Wijkman, "Circular Economy Could Bring 70 Percent Cut in Carbon Emissions by 2030," *The Guardian*, April 15, 2017.

18. "The Social Benefits of a Circular Economy," Green Alliance, 2015, green-alliance.org.uk/resources/The%20social%20benefits%20of%20a% 20circular%20economy.pdf

19. Competitive Circular Economy, Renault, group.renault.com/en /commitments/environment/competitive-circular-economy/

20. Mary Mazzoni, "10 Companies Going Zero Waste to Landfill," *Triple Pundit*, January 6, 2017, triplepundit.com/2017/01/10-companies-zero -waste-to-landfill/

21. "Economic Sustainability with Best-in-class Energy Savings," Philips, usa.lighting.philips.com/services/managed-services

22. Emad, "Michelin: Tires-as-a-Service," Harvard Business School, Open Knowledge, November 17, 2017, rctom.hbs.org/submission/michelin -tires-as-a-service/

23. Zeeteam, "Find Out What Has Made Airbnb Such a Successful Business Model," On-demand Startup, September 11, 2017, ondemandstartup .com/airbnb-business-model/

24. Mud Jeans, mudjeans.eu/lease-a-jeans/

25. Houdini Sportswear, houdinisportswear.com/en/sustainability

26. H&M, about.hm.com/en/sustainability/get-involved/recycle-your -clothes.html

27. Patagonia, patagonia.com/reuse-recycle.html

28. Walter Stahel, "The Circular Economy," *Nature*, March 23, 2016.

29. Keivan Zokaei et al., *Creating a Lean and Green Business System: Techniques for Improving Profits and Sustainability*, CRC Press, 2013.

30. Shannon Bouton et al., "Energy Efficiency: A Compelling Global Resource," 2009, McKinsey, mckinseyonsociety.com/energy-efficiency-a -compelling-global-resource/

31. *Pathways to a Low-carbon Economy: Version 2 of the Greenhouse Gas Abatement Cost Curve*, 2013, mckinsey.com/business-functions/sustain ability-and-resource-productivity/our-insights/pathways-to-a-low -carbon-economy

32. Joseph Romm, "The Triumph of Energy Efficiency: Waxman-Markey Could Save $3,900 Per Household and Create 650,000 Jobs by 2030," *Climate Progress*, June 9, 2009, thinkprogress.org/climate /2009/06/09/204217/waxman-markey-energy-efficiency-savings-jobs/

33. Energy Efficiency Market Report 2014, iea.org/publications/free publications/publication/EEMR2014.pdf

34. *Energy Efficiency Market Report 2014*, October 8, 2014, iea.org/news roomandevents/pressreleases/2014/october/global-energy-efficiency -market-an-invisible-powerhouse-at-least-usd-310byr.html

35. Fatih Birol, *Energy Efficiency Market Report 2015*, IEA 2015, iea.org /publications/freepublications/publication/MediumTermEnergy efficiencyMarketReport2015.pdf

36. Rachel Young, "Germany, Italy, EU, China, and France Top Global Energy Efficiency Rankings," American Council for an Energy Efficient Economy, July 17, 2014, aceee.org/press/2014/07/germany-italy-eu -china-and-france-to

37. W. V. Reid and Jose Goldemberg, "Are Developing Countries Already Doing as Much as Industrialized Countries to Slow Climate Change?" Climate Notes, July 1997, World Resources Institute, Washington, DC.

38. Dominique Mosbergen, "Air Pollution Causes 4,400 Deaths in China Every Single Day: Study," *Huffington Post*, August 14, 2015, huffington post.com/entry/air-pollution-china-deaths_us_55cd9a62e4b0ab468d 9cefa9

39. Jane Spencer, "Why Beijing Is Trying to Tally the Hidden Costs of Pollution As China's Economy Booms," *Wall Street Journal*, October 2, 2006, p. A3.

40. "China Vows to Take Due Responsibility to Curb Global Warming," *People's Daily, English*, March 6, 2007.

41. "China Plans US$925 Million Energy Efficiency Fund," Reuters, August 28, 2007, planetark.com/dailynewsstory.cfm/newsid/43964/story.htm

42. Zhihe Wang, Huili He, and Meijun Fan, "The Ecological Civilization Debate in China," *Monthly Review*, November 6, 2014, monthlyreview .org/author/zhihewang/

43. "China Greentech Market Could Grow to $1 Trillion Annually by 2013," September 11, 2009, *PWC*, pwc.blogs.com/press_room/2009/09/china -greentech-market-could-grow-to-1-trillion-annually-by-2013.html

44. "China's Coal Imports Fall Nearly Half in 12 Months as Anti-pollution Drive Bites," *The Guardian*, April 13, 2015.

45. Geoffrey Henderson et al., "5 Most Important Things to Know About China's 5-Year Plan," *EcoWatch*, March 18, 2016, ecowatch.com /2016/03/18/china-five-year-plan-climate/

46. Fiona Harvey, "China Aims to Drastically Cut Greenhouse Gas Emissions Through Trading Scheme," *The Guardian*, December 19, 2017.

47. "China and California Form Unlikely Partnership to Address Climate Change," *Think Progress*, September 16, 2013, thinkprogress.org/china -and-california-form-unlikely-partnership-to-address-climate-change -f11438c5713d#.wsgc9ggw8

48. Muyu Xu and Josephine Mason, "China Aims for Emission Trading Scheme in Big Step vs. Global Warming," *Reuters*, December 19, 2017, reuters.com/article/us-china-carbon/china-aims-for-emission-trading -scheme-in-big-step-vs-global-warming-idUSKBN1ED0R6

49. Edward Wong, "China Poised to Take Lead on Climate After Trump's Move to Undo Policies," *New York Times*, March 29, 2017.

50. Ed Crooks, "Coal Hits a Plateau," *Financial Times*, September 19, 2017.

51. "Turning Coal into Bitcoin? Dirty Secret of 2017's Hottest Market," *Economic Times*, December 15, 2017, economictimes.indiatimes.com /markets/stocks/news/turning-coal-into-bitcoin-dirty-secret-of-2017s -hottest-market/articleshow/62080307.cms

52. Ian Johnson, "China's Great Uprooting: Moving 250 Million into Cities," *New York Times*, June 15, 2013.

53. Peter Hilderson, Jones Lang LaSalle, Asia Pacific, Energy and Sustainability Services, *Global Sustainability Perspective*, February 2012.

54. Lester Brown, "China Forcing World to Rethink Its Economic Future," Earth Policy Institute, January 5, 2006, earthpolicy.org/Books/PB2 /index.htm

55. Rachel Young et al., *The 2014 International Energy Efficiency Scorecard*, American Council for an Energy Efficient Economy, July 2014, aceee.org /sites/default/files/publications/researchreports/e1402.pdf

56. "Policy Makers Summary," Environmental Performance Index, Yale Center for Environmental Law and Policy, January 23, 2018, epi.envirocenter .yale.edu/downloads/epi2018policymakerssummaryv01.pdf

57. Amit Ghani, "How Will India Manage Energy Efficiency," World Economic Forum, November 24, 2015, weforum.org/agenda/2015/11/how -will-india-manage-energy-efficiency/

58. Arshad R. Zargar, "'Gas chamber' Delhi 10 times more polluted than Beijing," *CBS News*, November 9, 2017, cbsnews.com/news/delhi-smog -chokes-india-capital-air-pollution-10-times-worse-beijing/

59. Kim Petrick and Amit Sinha, "Energy Efficiency: Opportunities in Emerging Markets," *Bain Insights*, August 26, 2015, bain.com/publi cations/articles/energy-efficiency-opportunities-in-emerging-markets .aspx

60. Natalie Pearson and Alex Nussbaum, "India's Modi Aims for Energy Efficiency, Not Obama CO_2 Cuts," *Bloomberg Business*, January 21, 2015,

bloomberg.com/news/articles/2015-01-21/india-s-modi-aims-for-energy
-efficiency-not-obama-emission-cuts

61. Anjali Jaiswas, "Building Efficient Cities," NRDC, nrdc.org/international
/india/real-estate-efficiency-codes.asp

62. Phillip Mihlmeste et al., *BRIC'd Up Energy Efficiency: Energy and Climate Policies in Brazil, Russia, India, and China*, ACEEE, 2010, aceee.org
/files/proceedings/2010/data/papers/2027.pdf

63. "South America: Widespread Exceptional Water Deficits for Much of
Brazil," June 22, 2017, isciences.com/blog/2017/6/20/south-america
-widespread-exceptional-water-deficits-for-much-of-brazil

64. Joseph Romm, *Climate Change: What Everyone Needs to Know*, Oxford
University Press, 2015.

65. Joseph Romm, "Energy Efficiency Is THE Core Climate Solution;
Part 1: The Biggest Low-Carbon Resource by Far," *Climate Progress*,
June 1, 2011, thinkprogress.org/energy-efficiencey-is-the-core-climate-
solution-part-1-the-biggest-low-carbon-resource-by-far-94ee37a548af/

66. "Energy Efficiency and Fossil Energy Technologies Prove Wise Investment for Department of Energy," National Research Council, July 17,
2001, www8.nationalacademies.org/onpinews/newsitem.aspx?Record
ID=10165

67. Emma Merchant, "America First? Trump Energy Cuts Would Eliminate
Billions of Dollars in Direct Savings to Consumers," *Greentech Media*,
November 15, 2017, greentechmedia.com/articles/read/trump-energy
-cuts-would-eliminate-billions-in-consumer-savings#gs.t8Thtxg

Chapter 5: Building A Better World

1. J.K. Rowling, *Harry Potter and the Prisoner of Azkaban*, 2013.

2. World Business Council for Sustainable Development, wbcsd.org/home
.aspx

3. "Green Building Facts," US Green Building Council, usgbc.org/articles
/green-building-facts

4. Alex Wilson et al., *Green Development, Integrating Ecology and Real
Estate*, Wiley and Sons, 1998.

5. "The Business Case for Green Building," US Green Building Council,
February 10, 2015, usgbc.org/articles/business-case-green-building

6. Ed LeBard, "Return on Investment for Green/LEED Projects," US
Green Building Council, 2010, greeneconomypost.com/return-on
-investment-for-green-leed-projects-10962.htm

7. Joe Romm, "Energy Efficiency, Part 4: How Does California Do It So
Consistently and Cost-effectively?" *Think Progress*, July 30, 2008,
thinkprogress.org/energy-efficiency-part-4-how-does-california-do
-it-so-consistently-and-cost-effectively-a82d2b48ea8e/

8. Joe Romm, "Why We Never Need to Build Another Polluting Power

Plant: Coal? Natural Gas? Nuke? We Can Wipe Them All off the Drawing Board by Using Current Energy More Efficiently. Are You Listening, Washington?" *Salon*, July 28, 2008, salon.com/2008/07/28/energy _efficiency/

9. hpbmagazine.org/attachments/article/12142/11W-Oberlin-College -Adam-Joseph-Lewis-Center-Oberlin-OH.pdf; oberlin.edu/news-info /98sep/orr_remarks.html

10. Bullitt Center, bullittcenter.org/

11. bullittcenter.org/vision/living-building-challenge/

12. Mary Thomas, *The Greenest Building: How the Bullitt Center Changes the Urban Landscape*, Ecotone Publishing, 2016.

13. Prince of Wales's Corporate Leaders Group, *EU Industry Commitment: Moving Towards Net Zero Buildings*, 2016, corporateleadersgroup.com /resources/pdfs/eu-industry-commitment.pdf

14. passivehouse.com/; see also, passipedia.org/basics/what_is_a_passive _house

15. "The World's First Passive House, Darmstadt-Kranichstein, Germany," *Passipedia*, passipedia.org/examples/residential_buildings/multi -family_buildings/central_europe/the_world_s_first_passive_house _darmstadt-kranichstein_germany

16. Passivhaus, "The World's Leading Fabric First Approach to Low Energy Buildings," passivhaus.org.uk/standard.jsp?id=122

17. *Energy Efficiency Market Report*, 2015, iea.org/publications/freepub- lications/publication/MediumTermEnergyefficiencyMarketReport 2015.pdf

18. *United States Building Energy Efficiency Retrofits*, Rockefeller Foundation, March 1, 2012, rockefellerfoundation.org/report/united-states-building -energy-efficiency-retrofits/

19. Harvey Bernstein and Michele Russo, *Business Case for Energy Efficient Building Retrofit and Renovation*, McGraw-Hill Construction, 2011, apps1.eere.energy.gov/buildings/publications/pdfs/alliances/business _case_for_energy_efficiency_retrofit_renovation_smr_2011.pdf

20. "Why Focus on Existing Buildings," Institute for Building Efficiency, April 29, 2010, buildingefficiencyinitiative.org/articles/why-focus -existing-buildings

21. *Power Forward 3.0: How the Largest U.S. Companies Are Capturing Business Value While Addressing Climate Change*, World Wildlife Fund, CERES, Calvert, CDP, April 25, 2017, c402277.ssl.cf1.rackcdn.com /publications/1049/files/original/Power_Forward_3.0_-_April_2017 _-_Digital_Second_Final.pdf?1493325339

22. Aether, aether.ee/

23. Sustainable Endowments Institute, endowmentinstitute.org/

24. Green Revolving Investment Tracking System, greenbillion.org/grits/

25. David Bornstein, "Investing in Energy Efficiency Pays Off, *New York Times*, February 6, 2015, opinionator.blogs.nytimes.com/2015/02/06 /investing-in-energy-efficiency-pays-off/

Chapter 6: Going Places: Efficiency in Vehicles

1. Bill Gates and Janet Lowe, *Bill Gates Speaks: Insight from the World's Greatest Entrepreneur*, John Wiley & Sons, 1998, p. 173.
2. "What Is the City's Commitment to Climate Action?" fcgov.com/climate action/
3. *What Are the Products and Uses of Petroleum?* US Energy Information Administration, September 21, 2015, eia.gov/tools/faqs/faq.cfm?id =41&t=6
4. *Consumption of Energy*, Eurostat Statistics Explained, May 2015, ec.europa.eu/eurostat/statistics-explained/index.php/Consumption _of_energy
5. "Global Plug-in Sales for 2016," EVVolumes.com, ev-volumes.com/news /global-plug-in-sales-for-2016/
6. *Model Year 2017: Alternative Fuel and Advanced Technology Vehicles*, afdc.energy.gov/uploads/publication/model-year-2017-vehicles.pdf
7. Camille von Kaenel, "Auto Sales Hit New Record as Americans Buy More Gas-Guzzling Cars," *Scientific American*, January 5, 2017.
8. *Fuel Economy Improvements Are Projected to Reduce Future Gasoline Use*, US Energy Information Administration, May 23, 2017, eia.gov/todayin energy/detail.php?id=31332
9. "Nonpetroleum Share of Transportation Energy at Highest Level Since 1954," Energy Information Administration, May 18, 2015, eia.gov/today inenergy/detail.cfm?id=21272
10. Daniel Gross, "This Chart Shows How Oil Is Losing Its Total Grip on American Transportation," *Slate*, May 21, 2015, slate.com/blogs/money box/2015/05/21/oil_use_in_transportation_this_chart_shows_how _it_s_losing_ground.html
11. Nancy Ryan, "Pathways to Deep Decarbonization in California: The Role of Transportation Electrification," Energy + Environmental Economics, November 10, 2015, renewablenow.biz/renewable-living.html
12. John O'Dell, "Will California's Zero-Emissions Mandate Alter the Car Landscape?" Edmunds.com, May 27, 2015, edmunds.com/fuel-economy /will-californias-zero-emissions-mandate-alter-the-car-landscape.html
13. Alex Klokus, *Humans of the Future*, facebook.com/humansofthefuture /videos/658614524296230/?pnref=story
14. Matt McFarland, "How to Get a Free Ride in a Self-driving Shuttle This Summer," *Washington Post*, July 16, 2016.
15. Andrew Winston, "The Inside Story of Diageo's Stunning Carbon Achievement," *Harvard Business Review*, February 20, 2013.

16. Rachel Young, *Germany, Italy, EU, China, and France Top Global Energy Efficiency Rankings*, ACEEE, July 17, 2014, aceee.org/press/2014/07 /germany-italy-eu-china-and-france-to

Chapter 7: Moving Money from Harm to Healing

1. Tom Toro, Cartoons, tomtoro.com/cartoons/
2. Milton Friedman, "The Social Responsibility of Business Is to Increase Its Profits," *New York Times Magazine*, September 13, 1970.
3. Peter Drucker, *People and Performance*, Harvard Business Review Press, 2007, p. 88.
4. Speech by Professor Clayton Christensen to Gartner Symposium ITExpo 2011, October 16-20, 2011, gartner.mediasite.com/mediasite/play /9cfe6bba5c7941e09bee95eb63f769421d?t=1320659595
5. Robin Greenwood and David Scharfstein, "The Growth of Finance," *Journal of Economic Perspectives*, Vol. 27, No. 2, Spring 2013, pp. 3–28.
6. Louis Jacobson, "Bernie Sanders Says Six Bank Companies Have Assets Equaling 60 Percent of U.S. GDP," *Politifact*, October 6, 2011, politifact .com/truth-o-meter/statements/2011/oct/06/bernie-s/bernie-sanders -says-six-bank-companies-have-assets/
7. Greenwood and Scharfstein, "The Growth of Finance."
8. Gautam Mukunda, "The Price of Wall Street's Power," *Harvard Business Review*, June 2014.
9. Bruce Bartlett, "'Financialization' as a Cause of Economic Malaise," *New York Times*, June 11, 2013.
10. David A. Stockman, "State-Wrecked: The Corruption of Capitalism in America," *New York Times Sunday Review*, March 30, 2013.
11. Jean-Louis Arcand et al., *Too Much Finance*, IMF Working Paper, 2012, p. 15, imf.org/external/pubs/ft/wp/2012/wp12161.pdf
12. Michael Hudson, "Tech Bubble: Who Benefited," *Counterpunch*, August 30, 2003, michael-hudson.com/2003/08/tech-bubble-who-benefited/
13. Adam Davidson, "Wall Street Is Using the Power of Dodd-Frank Against Itself," *New York Times*, May 27, 2015.
14. Viral V. Acharya and Matthew P. Richardson, "Causes of the Financial Crisis," *Critical Review*, Vol. 21, Nos. 2 & 3, pp. 195-210, November 30, 2009.
15. Davidson, "Wall Street Is Using the Power of Dodd-Frank Against Itself."
16. Jeff Cox, "Too Big to Fail Banks Just Keep Getting Bigger," *CNBC*, March 5, 2015, cnbc.com/2015/03/05/too-big-to-fail-banks-just-keep -getting-bigger.html
17. "Securities and Investment Industry Profile Summary," *Open Secrets*, 2015, opensecrets.org/lobby/indusclient.php?id=F07#
18. Steve Dunning, "Wall Street Costs the Economy 2% of GDP Each Year," *Forbes*, May 31, 2015, forbes.com/sites/stevedenning/2015/05/31/wall -street-costs-the-economy-2-of-gdp-each-year/#6a93b8d6171e

19. Sheelah Kolhatkar, "When Wall Street Writes Its Own Rules," *New York Times*, February 9, 2018.

20. Bernard Lietaer et al., "Options for Managing a Systemic Bank Crisis," *Sapiens*, 2.1, Vol. 2, No. 1, 2009, sapiens.revues.org/747

21. *Financial System Resilience Index: Building a Strong Financial System*, New Economics Foundation, 2015, b.3cdn.net/nefoundation/3898c6a7f8338 9375a_y1m6ixqbv.pdf

22. *Where Does Money Come From*, New Economics Foundation, 2012, neweconomics.org/where-does-money-come-from/

23. gov.uk/government/publications/bis-new-regulations-update-october -2015

24. John Fullerton, *Limits to Investment: Finance in the Anthropocene*, Great Transition Initiative, 2014, greattransition.org/publication/limits-to -investment

25. Ibid.

26. "Edge Effect Abundance," *The Field Guide*, fieldguide.capitalinstitute.org /edge-effect-abundance.html

27. Much more detail on the above can be found in the following NEF reports/books: *Where Does Money Come From*, neweconomics.org /publications/entry/where-does-money-come-from; *Stakeholder Banks*, neweconomics.org/publications/entry/stakeholder-banks; and new economics.org/publications/entry/reforming-rbs

28. Elizabeth Warren, "The Unfinished Business of Financial Reform," Senator Elizabeth Warren's Remarks at the Levy Institute's 24th Annual Hyman P. Minsky Conference, as prepared for delivery, April 15, 2015, warren.senate.gov/files/documents/Unfinished_Business_20150415.pdf

29. Ibid.

30. Neel Kashkari, "Lessons from the Crisis: Ending Too Big to Fail," Speech to Brookings Institution, February 16, 2016, minneapolisfed.org/news -and-events/presidents-speeches/lessons-from-the-crisis-ending-too -big-to-fail#_ftnref5

31. Global Alliance for Banking on Value, gabv.org/about-us

32. Andy Haldane, *BBC Newsnight* programme, July 24, 2015, bbc.co.uk /news/business-33660426

33. *Natural Capital at Risk*, trucost.com/_uploads/publishedResearch/TE EB%20Final%20Report%20-%20web%20SPv2.pdf

34. John Fullerton, "Evergreen Direct Investing: ESG 2.0?"; "Evergreen Direct Investing: The CEO Perspective," *Field Guide*, Capital Institute, 2013, fieldguide.capitalinstitute.org/evergreen-direct-investing.html

35. *The Coming Financial Climate*, UN Environment Programme, May 2015, apps.unep.org/redirect.php?file=/publications/pmtdocuments/-The _coming_financial_climate__The_Inquiry%E2%80%99s_4th_Progress _Report_(Summary)-2015ES_Englis.pdf

36. These arguments are set out in detail in the New Economics Foundation

report *Strategic QE*, neweconomics.org/publications/entry/strategic
-quantitative-easing

37. *Green Quantitative Easing*, Finance for the Future, financeforthefuture
.com/GreenQuEasing.pdf

38. Josh Ryan-Collins, *Sovereign Money: What It Is and Why It Matters*,
New Economics Foundation, April 29, 2014, neweconomics.org/blog
/entry/sovereign-money-what-it-is-and-why-it-matters

39. Martin Wolf, "Strip Private Banks of Their Power to Create Money, *Financial Times*, April 24, 2014, ft.com/content/7f000b18-ca44-11e3-bb92
-00144feabdc0

40. Joromir Benes and Michael Kumhof, *The Chicago Plan Revisited*, International Monetary Fund, 2012, imf.org/external/pubs/ft/wp/2012
/wp12202.pdf

41. For more on these, see the writings of Bernard Lietaer and Gwen
Hallsmith, lietaer.com/writings/books/creating-wealth/

42. bbc.co.uk/blogs/thereporters/robertpeston/2011/04/do_banks_use
_10bn_subsidy_wise.html

43. Wolf, "Strip Private Banks of Their Power to Create Money."

44. John Fullerton, *Financial Overshoot: From Stranded Assets to a Regenerative Economy*, capitalinstitute.org/wp-content/uploads/2014/09
/FINANCIAL-OVERSHOOTread.pdf

Chapter 8: Corporate Transformation

1. Annie Leonard, "The Cleanest Line," Solutions Series, Part 4: Solutions
in Business, Patagonia, May 7, 2014, patagonia.com/blog/2014/05
/solutions-series-part-4-solutions-in-business/

2. Personal communication, Ray Anderson to Hunter Lovins, Maui, April
8, 1997; for the speech Ray gave in 1994, see: raycandersonfoundation.org
/assets/pdfs/rayslife/original083194SpearinChest.pdf;

3. Interface website, "Sustainability: The Interface Story," interfaceglobal
.com/sustainability/interface-story.aspx

4. Ray Anderson, *A Better Way, Try It: The Business Case for Sustainability*,
raycandersonfoundation.org/assets/pdfs/rayslife/08-13-03-A-Better
-Way.pdf

5. Mikhail Davis, "Radical Industrialists: 20 Years Later, Interface Looks
Back on Ray Anderson's Legacy," *Green Biz*, September 3, 2014,
greenbiz.com/blog/2014/09/03/20-years-later-interface-looks-back-ray
-andersons-legacy

6. Interface website, "Company, Speakers Bureau," interfaceglobal.com
/Company/Speakers-Bureau/Speakers/David-Oakey.aspx

7. biomimicry.net/

8. Personal communication, Ray Anderson and David Oakey at a Dream
Team meeting of which Hunter Lovins was a member, Henderson, NV,
1997.

9. Personal communication, Ray Anderson and Mike Bertolucci at a Dream Team meeting, Interface Headquarters, Atlanta, GA, 1998.

10. Personal communication, Cargill representative to Hunter Lovins at NBIS conference September 27, 2004, Seattle, WA.

11. Interface website, "Sustainability," interfaceglobal.com/Sustainability /Environmental-Footprint/Climate.aspx

12. interfaceglobal.com/Sustainability/Environmental-Footprint/Energy .aspx

13. interfaceglobal.com/Sustainability/Environmental-Footprint/Waste .aspx

14. interfaceglobal.com/Sustainability/Environmental-Footprint.aspx

15. Davis, "Radical Industrialists."

16. Personal communication, Ray Anderson to Hunter Lovins, Natural Step Conference, San Francisco, May 2002; for the paper that resulted from this conversation, see Anderson, *A Better Way, Try It: The Business Case for Sustainability.*

17. Bruce Posner, "One CEO's Trip from Dismissive to Convinced," *MIT Sloan Management Review*, Fall 2009, sloanreview.mit.edu/article/one -ceos-trip-from-dismissive-to-convinced/

18. One of the early advocates that there is a business case for more sustainable behavior was Michael Russo, University of Oregon, business .uoregon.edu/faculty/michael-russo; *Natural Capitalism: The Next Industrial Revolution* (Hawken, Lovins, and Lovins) built on this work, and used the example of Interface to assert that this business case was robust.

19. This concept was created by Hunter Lovins, based on work with the electric utility industry in the 1980s and with Ray Anderson in the 1990s. It was used by Hunter as the basis of the Bottom Line 2001 conference held in April 2001 in San Francisco, natcapsolutions.org/integrated -bottom-line/. It subsequently formed the basis for the IIRC, integratedreporting.org/resource/international-ir-framework/, and SASB, sasb.org/

20. *Sustainability Pays*, Natural Capitalism Solutions, 2012, natcapsolutions .org/businesscasereports.pdf

21. *Carbon Disclosure Project*, cdp.net/CDPResults/CDP-SP500-leaders -report-2014.pdf

22. *The UN Global Compact: Accenture CEO Study on Sustainability 2013*, Architects of a Better World, 2013, unglobalcompact.org/docs/news _events/8.1/UNGC_Accenture_CEO_Study_2013.pdf

23. "UN Fears Business Sustainability Has Plateaued," Green Growth, green-growth.org.uk/article/un-fears-business-sustainability-has -plateaued

24. "UN Global Compact: Accenture Strategy CEO Study," acnprod.accen ture.com/us-en/insight-un-global-compact-ceo-study

25. Bob Willard, "The 5-Stage Sustainability Journey," July 27, 2010, sustain ability advantage.com/2010/07/27/the-5-stage-sustainability-journey/

26. World Commission on Environment and Development, *Our Common Future*, Oxford University Press, 1987, un-documents.net/our-common -future.pdf

27. John Elkington, "Enter the Triple Bottom Line," in Adrian Henriqes and Julie Richardson, eds., *The Triple Bottom Line: Does It All Add Up?* Earthscan, 2004.

28. Randy Hayes and Dan Imhoff, *Biosphere Smart Agriculture in a True Cost Economy*, Foundation Earth, 2015, fdnearth.org/files/2015/09 /FINAL-Biosphere-Smart-Ag-in-True-Cost-Economy-FINAL-1-page -display-1.pdf

29. This concept was created by L. Hunter Lovins in the 1990s, and used as the basis of the Bottom Line 2001 conference held in April 2001 in San Francisco.

30. Robert Eccles and Michael Krzus, *One Report: Integrated Reporting for a Sustainable Society*, John Wiley and Sons, 2010.

31. Sustainability Accounting Standards Board, sasb.org/

32. See, e.g., the Moskowitz Prize winners, responsiblebusiness.haas .berkeley.edu/research/moskowitz-past-winners.html, including Flammer, Caroline, "Does Corporate Social Responsibility Lead to Superior Financial Performance? A Regression Discontinuity Approach," October 2013, papers.ssrn.com/sol3/papers.cfm?abstract_id=2146282

33. Robert Eccles and Michael Krzus, *The Integrated Reporting Movement: Meaning, Momentum, Motives and Materiality*, Wiley Corporate, 2015.

34. Mozaffar Khan, George Serafeim, and Aaron Yoon, *Corporate Sustainability: First Evidence on Materiality*, Harvard Business School, Working paper 15-073, 2015, hbswk.hbs.edu/item/corporate-sustainability-first -evidence-on-materiality

35. International Integrated Reporting Council, integratedreporting.org/

36. Environmental Profit and Loss Account, about.puma.com/en/sustain ability/environment/environmental-profit-and-loss-account

37. "Integrated Reporting," *Novo Nordisk Annual Report*, 2016, novonordisk .com/sustainability/performance/Integrated-reporting.html

38. 2016 US CEO Survey Top Findings, pwc.com/us/en/ceo-survey/top -findings.html

39. William Brittlebank, *Biggest US Corporates Setting Ambitious Climate Targets: New Report*, Climate Group, April 20, 2017, theclimategroup.org /news/biggest-us-corporates-setting-ambitious-climate-targets-new -report

40. *UN Global Compact: The Power of Principles*, unglobalcompact.org/what -is-gc/mission/principles

41. World Business Council for Sustainable Development, *Low-carbon Technology Partnerships Initiative*, 2016, lctpi.wbcsd.org/

42. Business End of Climate Change, businessendofclimate.org/
43. Barbara Grady, "Mars, Bloomberg Vow with '6 Million Companies' to Act on Climate Change," *GreenBiz*, September 29, 2015, greenbiz.com /article/mars-bloomberg-vow-6-million-companies-act-climate-change
44. *Green Building Councils Commit to Green Area Twice the Size of Singapore*, World Green Building Council, December 3, 2015, worldgbc.org /activities/news/global-news/green-building-councils-commit-green -area-twice-size-singapore/
45. USGBC Statistics, January 2017, usgbc.org/articles/usgbc-statistics
46. *Gearing for Growth: Future Drivers of Corporate Productivity*, Economist Intelligence Unit, 2011, services.ricoh.com/images/uploads/literature /knowledge_center/Gearing_for_growth_RICOH_Mar21_WEB.pdf
47. gallup.com/services/191489/q12-meta-analysis-report-2016.aspx?g_ source=position2&g_medium=related&g_campaign=tiles
48. *Generation Y and the Workplace*, Johnson Controls, 2010, gbcsa.org.za /wp-content/uploads/2013/06/NZGBC-Gen-Y-and-The-Workplace -Annual-Report-2010.pdf
49. Anne Moore Odell, "Working for the Earth: Green Companies and Green Jobs Attract Employees," *GreenBiz*, October 16, 2007, greenbiz .com/news/2007/10/16/working-earth-green-companies-and-green -jobs-attract-employees
50. Shelly DuBois, "How Going Green Can Be a Boon to Corporate Recruiters," *Fortune*, June 2, 2011.
51. *Cone Communications 2015 Global CSR Survey*, conecomm.com/2015 -cone-communications-ebiquity-global-csr-study-pdf
52. Freya Williams, *Green Giants*, 2015, greengiantsbook.com/
53. Martinne Geller, "Unilever Says Its Socially Responsible Brands Outperform Rest," *Reuters*, May 4, 2015, reuters.com/article/us-unilever -sustainability-idUSKBN0NQ02G20150505
54. The Natural Step, "The Framework," thenaturalstep.org/our-approach/
55. Ray Anderson, *Mid-Course Correction*, Chelsea Green Publishing, 1998; *Confessions of a Radical Industrialist*, St. Martin's Press, 2009.
56. Paul Hawken, Amory Lovins, and Hunter Lovins, *Natural Capitalism: Creating the Next Industrial Revolution*, Little Brown, 1999.
57. Natural Capitalism Solutions, natcapsolutions.org
58. Hunter Lovins, *The Way Out: Kickstarting Capitalism to Save Our Economic Ass*, Farrar Straus Giroux, 2012.
59. Janine Benyus, Biomimicry Institute, biomimicryinstitute.org/
60. This concept was first introduced by Walter Stahel, product-life.org/, although it was later borrowed by Michael Braungart and Bill McDonough, who wrote a book by that title.
61. Ben Shiller, "A Blueprint for a Circular Economy: Reusing and Refurbishing for Prosperity," *Fast Company*, June 7, 2012, fastcoexist.com /1679241/a-blueprint-for-a-circular-economy-reusing-and-refurbishing -for-prosperity, thecirculareconomy.org/exec-summary

62. Interface Floor, interfaceglobal.com/

63. Download the biomimicry taxonomy at 1d59b73swr1f1swu2v451xcx
-wpengine.netdna-ssl.com/wp-content/uploads/2016/09/Biomimicry
_Taxonomy_AskNature_6.1_Color.pdf

64. Janine Benyus, "Biomimicry's Surprising Lessons from Nature's En-
gineers," TED, February 2005, ted.com/talks/janine_benyus_shares
_nature_s_designs; and "Biomimicry in Action," TED, July 2009, ted
.com/talks/janine_benyus_biomimicry_in_action

65. Ecovative, ecovativedesign.com/

66. Newlight Technologies, newlight.com/#sthash.0V84JiyG.dpuf; and
newlight.com/newlight-signs-20-year-contract-for-19-billion-pounds
-of-aircarbon-pha/

67. LanzaTech, lanzatech.com/company/

68. Jay Friedlander, "The Sustainable Tactics You Don't Know, but Should,"
Big Idea: SustainabilityBlog, *MIT Sloan Management Review*, July 12,
2016, sloanreview.mit.edu/article/the-sustainable-tactics-you-dont
-know-but-should/?utm_source=WhatCounts,+Publicaster+Edition
&utm_medium=email&utm_campaign=SU+7/12/16+-+Sustainability
+Tactics&utm_content=pathways+to+sustainability

69. Susan Arterian Chang, *The Field Guide to Investing in a Regenerative
Economy*, Capital Institute, fieldguide.capitalinstitute.org/

70. Joel Makower, "Why Aren't There More Ray Andersons?" *GreenBiz*,
August 6, 2012, greenbiz.com/blog/2012/08/06/why-aren%E2%80%99t
-there-more-ray-andersons

71. Ibid.

72. Unilever has consistently been ranked as the world's most sustainable
company, to the point that *GreenBiz* asked who are the sustainability
leaders *besides* Unilever, google.com/webhp?sourceid=chrome-instant
&ion=1&espv=2&ie=UTF-8#q=unilever%20most%20sustainable%20
company

73. "Growing Roots Program Seeks to Improve Fresh Food Access and
Education in City Communities," February 2016, unileverusa.com/news
/news-and-features/2016/growing-roots-program-seeks-to-improve
-fresh-food-access.html

74. "The Unilever Sustainable Living Young Entrepreneurs Awards,"
unilever.com/sustainable-living/join-in/Young-Entrepreneurs-Awards/

75. unilever.com/sustainable-living/the-sustainable-living-plan/our
-strategy/

76. Unilever, *Our Strategy for Sustainable Business*, unilever.com/sustainable
-living/the-sustainable-living-plan/our-strategy/

77. Personal communication, Kees Krythoff, president Unilever North
America Operations, Englewood Cliffs, Unilever Big Moment, May 16,
2016.

78. Robert Armstrong, "Hyena Capitalism Receives a Swift Kick from the
Unilever Giraffe," *Financial Times*, February 24, 2017.

79. Unilever, *Sustainable Living, Our Metrics*, 2017, unilever.com/sustainable
    -living/our-approach-to-reporting/our-metrics/
80. "Measure What Matters," B Impact Assessment, bimpactassessment.net/
81. "Become a Measure What Matters Partner," B Analytics, b-analytics.net/
82. "Walmart Announces Partnership with Carbon Disclosure Project
    to Measure Energy Used to Create Products," September 24, 2007,
    walmartstores.com/pressroom/news/6739.aspx
83. Jo Confino, huffingtonpost.com/author/jo-confino
84. Jo Confino, Review of *Green Giants*, greengiantsbook.com/
85. Jo Confino, "29 Qualities for Business Leaders to Create a Sustainable
    Society," *The Guardian*, 12 November 2014.
86. Bard MBA is only one of a few MBA programs in which sustainability
    and regenerative management are baked into every class, bgi.edu, bard
    .edu/mba/
87. hub.aashe.org/browse/academicprogram/13937/ms-in-regenerative
    -studies, unprme.org/index.php
88. Certified B Corporations, bcorporation.net/
89. Apparel Coalition, apparelcoalition.org/higgindex/
90. Patagonia, patagonia.com/us/patagonia.go?assetid=67372
91. "Yvon Chouinard: The Company as Activist," *GreenBiz*, March 1, 2013,
    greenbiz.com/video/2013/03/01/patagonia-responsible-company
92. "What Is NEXT?" DNV GL, 2014, dnvgl.com/news/what-is-next
    --6301
93. Bjorn Haugland, *Time to Make a Step Change*, DNV GL Sustainability,
    September 21, 2015, blogs.dnvgl.com/sustainability/2015/09/time-to
    -make-a-step-change/
94. Cecilie Arnesen Hultmann and Anne Louise Koefoed, *A Safe and Sus-
    tainable Future*, DNV GL, 2014, production.presstogo.com/fileroot6/gal
    lery/dnvgl/files/original/f7a21697d758474be04385ee5e4dd62e_hi.pdf

Chapter 9: Growing a Finer Future

1. Founder of the Biochar Company, soilreef.com/company/soilreef
   -company.php
2. *Status of the World's Soil Resources*, FAO, 2015, fao.org/documents/card
   /en/c/c6814873-efc3-41db-b7d3-2081a10ede50/
3. *Soil Erosion and Degradation*, World Wildlife Fund, worldwildlife.org
   /threats/soil-erosion-and-degradation
4. *Land Based Adaptation and Resilience*, UNCCD, 2014, p. 4, unccd.int
   /Lists/SiteDocumentLibrary/Publications/Land_Based_Adaptation
   _ENG%20Sall_web.pdf
5. *Soil Degradation: A Major Threat to Humanity*, Sustainable Food Trust,
   2015, sustainablefoodtrust.org/wp-content/uploads/2013/04/Soil
   -degradation-Final-final.pdf
6. Wes Jackson, "The 50-Year Farm Bill," *Solutions Journal*, Vol. 1, Issue 3,
   July 7, 2010.

7. afsic.nal.usda.gov/videos/histories/robert-rodale; see also, youtube.com /watch?v=e60ovdeevag&feature=youtu.be

8. *Why Regenerative Agriculture?* Regeneration International, regenerationinternational.org/why-regenerative-agriculture/

9. Mark Bittman, "How to Change the Food System and Feed the Nine Billion," *New York Times*, YouTube, November 13, 2014, youtube.com /watch?v=JWKa9DWSlz4

10. Karla Wolfensen, *Coping with the Food and Agriculture Challenge: Smallholders' Agenda*, FAO, 2013, p. 1, fao.org/fileadmin/templates/nr /sustainability_pathways/docs/Coping_with_food_and_agriculture _challenge__Smallholder_s_agenda_Final.pdf

11. William Cline, *Global Warming and Agriculture: Impact Estimates by Country*, Center for Global Development, 2007, cgdev.org/content /publications/detail/14090

12. "Fresh Water Resources and Their Management," in *Climate Change 2007*, Working Group II, IPCC, ipcc.ch/publications_and_data/ar4 /wg2/en/ch3s3-4.html

13. Lester R. Brown, *Plan B 4.0: Mobilizing to Save Civilization*, W.W. Norton, 2009, earthpolicy.org/index.php?/books/pb4/pb4_presentation

14. Rattan Lal, "The Solutions Underfoot: The Power of Soil," YouTube IIASA, November 3, 2015, youtube.com/watch?v=Uh0TwQyw37A

15. Lester R. Brown, *Rising Temperatures Raise Food Prices: Heat, Drought and a Failed Harvest in Russia*, Earth Policy Institute, August 10, 2010, www.earthpolicy.org/index.php?/plan_b_updates/2010/update89

16. *A Stronger UNCCD for a Land Degradation Neutral World*, UNCCD, 2013, p. 4, unccd.int/Lists/SiteDocumentLibrary/Rio+20/issue%20 brief%2004_09_13%20web.pdf

17. Jim Tankersley, "California Farms, Vineyards in Peril from Warming, US Energy Secretary Warns," *Los Angeles Times*, February 4, 2009.

18. NYC Hi Tech Staff, "California's Three-year Drought Not Over," *New York City High Tech News*, February 6, 2017, newyorkcityhightech.com /californias-three-year-drought-not-over/

19. Judith Schwartz, "Soil as Carbon Storehouse: New Weapon in Climate Fight?" *Yale Environment 360*, March 4, 2014, e360.yale.edu/feature /soil_as_carbon_storehouse_new_weapon_in_climate_fight/2744/

20. PriceWaterhouseCoopers, "Global Economies Must Lower Carbon Emissions at Five Times the Levels Currently Achieved," September 7, 2014, press.pwc.com/Global/global-economies-must-lower-carbon -emissions-at-fivetimes-the-levels-currently-achieved/s/f748001d-e73b -47c0-af8f-18ad9d1023b8

21. W.M. Post and K.C. Kwon, "Soil Carbon Sequestration and Land-use Change: Processes and Potential," *Global Change Biology*, 6, August 9, 1999, pp. 317–328.

22. *Status of the World's Soil Resources*, FAO, 2015, fao.org/documents/card /en/c/c6814873-efc3-41db-b7d3-2081a10ede50/

23. S. L. Baggott et al., *Greenhouse Gas Inventories for England, Scotland, Wales and Northern Ireland*, Division Research Programme of the Department for Environment, Food and Rural Affairs, November 2006, www.airquality.co.uk/.../0509211321_Reghg_report_2003_Main_Text_Issue_1.doc

24. J. T. Houghton et al., eds., *Climate Change 1995: The Science of Climate Change*, published for the Intergovernmental Panel on Climate Change by Cambridge University Press, New York, 1996.

25. A little soil and health science helps explain what is going on literally beneath our feet. Nitrogen, necessary for life, is a key component of DNA. People and other animals cannot obtain nitrogen by breathing it in; they have to eat it. Nitrogen in molecular form (N_2) is an inert element. To be biologically available, it must be converted to nitrate (NO_3), ammonium (NH_4), or organic nitrogen ($(NH_2)2CO$, otherwise known as plant protein). This biologically available nitrogen enters the soil when lightning oxidizes atmospheric nitrogen and rain brings it to Earth. Legumes like clover and alfalfa also "fix" atmospheric nitrogen in the soil, using soil microbes called Rhizobium to break the N_2 into forms useful to plants. Animals then get the nitrogen they need by eating plants. In healthy soil, microbes convert the nitrogen that enters the soil when living things decay, back into N_2, closing the loop and completing the nitrogen cycle. Artificial fertilizers upset this balance. Excessive use of artificial nitrogen, created from natural gas, drives the cycle ever faster, as the microbes in the soil that convert organic nitrogen back into N_2 gas are fueled by excess nitrogen and release it into the atmosphere. For more on this, see "The Nitrogen Cycle," users.rcn.com/jkimball.ma.ultranet/BiologyPages /N/NitrogenCycle.html; John A. Harrison, "The Nitrogen Cycle: Of Microbes and Men," Visionlearning, visionlearning.com/library/module _viewer.php?mid=98; J. T. Houghton et al., eds., *Climate Change 1995*.

26. Dan Charles, "Fertilized World," *National Geographic*, ngm.national geographic.com/2013/05/fertilized-world/charles-text?source= podrelated

27. J. T. Houghton et al., eds., *Climate Change 1995*.

28. www2.epa.gov/nutrientpollution/harmful-algal-blooms

29. scientificamerican.com/article/oceanic-dead-zones-spread/

30. A. R. Ravishankara et al., "Nitrous Oxide (N_2O): The Dominant Ozone-Depleting Substance Emitted in the 21st Century," *Science*, August 28, 2009.

31. C. Weber and H. S. Matthews, "Food-miles and the Relative Climate Impacts of Food Choices in the United States," *Environmental Science and Technology*, 42, 2008, pp. 3508–3513; Cool Food Campaign, *Meat and Dairy Fact Sheet*, fao.org/newsroom/en/news/2006/1000448/, and coolfoodscampaign.org/uploads/MeatandDairyFactSheet.pdf

32. "Livestock a Major Threat to Environment," *FAO News*, November 29, 2006.

33. Richard Black, "UN Body to Look at Meat and Climate Link," *BBC News*, March 24, 2010, news.bbc.co.uk/2/hi/science/nature/8583308.stm

34. Jessica Bellarby et al., *Cool Farming: Climate Impacts of Agriculture and Mitigation Potential*, Greenpeace Report, January 2008.

35. Suzanne Nelson, "Beef and Dairy Can Be Good for the Planet," indyweek.com/gyrobase/Content?oid=oid%3A194735

36. US Department of Agriculture, Economic Research Service, Feed Grains Database: Yearbook Tables, and Oil Crops Yearbook, ers.usda .gov/Data/Feedgrains/StandardReports/YBtable4.htm21; and usda .mannlib.cornell.edu/MannUsda/viewDocumentInfo.do?document ID=129061: 279-286

37. Charles, "Fertilized World."

38. Report on the International Conference on Organic Agriculture and Food Security, May 2007.

39. *Wake Up Before It's Too Late*, UNCTAD, 2013, unctad.org/en /PublicationsLibrary/ditcted2012d3_en.pdf

40. *The State of Food Insecurity in the World*, UNFAO, 2015, fao.org/3/a4ef2 d16-70a7-460a-a9ac-2a65a533269a/i4646e.pdf

41. *FAO Calls for "Paradigm Shift" Towards Sustainable Agriculture and Family Farming*, Food and Agriculture Organization, September 29, 2014, fao.org/news/story/en/item/250148/icode/

42. Unlike the term "green" used today to indicate sustainability and living in harmony with nature, the term "green" was used to indicate a resistance to communism, mirroring images of "red." The name was given by the US State Department, William Guad, in 1968. He explained that if people were well fed by the high-yielding crops of the new modernized agriculture system, they would be less motivated to become communist.

43. Daniel Zwerdling, "India's Farming 'Revolution' Heading for Collapse," National Public Radio, April 13, 2009, npr.org/templates/story/story .php?storyId=102893816.

44. Somini Sengupta, "On India's Farms: A Plague of Suicide," *New York Times*, September 19, 2006; for more recent information, see Vandana Shiva, navdanya.org/blog/?p=2136

45. Ibid.

46. Jenny Gustavsson, Christel Cederberg, Ulf Sonesson, Robert van Otterdijk, and Meybeck Alexandre, *Global Food Losses and Food Waste*, FAO, 2011, p. v, fao.org/docrep/014/mb060e/mb060e.pdf

47. Kate Lyons, "Cutting Food Waste by a Quarter Would Mean Enough for Everyone, Says UN," *The Guardian*, August 12, 2015.

48. The Land Institute, landinstitute.org/

49. Ibid.

50. David Burrows, "New Demand Driving Sustainable Food Growth," *Marketing Week*, May 29, 2015, marketingweek.com/2015/05/29/new -demand-driving-sustainable-food-growth/

51. "About Us," Development Research Communication and Services Centre (DRCSC) drcsc.org/aboutus.html
52. Ibid.
53. bie.berkeley.edu/cookstoves
54. biochar-international.org/aboutbiochar/informationaboutbiochar .html International Biochar Initiative
55. biocharmatters.org/
56. Tim Flannery, "An Open Letter on Biochar," Biochar International, August 2008, biochar-international.org/timflannery
57. Scott Bilby, "Flannery Talks Biochar and Why We Need to Move into the Renewable Age," *Beyond Zero Emissions*, January 11, 2008, beyond zeroemissions.org/media/radio/tim-flannery-talks-bio-char-and-why -we-need-move-renewable-age-080111
58. Biochar Company, soilreef.com/
59. "FST Fast Facts," Rodale Institute, rodaleinstitute.org/our-work /farming-systems-trial/farming-systems-trial-fst-fast-facts/
60. Soil Association, soilassociation.org/
61. Gaudin Lab, University of California at Davis, gaudin.ucdavis.edu/
62. Janet Cotter and Reyes Tirado, *Food Security and Climate Change: The Answer Is Biodiversity*, Greenpeace International, December 19, 2008, greenpeace.org/eu-unit/en/Publications/2009-and-earlier/food -security-and-climate-change/
63. L. Drinkwater et al., "Legume-based Cropping Systems Have Reduced Carbon and Nitrogen Losses," *Nature*, 396, 1998, pp. 262–265; D. Pimentel, "Environmental, Energetic and Economic Comparisons of Organic and Conventional Farming Systems," *BioScience*, 55, 2005, pp. 573–582; E. E. Marriott and M. M. Wander, "Total and Labile Soil Organic Matter in Organic and Conventional Farming Systems," *Soil Society of America Journal*, 70, 2006, pp. 950–959.
64. D. Gabriel et al., "Beta Diversity at Different Special Scales: Plant Communities in Organic and Conventional Agriculture," *Ecological Applications*, 16, 2006, pp. 2011–2021, cited in www3.interscience.wiley.com /journal/123417154/abstract?CRETRY=1&SRETRY=0
65. *Agricultural Practices and Carbon Sequestration*, Union of Concerned Scientists, October 1, 2009, ucsusa.org/assets/documents/food_and _agriculture/ag-carbon-sequest-fact-sheet.pdf
66. *Organic Market Report 2016*, Soil Association, March 16, 2016, soilassociation.org/news/2016/organic-market-report-2016/
67. *Organic Market Report 2017*, Soil Association, May 11, 2017, soilassociation.org/certification/market-research-and-data/the-organic -market-report/
68. *US Organic State of the Market*, Organic Trade Association, 2016, ota .com/sites/default/files/indexed_files/OTA_StateofIndustry_2016.pdf
69. Emily Monaco, "Global Organic Produce Market to Skyrocket to Nearly

$63 Billion by 2020," *Organic Authority*, December 2, 2015, organic authority.com/global-organic-produce-market-to-skyrocket-to-nearly -63-billion-by-2020/

70. *Organic Market Overview*, USDA, April 4, 2017, ers.usda.gov/topics /natural-resources-environment/organic-agriculture/organic-market -overview/

71. Judith Schwartz, *Cows Save the Planet*, Chelsea Green, 2013; see also rangemagazine.com/features/summer-15/range-su15-sr-cows_save _world.pdf

72. Savory Institute, savory.global/institute/

73. "An Introduction to Savory Hubs," YouTube, November 13, 2012, youtube.com/watch?v=SKWeqkq6tP4

74. Allan Savory, "Reversing Global Warming While Meeting Human Needs," YouTube, March 13, 2013, youtube.com/watch?v=uEAFTsFH_x4

75. Allan Savory, "A Global Strategy for Addressing Climate Change, savory.global/wp-content/uploads/2017/02/climate-change.pdf

76. bfi.org/challenge

77. "What Is Savory Global Network?" savory.global/network/

78. Sarah Eykyn, "Savory Institute Ignites Consumer Revolution," January 24, 2017, savory.global/wp-content/uploads/2017/02/Savory-Land-to -Market-Program.pdf

79. "Evidence," Savory Institute, savory.global/institute/#evidence

80. White Oak Pastures, whiteoakpastures.com/

81. Personal communication, Will Harris to Hunter Lovins, White Oak Pastures, April 9, 2017.

82. Susan Matthews, "An Organic Chicken Farm in Georgia Has Become an Endless Buffet for Bald Eagles," *Audubon Magazine*, Fall 2016, audubon .org/magazine/fall-2016/an-organic-chicken-farm-georgia-has-become -endless

83. "Organic Industry Surpasses $30 Billion Threshold in 2011," Sustainable Brands, April 23, 2012, sustainablebusiness.com/index.cfm/ go/news.display/id/23632; by 2015 the industry had surpassed $34 billion, growing at double digit rates every year, ota.com/news/press -releases/19031

84. Chris Rose, *Food and Values: A Recipe to Save British Farming*, Soil Association, 2000, soilassociationscotland.org/media/4940/policy _report_2006_food_values-1.pdf

85. Alana Herro, *Organic Farms Provide Jobs, High Yields*, Worldwatch Institute, 2013, worldwatch.org/node/3975

86. "Organic Foods Industry Creates More Than a Half Million Jobs," PR newswire, April 25, 2012, prnewswire.com/news-releases/organic-foods -industry-creates-more-than-a-half-million-jobs-148878215.html

87. John Ikerd, *Sustainable Agriculture as a Rural Economic Development Strategy*, University of Missouri, Cacapon Institute, 1994, cacapon

institute.org/html/SUSTAINABLE%20AGRICULTURE%20as%20 rural%20development%20strategy_Ikerd.htm

88. Maryn McKenna, "Is More Cattle Grazing the Solution to Saving Our Soil?" *The Plate*, *National Geographic*, December 23, 2015.

89. Personal communication, Tony Lovell to Hunter Lovins, London, August 5, 2014; see also slmpartners.com/

90. Grasslands, LLC, grasslands-llc.com/

91. Hana Ranch, About, hanaranch.com/new-page/; and Bio-logical Capital, biologicalcapital.com/company-history/

92. Joel Salatin, "Meet the Farmer, Parts 1–3," YouTube, April 29, 2012, youtube.com/playlist?list=PL6C0D6709117A0049

93. Joel Salatin, "On Creating Young Farmers," YouTube, April 27, 2016, youtube.com/watch?v=696uw1MqrCo

94. Gabe Brown, "Keys to Building a Healthy Soil," YouTube, December 8, 2014, youtube.com/watch?v=9yPjoh9YJMk

95. Gabe Brown, "Can We Really Regenerate Our Soils?" *Graze Magazine*, January 1, 2017, grazeonline.com/canweregeneratesoils

96. Sally Neas, "What's a Carbon Farmer? How California Ranchers Use Dirt to Tackle Climate Change," *Yes Magazine*, April 29, 2016, yesmagazine.org/planet/whats-a-carbon-farmer-how-california -ranchers-use-dirt-to-tackle-climate-change-20160429?utm_source =YTW&utm_medium=Email&utm_campaign=20160429; and Rebecca Dargie, "Could Carbon Farming Be the Answer for a 'Clapped-out' Australia?" *The Guardian*, April 28, 2016.

97. "California Farmers Use Carbon Sequestration to Reverse Climate Change," Foodtank, May 16, 2015, foodtank.com/news/2015/05 california-farmers-use-carbon-sequestration-to-reverse-climate-change; see protocols at capcoa.org/

98. "Carbon Farming Gaining Traction in the US," SustainableBusiness .com, November 19, 2014, sustainablebusiness.com/index.cfm/go/news .display/id/26014

99. "Can Land Management Enhance Soil Carbon Sequestration?" Marin Carbon Project, marincarbonproject.org/science/land-management -carbon-sequestration

100. "The Marin Carbon Project," carboncycle.org/marin-carbon-project/

101. Rebecca Ryals and Whendee Silver, "Effects of Organic Matter Amendments on Net Primary Productivity and Greenhouse Gas Emissions in Annual Grasslands," *Ecological Applications*, January 1, 2013, onlinelibrary.wiley.com/doi/10.1890/12-0620.1/abstract

102. David Johnson, "Atmospheric CO_2 Reduction: A Practical Solution!" Institute for Sustainable Agricultural Research, New Mexico State University, newscenter.nmsu.edu/Articles/view/10461/nmsu-researcher-s -carbon-sequestration-work-highlighted-in-the-soil-will-save-us; see also, David Johnson, *Carbon Sequestration: A Practical Approach*,

web.nmsu.edu/~johnsoda/Carbon%20Sequestration%20with%20IP
%20Agriculture.pdf

103. W. R. Teague et al., "The Role of Ruminants in Reducing Agriculture's Carbon Footprint in North America," *Journal of Soil and Water
Conservation*, Vol. 71, No. 2, March/April 2016.

104. David Johnson et al., "Development of Soil Microbial Communities
for Promoting Sustainability in Agriculture and a Global Carbon Fix,"
Peer J Preprints, 2015, peerj.com/preprints/789/

105. Ratan Lal, "Managing Soils and Ecosystems for Mitigating
Anthropogenic Carbon Emissions and Advancing Global Food
Security," *BioScience*, Vol. 60, no. 9, 2010, pp. 708-721. doi:10.1525/bio
.2010.60.9.8, bioscience.oxfordjournals.org/content/60/9/708.abstract

106. A.-M. Codur et al., *Hope Below Our Feet: Soil as a Climate Solu-
tion*. Retrieved from Global Development and Environment Institute
(GDAE), Tufts University, Medford, MA, 2017, ase.tufts.edu/gdae
/Pubs/climate/ClimatePolicyBrief4.pdf

107. Richard Teague, "Forages and Pastures Symposium: Cover Crops
in Livestock Production: Whole-system Approach, Managing Grazing
to Restore Soil Health and Farm Livelihoods," *Journal of Animal Science*,
doi:10.1093/jas/skx060, 2018, dx.doi.org/10.1093/jas/skx060

108. M. B. Machmuller et al., "Emerging Land Use Practices Rapidly
Increase Soil Organic Matter," *Nature Communications*, 6, 6995, 2015,
doi:10.1038/ncomms7995, nature.com/articles/ncomms7995#supplem
entary-information

109. W. R. Teague et al., "The Role of Ruminants in Reducing Agriculture's Carbon Footprint in North America." *Journal of Soil and Water
Conservation*, Vol. 71, no. 2, 2016, pp. 156-164. doi:10.2489/jswc.71.2.156,
jswconline.org/content/71/2/156.abstract

110. Personal communications, Seth Itzkan with Hunter Lovins, June 1,
2018.

111. Daniel Riodin, *The Blueprint: Averting Global Collapse*, Corinno
Press, 2013.

112. For a debate on reasonable numbers for soil carbon sequestration
on UK farms, see *National Trust Report on Carbon Footprints in
Various Beef Production Systems—And Expert Comment*, fcrn.org.uk
/research-library/national-trust-report-carbon-footprints-various-beef
-production-systems-%E2%80%93-and

113. William Becker, "Carbon Sinks Are the Next Big Thing (Part 1),"
Huffington Post, April 1, 2016, huffingtonpost.com/william-s-becker
/sinks-are-the-next-big-th_b_9517398.html

114. Keith Paistian et al., "Climate-smart Soils," *Nature*, 532, April 7, 2016,
pp. 49–57.

115. Robert Berwyn, "Far from Turning a Corner, Global CO2 Emissions
Still Accelerating," *Inside Climate News*, May 19, 2016, insideclimatenews

.org/news/19052016/global-co2-emissions-still-accelerating-noaa-greenhouse-gas-index

116. Tim Redford, "Soil Could Save Earth from Overheating," *Climate News Network*, April 17, 2016, climatenewsnetwork.net/soil-could-save-earth-from-overheating/

117. Carbon Underground, thecarbonunderground.org/

118. Soil4Climate Resources, soil4climate.org/resources/

119. 2014 National Climate Assessment: nca2014.globalchange.gov/report

120. John Richardson, "When the End of Human Civilization Is Your Day Job, *Esquire*, July 7, 2015.

121. Personal communication, Allan Savory to Hunter Lovins, Boulder, CO, December 1, 2015.

122. 4 Per 1000 Initiative, CGIAR, 4p1000.org/

123. "Join the 4 per 1000 Initiative," agriculture.gouv.fr/telecharger/85964?token=9be0ed8f9a0a5c07599ea97c354a5c3f

124. James McWilliams, "All Sizzle and No Steak," *Slate*, April 22, 2013, slate.com/articles/life/food/2013/04/allan_savory_s_ted_talk_is_wrong_and_the_benefits_of_holistic_grazing_have.html; Christopher Ketchum, "Allan Savory's Holistic Management Theory Falls Short on Science," *Sierra Magazine*, February 23, 2017; and George Monbiot, "Eat More Meat and Save the World: The Latest Implausible Farming Miracle," *The Guardian*, August 4, 2014. See also, Hunter Lovins, "Why George Monbiot Is Wrong: Grazing Livestock Can Save the World, *The Guardian*, August 19, 2014.

125. pastoralismjournal.com/content/1/1/19

126. Dan Daggett, *Gardeners of Eden: Rediscovering Our Importance to Nature*, Thatcher Charitable Trust/EcoResults, Santa Barbara, 2005.

Chapter 10: Triumph of the Sun: The Mother of All Disruptions

1. Thomas Edison, in conversation with Henry Ford and Harvey Firestone (1931); quoted in James Newton, *Uncommon Friends: Life with Thomas Edison, Henry Ford, Harvey Firestone, Alexis Carrel & Charles Lindbergh*, 1987, p. 31.

2. Jeremy Leggett, jeremyleggett.net/; see also, blueandgreentomorrow.com/features/jeremy-leggett-high-chance-of-a-tipping-point-in-retreat-from-fossil-fuels-soon/

3. Tom Randall, "Wind and Solar Are Crushing Fossil Fuels," *Bloomberg New Energy Finance*, April 6, 2016, bloomberg.com/news/articles/2016-04-06/wind-and-solar-are-crushing-fossil-fuels

4. Paul Gilding, "Fossil Fuels Are Finished: The Rest Is Just Detail," *REneweconomy*, July 13, 2015, reneweconomy.com.au/2015/fossil-fuels-are-finished-the-rest-is-just-detail-71574

5. Jeremy Leggett, "State of the Transition: Might The Fossil Fuel Industries Implode Faster Than the Clean Energy Industries Can

Grow to Replace Them?" August 3, 2016, jeremyleggett.net/2016/08
/state-of-the-transition-july-2016-might-the-fossil-fuel-industries
-implode-faster-than-the-clean-energy-industries-can-grow-to-replace
-them/

6. Mark Campanale, "Is Carbon Risk Fueling the Next Big Financial
    Bubble?" Carbon Tracker, November 10, 2015, cepsech.eu/sites/default
    /files/Mark%20Campanale%20Presentation.pdf

7. Robert Lenzner, "The Recessions of 1973, 1980, 1991, 2001, 2008 Were
    Caused by High Oil Prices," *Forbes*, September 1, 2013.

8. Bryan Rich, "Cheap Oil Edging Us Toward Global Economic Collapse,"
    Forbes, February 6, 2016.

9. Paley Commission, The President's Materials Policy Commission (Paley
    Commission), *Resources for Freedom*, 5 Volumes, Washington, DC, Gov-
    ernment Printing Office, 1952.

10. Richard Heinberg of the Post Carbon Institute is one prominent advo-
    cate of this position, postcarbon.org/

11. Ron Bousso, "Global Oil, Gas Discoveries Drop to 70-year Low: Rystad
    Energy," *Reuters*, January 18, 2017, reuters.com/article/us-oil-exploration
    -idUSKBN1521TA

12. Daniel Yergin, danielyergin.com/

13. Tam Hunt, "What Happened to Peak Oil?" *Greentech Media*,
    greentechmedia.com/articles/read/what-happened-to-peak-oil

14. Fereidoon Sioshansi, "Peak Oil? Sooner Than You Think,"
    REneweconomy, March 20, 2017, reneweconomy.com.au/peak-oil-sooner
    -than-you-think-59142

15. Jeremy Grantham, on *Charlie Rose Show*, May 11, 2013, charlierose.com
    /videos/30816

16. Jeremy Grantham, "Jeremy Grantham: In the Face of Finite Resources,
    It's Time to Think About 'Peak Everything,'" *Money Morning*, May 19,
    2011, moneymorning.com/2011/05/19/in-the-face-of-finite-resources-its
    -time-to-think-about-peak-everything/

17. Moises Naim and Francisco Toro, "Venezuela Is Falling Apart," *The
    Atlantic*, May 12, 2015.

18. Moritz Borgman, "Potentially Game-changing Saudi Arabian Govern-
    ment Restructuring Bolsters 9.5 GW Renewable Energy Targets
    by 2023," *Apericum*, May 9, 2016, apricum-group.com/saudi-arabia
    -announces-9-5-gw-renewable-energy-target-new-king-salman
    -renewable-energy-initiative/

19. Matt Egan, "Saudi Arabia to Run Out of Cash in Less Than 5 Years,"
    CNN Money, October 26, 2015, money.cnn.com/2015/10/25/investing
    /oil-prices-saudi-arabia-cash-opec-middle-east/

20. "Cost of Oil Production by Country," knoema.com/vyronoe/cost-of-oil
    -production-by-country

21. Petra Cahill and Laura Saravia, "Venezuela Protests and Economic
    Crisis: What Is Going On?" *NBC News*, May 6, 2017, nbcnews.com

/storyline/venezuela-crisis/venezuela-protests-economic-crisis-what
-going-n755306

22. *World Energy Outlook 2015*, International Energy Agency, November 10,
    2015, worldenergyoutlook.org/weo2015/#d.en.148701

23. *Energy Technology Perspectives 2015*, iea.org/publications/freepublications
    /publication/EnergyTechnologyPerspectives2015ExecutiveSummary
    Englishversion.pdf

24. *Turn Down the Heat*, World Bank, November 2012, documents.world
    bank.org/curated/en/865571468149107611/pdf/NonAsciiFileName0
    .pdf

25. Dahr Jamail, "The Coming 'Instant Planetary Emergency,'" *The Nation*,
    December 17, 2013, thenation.com/article/coming-instant-planetary
    -emergency/

26. Johan Rockström, Malte Meinshausen, and John Schellnhuber, "A
    Roadmap for Rapid Decarbonization," *Science Magazine*, Policy Forum,
    Climate Policy, March 2017.

27. Johan Rockström, "Curbing Emissions with a New 'Carbon Law,'" Stock-
    holm Resilience Centre, March 2017, stockholmresilience.org/research
    /research-news/2017-03-23-curbing-emissions-with-a-new-carbon-law
    .html

28. Manyan Ranjan et al., "Project: The Feasibility of Air Capture," MIT,
    2010, sequestration.mit.edu/research/aircapture.html

29. citivelocity.com/citigps/ReportSeries.action?recordId=21

30. Tom Randall, "Wind and Solar Are Crushing Fossil Fuels," *Bloomberg
    New Energy Finance*, April 6, 2016, bloomberg.com/news/articles/2016
    -04-06/wind-and-solar-are-crushing-fossil-fuels

31. Sophie Vorrath, "Fossil Fuels Subsidies Cost World $5.3 Trillion A
    Year: $10 Million a Minute," *Clean Technica*, May 22, 2015, cleantechnica
    .com/2015/05/22/fossil-fuels-subsidies-cost-world-5-3-trillion-a-year
    -10-million-a-minute/

32. Brad Plumer, "One Upside of Cheap Oil: Countries Are Ditching Their
    Fossil-Fuel Subsidies," *Vox*, vox.com/2015/1/29/7945525/fossil-fuel
    -subsidies

33. Giles Parkinson, "Deutsche Bank Predicts Solar Grid Parity in 80% of
    Global Market by 2017," *Clean Technica*, April 17, 2015, cleantechnica
    .com/2015/01/14/deutsche-bank-predicts-solar-grid-parity-80-global
    -market-2017/

34. The Conversation, "When Will Rooftop Solar Be Cheaper Than the
    Grid?" *US News and World Report*, March 31, 2016, usnews.com/news
    /articles/2016-03-31/when-will-rooftop-solar-be-cheaper-than-the-grid

35. *So What Is a Kilowatt-hour?* Duke Energy, duke-energy.com/pdfs/MyH
    ER%20What%20is%20a%20Killowatt-Hour%20Energy%20Chart.pdf

36. *What's in a Megawatt?* Solar Energy Industries Association, seia.org
    /policy/solar-technology/photovoltaic-solar-electric/whats-megawatt

37. Craig Severance, *Business Risks and Costs of New Nuclear Power*, January 2, 2009, energyeconomyonline.com/uploads/Business_Risks_and_Costs_of_New_Nuclear_Power_Reprint_-_Jan_2__2009_Craig_A._Severance.pdf

38. *Solar Energy Emerging As Cheapest Power Source in Many Parts of the World*, February 2015, agora-energiewende.org/topics/optimisation-of-the-overall-system/detail-view/article/solar-energy-emerging-as-cheapest-power-source-in-many-parts-of-the-world/

39. Moritz Borgmann, "Dubai Shatters All Records for Cost of Solar with Earth's Largest Solar Power Plant," *Apericum*, May 2, 2016, apricum-group.com/dubai-shatters-records-cost-solar-earths-largest-solar-power-plant/; Anna Hirtenstein, "New Record Set for World's Cheapest Solar Now Undercutting Coal," *Bloomberg*, May 3, 2016, bloomberg.com/news/articles/2016-05-03/solar-developers-undercut-coal-with-another-record-set-in-dubai

40. *Full Report*, National Bank of Abu Dhabi, 2015, nbad.com/content/dam/NBAD/documents/Business/FOE_Full_Report.pdf

41. "DONG Energy Awarded Three German Offshore Wind Projects," April 13, 2017, DONG Energy, dongenergy.com/en/media/newsroom/news/articles/dong-energy-awarded-three-german-offshore-wind-projects

42. Stephen Lacey, "Cheapest Solar Ever: Austin Energy Gets 1.2 Gigawatts of Solar Bids for Less Than 4 Cents," *Greentech Media*, greentechmedia.com/articles/read/cheapest-solar-ever-austin-energy-gets-1.2-gigawatts-of-solar-bids-for-less

43. Tom Randall, "California Just Had a Stunning Increase in Solar," *Bloomberg Business*, March 26, 2015, bloomberg.com/news/articles/2015-03-26/california-just-had-a-stunning-increase-in-solar

44. Bentham Paulos, "California Has More Solar Power Than You Think—A Lot More," *Greentech Media*, August 11, 2016, greentechmedia.com/articles/read/california-has-more-solar-than-you-think

45. Tom Randall, "Fossil Fuels Just Lost the Race Against Renewables," *Bloomberg Business*, April 14, 2015, bloomberg.com/news/articles/2015-04-14/fossil-fuels-just-lost-the-race-against-renewables

46. Tom Randall, "World Energy Hits a Turning Point: Solar That's Cheaper Than Wind," *Bloomberg Technology*, December 14, 2016, bloomberg.com/news/articles/2016-12-15/world-energy-hits-a-turning-point-solar-that-s-cheaper-than-wind

47. Rakteem Katakey, "Energy Giant Shell Says Oil Demand Could Peak in Just Five Years," *Bloomberg*, November 2, 2016 bloomberg.com/news/articles/2016-11-02/europe-s-biggest-oil-company-thinks-demand-may-peak-in-5-years

48. Michael Biesecker, "Renewable Energy Surges Past Nuclear for 1st Time in Decades," *US News and World Report*, July 6, 2017, usnews.com/news

/business/articles/2017-07-06/renewable-energy-surges-past-nuclear
-for-1st-time-in-decades

49. *Global Energy Markets Transition Drives Thermal Coal into Structural Decline*, IEEFA, January 14, 2015, ieefa.org/global-energy-markets/

50. "South Africa Doubles Down on Renewables With Plans for 6.3GW Auction," *REneweconomy*, reneweconomy.com.au/2015/south-africa -doubles-down-on-renewables-with-plans-for-6-3gw-auction-49192

51. "South Africa Saved $69 Million from Solar, Wind Energy in 2014," *Clean Technica*, February 17, 2015, cleantechnica.com/2015/02/17/south -africa-saved-69-million-solar-wind-energy-2014/

52. "Green Jobs Debate Should Look Beyond Short-Term Benefits, Says UKERC Report," November 5, 2014, ukerc.ac.uk/news/green-jobs -debate-should-look-beyond-short-term-benefits-says-ukerc-report .html

53. "Medupi Power Station," SourceWatch, sourcewatch.org/index.php /Medupi_Power_Station

54. "Top Chinese Manufacturers Will Produce Solar Panels for 42 Cents per Watt in 2015," *Solar Reviews*, solarreviews.com/news/top-chinese -manufacturers-will-produce-solar-panels-for-42-cents-per-watt-in-2015/

55. Ibid.

56. "South Africa's Push for Renewables," Oxford Business Group, May 26, 2016, oxfordbusinessgroup.com/news/south-africa%E2%80%99s-push -renewables

57. "South Africa Plans to Procure 6.3GW More RE in Future Rounds," *RECHARGE*, April 16, 2015, rechargenews.com/wind/1397249/south -africa-plans-to-procure-63gw-more-re-in-future-rounds

58. *Utility-scale Renewable Energy: 2017 Market Intelligence Report*, Green Cape, greencape.co.za/assets/Uploads/GreenCape-Renewable-Energy -MIR-2017-electronic-FINAL-v1.pdf

59. "Latin Lessons as the World Marches Towards Paris," *RECHARGE*, April 2, 2015, rechargenews.com/wind/1395357/latin-lessons-as-the -world-marches-towards-paris

60. "2015 OUTLOOK: Brazil Gets Serious About Solar," *RECHARGE*, January 2, 2015, rechargenews.com/solar/1387554/2015-OUTLOOK -Brazil-gets-serious-about-solar

61. "IBM Research Launches Project 'Green Horizon' to Help China Deliver on Ambitious Energy and Environmental Goals," January 7, 2014, www-03.ibm.com/press/us/en/pressrelease/44202.wss

62. ieefa.org/global-energy-markets/

63. "China to Approve Over 17.8GW of PV in 2015, *Bloomberg New Energy Finance*, about.bnef.com/landing-pages/china-approve-17-8gw-pv-2015/

64. Henry Linden, "China Hit Record Wind and Solar Year in 2015, *Sustainovate*, February 5, 2016, sustainovate.ae/en/industry-news/detail /china-wind-energy-installations-climbed-to-record-highs-in-2015

65. *China 2050 High Renewable Energy Penetration Scenario and Roadmap Study*, China National Renewable Energy Centre, April 20, 2015, rff.org/Documents/Events/150420-Zhongying-ChinaEnergyRoadmap -Slides.pdf

66. Personal communication to author, Wang Yimin, State Grid Corp. of China, June 24, 2014, United Nations Global Compact Meeting, UNHQ, New York.

67. Anindya Uphadhyay, "Narendra Modi Lures India's Top Fossil Fuel Companies to Back Solar Boom," *Live Mint*, July 22, 2016, livemint.com /Industry/n6JGIUiAK3dBZHvUxWprWO/Narendra-Modi-lures -Indias-top-fossil-fuel-companies-to-bac.html

68. Ben Parr and Don Henry, "India Is Focused on Energy and Poverty, but It Can Still Sign a Global Climate Deal," *The Conversation*, November 24, 2015, theconversation.com/india-is-focused-on-energy-and-poverty-but -it-can-still-sign-a-global-climate-deal-47868

69. Gireesh Chandra Prasad, "Renewables to Help Meet 40% of India's Power Needs by 2030: Power Minister," *Live Mint*, October 12, 2017, livemint.com/Politics/w4qIZS90KxaHQEVHqwJEHP/Renewables -to-help-meet-40-of-Indias-power-needs-by-2030.html

70. Mayank Aggarwal, "Modi and Hollande Launch Solar Alliance," *Live Mint*, December 1, 2015, livemint.com/Politics/KpAZtkrkhnxvjfTDcH TRZO/France-India-to-launch-global-solar-alliance.html

71. L. Hunter Lovins, "The Veil of Energy Poverty," *Unreasonable.IS*, December 2014, unreasonable.is/energy-poverty/

72. Saurabh Mahaptra, "India Plans to Increase Rooftop Solar Subsidy by 5X, to $3.7 Billion," *Clean Technica*, December 31, 2017, cleantechnica.com /2017/12/31/india-plans-increase-rooftop-solar-subsidy-5x-3-7-billion/

73. Saurabh Mahaptra, "Indian State of Karnataka Announces 860 Megawatt Solar Tender," *Clean Technica*, December 25, 2017, cleantechnica .com/2017/12/25/indian-state-karnataka-announces-860-megawatt -solar-tender/; Saurabh Mahaptra, "Indian State Plans Massive Solar Project at Retired Coal Power Plant," *Clean Technica*, December 31, 2017, cleantechnica.com/2017/12/31/indian-state-plans-massive-solar -project-retired-coal-power-plant/

74. *India Energy Statistics Report*, mospi.nic.in/Mospi_New/upload/Energy _stats_2015_26mar15.pdf

75. selco-india.com/

76. *The Business Case for Off-grid Energy in India*, Climate Group, Goldman Sachs, 2014, theclimategroup.org/sites/default/files/archive/files/The -business-case-for-offgrid-energy-in-India.pdf

77. Jon C. Ogg, "Ahead of Model 3: Tesla Value for 2019 Versus Ford and GM Today," *24/7 Wall St*, March 29, 2016, 247wallst.com/autos/2016 /03/29/ahead-of-model-3-tesla-value-for-2019-versus-ford-and-gm -today/

78. Dana Hull, "Tesla Inc Now Has a Market Cap Bigger Than Ford's—and GM's," *Bloomberg Financial Post*, April 3, 2017, business.financialpost.com /news/transportation/tesla-the-smallest-and-youngest-carmaker-now -has-a-market-cap-that-is-bigger-than-fords

79. Jeremy Leggett, "State of the Transition: April 2016, Unfolding Like the Plot of an Epic Novel," May 3, 2016, jeremyleggett.net/2016/05/state-of -the-transition-april-2016-unfolding-like-the-plot-of-an-epic-novel/

80. "Tesla's Musk Sells $10 Million in Flamethrowers in Four Days," *Reuters*, February 1, 2018, reuters.com/article/us-musk-flamethrower/teslas -musk-sells-10-million-in-flamethrowers-in-four-days-idUSKBN1FL544

81. teslamotors.com/gigafactory

82. Doug Arent, "After Paris the Smart Bet Is on a Clean Energy Future," *GreenMoney Journal*, July/August 2016, greenmoneyjournal.com/july -august-2016/after-paris-the-smart-bet-is-on-a-clean-energy-future/

83. "New Energy Outlook," *Bloomberg*, 2016, bloomberg.com/company/new -energy-outlook/

84. Davila Fragoso, "The Electric Car Market Is Growing 10 Times Faster Than Its Dirty Gasoline Equivalent," *Think Progress*, October 13, 2016, thinkprogress.org/electric-vehicle-sales-are-soaring-worldwide-5718b58 441c7

85. "China Moves to Increase Number of Electric Vehicles on Its Roads," *All Things Considered*, National Public Radio, April 25, 2017, npr.org /sections/parallels/2017/04/25/525412342/china-moves-to-increase -number-of-electric-vehicles-on-its-roads

86. Jon LeSage, "China's Ban on Gas-Powered Cars Could Cripple the Oil Market," September 12, 2017, *Business Insider*, businessinsider.com/china -ban-gas-powered-cars-effect-on-oil-market-2017-9

87. Personal communication, Tony Seba to Hunter Lovins, Boulder Colorado, April 7, 2018.

88. Zachary Shahan, "USA Fully Electric Car Sales Up 47% in 2017," *Clean Technica*, September 9, 2017, cleantechnica.com/2017/09/09/usa-fully -electric-car-sales-82-2017/

89. Anna Hirtenstein, "Global Electric Car Sales Jump 63 Percent," *Bloomberg*, November 30, 2017, bloomberg.com/news/articles/2017-11-21 /global-electric-car-sales-jump-63-percent-as-china-demand-surges

90. Chris Busch, "California Considers a Ban on Gasoline and Diesel Car Sales. Can It Work?" *Forbes*, October 16, 2017.

91. Joe Romm, "37% of Norway's New Cars Are Electric. They Expect It To Be 100% in Just 8 Years," *Think Progress*, February 21, 2017, thinkprogress .org/norway-aims-to-end-sales-of-fuel-burning-car-by-2025-as-ev -market-soars-edeac854f1e/

92. Zlata Rodionova, "Half of All New Cars in Norway Are Now Electric or Hybrid," *The Independent*, March 7, 2017, independent.co.uk/news /business/news/norway-half-new-cars-electric-hybrid-ofv-vehicle -registrations-a7615556.html

93. Hunter Lovins' personal experience. She also charges the car from the solar panels on her ranch, voanews.com/media/video/electric-cars /3165475.html

94. Tom Randall, "Here's How Electric Cars Will Cause the Next Oil Crisis," *Bloomberg*, February 25, 2016, bloomberg.com/features/2016-ev -oil-crisis/

95. Personal communication, Rhea Suh, NRDC, July 8, 2016.

96. Solar Hale, iterate.ai/Startup/SolarHale; solarhale.com

97. Gabriel Kahn, "Did California Figure Out How to Fix Global Warming? The Golden State's Accidental History," *Mother Jones*, March/April 2016.

98. We predicted precisely this outcome in the 1982 book *Brittle Power*, natcapsolutions.org/publications_files/brittlepower.htm.

99. Jeff McMahon, "Steven Chu Solves Utility Companies' Death Spiral," *Forbes*, March 21, 2014.

100. Gilbert Kreijger and Lara Hilmarsdottir, "Power Outage," *Handelsblatt*, global.handelsblatt.com/edition/53/ressort/companies-markets /article/power-struggle

101. *Levelized Cost of Energy Analysis, Version 10.0*, Lazard, December 15, 2016, lazard.com/media/438038/levelized-cost-of-energy-v100.pdf

102. Giles Parkinson, "Solar Plus Storage 'Already Cheaper Than Gas,'" *Echo Netdaily*, March 24, 2017, echo.net.au/2017/03/solar-plus-storage -already-cheaper-gas/

103. Christopher Irby, *Public Service Company: 2016 Electric Resource Plan Proceeding*, Number: 16A-0396E Filing Number: G_740080 Document Title: Proceeding No. 16A-0396E_HIGHLY CONFIDENTIAL 30-Day Report, Proceeding No. 16A-0396E_PUBLIC 30-Day Report _FINAL Deemed Submitted: Thu 12/28/2017 04:51 pm

104. Pilita Clark, Andrew Ward, and Neil Hume, "Oil Groups Threatened by Electric Cars," *Financial Times*, October 18, 2016.

105. Brian Parkin, "Batteries May Trip 'Death Spiral' in $3.4 Trillion Credit Market, *Bloomberg Markets*, October 18, 2016, bloomberg.com /news/articles/2016-10-18/batteries-may-trip-death-spiral-in-3-4 -trillion-credit-market

106. Adam Peltz, "Looking to the States to Improve Natural Gas Storage Policies," Environmental Defense Fund, February 24, 2017, breaking energy.com/2017/02/24/looking-to-the-states-to-improve-natural -gas-storage-policies/?

107. Tom Randall, "Tesla's Battery Revolution Just Reached Critical Mass," *Bloomberg Technology*, January 30, 2017, bloomberg.com/news /articles/2017-01-30/tesla-s-battery-revolution-just-reached-critical -mass

108. Megan Geuss, "After Just 6 Months of Planning and Building, a Substation in CA Can Supply 80MWh," *Ars Technica*, January 2017, arstechnica.com/information-technology/2017/01/a-look-at-the-new -battery-storage-facility-in-california-built-with-tesla-powerpacks/

109. Julian Spector, "Tesla Fulfilled Its 100-Day Australia Battery Bet: What's That Mean for the Industry?" *Greentech Media*, November 27, 2107, greentechmedia.com/articles/read/tesla-fulfills-australia-battery -bet-whats-that-mean-industry#gs.Ntm_jj8

110. Nick Harmsen, "Elon Musk's Tesla Plans to Give Thousands of Homes Batteries: Here's How It Would Work," *Australian Broadcasting Company News*, February 4, 2018, abc.net.au/news/2018-02-04/how -tesla-sa-labor-free-battery-scheme-would-work/9394728

111. "Expeditionary—Marine Corps and U.S. Army," simpliphipower .com/expeditionary-marine-corps-and-u-s-army/

112. "Humanitarian: Kisokwe Primary School of Tanzania," simpliphi power.com/humanitarian-kisokwe-primary-school-of-tanzania/

113. "98% Efficient Storage Solutions w/o Hazardous Cobalt/Heat Mitigation Requirements," simpliphipower.com/simpliphi-power -showcases-98-efficient-storage-solutions-without-hazardous-cobalt-or -heat-mitigation-requirements-at-solar-power-international/

114. greenenergystorage.eu/en/

115. James Conca, "Vanadium-flow Batteries: The Energy Storage Break-through We've Needed," *Forbes*, December 13, 2016.

116. This research is being directed by Clare Grey of Cambridge Univer-sity, ch.cam.ac.uk/person/cpg27

117. RE100, there100.org/companies

118. Urs Holzle, "100% Renewable Is Just the Beginning," Google Envi-ronment, environment.google/projects/announcement-100/

119. *Our Carbon Positive Ambition*, Unilever Sustainable Living, unilever .com/sustainable-living/what-matters-to-you/moving-to-renewables .html

120. Eric Roston and Brian Eckhouse, "Waging America's Wars Using Renewable Energy," *Bloomberg*, July 6, 2016, bloomberg.com/news /articles/2016-07-05/waging-america-s-wars-using-renewable-energy

121. Ramez Naam, "How Cheap Can Solar Get? Very Cheap Indeed," August 10, 2015, rameznaam.com/2015/08/10/how-cheap-can-solar-get -very-cheap-indeed/

122. Ramez Naam, "How Steady Can the Wind Blow?" August 30, 2015, rameznaam.com/2015/08/30/how-steady-can-the-wind-blow/

123. Ramez Naam, "How Cheap Can Energy Storage Get?" October 14, 2015, rameznaam.com/2015/10/14/how-cheap-can-energy-storage-get/

124. Ramez Naam, "How Cheap Electric Vehicles Can Get?" April 12, 2016, rameznaam.com/2016/04/12/how-cheap-can-electric-vehicles-get/

125. Ramez Naam, "How Far Can Renewals Go? Pretty Darn Far," Jan-uary 31, 2016, rameznaam.com/2016/01/31/how-far-can-renewables-go -pretty-darn-far/

126. Jigar Shah, *Creating Climate Wealth*, ICOSA 2013, creatingclimate wealth.co/

127. Jigar Shah, "What Einstein Might Say After People's Climate March," *Capital Content*, October 21, 2014, capital-content.com/2014/10/21/what -einstein-might-say-after-peoples-climate-march/

128. "Solar Guru Jigar Shah on His New Book: *Creating Climate Wealth*," *Solar Plaza*, July 9, 2013, solarplaza.com/channels/archive/11143/solar -guru-jigar-shah-on-his-new-book-creating-cli/

129. Gabriel Kahn, "Did California Figure Out How to Fix Global Warming? The Golden State's Accidental History," *Mother Jones*, March/ April 2016.

130. Paul Gilding, "Fossil Fuels Are Finished: The Rest Is Just Detail," *REneweconomy*, July 13, 2015, reneweconomy.com.au/2015/fossil-fuels -are-finished-the-rest-is-just-detail-71574

131. ucsusa.org/sites/default/files/attach/2015/07/The-Climate -Deception-Dossiers.pdf

132. *International Energy Outlook 2016*, Chapter 5, Electricity, Energy In- formation Administration, May 11, 2016, eia.gov/forecasts/ieo/electricity .cfm

133. William Becker, "Carbon Sinks, The Next Big Thing (Part 3)," *Huffington Post*, March 26, 2016, huffingtonpost.com/william-s-becker /carbon-sinks-the-next-big_b_9550830.html?utm_hp_ref=green &ir=Green

134. Hunter Lovins, "The Triumph of Solar in the Energy Race," *Unrea- sonable.IS*, August 7, 2015, unreasonable.is/triumph-of-the-sun/; Paul Gilding, "Fossil Fuels Are Finished: The Rest Is Just Detail"; Jeremy Leg- gett, jeremyleggett.net/; see also blueandgreentomorrow.com/features /jeremy-leggett-high-chance-of-a-tipping-point-in-retreat-from-fossil -fuels-soon/

135. Vanessa Dezem and Javiera Quiroga, "Chile Has So Much Solar Energy It's Giving It Away for Free," *Bloomberg*, June 1, 2016, bloomberg .com/news/articles/2016-06-01/chile-has-so-much-solar-energy-it-s -giving-it-away-for-free

136. Jesper Starn, "There Was So Much Wind Power in Germany This Weekend, Consumers Got Free Energy," *Bloomberg*, October 30, 2017, bloomberg.com/news/articles/2017-10-30/record-winds-in-germany -spur-free-electricity-at-weekend-chart

137. Doug Arent, "After Paris the Smart Bet Is on a Clean Energy Future," *GreenMoney Journal*, July/August 2016, greenmoneyjournal.com/july -august-2016/after-paris-the-smart-bet-is-on-a-clean-energy-future/

138. Mike Munsell, "US Solar Market Grows 95% in 2016, Smashes Re- cords," *Greentech Media*, February 15, 2017, greentechmedia.com/articles /read/us-solar-market-grows-95-in-2016-smashes-records

139. Tony Seba, *Clean Disruption of Energy and Transportation: How Silicon Valley Will Make Oil, Nuclear, Natural Gas, Coal, Electric Utilities and Conventional Cars Obsolete by 2030*, May 20, 2014.

140. Tony Seba, "Tony Seba: Clean Disruption—Energy & Transportation," Colorado Renewable Energy Society, YouTube, June 9, 2017, youtube.com/watch?v=2b3ttqYDwFo

141. Young Rae Kim, "A Look at McKinsey & Company's Biggest Mistakes," September 12, 2013, equities.com/news/a-look-at-mckinsey-company-s-biggest-mistakes

142. Zachery Davies Boren, "There Are Officially More Mobile Devices Than People in the World," *The Independent*, October 7, 2014, independent.co.uk/life-style/gadgets-and-tech/news/there-are-officially-more-mobile-devices-than-people-in-the-world-9780518.html

143. Tam Hunt, "Swanson's Law and Making US Solar Scale Like Germany," *Greentech Media*, November 24, 2014, greentechmedia.com/articles/read/Is-there-really-a-Swansons-Law

144. Steve Bushong, "Futurist Ray Kurzweil Predicts Solar Industry Dominance in 12 Years," *Solar Power World*, March 30, 2016, solarpowerworldonline.com/2016/03/futurist-ray-kurzweil-predicts-solar-industry-dominance-12-years/

145. Mark Z. Jacobson and Mark Delucci, "A Plan to Power 100 Percent of the Planet with Renewables," *Scientific American*, November 1, 2009.

146. The Solutions Project, thesolutionsproject.org/infographic/

147. Manish Ram et al., *Global Energy System Based on 100% Renewable Energy - Power Sector*, Research Gate, Technical Report, November 2017, researchgate.net/publication/320934766_Global_Energy_System_based_on_100_Renewable_Energy_-_Power_Sector

148. Tony Seba, "How to Lose $40 Trillion," tonyseba.com/how-to-lose-40-trillion/

149. Tony wrote that in 2012. By 2015, the IEA was saying that the number would be $48 trillion by 2035. Either way, it is a huge sum, which the IEA proposes be spent essentially entirely on oil, gas, coal, and nuclear. iea.org/newsroomandevents/pressreleases/2014/june/world-needs-48-trillion-in-investment-to-meet-its-energy-needs-to-2035.html

150. Eric Roston, "By the Time You Read This, They've Slapped a Solar Panel on Your Roof," *Bloomberg*, February 25, 2015, bloomberg.com/news/articles/2015-02-25/in-the-time-it-takes-to-read-this-story-another-solar-project-will-go-up?hootPostID=56325fde82327ff748ea1971f77f62ab

151. Sam Morgan, "China Eclipses Europe as 2020 Solar Power Target Is Smashed," EURACTIV, August 30, 2017, euractiv.com/section/energy/news/china-eclipses-europe-as-2020-solar-power-target-is-smashed/

152. Christian Roselund, "California's Big Utilities to Reach 50% Renewable Energy in 2020," *PV Magazine*, November 14, 2017, pv-magazine-usa.com/2017/11/14/californias-big-utilities-to-reach-50-renewable-energy-in-2020/

153. John Parnell, "Solar Will Drop Below Two Cents in 2017: GTM," *PV Tech*, April 6, 2017, pv-tech.org/news/solar-will-drop-below-two-cents-in-2017-gtm

154. Anthony Dipaola, "Saudi Arabia Gets Cheapest Bids for Solar Power in Auction," *Bloomberg*, October 3, 2017, bloomberg.com/news/articles/2017-10-03/saudi-arabia-gets-cheapest-ever-bids-for-solar-power-in-auction

155. Morgan Watkins, "Even the Kentucky Coal Museum Is Going Solar," *USA Today*, April 8, 2017.

156. Julian Spector, "Study: We're Still Underestimating Battery Cost Improvements," *Greentech Media*, August 17, 2017, greentechmedia.com/articles/read/were-still-underestimating-cost-improvements-for-batteries

157. "Solar Energy Now Cheaper Than Fossil Fuels Even Without Subsidies," *ZME Science*, June 14, 2017 zmescience.com/ecology/climate/solar-energy-cheap/

158. Alex Davies, "General Motors Is Going All Electric," *Wired*, October 2, 2017, wired.com/story/general-motors-electric-cars-plan-gm/

159. Tom Chi, YouTube, bsahely.com/2017/11/11/watch-everything-is-connected-heres-how-tom-chi-tedxtaipei-on-youtube/

160. Fred Lambert, "Tesla's Global Fleet Reaches Over 5 Billion Electric Miles Driven Ahead of Model 3 Launch," *Electrek*, July 12, 2017, electrek.co/2017/07/12/tesla-global-fleet-electric-miles-model-3-launch/

161. Fred Lambert, "Understanding the Fatal Tesla Accident on Autopilot and the NHTSA Probe," *Electrek*, June 2016, electrek.co/2016/07/01/understanding-fatal-tesla-accident-autopilot-nhtsa-probe/

162. Tracey Lindeman, "Don't Let the First Pedestrian Death by Uber's Self-Driving Car Freak You Out," *Vice*, 20 March 2018, motherboard.vice.com/en_us/article/mbxjyv/autonomous-uber-kills-pedestrian-in-tempe-arizona-self-driving-car

163. Brett Williams, "Waymo Self-driving Cars Have Driven Over 4 Million Miles," *Mashable*, November 28, 2017, mashable.com/2017/11/28/waymo-4-million-miles-self-driven/#6s_WfyK9vsqy

164. David Welch, "GM's Self-Driving Cars to Be Ready for Ride-Sharing in 2019," November 30, 2017, *Bloomberg*, bloomberg.com/news/articles/2017-11-30/gm-sees-self-driving-ride-share-service-ready-for-roads-in-2019

165. Shawn Langlois, "Hello, Self-driving Cars, and Goodbye to 4.1 Million Jobs?" *Market Watch*, September 17, 2016, marketwatch.com/story/hello-self-driving-cars-goodbye-41-million-jobs-2016-09-15

166. Louis Jacobson, "Are There Three Times as Many Solar Energy Jobs as Coal Jobs?" *Politifact*, April 25, 2017, politifact.com/illinois/statements/2017/apr/25/brad-schneider/are-there-three-times-many-solar-energy-jobs-coal-/

167. Jeremy Deaton, "Americans Are Now Twice as Likely to Work in Solar as in Coal," *Think Progress*, February 7, 2017, thinkprogress.org /solar-jobs-report-2016-8f0e7c7b91c4/

168. Hiroko Tabuchimarch, "Coal Mining Jobs Trump Would Bring Back No Longer Exist," *New York Times*, March 29, 2017.

169. *Renewable Energy and Jobs: Annual Review 2016*, International Renewable Energy Agency 2016, irena.org/DocumentDownloads /Publications/IRENA_RE_Jobs_Annual_Review_2016.pdf

170. "IN DEMAND: Clean Energy, Sustainability and the New American Workforce," Environmental Defense Fund, 2017, edfclimatecorps .org/sites/edfclimatecorps.org/files/edf_in_demand_clean_energy _sustainability_and_the_new_american_workforce.pdf?_ga=2.158875 770.156343590.1524761103-1372380723.1524761103

171. *Report: Clean Energy Jobs Overwhelm Coal, Oil and Gas, in 41 States and D.C.*, Sierra Club, 2017, docdroid.net/G6njmYC/sierra-club-clean -energy-jobs-report-final-1.pdf.html

172. Mahmoud Habboush, "Renewable Energy Powers Jobs for Almost 10 Million People," *Bloomberg*, May 23, 2017, bloomberg.com/news /articles/2017-05-23/renewable-energy-powers-jobs-for-almost-10 -million-people

173. "2.5 Million Clean Energy Workers in the USA," *Energy Matters*, March 31, 2016, energymatters.com.au/renewable-news/usa-clean -energy-em5407/

174. Jake Richardson, "2.5 Million Americans Work in Clean Energy (Report)," *Clean Technica*, March 30, 2017, cleantechnica.com/2016/03 /30/2-5-million-americans-work-clean-energy-report/

175. johnsoncontrols.com/content/dam/WWW/jci/be/global_work place_innovation/oxygenz/Oxygenz_Report_-_2010.pdf

176. Kayla Shultz, "Wind and Solar Create More Jobs When They Are Locally Owned," *Yes Magazine*, October 22, 2012, yesmagazine.org /planet/locally-owned-renewable-energy-better-for-the-environment -and-your-town

177. See also the Club of Rome report on the Circular Economy: clubof rome.org/wp-content/uploads/2016/03/The-Circular-Economy-and -Benefits-for-Society.pdf

178. Fiona Harvey, "Switching to a Green Economy Could Mean Millions of Jobs, Says UN," *The Guardian*, May 31, 2012.

179. Carbon Tracker, carbontracker.org/report/no-rhyme-or-reason-eia -energy-outlook-coal-companies-risk-disclosure/

180. Carbon Tracker, carbontracker.org/wp-content/uploads/2014/09 /Unburnable-Carbon-Full-rev2-1.pdf

181. John Fullerton, "The Big Choice," *Future of Finance Blog*, Capital Institute, July 19, 2011, capitalinstitute.org/blog/big-choice-0/

182. Bill McKibben, "Global Warming's Terrifying New Math," *Rolling Stone*, July 19, 2012.

183. John Fullerton, "Beyond Divestment," 28 March 2013, capitalinstitute
.org/blog/beyond-divestment/

184. "Fossil Fuel Divestment: A $5 Trillion Challenge," *Bloomberg New
Energy Finance*, about.bnef.com/content/uploads/sites/4/2014/08
/BNEF_DOC_2014-08-25-Fossil-Fuel-Divestment.pdf

185. *Investing in a Time of Climate Change*, Mercer, 2015, mercer.com
/content/dam/mercer/attachments/global/investments/mercer-climate
-change-report-2015.pdf

186. Karl Mathiesen, "Coal Investments Are Increasingly Risky, Say Bank
of America," *The Guardian*, May 7, 2015.

187. *Global Energy Markets Transition Drives Thermal Coal Into Structural Decline*, January 14, 2015, ieefa.org/global-energy-markets/

188. Emily Schwartz Greco, "King Coal Catches Black Lung," Other
Words, February 18, 2015, otherwords.org/king-coal-catches-black-lung
/?utm_source=feedly&utm_reader=feedly&utm_medium=rss&utm
_campaign=king-coal-catches-black-lung

189. Graham Readfearn, "How Bill Gates and Peabody Energy Share
Vision for Coal Powered Future Through Views of Bjorn Lomborg,"
Desmog Blog, October 28, 2014, desmogblog.com/2014/10/28/how-bill
-gates-and-peabody-energy-share-vision-coal-powered-future-through
-views-bjorn-lomborg

190. L. Hunter Lovins, "The Veil of Energy Poverty," *Unreasonable.IS*,
December 2014, unreasonable.is/energy-poverty/

191. Tiffany Kary, Tim Loh, and Jim Polson, "Coal Slump Sends Mining
Giant Peabody Energy Into Bankruptcy," *Bloomberg*, April 13, 2016,
bloomberg.com/news/articles/2016-04-13/peabody-majority-of-its-u-s
-entities-file-for-chapter-11

192. Ibid.

193. Mark Gottlieb, "Peabody Energy: Confirmation Hearing Smashes
Long-Standing U.S. Bankruptcy Laws," *Seeking Alpha*, March 27, 2017,
seekingalpha.com/article/4058090-peabody-energy-confirmation
-hearing-smashes-long-standing-u-s-bankruptcy-laws

194. Tracy Rucinski and Tom Hals, "Coal Revival Means Big Stock
Bonuses at Bankrupt Peabody," *Reuters*, February 28, 2017, reuters.com
/article/us-peabody-energy-bankruptcy-bonuses-ana-idUSKBN1670HM

195. Matt Egan, "Big Oil Loses $200 Billion from Oil Price Crash," *CNN
Money*, January 7, 2015, money.cnn.com/2015/01/07/investing/big-oil
-price-energy-stocks/

196. Matt Egan, "Warning: ExxonMobil May Be in Irreversible Decline,"
CNN Money, October 26, 2016, money.cnn.com/2016/10/26/investing
/exxonmobil-stock-oil-prices/index.html

197. Tom Randall, "Bankers See $1 Trillion of Zombie Investments
Stranded in the Oil Fields," *Bloomberg*, December 17, 2014, bloomberg
.com/news/articles/2014-12-18/bankers-see-1-trillion-of-investments
-stranded-in-the-oil-fields

198. *The Crude Downturn for Exploration and Production Companies*, Deloitte Center for Energy Solutions, 2016, www2.deloitte.com /content/dam/Deloitte/us/Documents/energy-resources/us-er-crude -downturn.pdf

199. "Spotlight on Oil and Gas Megaprojects," *EY*, August 14, 2014, p. 4.

200. Jillian Ambrose, "IEA Warns $1.3 Trillion of Oil and Gas Could Be Left Stranded," *The Telegraph*, March 20, 2017.

201. Personal communication, Mark Campanale to Hunter Lovins at the Green Accord Economia E Finanza Nell'Era No-Carbon, Larderello, Italy, November 4, 2017.

202. Nafeez Ahmed, *AlterNet*, April 30, 2016, alternet.org/environment /we-could-be-witnessing-death-fossil-fuel-industry-will-it-take-rest -economy-down-it

203. Alexander Pleiffer et al., "The '2°C Capital Stock' for Electricity Generation: Committed Cumulative Carbon Emissions from the Electricity Generation Sector and the Transition to a Green Economy," *Applied Energy*, March 24, 2016, sciencedirect.com/science/article/pii /S0306261916302495

204. Lord Nicholas Stern, *Stern Review: The Economics of Climate Change*, 2006, mudancasclimaticas.cptec.inpe.br/~rmclima/pdfs/destaques /sternreview_report_complete.pdf

205. "Would You Drive a Motorcycle Without a Helmet?" Deutsche Bank, October 15, 2013, db.com/cr/en/concrete-the-impacts-and-risk-of -climate-change.htm

206. Siobhan Wagner, "Insurers' Climate Risk May Be Financial Problem for All," *Bloomberg Briefs*, July 21, 2016, newsletters.briefs.bloomberg .com/document/PqlftUTVta9ODKfrRCu79Q--_9ez1sxeg2vpza03wq1 /front

207. *Global Climate Index 2016: Insurance Sector Analysis*, Asset Owners Disclosure Project, July 21, 2016, aodproject.net/global-climate-500-index -2016-insurance/

208. Damian Carrington, "Bank of England Warns of Huge Financial Risk from Fossil Fuel Investment," *The Guardian*, March 3, 2015.

209. Thomas Coleman and Alex LePlante, *Climate Change: Why Financial Institutions Should Take Note*, Global Risk Institute, 2016, globalrisk institute.org/publications/climate-change-why-financial-institutions -should-take-note/

210. Julia Pyper, "California Wildfires Spark Utility Investigations and New Regulations," *Greentech Media*, December 18, 2017, greentechmedia.com /articles/read/california-wildfires-spark-utility-investigations-and-new -regulations

211. "$306bn in One Year: US Bill for Natural Disasters Smashes Record," *The Guardian*, January 8, 2018.

212. Milton Friedman, "The Social Responsibility of Business Is to Increase Its Profits," *New York Times Magazine*, September 13, 1970.

213. "US SIF Commends Department of Labor Repeal of 2008 Bulletin Discouraging Fiduciaries from Incorporating Social and Environmental Investment Factors," Forum for Sustainable and Responsible Investment, October 22, 2015, ussif.org/blog_home.asp?Display=64

214. This conference was presented by the Link Foundation and Progressive Asset Management, www.progressive-asset.com.

215. Katy Lederer, "The New Economics of Climate Change," *New Yorker*, July 30, 2015.

216. Personal communication to Hunter Lovins, who helped organize the conference, Mark Hopkins Hotel, San Francisco, April 2001.

217. The Impact of Sustainable and Responsible Investment, USSIF Foundation, June 2016, ussif.org/files/Publications/USSIF_ImpactofSRI_FINAL.pdf

218. Investor Network on Climate Change, ceres.org/investor-network/incr

219. "Reducing Systemic Risks: The Securities and Exchange Commission and Climate Change," CERES, 2014, ceres.org/files/investor-files/sec-guidance-fact-sheet

220. "Interpretive Bulletin Relating to the Fiduciary Standard Under ERISA in Considering Economically Targeted Investments: A Rule by the Employee Benefits Security Administration," *Federal Register*, October 26, 2015, federalregister.gov/articles/2015/10/26/2015-27146/interpretive-bulletin-relating-to-the-fiduciary-standard-under-erisa-in-considering-economically

221. "The Impact of Sustainable and Responsible Investment," Forum for Sustainable and Responsible Investment, June 2016, ussif.org/files/Publications/USSIF_ImpactofSRI_FINAL.pdf

222. "Global Sustainable Investment Alliance Releases Biennial Global Sustainable Investment Review 2016," US SIF, March 27, 2017, ussif.org/blog_home.asp?Display=85

223. "The Impact of Sustainable and Responsible Investment," Forum for Sustainable and Responsible Investment, June 2016, ussif.org/files/Publications/USSIF_ImpactofSRI_FINAL.pdf

224. Andy Behar, "Exclusive Interview: Andrew Behar, CEO of As You Sow," *Blue and Green Tomorrow*, November 10, 2015, blueandgreentomorrow.com/environment/exclusive-interview-andrew-behar-ceo-of-as-you-sow/

225. Katy Lederer, "The New Economics of Climate Change," *New Yorker*, July 30, 2015.

226. "Ellen Dorsey, the Alliance for Sustainable Colorado's 2015 Hero for Sustainability," Alliance for Sustainable Colorado, 2015, sustainablecolorado.org/wp-content/uploads/2015/05/remarks-for-denver.pdf

227. math.350.org/

228. Cary Krosinsky, "Why the 'Do the Math Tour' Doesn't Add Up," *GreenBiz*, November 27, 2012, greenbiz.com/blog/2012/11/19/do-math-tour-doesnt-add-up

229. *Stranded Assets and the Fossil Fuel Divestment Campaign: What Does Divestment Mean for the Valuation of Fossil Fuel Assets?* Oxford Stranded Assets Programme, October 2013, smithschool.ox.ac.uk/research -programmes/stranded-assets/SAP-divestment-report-final.pdf

230. Alan Rusbridger, "Keep It in the Ground," *The Guardian*, March 16, 2015.

231. *The Global Fossil Fuel Divestment and Clean Energy Investment Movement*, Arabella Advisors, December 2016, arabellaadvisors.com/wp-content /uploads/2016/12/Global_Divestment_Report_2016.pdf

232. gofossilfree.org/commitments/

233. Julie Fox Gorte and Steve Falci, "The Smart Way to Divest Fossil Fuels," *Reuters*, March 2, 2015, sustainability.thomsonreuters.com/2015/03/03 /executive-perspective-the-smart-way-to-divest-fossil-fuels/

234. Peter Lehner, "Divestment Outperforms Conventional Portfolios for Past 5 Years," *NRDC Switchboard*, February 13, 2015, switchboard.nrdc .org/blogs/plehner/divestment_outperforms_convent.html

235. Patrick Collinson, "Fossil Fuel-Free Funds Outperformed Conventional Ones, Analysis Shows," *The Guardian*, April 10, 2015.

236. Adam Vaughn, "World's Biggest Sovereign Wealth Fund Proposes Ditching Oil and Gas Holdings," *The Guardian*, November 16, 2017.

237. Fabio Benedetti Valentini and Russell Ward, "BNP to Halt Shale Oil Financing, Expand Funds for Renewables," *Bloomberg*, October 10, 2017, bloomberg.com/news/articles/2017-10-11/bnp-paribas-to-halt-shale-oil -financing-in-climate-change-pledge

238. Change Finance, change-finance.com/

239. New York Stock Exchange, November 7, 2017, livestream.com/NYSE /changefinance/videos/165572663

240. Press Release, 350.org, 350.org/press-release/divest-new-york-victory/

241. Mission 2020, mission2020.global/

242. Elizabeth Kolbert, "The Weight of the World: Can Christiana Figueres Persuade Humanity to Save Itself?" *New Yorker*, August 24, 2015.

243. Clean Energy Investment, End of Year 2016," *Bloomberg New Energy Finance*, 2016, about.bnef.com/clean-energy-investment/

244. Jessica Shankleman, "As Oil Crashed Renewables Attract Record $329 Billion," *Bloomberg*, January 13, 2016, bloomberg.com/news /articles/2016-01-14/renewables-drew-record-329-billion-in-year-oil -prices-crashed

245. "Clean Energy Investment, End of Year 2016," *Bloomberg New Energy Finance*, 2016, about.bnef.com/clean-energy-investment/

246. "Carbon Clean 200," *As You Sow*, 2017, clean200.org/report-form

247. "Cleantech Companies Delivered Triple the Returns of Fossil Fuel Companies Over Past Decade," *Sustainable Brands*, August 15, 2016, sustainablebrands.com/news_and_views/cleantech/sustainable_brands /cleantech_companies_delivered_triple_returns_fossil_fuel

248. "Moody's Says Green Bond Issuance Set for Another Record Year," *Reuters*, January 19, 2017, reuters.com/article/bonds-greenfinance -idUSL4N1F91C0

249. "Climate Changing for 'Green Bonds' Even in Face of Trump Skepticism, *Reuters*, January 12, 2017, reuters.com/article/us-global-bonds -greenbonds-idUSKBN14W2FX

250. Joe Rennison, Adam Samson, and Tim Bradshaw, "Apple Raises $1bn Through 'Green Bond' in Environmental Push," *Financial Times*, June 13, 2017.

251. Catherine Tweed, "IEA: $44 Trillion in Energy Investment Won't Limit Climate Change to 2 Degrees," *Greentech Media*, November 18, 2016, greentechmedia.com/articles/read/iea-44-trillion-in-energy-investment -wont-limit-climate-change-to-2-degrees

252. "Green Bond Issuance up 42% in First Quarter of 2017," Climate Action Programme, UN, April 19, 2017, climateactionprogramme.org/news /green-bond-issuance-up-42-in-first-quarter-of-2017

253. Bevis Longstreth, "The Financial Case for Divestment of Fossil Fuel Companies by Endowment Fiduciaries," *Huffington Post Blog*, January 23, 2014, huffingtonpost.com/bevis-longstreth/the-financial-case-for -di_b_4203910.html

254. Hunter Lovins, YouTube, August 23, 2017, youtube.com/watch?v=bkBK 5sb2V5U

Section 4: Systemic Change: Policies to Get Us Out of the Mess

1. ecology.com/2011/10/24/wangari-maathai-quotes/

2. Security is defined by *Webster's Dictionary* as "Freedom from fear of privation or attack." Privation is defined as "Lack of basic necessities or comforts of life."

3. Paul Hawken, Amory Lovins, and Hunter Lovins, *Natural Capitalism: Creating the Next Industrial Revolution*, Chapter 13, Little Brown, 1999.

4. Don Hazen, "Google, Facebook, Amazon Undermine Democracy: They Play a Role in Destroying Privacy, Producing Inequality," *Salon*, April 23, 2017, salon.com/2017/04/23/google-facebook-amazon-undermine -democracy-they-play-a-role-in-destroying-privacy-producing -inequality_partner/

5. Alan Murray, "When Two Models of Capitalism Collide," *Fortune*, February 21, 2017.

6. Vivienne Walt, "Unilever CEO Paul Polman's Plan to Save the World," *Fortune*, February 17, 2017.

Chapter 11: Level the Playing Field

1. Nelson Mandela, letter to Senator Douglas Lukhele, written on Robben Island, August 1, 1970, facebook.com/nelsonmandela/posts /686878751322917

2. "Who, What, Why: What Is the Gini Coefficient?" *BBC News*, March 12, 2015, bbc.com/news/blogs-magazine-monitor-31847943

3. There is a challenge getting accurate data. There is also confusion between income inequality and absolute wealth. Discrepancies in data make it hard to say which country has the highest level of inequality. Most available measures point to parts of Latin America and the southern tip of Africa as having the least equal income distributions. But this is shifting, and generally worsening. When income inequality is measured as the ratio between the top quintile and bottom quintile, a similar picture emerges, with Colombia, Nepal, and Zambia showing high levels of inequality.

4. David Meyer, "The Richest 1% Now Own More Than 50% of the World's Wealth," *Fortune*, December 14, 2017.

5. Christopher Ingraham, If You Thought Income Inequality Was Bad, Get a Load of Wealth Inequality," *Washington Post*, May 21, 2015.

6. Jack Holmes, "More Than Half of Americans Reportedly Have Less Than $1,000 to Their Name." *Esquire*, January 12, 2016.

7. Laurie Goering, "Growing Wealth Inequality 'Dangerous' Threat to Democracy: Experts," *Reuters*, April 15, 2016, uk.reuters.com/article /us-democracy-wealth-inequality/growing-wealth-inequality-dangerous -threat-to-democracy-experts-idUKKCN0XC1Q2

8. Noam Scheiber and Patricia Cohen, "For the Wealthiest, a Private Tax System that Saves Them Billions, *New York Times*, December 29, 2015.

9. Matt Fuller and Arthur Delaney, "Senate Passes Massive Tax Cuts for the Rich in Middle of the Night," *Huffington Post*, December 2, 2017, huffingtonpost.com/entry/senate-passes-tax bill_us_5a21da79e4b0a0 2abe91412e

10. Nicholas Confessore, Sarah Cohen, and Karen Yourish, "The Families Funding the 2016 Presidential Election," *New York Times*, October 10, 2015.

11. Nick Robins-Early, "The Top 1 Percent Owns Over Half of the World's Household Wealth," *Huffington Post*, November 14, 2017, huffingtonpost .com/entry/top-1-percent-world-wealth_us_5a0b2ffde4b0bc648a0e4afa

12. Daniel Kurt, "Are You in the Top One Percent of the World?" *Investopedia*, December 14, 2017, investopedia.com/articles/personal-finance /050615/are-you-top-one-percent-world.asp

13. Tom Metcalf and Jack Witzig, "World's Wealthiest Became $1 Trillion Richer in 2017," *Bloomberg*, December 26, 2017, bloomberg.com/news /articles/2017-12-27/world-s-wealthiest-gain-1-trillion-in-17-on-market -exuberance

14. The Gini coefficient (Gini index or Gini ratio) is a measure of statistical dispersion representing the income distribution of a nation's people, used as a measure of inequality; data.worldbank.org/indicator/SI.POV .GINI

15. Faiza Shaheen, *Reducing Economic Inequality as a Sustainable Development Goal*, New Economics Foundation, July 1, 2014, neweconomics.org /publications/entry/reducing-economic-inequality-as-a-sustainable -development-goal

16. Tariq Banuri, "Twelve Theses: Sustainable Development Agenda for Climate Change," UN DESA, September 2007, un.org/en/development /desa/policy/cdp/cdp_news_archive/egm_climatechange/banuri.pdf

17. Peter Edward and Andy Sumner, "The Future of Global Poverty in a Multi-Speed World: New Estimates of Scale and Location, 2010-2030," Centre for Global Development Working Paper 327, 2013, cgdev.org /sites/default/files/future_of_global_poverty.pdf. The poverty threshold is now $1.90 US per day, although $1.25 US per day in the 1990s should probably be set at $2.50 US today.

18. Faiza Shaheen, *Ten Reasons to Care About Economic Inequality*, Innovative Social Enterprise Development Network, 2011, isede-net.com /sites/default/files/social_economy/Ten_Reasons_to_Care_About _Economic_Inequality_0.pdf

19. Helen Kersley and Faiza Shaheen, *Addressing Inequality at Root*, New Economics Foundation, 2014, neweconomics.org/publications/entry /addressing-economic-inequality-at-root

20. Betsey Martens, Bringing School Home, bringingschoolhome.org /about/

21. William Doyle, "How Finland Broke Every Rule—and Created a Top School System," *Hechinger Report*, February 18, 2016, hechingerreport .org/how-finland-broke-every-rule-and-created-a-top-school-system/

22. Andrew Chamberlain, "CEO to Worker Pay Ratios: Average CEO Earns 204 Times Median Worker Pay," *Glass Door*, August 25, 2015, glassdoor.com/research/ceo-pay-ratio/

23. Gill Flora, "The Meaning of Work: Lessons from Sociology, Psychology, and Political Theory," *Journal of Socio-Economics*, 28, 1999, pp. 725–743.

24. Frank Pittman, *Man Enough: Fathers, Sons, and the Search for Masculinity*, Reprint edition, TarcherPerigee, October 1, 1994.

25. Personal communication, from Ashok Khosla to Hunter Lovins, International Expert Working Group, Thimphu, Bhutan, January 2013.

26. "The Importance of Startups in Job Creation and Job Destruction, Kauffman Foundation," 2010, kauffman.org/what-we-do/research /firm-formation-and-growth-series/the-importance-of-startups-in-job -creation-and-job-destruction

27. Mark Thoma, "How Much Does It Cost to Create a Job?" *Economist's View*, November 24, 2008, economistsview.typepad.com/economistsview /2008/11/how-much-does-i.html

28. "CBO: Obama Stimulus May Have Cost As Much As $4.1 Million a Job, American Enterprise Institute, May 2012, aei.org/publication/cbo -obama-stimulus-may-have-cost-as-much-as-4-1-million-a-job/

29. Gunther Pauli, The Blue Economy, theblueeconomy.org/

30. Personal communication, from Daniel Epstein to Hunter Lovins, London, December 4, 2017, unreasonablegroup.com/

31. Frederik Obermaier et al., "About the Panama Papers," *Sueddeutsche Zeitung*, 2016, panamapapers.sueddeutsche.de/articles/56febffoa1bb8 d3c3495adf4/

32. Luke Harding, "What Are the Panama Papers? A Guide to History's Biggest Data Leak," *The Guardian*, April 5, 2016.

33. Will Fitzgibbon and Diaz-Struck Emilia, "Panama Papers Have Had Historic Global Effects—and the Impacts Keep Coming," Center for Public Integrity, December 1, 2016, publicintegrity.org/2016 /12/01/20500/panama-papers-have-had-historic-global-effects-and -impacts-keep-coming

34. Elizabeth Barlow, "Buckminster Fuller," in "The New York Magazine Environmental Teach-In," *New York Magazine*, March 30, 1970, p. 30.

35. James Murray, "2017: A Year of Dark Hours and Green Optimism," *Business Green*, December 22, 2017, businessgreen.com/bg/blog-post/3023 480/2017-a-year-of-climate-optimism-and-daunting-reality

36. Such schemes are also called Basic Income Guaranteed (BIG).

37. Sonia Sodha, "Is Finland's Basic Universal Income a Solution to Automation, Fewer Jobs and Lower Wages?" *The Guardian*, February 19, 2017.

38. Chakrabortty Aditya, "A Basic Income for Everyone? Yes, Finland Shows It Really Can Work," *The Guardian*, October 31, 2017; Antti Jaihiainen and Joona-Hermanni Makinen, "Why Finland's Basic Income Experiment Isn't Working," *New York Times*, July 20, 2017.

39. Ben Shiller, "A Dutch City Is Experimenting With Giving Away a Basic Income of $1,000 a Month," *Fast Company*, January 22, 2016, fastcompany .com/3055679/a-dutch-city-is-experimenting-with-giving-away-a-basic -income-of-1000-a-month

40. Kathleen Pender, "Oakland Group Plans to Launch Nation's Biggest Basic-Income Research Project," *San Francisco Chronicle*, September 21, 2017.

41. Seung Y. Lee, "Y Combinator Needs to Make Its Universal Basic Income Experiment in Oakland Public and Transparent," *San Francisco Examiner*, April 17, 2017.

42. James Browne and Herwig Immervoll, *Basic Income as a Policy Option*, OECD, May 2017, oecd.org/els/soc/Basic-Income-Policy-Option-2017 -Brackground-Technical-Note.pdf

43. Chris Giles, "Universal Basic Income Would Fail to Cut Poverty, Says OECD," *Financial Times*, May 27, 2017.

44. Filipe Costa, "A Universal Basic Income Would Destroy Our Economy," *Master Investor*, June 3, 2016, masterinvestor.co.uk/economics/universal -basic-income-destroy-economy/

45. Patrick Kulp, "Universal Basic Income Could Find More Mainstream

Traction in 2017," *Mashable*, January 5, 2017, mashable.com/2017/01/05
/universal-basic-income-2017-year-ahead/

46. Byrd Pinkerton, "What a Kenyan Village Can Teach Us About a Universal Basic Income," *Vox*, May 12, 2017, vox.com/2017/5/12/15600280
/kenyan-village-universal-basic-income-give-directly-podcast

47. Thomas Colson, "The Indian Government Is Considering Introducing a Universal Basic Income," *Business Insider*, January 3, 2017, businessinsider
.com/india-indian-government-set-to-endorse-universal-basic-income
-free-money-economic-survey-2017-1

48. This map updates experiments: infozaps.com/images/UBI_Pilots_2017
_a.jpg

49. James Manyika et al., "What the Future of Work Will Mean for Jobs, Skills, and Wages," McKinsey Global Institute, November 2017, mckinsey.com/global-themes/future-of-organizations-and-work/what
-the-future-of-work-will-mean-for-jobs-skills-and-wages

50. "European Parliament Calls for Robot Law, Rejects Robot Tax," *Reuters*, February 16, 2017, reuters.com/article/us-europe-robots-lawmaking-id
USKBN15V2KM

51. Kevin Delany, "The Robot That Takes Your Job Should Pay Taxes, Says Bill Gates," *Quartz*, February 17, 2017, qz.com/911968/bill-gates-the
-robot-that-takes-your-job-should-pay-taxes/

52. Michael Jacobs and Mariana Mazzucato, *Rethinking Capitalism*, Wiley Blackwell, 2016, marianamazzucato.com/rethinking-capitalism/

53. Randall Wray, "Job Guarantee," *New Economic Perspectives*, August 23, 2009, neweconomicperspectives.org/2009/08/job-guarantee.html

54. Personal communication, Randall Wray to Hunter Lovins, April 27, 2017.

55. Emma Seery and Ana Caistor Arendar, *Even It Up: Time to End Extreme Inequality*, Oxfam, 2014, oxfam.org/sites/www.oxfam.org/files/file
_attachments/cr-even-it-up-extreme-inequality-291014-en.pdf

56. Julia Kollewe, "Global Luxury Goods Market Exceeds €1tn," *The Guardian*, October 29, 2015.

57. Shanta Rao, "Funding Needs for UN's 2030 Development Agenda," *IDN-InDepthNews*, May 28, 2017, globalpolicywatch.org/blog/2017/05
/29/funding-needs-for-uns-2030-development-agenda/

58. *Reducing Economic Inequality as a Sustainable Development Goal Measuring up the Options for Beyond 2015*, New Economics Foundation, 2014, b.3cdn.net/nefoundation/226c9ea56ee0c9e510_gqm6b9zpz.pdf

59. UN Framework Convention on Climate Change, Clean Development Mechanism, unfccc.int/kyoto_protocol/mechanisms/clean_develop
ment_mechanism/items/2718.php

Chapter 12: Meet Basic Needs for All

1. Poor As Folk, poorasfolk.com/2016/03/31/the-fight-is-never-about
-grapes-or-lettuce-its-always-about-the-people-cesar-chavez/

2. Randy Hayes, "The Great U-Turn from Cheater Economics to True-Cost Economics," Synergetic Press, YouTube, February 5, 2014, youtube.com/watch?v=b-yRWsOBlBg

3. "Environmental and Labour Taxation," European Environment Agency, November 30, 2017, eea.europa.eu/airs/2017/resource-efficiency-and-low-carbon-economy/environmental-and-labour-taxation#tab-related-briefings

4. Jasse Droege, "The Great Green Tax Shift: Evidence from Germany," *The Aspiring Economist*, April 20, 2016, theaspiringeconomist.wordpress.com/tag/pollution-taxes/

5. Martin Gilens and Benjamin I. Page, "Testing Theories of American Politics: Elites, Interest Groups, and Average Citizens," doi:10.1017/S1537592714001595, American Political Science Association, 2014, scholar.princeton.edu/sites/default/files/mgilens/files/gilens_and_page_2014_-testing_theories_of_american_politics.doc.pdf

6. *New Report: Valuing the SDG Prize in Food and Agriculture*, Business and Sustainable Development Commission, October 2016, s3.amazonaws.com/aws-bsdc/Valuing-SDG-Food-Ag-Prize-Paper.pdf

7. Georg Menz, "Neoliberalism Died Last Fall," Humanities and Social Sciences Net Online, 2009, h-net.org/reviews/showrev.php?id=23729

8. Jenna Kegel, "Here's What Is Happening to the States That Increased Minimum Wage This Year," Mic, 2014, mic.com/articles/92983/here-s-what-is-happening-to-the-states-that-increased-minimum-wage-this-year#.5ECvIjEDc

9. Ben Wolcott, "2014 Job Creation Faster in States that Raised the Minimum Wage," *CEPR Blog*, June 30, 2014, cepr.net/blogs/cepr-blog/2014-job-creation-in-states-that-raised-the-minimum-wage

10. Shawn Humphrey, "The Cooperative Model in Microfinance: More Current and Pertinent than Ever," *Développement International Desjardins*, April 15, 2014, monthofmicrofinance.org/engage/blog/the-cooperative-model-in-microfinance-more-current-and-pertinent-than-ever/

11. Nick Hanauer, "The Pitchforks Are Coming…For Us Plutocrats," *Politico Magazine*, July/August 2014, politico.com/magazine/story/2014/06/the-pitchforks-are-coming-for-us-plutocrats-108014

12. Maya Gainer, "How Kenya Cleaned Up Its Courts," *Foreign Policy*, July 9, 2016, foreignpolicy.com/2016/07/09/how-kenya-cleaned-up-its-courts/

13. Ibid.

14. Jeffrey Dorfman, "Forget Debt As a Percent of GDP, It's Really Much Worse," *Forbes*, July 12, 2014.

15. Angelo Young, "Puerto Rico's Debt Addiction Was Fed by Banks That Passed Risk to Bond Buyers," *International Business Times*, July 1, 2015, ibtimes.com/puerto-ricos-debt-addiction-was-fed-banks-passed-risk-bond-buyers-1990649

16. "Debt Relief Under the Heavily Indebted Poor Countries (HIPC) Initiative," IMF, April 8, 2016, imf.org/external/np/exr/facts/hipc.htm

17. *Debt Relief Facts*, World Bank, April 2017, pubdocs.worldbank.org/en /702021492519096192/Debt-relief-facts-April-2017.pdf

18. Many of the world's innovations are coming from the slums. See Slum Dwellers International: sdinet.org/

19. Laurie Goering, "Growing Wealth Inequality 'Dangerous' Threat to Democracy: Experts," *Reuters*, April 15, 2016, uk.reuters.com/article/us -democracy-wealth-inequality/growing-wealth-inequality-dangerous -threat-to-democracy-experts-idUKKCN0XC1Q2

20. Hunter Lovins, "Development As If the World Mattered," *World Affairs Journal*, 2005, rightlivelihood.org/fileadmin/Files/PDF/Literature _Recipients/Lovins/Lovins_H_-_Developments_as_if_the_world _mattered.pdf

21. "Energy Access: Why Coal Is Not the Way out of Energy Poverty," Carbon Tracker, November 12, 2014, carbontracker.org/reports/energy access/

22. *Global Trends in Renewable Energy Investing*, UN Environment Pro- gramme, fs-unep-centre.org/sites/default/files/publications/global trendsinrenewableenergyinvestment2016lowres_0.pdf

23. Marlowe Hood, "China Takes Global Lead in Clean Energy: Report," *Phys. Org*, January 7, 2017, phys.org/news/2017-01-china-global-energy .html#nRlv

24. Gar Alperowitz, garalperovitz.com/about-gar/

25. Fred Freundlich et al., "Institutional Innovation in Mondragon: Context, Shape and Consequences," Research Gate, January 2012, researchgate .net/publication/220004070_Institutional_Innovation_in_Mondragon _Context_Shape_and_Consequences

26. Peter Eavis, "The Mystery of Spain's Perpetual Jobs Problem," *New York Times*, May 2, 2016.

27. Giles Tremlett, "Mondragon, Spain's Giant Co-Operative Where Times Are Hard But Few Go Bust," *The Guardian*, March 7, 2013.

28. ica.coop/; ICA's 2011 report can be found at ica.coop/en/global-300

29. Craig Morris, "Citizens Own Half of German Renewable Energy," *En- ergy Transition*, October 29, 2013, energytransition.org/2013/10/citizens -own-half-of-german-renewables/; and "Citizen Ownership of Grids," July 19, 2013, energytransition.org/2013/07/citizen-ownership-of-grids/

30. Oscar Perry Abello, "NYC Set to Triple Number of Worker Coopera- tives," *Next City*, January 11, 2016, nextcity.org/daily/entry/nyc-worker -cooperatives-jobs-increase

31. Evergreen Cooperatives, evgoh.com/about-us/

32. Gar Alperowitz, "The Cooperative Economy: A Conversation with Gar Alperovitz," June 5, 2014, garalperovitz.com/2014/06/cooperative -economy-conversation-gar-alperovitz/

33. Jessica Reeder, "Cooperative Businesses Provide a New-Old Model for Job Growth," *Christian Science Monitor*, April 2, 2012.
34. "Cooperatives in Social Development," Resolution adopted by the General Assembly on December 18, 2009 [on the report of the Third Committee (A/64/432)] 64/136. un.org/en/ga/search/view_doc.asp?symbol=A/RES/64/136
35. Graham Turner and Cathy Alexander, "Limits to Growth Was Right. New Research Shows We're Nearing Collapse," *The Guardian*, September 1, 2014.
36. *World Population Prospects, Key Findings and Advanced Tables*, UN, 2015, esa.un.org/unpd/wpp/publications/files/key_findings_wpp_2015.pdf
37. Wolfgang Lutz, A Population Policy Rationale for the Twenty-First Century, *Population and Development Review*, Vol. 30, No. 3, September 2014, pp. 527–544.
38. Ashok Khosla, *To Choose Our Future*, Academic Foundation, 2016.
39. Ibid.
40. "Working for the Few," Oxfam, January 20, 2014, oxfam.org/sites/www.oxfam.org/files/bp-working-for-few-political-capture-economic-inequality-200114-summ-en.pdf

Chapter 13: Confront the Myth of Growth

1. Kenneth Boulding, *Adbusters*, February 14, 2011, adbusters.org/article/kenneth-boulding/
2. Ray Williams, "Why the GDP Is Not a Good Measure of a Nation's Well-Being," *Psychology Today*, September 12, 2013.
3. Gallup-Healthways Well-Being Index, well-beingindex.com/
4. L. Hunter Lovins and Michael Kinsley, *Paying for Growth, Prospering from Development*, Natural Capitalism Solutions, 1996, natcapsolutions.org/publications_files/PayingForGrowth_ChronPilot_Sep1997.pdf
5. Erik Brynjolfsson and Andrew McAfee, *The Second Machine Age*, W.W. Norton, 2017.
6. Mike McPhate, "Use of 'Affluenza' Didn't Begin With Ethan Couch Case," *New York Times*, December 29, 2015.
7. Josh Allan Dykstra, "Why Millennials Don't Want to Buy Stuff," *Fast Company*, July 13, 2012, fastcompany.com/1842581/why-millennials-dont-want-buy-stuff
8. Tim Jackson and Peter Victor, "Credit Creation and the 'Growth Imperative,'" PASSAGE Working Paper 15-01, prosperitas.org.uk/assets/passage-wp_15-01.pdf
9. Peter Victor, "The 'Lowgrow' Model of the Canadian Economy," Proceedings, Fenner Conference on the Environment, 2014, ies.unsw.edu.au/sites/all/files/uploads/2014_FennerConf/proceedings/pres/T3_2_Victor_Fenner-Conf-IES-UNSW_2014.pdf
10. Anna Coote et al., *21 Hours*, New Economics Foundation, 2010, neweconomics.org/publications/entry/21-hours

11. J. Steven Landefeld, "GDP: One of the Great Inventions of the 20th Century," Bureau of Economic Analysis, 2000, bea.gov/scb/account _articles/general/0100od/maintext.htm

12. GDP is a hard metric to leave behind, however, as it correlates pretty well with increases in income, and without a doubt, the increased velocity of economic activity has been the engine that has lifted millions of people out of poverty the world around. For a detailed discussion of the need for a new metric, see Robert Costanza et al., "Development: Time to Leave GDP Behind," *Nature*, January 15, 2014.

13. Herman Daly, "Farewell Speech," Whirled Bank Group, 1994, whirledbank.org/ourwords/daly.html

14. *Wellbeing in Four Policy Areas: Report by the All-Party Parliamentary Group on Wellbeing Economics*, New Economics Foundation, September 2014, b.3cdn.net/nefoundation/ccdf9782b6d8700f7c_lcm6i2ed7.pdf

15. Hazel Henderson, "A Systems Approach: Calvert-Henderson Quality of Life Indicators," Hazelhenderson.com, January 6, 2002, hazelhenderson .com/2002/01/06/a-systems-approach-calvert-henderson-quality-of -life-indicators/; The Calvert Henderson Indicators were used by the "Foresighting the New Technology Wave SIG I: Quality of Life," effort in Europe, cordis.europa.eu/pub/foresight/docs/ntw_sig1_en.pdf

16. Happy Planet Index, happyplanetindex.org/

17. Christine Berry, *Wellbeing in Four Policy Areas*, New Economics Foundation, September 9, 2014, neweconomics.org/publications/entry /wellbeing-in-four-policy-areas

18. Mark Williamson, "Why Does Happiness Matter," *The Guardian*, November 3, 2014.

19. Change Course Conference of the Club of Rome, December 8–11, 2012, youtube.com/watch?v=6aedyx2xZuM

20. OECD Better Life Index, oecdbetterlifeindex.org/#/11111111111

21. Herman E. Daly and John B. Cobb, Jr., *For the Common Good: Redirecting the Economy Toward Community, the Environment, and a Sustainable Future*, Beacon Press, Boston, 1989.

22. Redefining Progress, "Genuine Progress Indicator," San Francisco, 1995.

23. J. Talberth, C. Cobb, and N. Slattery, "The Genuine Progress Indicator 2006: A Tool for Sustainable Develoment," Redefining Progress, Oakland, CA, 2007.

24. S. M. Posner and Robert Costanza, "A Summary of ISEW and GPI Studies at Multiple Scales and New Estimates for Baltimore City, Baltimore County, and the State of Maryland," *Ecological Economics*, 70, 1972, 2011.

25. Richard Wilkinson and Kate Pickett, *The Spirit Level: Why Greater Equality Makes Societies Stronger*, Bloomsbury Press, New York, 2009.

26. M. Smith, K. Hargroves and C. Desha, *Cents and Sustainability: Decoupling Economic Growth from Negative Environmental Pressure*, Earthscan, 2010.

Chapter 14: A Values Shift

1. Tunku Varadarajan, "The Moment You Give Up Your Principles, and Your Values, You Are Dead, Your Culture Is Dead, Your Civilisation Is Dead. Period," *The Telegraph*, September 4, 2005, telegraph.co.uk/news /worldnews/europe/italy/1497614/The-moment-you-give-up-your -principles-and-your-values-you-are-dead-your-culture-is-dead-your -civilisation-is-dead.-Period.html

2. bfi.org/about-fuller/big-ideas/world-game

3. Personal communication Donna Morton to Hunter Lovins, April 20, 2014.

4. Sebastian Junger, *Tribe: On Homecoming and Belonging*, HarperCollins-Canada, 2016.

5. *Global Agenda Council on Values: A New Social Covent*, www3.weforum .org/docs/WEF_GAC_Values_2013.pdf

6. David Cadman, *Peacefulness: Being Peace and Making Peace*, Spirit of Humanity Press, September 28, 2017.

7. Garrett Hardin, "The Tragedy of the Commons," *Science Magazine*, December 13, 1968, science.sciencemag.org/content/162/3859/1243

8. Fran Korten, "Elinor Ostrom Wins Nobel for Common Sense," *Yes Magazine*, February 26, 2010, yesmagazine.org/issues/america-the-remix /elinor-ostrom-wins-nobel-for-common-s-sense

9. Amy R. Poteete, Marco A. Janssen, and Elinor Ostrom, *Working Together: Collective Action, the Commons, and Multiple Methods in Practice*, Princeton University Press, 2010.

10. "Elinor Ostrom—Facts," 2009, Nobelprize.org, nobelprize.org/nobel _prizes/economic -sciences/laureates/2009/ostrom-facts.html

11. commonstransition.org/what-is-commons-transition/

12. David Bollier, "The Commons, Short and Sweet," July 15, 2011, bollier.org /commons-short-and-sweet

13. Ibid.

14. Michel Bauwens, "Commons Transition Plan," Commons Transition Wiki, wiki.commonstransition.org/wiki/Commons_Transition_Plan

15. Ibid.

16. Common, common.is/about/

17. Peter Barnes, *Who Owns the Sky*, Island Press, 2001.

18. Robert Costanza, "Claim the Sky," *Solutions Journal*, Vol. 6, No. 1, January 2015, pp. 21–24.

19. Ibid.

20. Chelsea Harvey, "Trump Could Face the 'Biggest Trial of the Century'—Over Climate Change," *Washington Post*, December 1, 2016; and Neela Banerjee, "Appeals Court Takes Up Youth Climate Change Lawsuit Against Trump," *Inside Climate News*, November 17, 2017, insideclimate news.org/news/17112017/climate-change-lawsuit-kids-donald-trump -administration-our-childrens-trust

21. Dana Varinsky, "The Trump Administration Is Doing Everything It Can to Keep a Huge Climate Lawsuit from Going to Trial," *Business Insider*, March 12, 2017, businessinsider.com/trump-landmark-climate-change -lawsuit-2017-3

Chapter 15: Reinventing Governance

1. Cesar Chavez, Address to the Commonwealth Club, November 9, 1984.
2. Elinor Ostrom, "How Do Institutions for Collective Action Evolve?" Annual Neale Wheeler Watson Lecture presented at the Nobel Museum, Stockholm, Sweden, April 12, 2008.
3. Michael Stagnaroa et al., "From Good Institutions to Generous Citizens: Top-down Incentives to Cooperate Promote Subsequent Prosociality but Not Norm Enforcement," *Science Direct*, February 27, 2017, science direct.com/science/article/pii/S001002771730025
4. Edelman, *2017 Edelman Trust Barometer*, Global Report, January 17, 2017, edelman.com/global-results/
5. Gregory Wallace, "Voter Turnout at 20-year Low in 2016," CNN, November 30, 2016, cnn.com/2016/11/11/politics/popular-vote-turnout -2016/index.html
6. Fareed Zakaria, "Populism on the March: Why the West Is in Trouble," *Foreign Affairs*, March 2017, foreignaffairs.com/articles/united-states /2016-10-17/populism-march
7. George Monbiot, "All About That Base," *The Guardian*, January 26, 2018.
8. Personal communication, Eban Goodstein to Hunter Lovins, August 23, 2017.
9. Randall Wray, "Is Euroland the Next Argentina?" Working Paper 23, Center for Full Employment and Price Stability, University of Missouri, Kansas City, cfeps.org/pubs/wp-pdf/WP23-Wray.pdf
10. Robert Putnam, *Bowling Alone: The Collapse and Revival of American Community*, Touchstone Books, 2001.
11. Nancy LeTourneau, "Some Shocking Data on the Potential for a Blue Wave in 2018," *Washington Monthly*, December 20, 2017, washington monthly.com/2017/12/20/some-shocking-data-on-the-potential-for-a -blue-wave-in-2018/
12. Z. Byron Wolf, "The Senate Voted on a Tax Bill Pretty Much Nobody Had Read," CNN, December 2, 2017, cnn.com/2017/12/01/politics /senate-vote-still-writing-tax-bill/index.html
13. Martin Gilens and Benjamin I. Page, "Testing Theories of American Politics: Elites, Interest Groups, and Average Citizens," *Perspectives on Politics*, Vol. 12, No. 3, September 2014, pp. 564–581.
14. Tom Huddleston, Jr., "CBS Chief: Trump's Success Is 'Damn Good' for the Network," *Fortune Magazine*, March 1, 2016.
15. Neil Postman, *Amusing Ourselves to Death*, Penguin, December 27, 2005.

16. Martin Baron, quoted in Jim Rutenberg, "Media's Next Challenge: Overcoming the Threat of Fake News," *New York Times*, November 6, 2016.
17. Laura Seydel, "On Both the Left And Right, Trump Is Driving New Political Engagement," March 3, 2017, National Public Radio, npr.org /2017/03/03/518261347/on-both-left-and-right-trump-is-driving-new -political-engagement

Chapter 16: Bringing It Home

1. Jon Pareles and Pete Seeger, 1994, quoted in "Pete Seeger, Champion of Folk Music and Social Change, Dies at 94," *The New York Times*, January 28, 2014.
2. This concept of the Just City, and the presentation of it here, is courtesy of Eban Goodstein, Director of the Bard Center for Environmental Policy and the Bard MBA, bard.edu/mba/
3. *Shanghai Manual: A Guide for Sustainable Urban Development in the 21st Century*, Sustainable Development Knowledge Platform, UNDESA, 2012, sustainabledevelopment.un.org/index.php?page=view&type=400 &nr=633&menu=35
4. Plan Bay Area, Greenbelt Alliance, greenbelt.org/plan-bay-area/
5. "Our Home, Our Environment, Our Future," mewr.gov.sg/ssb/
6. "Danish Strategy for Sustainable Development," Danish Ministry for Environment and Food, 2014, eng.mst.dk/topics/sustainability /sustainable-development-in-denmark/
7. USA—Oregon (Portland)—Sustainable City, EcoTipping Points Project, posted June 2006, ecotippingpoints.org/our-stories/indepth/usa -portland-sustainable-regional-planning.html
8. Zach Dyer, "Costa Rica Ranked 2nd in the World for 'Environmental Sustainability,'" *Tico Times*, September 23, 2013, ticotimes.net/2013 /09/24/costa-rica-ranked-2nd-in-the-world-for-environmental -sustainability
9. Jane Jacobs, *Cities and the Wealth of Nations*, Vintage, 1985.
10. UN forecast from 2014, at un.org/development/desa/en/news /population/world-urbanization-prospects.html
11. Jason Deign, "Microgrids with 50 Percent Solar Do Not Need Storage," *Greentech Media*, September 30, 2015, greentechmedia.com/articles /read/microgrids-with-50-percent-solar-do-not-need-storage
12. Alex Tapscott, "Blockchain Is Eating Wall Street," TEDx Talks, YouTube, October 26, 2016, youtube.com/watch?v=WnEYakUxsHU
13. Michael Shuman, *Local Dollars, Local Sense*, 2012, and *The Local Economy Solution*, Chelsea Green, 2014.
14. Natural Capitalism Solutions, LASER, natcapsolutions.org/LASER /LASERguide.pdf
15. "Challenges and Opportunities in Lagos: Interview with Lookman

Oshodi," Sustainable Cities Collective, November 15, 2014, sustainable citiescollective.com/futurecapetown/1011351/challenges-and -opportunities-lagos-interview-lookman-oshodi

16. Kate Abbey-Lambertz, "You May Not Know These Black Millennials, But They're Helping Detroit Make Its Comeback," *Huffington Post*, January 21, 2016, huffingtonpost.com/entry/detroit-revival-black-millennials _us_55ddaf6ae4b08cd3359def3f

17. Jeffrey Sachs and Andrew Warner, "Natural Resource Abundance and Economic Growth," National Bureau of Economic Research, December 1995, nber.org/papers/w5398

18. Jane Jacobs, *The Death and Life of Great American Cities*, Reissue edition, Vintage, December 1, 1992.

19. Forum for the Future, "Sustainable Urban Enterprise: Creating the Right Business Environment in Cities," forumforthefuture.org/project /sustainable-urban-enterprise-creating-right-business-environment -cities/overview

20. "Oregon Businesses Band Together to Support Local B Corps Wanna-bes," *Portland Business Journal*, March 17, 2016, bizjournals.com /portland/blog/sbo/2016/03/oregon-businesses-band-together-to -support-local-b.html

21. Iris Kunze and Andrea Philipp, *WP 4 | CASE STUDY Report: Co-housing: The Eco-District of Vauban and the Cohousing Project GENOVA*, Transformative Social Innovation Theory, 2016, iriskunze.files.word press.com/2016/04/cohousing_vauban_2015_07_16_report_ik_ap _publication_transit.pdf

22. Jennifer Lasseter, "Growing Green Businesses in Austin," *GreenBiz*, April 30, 2013, greenbiz.com/blog/2013/04/30/growing-green-businesses -austin

23. New Internationalist, "World Development Book Case Study: Sustainable Urban Development in Curitiba," 2010, newint.org/books /reference/world-development/case-studies/sustainable-urban -development-curitiba/

24. Neal Peirce and Gregory Scruggs, "Bogotá Mayor Enrique Peñalosa on Making Better Cities," Citiscope, Global Goals, Local Solutions, October 7, 2016, citiscope.org/story/2016/bogota-mayor-enrique-penalosa -making-better-cities

25. Rick Wartzman, "What Unilever Shares with Google and Apple," *Fortune*, January 7, 2015.

26. Amanda Sakuma, "No Safe Place," MSNBC, Fall 2017, msnbc.com /specials/migrant-crisis/sanctuary-cities

27. Ron Pernick, "Clean Energy Jobs Mean Business," Renewable Energy World, March 14, 2017, renewableenergyworld.com/ugc/articles/2017 /03/13/clean-energy-jobs-mean-business.html

28. We Are Still In, wearestillin.com/

29. Madeleine Perkins, "A Group Representing $6.2 Trillion of the US Economy Says They're 'Still in' the Paris Climate Agreement," *Business Insider*, June 5, 2017, businessinsider.com/we-are-still-in-group -represents-62-trillion-of-the-us-economy-plans-to-stay-in-paris -agreement-2017-6

30. "Historic Paris Agreement on Climate Change: 195 Nations Set Path to Keep Temperature Rise Well Below 2 Degrees Celsius," UN Framework Convention on Climate Change, 2015, newsroom.unfccc.int/unfccc -newsroom/finale-cop21/

31. Fiona Harvey, "Paris Climate Change Agreement Enters into Force," *The Guardian*, November 3, 2016.

32. Amanda Ji, "The Carbon Tax in Norway, UBC Blogs, blogs.ubc.ca /amandaji/2014/03/12/the-carbon-tax-in-norway/

33. Simone McCarthy, "Is Norway Ready To Go Carbon Neutral?" *Christian Science Monitor*, June 18, 2016, csmonitor.com/Environment/2016/0618 /Is-Norway-ready-to-go-carbon-neutral

34. Patrick Doherty, "A $2 Trillion Object Lesson in Sustainability from Saudi Arabia," March 17, 2017, brinknews.com/a-2-trillion-object-lesson -in-sustainability-from-saudi-arabia/. It is worth noting that the fund the Saudi's have created for this purpose would enable them to buy Apple, Google, Microsoft, and Berkshire Hathaway, with enough left over to buy several large islands.

35. un.org/sustainabledevelopment/sustainable-development-goals/

36. Joel Jaeger, Ferzina Banaji, and Talia Calnek-Sugin, "By the Numbers: How Business Benefits from the Sustainable Development Goals," World Resources Institute Blog, April 5, 2017, wri.org/blog/2017/04 /numbers-how-business-benefits-sustainable-development-goals

37. "Business and Sustainable Development Commission, Better Business Better World," January 2017, report.businesscommission.org/uploads /Executive-Summary.pdf

38. Mohandas Gandhi, quoted in the statement by Amit Narang, Counsellor, Permanent Mission of India, on the adoption of the Outcome Document of the "Agenda 2030 for Sustainable Development" Final Session of Intergovernmental Negotiations on Post-2015 Development Agenda, August 2, 2015, drive.google.com/file/d/0B6oVHokeZxvdbkR1WHRr UXZacTQ/view?pli=1

39. Tim Wallace and Alicia Parlapiano, "Crowd Scientists Say Women's March in Washington Had 3 Times More People Than Trump's Inauguration," *New York Times*, January 22, 2017.

40. Matt Broomfield, "Women's March against Donald Trump is the largest day of protests in US history, say political scientists," *The Independent*, January 23, 2017, independent.co.uk/news/world/americas

/womens-march-anti-donald-trump-womens-rights-largest-protest
-demonstration-us-history-political-a7541081.html

41. "Germany Gets 50 Percent of Its Electricity from Solar for the First
Time," *The Week*, June 20, 2014, theweek.com/speedreads/451299
/germany-gets-50-percent-electricity-from-solar-first-time

42. Kiley Kroh, "China's Gigantic New Commitment to Renewable Energy
Explained," *Climate Progress*, November 12, 2014, thinkprogress.org
/climate/2014/11/12/3591433/china-renewable-energy-commitment/

43. Clean Energy Action, cleanenergyaction.org/learn-more
/municipalization/

44. City of Boulder, bouldercolorado.gov/lead/climate-action-ramp-up
-renewables-focus-area

45. Leanna Garfield, "From Oslo to Paris, These Major Cities Have Plans
to Go Car-free," *World Economic Forum*, February 10, 2017, weforum.org
/agenda/2017/02/these-major-cities-are-starting-to-go-car-free/

46. Leanna Garfield, "Oslo Just Declared That It Will Become the First
Major City to Ban Cars," October 20, 2015, *Business Insider*, business
insider.com/oslo-bans-cars-from-its-city-center-2015-10

47. change-finance.com/

48. Fiona Harvey, "Global Emissions Stall In 2014 Following Slowdown in
China's Economy," *The Guardian*, March 13, 2015.

49. "IEA Finds CO_2 Emissions Flat for Third Straight Year Even As Global
Economy Grew in 2016," International Energy Agency, March 17, 2017,
iea.org/newsroom/news/2017/march/iea-finds-co2-emissions-flat-for
-third-straight-year-even-as-global-economy-grew.html

50. Zeke Hausfather, "Emissions Set to Rise 2% in 2017 after Three-year
'Plateau,'" *Carbon Brief*, November 13, 2017, carbonbrief.org/analysis
-global-co2-emissions-set-to-rise-2-percent-in-2017-following-three
-year-plateau

51. Joshua Hill, "China Installs Nearly 10 Gigawatts Of Solar In First
Quarter, Up 22%," *CleanTechnica*, April 24, 2018, cleantechnica.com/2018
/04/24/china-installs-nearly-10-gigawatts-of-solar-in-first-quarter-up
-22/

Section 5: A Finer Future Is Possible

1. Martin Luther King, Jr., "Beyond Vietnam: A Time to Break Silence,"
Speech at Riverside Church, New York City, April 4, 1967, american
rhetoric.com/speeches/mlkatimetobreaksilence.htm

2. Jacob Sugarman, "The Koch Brothers Are Plotting a Right-wing Takeover of America's Judicial System, *Salon*, February 5, 2018, salon.com
/2018/02/05/the-koch-brothers-are-plotting-a-right-wing-takeover-of
-americas-judicial-system_partner/; see also Alex Kotch, "Koch Brothers
Could Be $1 Billion Richer Each Year from GOP Tax Bill," *IBT*, January

24, 2018, ibtimes.com/political-capital/koch-brothers-could-be-1-billion -richer-each-year-gop-tax-bill-2644857

3. Ban Ki Moon, "Secretary-General, Introducing Report in General Assembly, Outlines 'Generational Opportunities' to Shape Tomorrow's World by Today's Decisions," United Nations, September 21, 2011, un.org/press/en/2011/sgsm13823.doc.htm

4. Eva Alfredsson and Anders Wijkman, "The Inclusive Green Economy," MISTRA 2014, mistra.org/download/18.2f9de4b14592a1589d1 72e2/1400765561079/Mistra_Prestudy_TheInclusiveGreenEconomy _April2014+(1).pdf

5. Chris Laszlo, weatherhead.case.edu/executive-education/instructors /chris-laszlo

6. goodreads.com/quotes/481614-the-future-belongs-to-those-who-give -the-next-generation

7. Moyers and Company, "Wendell Berry Reads A Poem on Hope," 3 October 2013, youtube.com/watch?v=2j_r4jb9AYw

8. Donella Meadows et al., *Beyond the Limits*, 1992, Chelsea Green Publishing.

9. This is the title of the brilliant book by Jonah Sachs on the power and essential nature of narrative: *Winning the Story Wars: Why Those Who Tell and Live the Best Stories Will Rule the Future*, Harvard Business Review Press, 2012.

10. Alex Steffen, *World Changing, Revised and Updated Edition: A User's Guide for the 21st Century*, Henry N. Abrams, 2011.

11. Alex Steffen, "A Talk Given at a Conservation Meeting a Hundred Years from Now," November 3, 2015, alexsteffen.com/future_conservation _meeting_talk

Index

About the Authors

Norm Clasen

L. HUNTER LOVINS, *Time Magazine's* Millennium Hero for the Planet, is a business professor, President and Founder of Natural Capitalism Solutions, and co-author of *The Way Out* and the best-selling *Natural Capitalism*.

STEWART WALLIS is Executive Chair of WEAll, the Wellbeing Economy Alliance, an Honorary Professor at Lancaster University and formerly Executive Director of the New Economics Foundation.

ANDERS WIJKMAN is Co-Chair of the Club of Rome, a former EU parliamentarian, Chair Climate-KIC, the largest public-private partnership for climate innovation in the EU, and co-author of *Bankrupting Nature* and *Come On!*

JOHN FULLERTON is the Founder of Capital Institute and a former Managing Director of JP Morgan. He is the author of *Regenerative Capitalism: How Universal Principles and Patterns Will Shape Our New Economy.*

Also Available from New Society Publishers

The Clean Money Revolution

Reinventing Power, Purpose, and Capitalism

JOEL SOLOMON WITH TYEE BRIDGE

6 × 9" / 288 pages
US/Can $19.99
PB ISBN 978-0-86571-892-0
EBOOK ISBN 978-1-55092-685-9

Invest like you Give A Damn

Make Money, Change the World,

Sleep Well at Night

MARC DE SOUSA-SHIELDS

6 × 9" / 256 pages
US/Can $18.99
PB ISBN 978-0-86571-848-7
EBOOK ISBN 978-1-55092-643-9

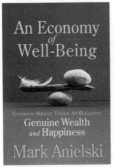

An Economy of Well-Being

Common-Sense Tools for Building

Geniune Wealth and Happiness

MARK ANIELSKI

6 × 9" / 240 pages
US/Can $19.99
PB ISBN 978-0-86571-873-9
EBOOK ISBN 978-1-55092-666-8

In the Business of Change

How Social Entrepreneurs are

Disrupting Business as Usual

ELISA BIRNBAUM

6 × 9" / 192 pages
US/Can $17.99
PB ISBN 978-0-86571-871-5
EBOOK ISBN 978-1-55092-664-4

ABOUT NEW SOCIETY PUBLISHERS

New Society Publishers is an activist, solutions-oriented publisher focused on publishing books for a world of change. Our books offer tips, tools, and insights from leading experts in sustainable building, homesteading, climate change, environment, conscientious commerce, renewable energy, and more—positive solutions for troubled times.

We're proud to hold to the highest environmental and social standards of any publisher in North America. This is why some of our books might cost a little more. We think it's worth it!

- We print all our books in North America, never overseas

- All our books are printed on **100% post-consumer recycled paper**, processed chlorine-free, with low-VOC vegetable-based inks (since 2002)

- Our corporate structure is an innovative employee shareholder agreement, so we're one-third employee-owned (since 2015)

- We're carbon-neutral (since 2006)

- We're certified as a B Corporation (since 2016)

At New Society Publishers, we care deeply about *what* we publish—but also about *how* we do business.

Download our catalog at https://newsociety.com/Our-Catalog or for a printed copy please email info@newsocietypub.com or call 1-800-567-6772 ext 111.

New Society Publishers
ENVIRONMENTAL BENEFITS STATEMENT

For every 5,000 books printed, New Society saves the following resources:[1]

44	Trees
3,988	Pounds of Solid Waste
4,388	Gallons of Water
5,724	Kilowatt Hours of Electricity
7,250	Pounds of Greenhouse Gases
31	Pounds of HAPs, VOCs, and AOX Combined
11	Cubic Yards of Landfill Space

[1] Environmental benefits are calculated based on research done by the Environmental Defense Fund and other members of the Paper Task Force who study the environmental impacts of the paper industry.

Certified
B Corporation

FSC
www.fsc.org

MIX
Paper from responsible sources
FSC® C016245

new society
PUBLISHERS
www.newsociety.com